Amelia Opie

Amelia Opie portrait by her husband John Opie. Earland challenged (correctly) Jope Rogers' assertion that it was painted in 1787 when Amelia was still Miss Alderson, as the couple had not met then. The dress and the background are the same as in the portrait Opie painted in the early weeks of their marriage. The portrait was handed down from Amelia's cousin Margaret Thompson to her daughter Sarah Isabella, wife of an Oxford tutor William Sidgwick , and then to their son Nevil Vincent Sidgwick, fellow of Lincoln College, Oxford. In her *Recollections of Mrs Opie* (1884) Mrs Sidgwick writes in some detail of 'a portrait of Mrs Opie' which she knows well (undoubtedly the one she owned): 'I think Opie never surpassed this head…it presents her when she fascinated her painter husband, but in its youthful features I never fail to trace the sweet lines of her dear old face.'
(Ashmolean Museum of Art & Archaeology)

Amelia Opie

The Quaker Celebrity

Ann Farrant

In memory of my parents:

Ivan and Peggy French

Also by Ann Farrant:
Sibling Bereavement: Helping Children Cope with Loss
(Cassell, 1998)

ISBN 978-1-870948-65-4
First published 2014

Published by
JJG Publishing
Sparrow Hall
Hindringham
Norfolk NR21 0DP

Designed by Graham Hiles
Printed in China through Colorcraft Ltd, Hong Kong

Contents

Foreword

I enrolled as a mature student on the University of East Anglia MA in Life Writing course (when it was in its second year) because I was an enthusiastic reader of biographies and memoirs and was thinking about attempting such a project myself. Although daunted at the prospect of entering the academic world, having spent my working life as a journalist for newspapers and magazines and for the BBC as a regional television news producer, I soon settled in and found the MA programme inspiring and stimulating.

For my dissertation I chose to write something biographical about Amelia Opie. I was busy with free-lance work and many other demands on my time and energy and thought that, living in Norwich, I could do much of my research locally, as indeed was the case, initially. Amelia Opie (née Alderson) was born in Norwich and spent most of her long life in the city. Once I got going, I realised that there was masses of material, not just in her home county but in libraries across the UK and in America, much of it unpublished. However, as the MA dissertation required only 15,000 words, there was no need to go further afield than Norwich, London and Oxford at that stage.

Thanks to the encouragement of my supervisor, the distinguished biographer Professor Richard Holmes, and the continuing support of Professor Kathryn Hughes, also a distinguished biographer, who took over the core MA biography course at short notice, I felt it worth my while – once I had achieved the MA – to press on with further research into Amelia Opie's life, with a view to writing a new biography of her. I was fortunate to receive two literary awards for my dissertation which helped to fund my first research trip to America; later the Friends of the Norwich Museums offered me a bursary to help fund a second research trip to the USA,

The project has taken far longer than I anticipated. For personal reasons I have been unable to maintain a steady programme of research and writing. Time spent at home and abroad, transcribing Amelia's many hundreds of letters and poring over her albums, checking family trees, perusing literary diaries and memoirs, has been sporadic. Although born in Norwich, as Amelia was, I knew very little about her before I chose her as my dissertation subject. It was interesting to observe, from a new perspective, some of the buildings and places which she knew well. I was intrigued to discover that when she first became acquainted with the Gurney family, they lived at Gurney Court, the north wing of which was occupied by my maternal great grandfather and his family from 1896 for ten years. Amelia and her father were also acquainted with William Tooke Harwood, who married Thomas Holcroft's daughter Ann and lived with her at College Farm, Thompson, where my paternal great great grandfather was the tenant from 1863 to 1888.

Ann Farrant, 2014

Acknowledgements

Along the way I have met and been befriended by some delightful people, many of whom have gone out of their way to assist me. It is customary for authors to acknowledge such help and I am pleased to do so. In the time it has taken me to do my research I imagine that some of the people named here have moved on; nevertheless I will place them in the context of their workplace at the time of our meeting or correspondence and trust they will find that acceptable. As long and detailed lists can be tedious for the reader I will keep it simple:

John Anderies, Diana Peterson and Ann Upton (Haverford College Library); Stuart Amey; Dr B.C. Barker-Benfield (Bodleian Library); Philippa Bassett (Birmingham University Library); Roger and the late Jane Bellinger; June Bridgeman; Joanna Clark, Jennifer Milligan and Heather Rowland (Religious Society of Friends Library); Dr Pamela Clemit (University of Durham); Elizabeth Denlinger and Charles Carter (New York Public Library); Jill Cogen, Susi Krasnoo and Mona Shulman (Huntington Library); Fiona Courage (University of Sussex library); Paul Cox (National Portrait Gallery Archive and Library); Kristel de Wulf; Gurney family members; Virginia Elwood-Akers (Los Angeles); Wayne Hammond (Chapin Library, Williams College); Viv Hendra (Lander Gallery); Professor Richard Holmes; Professor Kathryn Hughes (UEA); Emma Jarvis (Norfolk & Norwich University Hospital Archive); Sam Johnson (Cornwall Record Office); Caroline Kelly (University of Nottingham); Geoffrey Kelly (historical research consultant); Leona Levine and Rosemary Salt (Friends of the Norwich Museums); Professor David McKitterick and Ruth Bridgen (Trinity College, Cambridge); Susanna Morikawa, Christopher Densmore and Pat O'Donnell (Friends Historical Library, Swarthmore College); Rochelle Mortimer-Massingham (Cromer Museum); Maria Molestina and Christine Nelson (The Morgan Library); Norfolk Record Office staff; Rhodes House Library staff; Sandra Robertson (Sessions of York); Arthur R.B. and Betty Robinson; St Bride Printing Library staff; Deirdre Sharp (UEA library); Sandra Stelts (Pennsylvania State University library); the late John Turner of Hempnall, Norfolk; Norma Watt (Norfolk Museums Art Department); Dr Clive Wilkins-Jones and staff (Norwich Heritage Centre); Wisbech and Fenland Museum staff; Christopher and Patricia Woods.

In conclusion, I must express thanks to my partner John Benjafield, whose expertise in early photography and many related subjects, has been of great help and whose unflagging support over the years has been invaluable.

Illustration acknowledgements

Ashmolean Museum of Art & Archaeology, Oxford
The Carl H Pforzheimer Collection of Shelley & his Circle, The New York Public Library, Astor, Lenox & Tilden Foundations
Haverford College Special Collections, Haverford, Pennsylvania
Lander Gallery, Truro
National Portrait Gallery
Norfolk & Norwich University Hospital Archive
Norfolk County Council Library & Information Service
Norfolk Record Office
Norwich Castle Museum & Art Gallery
Religious Society of Friends Library, London
Suffolk Record Office, Ipswich Branch

The author acknowledges the financial suport of Norwich Heart and the Harry Watson Bursary.

Introduction

O n a May morning in 1851, an hour before the doors of the Great Exhibition in London were opened to the general public, an elderly lady in a silk Quaker dress and bonnet, sitting in a wheelchair, was already inside the Crystal Palace in Hyde Park, one of the few privileged people allowed in early because of age or infirmity. Among the other early wheelchair arrivals she recognised an old acquaintance. 'Where did you get that chair?' asked the friend, noting the superiority of the other's conveyance, 'I quite envy it.' Whereupon the Quaker lady proposed a chair race.

The playful challenger was the 81-year-old Amelia Opie (née Alderson) on her last visit to the capital which she had first visited as an attractive young woman, the adored daughter of a widowed surgeon, a leading light in her home city of Norwich, a budding writer, an accomplished singer and musician. In the intervening years she had become a best-selling novelist and poet, the wife of a Royal Academician, an active supporter of the anti-slavery movement, an assured performer on the social scene; she had befriended and been befriended by writers, artists, politicians, philosophers, actresses, publishers, philanthropists and aristocrats; in her fifties, to the amazement of her fashionable acquaintances, she had become a member of the Society of Friends.

Opened by Queen Victoria on May 1st, the Great Exhibition achieved worldwide publicity. Regional newspapers reported on local exhibitors taking part; Norwich manufacturers were showing shawls, textiles, boots and shoes, wrought iron goods and furniture at the huge international event, which had attracted an outstanding range of items from exhibitors across the globe. Extra trains were laid on from the provinces and London was buzzing with visitors from home and abroad. Like her fellow citizens, Amelia was enthralled by what she heard of the Great Exhibition, but she had not been to London for three years, fearing that her 'helplessness' as she called her lameness, would make her a burden to other people. However, she decided to accept the hospitality offered by an old friend, believing she could purchase a 'chair on wheels' in the capital and have the chance to see the *outside* of the Crystal Palace.

In the event, Amelia saw more than the outside of the splendid construction; she was able to cross its threshold in a new wheelchair and to spend some time there. She stayed in London for six weeks, attending Quaker Meetings, visiting favourite shops and calling on friends and acquaintances, believing, as indeed proved to be the case, that this would be her last visit to the capital. Back in her native city, she settled down in her house near the Norman castle – the home in which she was to end her days. She had moved into the property on Castle Meadow in 1848 from lodgings in the city; as she explained to a friend, 'a lodging house is not the proper residence of an old woman and I have for sometime longed to have a home of my own to die in.'[1]

Intimations of mortality were not in the forefront of her mind sixty years earlier when London had been a Mecca for the youthful Amelia Alderson. During prolonged visits in the 1790s she attended the treason trials of Thomas Hardy, John Thelwall and Horne Tooke, flirted with William Godwin and Thomas Holcroft, exchanged confidences with Mary Wollstonecraft and Elizabeth Inchbald, and associated with the celebrated Sarah Siddons and her theatrical siblings. In a heady atmosphere of social and intellectual challenges, the provincial doctor's daughter enjoyed life in London to the full. Yet, even while participating happily in all that the capital had to offer, she felt a tug from the city and county of her birth, as she owned in a letter to her friend Susannah Taylor:

> ...but still I sigh for home, that is, I sigh for a day or two of confidential intercourse with you and others, and to wash off the dirt of London in the sea of Cromer; to write poetry on the shore; to live over again every scene there that memory loves...and having rioted in all that my awakened fancy can give, return to Norwich, and endeavour to make one of my plays, at least, fit to be offered to one of the managers of the winter theatres.[2]

Amelia's affection for her home city was, in part, rooted in the deep bond between her and her father, Dr James Alderson. During extended visits away from home, when she was still single, her father was continually in her thoughts. She was devoted to him. When she went to live in London, following her marriage to John Opie, she went frequently to Norwich to stay with her father; when John died, she packed up and returned to live with Dr Alderson. His death, when she was 55, caused her intense grief and she continued to mourn him for the rest of her life.

Amelia Opie's first best-selling novel, *The Father and Daughter*, concludes with her penitent heroine Agnes Fitzhenry dying of grief and being buried with her long-suffering father, re-united in death, after an estrangement of many months. Some 50 years after its publication Amelia was herself buried in her father's grave. She wrote the novel during her marriage to a man who fully understood his wife's desire to write and encouraged her to persevere. But *The Father and Daughter* was dedicated not to the author's supportive husband but to her adored parent.

Chapter One

Amelia Alderson was born on Sunday, November 12th, 1769, in the parish of St George's, Colegate, in Norwich. Her mother, who was far from robust, died on December 31st, 1784, at the age of 38. Amelia's immediate response was not recorded, but in later years she chose to express her bereavement in elegiac poems. In 1791 she wrote a sonnet recalling 'scenes of my childhood'[1] after a visit to Cromer on the north Norfolk coast, which she used to visit with her mother; however, its funereal tone did little to capture a mother and child enjoying the pleasures of the seaside. A few years later Amelia reminisced about her mother in *Epistle to a Friend on New Year's Day, 1802*, which was published in her first book of poems.[2] Reflecting on the anniversary of her mother's death, the passing of another year and her regrets over duties not fulfilled and precious hours wasted, she wrote of remorse over 'squandering the time that can return no more'.

The poem was a serious attempt at re-creating an image of a mother much missed. The bereaved daughter, admitting that once she had overcome 'the first conflict' of her loss, 'life's opening joys' beguiled her grief and 'the dear maternal image sunk and drowned'. But now, with memories of that long-lost parent recovered and restored, she wanted to address a tribute to her 'anxious care for others' and her 'patient sweetness'. The homage concluded with an acknowledgement that while her mother was alive Amelia had often been diverted from her company by other pleasures, had been impatient of restraints, tired of her lessons:

> Then, by thy couch I loved not to abide,
> To tend thee now would be my joy, my pride:
> Then, I thy well-meant frown abhorred to see,
> Now, 'twere more dear than others' smiles to me....

Fifty years after the death a poem entitled simply *In Memory of My Mother* appeared in her *Lays for the Dead*. As Mrs Opie, she had been a published poet for four decades and the work was more assured, taking for its theme a visit to the church at Holt in Norfolk, where Mrs Alderson was buried with her paternal ancestors. Again, the tone was of regret for the way in which her 'heedless youth' so ill repaid the mother's 'watchful care', but still, the image of a real flesh and blood mother eluded her. Rather, she created a shadowy, gentle figure whose kindly discipline, the daughter – now a mature woman – could at last appreciate.

Much more vivid was the account of her childhood found among Amelia's papers by her first biographer Cecilia Lucy Brightwell. In these recollections she wrote how Mrs Alderson had instilled in her the importance of non-racist attitudes and respect for other people. Her mother, whom she believed to be 'as firm from principle, as she was gentle in disposition', took steps to cure her of her numerous fears, one of which was terror of a black man:

> The African of whom I was so terribly afraid was the footman of a rich merchant from Rotterdam, who lived opposite our house; and, as he was fond of children, Aboar (as he was called) used to come up to speak to little missey as I stood at the door in my nurse's arms, a civility which I received with screams and tears and kicks. But, as soon as my parents heard of this ill-behaviour they resolved to put a stop to it, and missey was forced to shake hands with the black the next time he approached her, and thenceforward we were very good friends. Nor did they fail to make me acquainted with negro history; as soon as I was able to understand, I was shewn [sic] on the map where their native country was situated; I was told the sad tale of negro wrongs and negro slavery; and I believe that my early and ever-increasing zeal in the cause of emancipation was founded and fostered by the kindly emotions which I was encouraged to feel for my friend Aboar and all his race.[3]

For the first four years of her life Amelia's mother had been cared for by a black nurse – one to whom she was particularly close since her parents both died when she was a toddler. Mrs Alderson, also named Amelia, was the daughter of Joseph Briggs, a Norfolk rector's eldest son, who worked as writer for the East India Company in Bengal. Joseph married his wife Mary Worrall in Calcutta in May, 1742, when he was in his early 20s.* Amelia, their only child, was born four years later. Joseph died in May, 1747; Mary the following December, of smallpox.[4] The orphaned Amelia was taken into the care of Joseph's

---

* In the Bengal marriages register (BL, India Office records, N/1/1 f.254) Joseph Briggs's bride is named as Mrs Mary Worrall. At that time 'Mrs' was the title for unmarried women of social standing.

good friend Captain James Irwin, who also worked for the East India Company. He undertook to arrange for the little girl to be sent home to England – a long journey of several months by sea – in the care of her black nurse Savannah.

By the summer of 1749 Amelia Briggs was in Holt in Norfolk, with her paternal grandmother Grace Briggs, widow of Dr Henry Briggs, who was Rector of Holt for 26 years. When appointed rector in 1722, Briggs, a scholar and historian. was already Lord of the Manor of Holt through his mother's Hobart ancestors. On his death in 1748, his second son William took over the family affairs and was in correspondence with Captain Irwin over the orphan's welfare. In a letter, telling Irwin that Amelia had arrived safely in England at the end of May 1749, he wrote:

> Your great care of my niece has given very sensible pleasure to all her relations, and all unite with me to return you sincere and hearty thanks; at present we can only express our gratitude in words....
>
> My very great affection for my dear brother Joseph naturally leads me to love and care for the little orphan as if it was my own. She will never want while I have it in my power to assist her. She will be a burden to none of her relations, for before she will have any occasion for it, she will be in possession of a very handsome annuity.[5]

William Briggs, newly married to Elizabeth Perronet, was living in London, where he worked in the Customs House and was a book steward for John Wesley at the Foundery at Moorfields, one of the first Methodist missionary centres. Elizabeth's father, the Rev Vincent Perronet, of Shoreham in Kent, was a close associate and adviser of the Wesley brothers. John Wesley was a life-long opponent of slavery and the slave trade; it appears that William was of the same mind. In his letter of thanks to Captain Irwin he made a point of seeking assurances about the future of his niece's nurse:

> The black girl, her nurse, is not reconciled to England; and, thinking she never shall be so, she is determined to return to Bengal by the Christmas ships. As my mother will give her entire liberty to be at her own disposal, I believe her design is to enter into service, as other free women do. If it be in your power, you are very much desired by all my niece's friends to prevent Savannah's being bought or sold as a negro.[6]

Amelia Alderson was proud of her maternal ancestry. Her mother was descended from Augustine Briggs (1617-84), born and educated in Norwich, an ardent Royalist, who was MP for the city four times and after whom Briggs's Lane in the city was named.* She minded that the vault containing the body of her worthy ancestor in the city's St Peter Mancroft Church was no longer in the possession of the family. In a pocket book in which she wrote an account of the Briggs family pedigree dating back to the early 13th century she stated:

> [The vault] has been since appropriated by the Dean and Chapter to another family, as it was supposed no one was alive to claim it; but I, A Opie, am the lineal descendant and representative of this excellent man, and the vault was my property.[7]

The loss of the vault rankled for many years. She returned to the subject again in a letter to her second cousin, the artist Henry Perronet Briggs, who was a grandson of William:

> The late Dean's widow sent me thro' her nephew-in-law the other day, a humble petition requesting my leave to be buried in St Peter's Church forgetting that *years ago* I gave up to her and her family my *right* in Augustine Briggs's vault. He is there in the large chamber he built for his descendants, who removed to Holt and lie, my dear mother with them, in the family vault there – which is now *full* I believe.[8]

The Briggs ancestors who settled in Holt were descendants of Augustine through his most famous son William, whose wife Hannah was daughter of the Royalist Squire of Holt, Edmund Hobart, and great grand-daughter of Sir Henry Hobart, Lord Chief Justice to James I. Like the Briggses, the Hobarts were long-established residents of Norfolk. Hannah's grandfather James Hobart was Lord of the Manor of Holt in the early 1600s; his brother Henry bought and rebuilt Blickling Hall.† Hannah and William, a celebrated oculist, physician to William III and a fellow of the Royal College of Surgeons, were the parents of Dr Henry Briggs.

A few years before he took up his appointment in Holt, a fire

---

* Now known as Brigg Street. Amelia, too, gave her name to a street in Norwich. A passageway known as Devil's Alley ran alongside her last home on Castle Meadow; when the house was pulled down the alley was widened and renamed Opie Street.

† Now owned by the National Trust and regarded as one of England's great Jacobean houses.

destroyed almost the whole town and gutted the church. He determined to rebuild it and enlisted the support of fellow Norfolk man,
the Prime Minister Sir Robert Walpole, and Charles, Viscount Townshend, Secretary of State, who was Walpole's brother-in-law. They
gave £50 each and George, Prince of Wales (later George II) to whom
Briggs was chaplain, gave £100. Walpole and Townshend each gave a
silver alms dish, the Prince gave a silver flagon and Briggs gave a silver
communion cup. By 1727 all was complete.

Henry Briggs also enlarged the Parsonage House – possibly needing ample accommodation for his growing family. He and his wife
Grace (née Everard), daughter of a Liverpool merchant, had five sons,
all of whom were educated at Gresham's School in Holt, and one
daughter Elizabeth.

Small wonder that Amelia was so proud of and interested in her
Briggs ancestors. Much of her correspondence with Henry Perronet
Briggs contained references to their forefathers which she had gleaned
from various sources, including Blomefield's *History of Norfolk*, to
which her great-grandfather had contributed information about Holt.
She delighted in addressing her cousin as 'Dear Pontibus', having as-
certained that the Briggs were descended from an ancient family of
Salle, in Norfolk, who assumed the surname of De Ponte or Pontibus.
As she explained it, this meant 'at Brigg or Brigges' because they had
dwelt 'by the bridge or bridges'.

Throughout her long life Amelia mixed easily with people from all
levels of society and was a willing supporter of good causes. However,
she also took great pleasure in friendships with the aristocracy; she
was acutely aware of social niceties and would assert her authority
on such matters if the need arose. In her 73rd year she responded
sharply to an appeal from a writer who wanted her to subscribe to
his new book and who had been unfortunate enough to address his
letter incorrectly:

> But *pray* do not call me *Mrs* Amelia Opie. I am not Mrs Amelia
> Opie but Mrs Opie or among friends Amelia Opie. I am not an old
> maid but the widow of a distinguished man and it is an offence to
> my husband's memory to call me as *single* unmarried women are
> designated.... Mrs Opie, Norwich, is my *lawful* and proper desig-
> nation.[9]

She became the widow of that 'distinguished man', the artist John
Opie, in 1807 after a marriage lasting only nine years, but she enjoyed

a much longer relationship of fifty-six years with another eminent man, her father. Dr James Alderson was well known and respected in Norwich where he had settled as a young married man. He numbered many of the city's wealthiest and most influential people among his patients and made a handsome living attending to their medical needs; but he also devoted many hours a week to treating the poor, free of charge, and was one of the trustees of a charity, the bequest of a vicar, which gave financial help to poor boys seeking trade apprenticeships.[10]

The son of a dissenting minister, he married Amelia Briggs in January 1769[11]. Amelia, their only child, was baptised in the 'new chapel' for the Society of Protestant Dissenters opened in 1756, their old meeting house on the same site having been demolished. The Octagon Chapel in Colegate was just round the corner from the Alderson family home in Snailgate.* The elegant building – with eight fluted columns supporting its roof and a domed ceiling supported by arches resting on the columns – was designed by Thomas Ivory, the city's leading architect of the time.

Amelia was baptised by Samuel Bourn[12], son of an eminent dissenting minister in Birmingham, who had been co-pastor at the chapel since its opening. The Octagon numbered among its congregation many intellectuals and radical thinkers. William Taylor, who went on to become a distinguished writer and German scholar, was also baptised by Bourn. He continued to attend services at the chapel in his adult life, wrote some hymns for the congregation and was buried in the Octagon graveyard. James Smith, who later founded the Linnaean Society, and Robert Woodhouse, a cousin of Amelia's, who became Lucasian professor of mathematics at Cambridge, were both members of Bourn's congregation. The Martineau family, whose talented members would later include Harriet, the author, and James, the theologian, also attended the Octagon Chapel

Amelia's paternal grandfather James Alderson was born in the old county of Westmorland (now part of Cumbria) and trained at a nonconformist academy in Kendal. In 1738, at the age of 24, he was appointed minister for the dissenting congregation at Lowestoft in Suffolk, where he remained until his death in 1760. A local historian remembered Mr Alderson as 'a very worthy, well disposed man, of

---

* Brightwell names it as Calvert Street, but in 1769 it was known as Snailgate. Dr Alderson moved the family to a house in Colegate while Amelia was growing up. When she married, he returned to Snailgate; in Thomas Peck's *Norwich Directory* of 1802 he is listed as the occupant of 3, Snailgate.

an exceeding affable and peaceful disposition, much esteemed by the whole circle of his congregation; and as he lived much respected, so he died universally lamented.'[13]

The minister married a Lowestoft woman, 20-year-old Judith Mewse, in 1740 and over the next 17 years she gave birth to nine children, of whom two died in infancy. Richard, the eldest son, died at the age of 18 in the same year as his father, leaving James Alderson, 17, as the eldest of the remaining siblings – Judith, 11; Thomas, 9; Robert, 7; Elizabeth, 5; John, 3. Little is known about James's medical training but it is possible that he went to London for at least some part of it. During the 18th century it was common practice for aspiring doctors to be apprenticed to an established practitioner for five to seven years. This was the time when several provincial hospitals were being set up, primarily to treat the poor and needy, but also to advance medical knowledge and give some training to student doctors. Many of the well-known London hospitals were established in the 18th century and surgery was the main subject taught in them.

In 1759, a year before he died, Richard Alderson was in London from where he wrote to tell his father about having dinner with a Mr Cruttenden at his house, which he reached 'after a very pleasant walk through Moorfields'.[14] It seems likely that this was Joseph Cruttenden, a member of the Company of Surgeons (later the Royal College of Surgeons), who lived in the parish of St Giles, Cripplegate, barely a quarter of a mile away from Moorfields. Replying to 'Dear Dickey', his father wrote that 'your uncle greatly approves your scheme for James'.[15] Possibly Richard was making inquiries about medical training for his younger brother. Richard himself may have been thinking of becoming a dissenting minister like his father. In the same letter home he wrote of going 'to hear Mr Godwin',* to which James senior replied: 'I think Mr Godwin cannot be ye most acceptable preacher, however, he is I suppose a pious and good man and under your circumstances it was right to attend him.'

James, bereaved of his father and older brother within months of each other, took his filial duties seriously and remained close to his widowed mother, who lived to be 90 years old. She eventually moved to Norwich, where James, his sister Judith and brother Robert had all settled, sharing a home with her unmarried daughter Elizabeth

---

* Possibly William Godwin's grandfather Edward Godwin, a dissenting minister, who was pastor of the Little St Helen's meeting house off Bishopsgate Street, and well known in London religious circles.

Alderson, who also lived to a ripe old age.

In the late 18th century Norwich was the third largest city in England with a population of about 38,000. For the well-to-do there were many fine city houses with extensive gardens, but the poor were crammed into small dwellings around mean yards in narrow back streets. Poor sanitation, overcrowded tenement buildings, unhealthy diets and low wages among a high percentage of the population meant that those most in need of medical treatment were the least able to afford it. A scheme to alleviate the problem was mooted in the August following Amelia's birth, when a public meeting was called at the Norwich Guildhall to draw up plans for a hospital which would offer free medical care to 'the deserving poor' of the city and county. A committee was formed, books for subscriptions opened and within a month a piece of land 'without St Stephen's Gates' – the city at that time still having its medieval walls and 12 original toll gates – had been leased from the Norwich Corporation for 500 years at £6 per annum.[16] James Alderson was present at the meeting at which the lease was signed; a month later he attended the committee which agreed the rules and orders for the new venture.[17]

The Norfolk and Norwich Hospital opened for its first out-patients in July 1772; its first in-patients were admitted in November that year. Dr Alderson was appointed one of its three assistant surgeons – there were also four physicians and three surgeons – and all gave their services gratis. He was promoted to full surgeon in 1777 and physician in 1793, retiring in 1821. It was an exacting role. The medical men took it in turn to examine those recommended as 'a real object of charity' by subscribers to the institution as in-patients every Saturday morning and to prescribe to out-patients every Tuesday morning. In addition they were expected to visit patients in hospital, to be consulted on difficult cases, to be available for emergencies, to supervise the purchase of drugs and medicines, to give instruction to medical trainees and to attend some meetings of the hospital board of governors.[18]

Although the medical men gave their services free, salaries had to be paid to a matron, nine nurses, a secretary, apothecary, cook, room maid and others including an assistant to work the horse 'for raising water'. Most of the physicians and surgeons, including Dr Alderson, were also subscribers. They were given an annual report from the auditors:

Thus the subscribers and other benefactors have the satisfaction of seeing how their money is applied, how far their benevolent and Christian intentions are made productive of real comfort and relief to the distresses of their fellow creatures. An account of this kind, it is presumed will best shew [sic] the extensive utility of the institution....[19]

At the time of Amelia's birth there were 899 people housed in the city's two workhouses, both of which were within a few minutes' walking distance from her parents' home. In the November of her fourth birthday, her father was appointed a city surgeon, that is, one of the four surgeons to the Corporation of Guardians of the Poor. This body had been set up in Norwich in 1712 to run two workhouses – to maintain the poor and provide them with employment. He had sought election to the post in June 1773, but was beaten by a fellow contender, 19 votes to 18. Thomas Bland, a member of the Corporation, wrote to his friend John Gurney, who was away from Norwich at the time, explaining the procedure and bemoaning the fact that 11 of Alderson's supporters had not turned up to vote:

I know thou wilt be not a little mortified to hear he is thrown out by the same means that many an Election has been lost, viz his Friends being over assured; they laughed at him for expressing any Apprehension about his Success, several went out of Town... poor Jemmy is thoroughly disappointed, having set his Heart on the place, and been so often assured by his Friends there was not the smallest Doubt of his success.[20]

On November 7th, when at last he was elected by the Guardians of the Poor to be a city surgeon, Dr Alderson's fellow assistant surgeon at the hospital, Edward Rigby,* was at the same time appointed 'male midwife' to the workhouses. The commitment which her father made to the poor and needy made a lasting impression on the tender-hearted Amelia. Years later, recalling his work she said:

He prescribed for about four or five hundred persons at his house every week. The forms [benches] in our large hall in a morning were so full from half-past eight till eleven, that I could scarcely pass.[21]

---

* Dr Rigby, a frequent visitor to the Alderson household, campaigned for better conditions in the workhouses and for vaccination against smallpox. During a serious outbreak in the city in 1812 he persuaded the workhouse guardians to offer a reward of 2s 6d to every poor person in Norwich 'who shall be vaccinated by a city surgeon'.

Her attachment to her father was so strong he could well be seen as a threat to any potential suitor for his vivacious daughter. When the artist John Opie first declared his feelings for Amelia she rejected him, but had to admit in a letter to Susannah Taylor:

> ...the attraction Mr O held out, that staggered me beyond anything else; it was that, if I was averse to leaving my father, he would joyfully consent to his living with us. What a temptation to me, who am every moment sensible, that the claims of my father will always be, with me, superior to any claims that a lover can hold out![22]

In the same letter she owned she was 'certain' her father would disapprove, not only of Opie but of '*any* connexion [sic]' for her. There was no hint of self-pity or resentment in her claim; she was simply acknowledging the truth. She and her father were – to their mutual satisfaction – inextricably linked.

Chapter Two

It is reasonable to assume that Amelia's bond with her father became even deeper after her mother died. At the age of 15, she took on the roles of mistress of the household, hostess to her father's guests and his companion at social events. But Mrs Alderson was, undoubtedly, a significant figure in her daughter's early years. Not only did she relieve Amelia's fear of black people and awaken her life-long concern for the plight of slaves, she also helped her to overcome a terror of mad people and, in so doing, helped her to understand some of the consequences of poverty.

The terror was provoked by seeing two 'deranged' women who passed by the Alderson house every day. In her recollections of childhood she wrote:

> ...these poor visited creatures were to me objects of such terror, that when I saw them coming (followed usually by hooting boys) I used to run away to hide myself. But as soon as my mother was aware of this terror she resolved to conquer it; and I was led by her to the door the next time one of these women was in sight; nor was I allowed to stir till I had heard her kindly converse with the poor afflicted one, and then I was commissioned to put a piece of money into her hand. I had to undergo the same process with the other woman, but she tried my nerves more than the preceding one, for she insisted on shaking hands with me... however, the fear was in a measure conquered, and a feeling of deep interest, not unmixed with awe, was excited in my mind, not only towards these women, but towards insane persons in general; a feeling that has never left me.[1]

Her interest in mad people was intensified when she was out walking with her 'beloved parents' and went past the 'city asylum for lunatics, called the bedlam'.* The trio used to stop before the iron gates and

---

* Probably the Bethel Hospital, built in Norwich in 1713 by Mary Chapman (née Mann), daughter of a former mayor of Norwich and widow of a clergyman, in gratitude for being 'blessed with the use of my reason and understanding' and out of compassion for 'such persons as are afflicted with lunacy or madness...and are poor inhabitants in the said city'. (Frederick Bateman & Walter Rye, *The History of the Bethel Hospital at Norwich* (Norwich: Gibbs & Waller, 1906), p.15.)

observe the inmates at the windows, who would sometimes ask for money so they could buy snuff. The imaginative child saw this as a chance to make further contact with the inhabitants; she walked there alone one day and when she held up a penny, 'a customer soon appeared at one of the windows' and begged her to throw it over the door to the ground where they walked. Amelia found herself trembling with fright as she stood listening for the inmate waiting on the other side and heard 'the clanking of his chain'.

Her first beneficiary was a man called Goodings with whom she struck up a friendship. From her weekly allowance she began to buy flowers for him after he admired a nosegay she was wearing one day:

> ...some of my happiest moments were those when I visited the gates of bedlam; and so often did I go, that I became well known to its inmates, and I have heard them say 'Oh! There is the little girl from St George's' (the parish in which I then lived).[2]

When her obsession with the pitiful inmates was at its height, Dr Alderson asked a friend whose house overlooked the grounds of the 'bedlam' to allow his daughter to stand at one of its open windows and 'see the lunatics walk'. On the first visit she was able to talk with Goodings and others. Most fascinating of all was an 'unseen lunatic', a woman who, Amelia was informed, had been 'crossed in love' and who, in her cell, opposite the open window, sang song after song. But she was only allowed two such visits:

> I believe my parents thought the excitement was an unsafe one, as I was constantly talking of what I had said to the mad folks, and they to me; and it was so evident that I was proud of their acquaintance, and of my own attachment to them, that I was admonished not to go so often to the gates of the bedlam.[3]

Warned against visiting the mad people so frequently, Amelia found no difficulty in transferring her passion elsewhere and 'dancing and French school soon gave another turn to my thoughts, and excited in me other views and feelings.' This capacity to move easily and enthusiastically from serious to frivolous subjects and back again never left her.

Amelia took French lessons from the Rev John Bruckner, who had been persuaded to leave his pastorship in Leiden in Holland in 1753, when he was 27, and come to Norwich to be the pastor of the city's Walloon (French Protestants) Church. A few years later he also took charge of the city's Dutch Protestant Church. A cultured, scholarly man, educated at Franeker University,* Bruckner could preach in Dutch, English, French and Latin. Another of his pupils was William Taylor, whose biographer wrote:

> Mr Bruckner was a man of vigorous intellectual powers, discriminating habits and quick observation. He grounded his pupil, not only in the elements of the French tongue, but also in the general principles of language.[4]

The pastor was also a published author† and a subscriber to the Norfolk and Norwich Hospital, where he regularly took his turn as one of the two 'house visitors' appointed each week to tour the wards and ensure that all was well with the patients.[5] Under his tuition, Amelia did very well in French. Her fluency in the language stood her in good stead when she paid visits to Paris and corresponded with French friends.

Her affection for the Rev Bruckner persisted into adult life, when she was away from home meeting new people in London. After her marriage in 1798 she asked her husband to paint for her a portrait of her old French master, which was exhibited at the Royal Academy in 1800 as *Portrait of a Gentleman*[6]. The portrait remained one of her most treasured possessions. When young visitors came to her house, she enjoyed explaining – with some dramatic licence – how it had come to be painted, as Caroline Fox, on a visit to her Gurney relations in Norwich and Norfolk, reported in her journal on October 22nd, 1843: 'Dined with Amelia Opie: she was in great force and really jolly. Exhibited her gallery containing some fine portraits by her husband, one being of her old French master, which she insisted on Opie painting before she would accept him.'[7]

Reminiscing about her schooldays in a letter to Susannah in January 1800, Amelia wrote:

> I feel the older I grow, the more tenderly I cling to the scenes, and recollections, and companions of my early hours. When I now look at Mr Bruckner's black cap, my memory gets astride on the tassel of

---

* Founded in 1585, the second oldest university in the Netherlands, with departments in theology, law, medicine, philosophy, mathematics and physics. Closed by the French in 1811.

† Dr Bruckner's best known work was *Criticisms on the Diversions of Purley in a letter to Horne Tooke* (London: T Cadell, 1790). It was published under the nom-de-plume 'I Cassander', a reference to the place of his birth, the Flemish island of Cadsand.

it, and off she gallops at a very pleasant rate; wooden desks, green bags, blotted books, inked hands, faces and gowns, rise in array before me.[8]

Dr Bruckner took his own life in May 1804. In the *Norwich Mercury*'s death notice he was described as 'beloved for his affability and attention; respected for his probity and prudence; and admired for his learning and good sense'. Amelia wrote her own poetic tribute to her beloved teacher in *Portrait the Third*, one of six odes inspired by portraits hanging in her home, published in 1834 in *Lays for the Dead*, her last book of poems:

> ...And he my childhood's friend, kind, pious, wise,
> Rais'd his own hand against his honour'd life!
> Thence, while I gaze upon that awful brow
> My sportive childhood sometimes wreath'd in smiles,
> Sad recollections suddenly arise,
> And grateful memory's joy is quench'd in tears.[9]

Another of Amelia's teachers, fondly remembered, was Judith Dixon 'with her plump good-humoured face'. Only seven years older than her pupil, Judith (later Mrs Beecroft) was a friend of Anna Letitia Barbauld, the poet, essayist and writer for children. Anna was married to the Rev Rochemont Barbauld, a graduate of Warrington Academy in Lancashire, where her father, the Rev John Aikin, a Presbyterian Dissenter, was a tutor. The son of a Church of England clergyman, Rochemont converted to dissent at the academy and later became a zealous Unitarian. He accepted a post as minister to a dissenting congregation at Palgrave in Suffolk, where he and Anna established a boys' school, which they ran from 1774 until 1785. One of their first boarders was Mr Bruckner's promising pupil William Taylor.

Amelia's uncle Robert Alderson was educated at the Warrington Academy, where he was tutored in divinity by Anna's father. He was ordained at Palgrave and in December 1776 was appointed minister at the Octagon Chapel where he had been assisting Samuel Bourn for three years. Another pupil from the academy was William Enfield, one of Anna's life-long friends, who settled in Norwich in 1785 when he took over at the Octagon Chapel. During their stay in East Anglia the Barbaulds developed friendships with many people in Norwich, including the Aldersons, Martineaus and others connected with the Octagon Chapel. In the following years, when they moved first to

Hampstead and then to Stoke Newington, they paid frequent visits to the city.

Anna Barbauld's particular friend in Norwich was Susannah Taylor, wife of John Taylor, a deacon at the Octagon Chapel and grandson of Dr John Taylor, one of its co-founders. Susannah and John were married in 1777 and went on to have five sons and two daughters. John served an apprenticeship in the city's thriving textile business and then set up on his own as a yarn-maker in 1773. He was treasurer to the Octagon's charity schools, wrote poetry for local publications and helped to found a subscription library in 1784. This was a scheme initiated by his cousin Philip Meadows Martineau* who had studied medicine in Edinburgh, and was appointed assistant surgeon to Amelia's father at the Norfolk and Norwich Hospital in 1777. When Dr Alderson became a physician in 1793, Martineau succeeded him as surgeon.

The Taylors, whose literary acquaintances over the years included William Godwin, Robert Southey and Henry Crabb Robinson, were friends and near neighbours of the Aldersons. Amelia became close to Susannah, 13 years her senior, whom one of her sons later recalled as having 'discharged her duties as wife, mother and friend in an exemplary manner'.[10] Mrs Barbauld, too, believed Susannah Taylor to be an exemplar. After leaving Norwich the Barbaulds spent nearly a year touring France, ending their trip in Paris from where, in June 1786, Anna wrote to her friend:

> ...when I see the Parisian ladies covered with rouge and enslaved by fashion, cold to the claims of maternal tenderness, and covering licentiousness with the thin veil of a certain factitious decency of manners, my thoughts turn away from the scene, and delight to contemplate the charming union formed by deep affection and lasting esteem – the mother endowed with talents and graces to draw the attention of polite circles, yet devoting her time and cares to her family and children – English delicacy, unspoiled beauty, and unaffected sentiment – when I think of these (and *your* friends will not be at a loss to guess where I look for them) it gives the same relief to my mind as it would to my eye when wearied and dazzled by their sand-walks and terraces, if it could repose upon the cheerful and soft green of our lawny turf.[11]

---

* John Taylor's mother Margaret and Philip Meadows Martineau's mother Sarah were the daughters of Philip Meadows, Mayor of Norwich in 1734.

Returning to England and living in Hampstead, the Barbaulds' London associates, as in Norfolk, were radical intellectuals and literary figures – the circle which Amelia Alderson became part of when she began to make regular trips to the capital in her twenties and about which she wrote to Susannah. Like Amelia, Mrs Barbauld was an ardent supporter of the anti-slavery campaign; her popular *Hymns in Prose for Children* (1781) included lines on a Negro slave woman, pining in captivity and weeping over her sick child. The writer Hannah More, at the request of the Abolition Society, penned *Slavery: A Poem* (1788) in which she declared that the slave trade was a blemish on the national character and urged her compatriots to hasten its abolition. In the same year the poet William Cowper was asked by supporters of the abolition campaign to write verses which might capture the attention of the public. His *The Negro's Complaint* was set to music and became a popular success.

The anti-slavery campaign had been gaining followers in a rather piecemeal fashion across the country since the 1760s. Quakers were the prime movers in the first instance. Across the Atlantic their American counterparts were also pushing for reform. Joseph Oxley, of the Norwich Society of Friends, travelled through the American colonies visiting Quaker meetings in the early 1770s. His information about slavery was passed on to Anthony Benezet, a Quaker and campaigner, who had been the driving force in setting up a school for negro children in Philadelphia. Benezet wrote to John and Henry Gurney, of the Norwich Society of Friends, in 1772, confirming Oxley's reports, adding that 'the pushing and bringing of the miserable specimens [the negro slaves] from their native land' was a matter of great concern.[12]

In 1783 the Quakers' Yearly Meeting decided to petition Parliament against the Slave Trade; in March 1785, the Norfolk Quaker Meeting agreed to set up a local committee to involve itself in the anti-slavery work. Nationally, the movement really took off in April 1787, when a Society for Effecting the Abolition of the Slave Trade was set up. It was led by the Quaker Granville Sharp and the committee included Thomas Clarkson, from Wisbech, whose interest in slavery began when he researched the subject for an essay, which won him a major prize when he was a student at Cambridge University. Clarkson was instrumental in persuading William Wilberforce, the West Riding MP, to plead the cause in Parliament. It was to be a long campaign before the Abolition Bill, making it unlawful for British ships to participate in the Atlantic slave trade, was passed in 1807.

In Norwich there was strong support for the cause; many citizens took to abstaining from buying sugar as a protest against slavery in the plantations of the West Indies. An anonymous member of the Society of Universal Goodwill in London and Norwich wrote *An Inquiry into the origin, progress and present state of Slavery, with a plan for the gradual, reasonable and secure Emancipation of Slaves* which was published in 1789 and widely circulated in the city. In February 1792, leading citizens held a meeting at which they unanimously agreed to send to the Commons a petition against the African Slave Traffic. When the Quarterly Assembly of the Corporation met later in the month it drew up a parallel petition for the abolition of a trade 'so disgraceful to a Christian country and incompatible with the sentiments of feelings of humanity'. In March that year the Norwich Revolution Society voted a subscription of £10 10s 0d to the Anti-Slave Trade Committee. A vote in the Commons on April 2nd in favour of gradual abolition – the protagonists had wanted instant abolition – was greeted by the ringing of the bells of St Peter Mancroft for two days running and 'the general joy of the citizens in the triumph of humanity', as reported in the *Norfolk Chronicle*. The euphoria was short-lived because the Lords insisted that evidence given in the Commons must be repeated before them; thus the business was postponed for a year by which time the country was at war with France and the anti-slavery issue was dropped for the time being.

Throughout the campaign, not only Anna Barbauld and Hannah More, but other women writers, among them Ann Yearsley, Helen Maria Williams and Norwich-born Elizabeth Bentley, also espoused the abolitionist cause. Elizabeth Bentley wrote *On the Abolition of the African Slave Trade* in which she suggested that all decent citizens must wish to see the breaking of the chains of 'inglorious slavery'. The poem, dated July 1789, was included in her *Genuine Poetical Compositions on Various Subjects*, published in Norwich in 1791. The book's subscribers included 'Miss Alderson' and 'John Taylor and Mrs [Taylor]'.

Amelia's first anti-slavery poem, *The Negro Boy's Tale: A Poem Addressed to Children*, was written in 1790. It was included in her first book of poems in 1802 and re-issued in 1824 as a slim volume for children with a new preface by the author. Like most of her contemporaries, she adopted a child-like pidgin English for the words of her slaves, as a way of expressing the racial difference. The champion of the tale is Anna, whose challenging behaviour represents the ongoing struggle in the fight for freedom.*

The long narrative poem tells of Zambo, a Negro boy, snatched from his mother by 'bad vite men' and set to work as a slave under the lash in Jamaica. Believing that if he can get to England he will be set free and have the chance to return to his native land, he appeals to Anna, the daughter of a sea captain about to set sail for home, to take him aboard:

> 'Missa,' poor Zambo cried, 'sweet land
> Dey tell me dat you go to see,
> Vere, soon as on de shore he stand,
> De helpless Negro slave be free.

Anna knows he will still be a slave in England but believes she might be able to find him less brutal employers. When her father refuses to take on Zambo, the young slave boy plunges into the sea in a desperate attempt to reach the vessel, whereupon the captain repents and a rope is thrown to help him on board. But it is too late and the poor child drowns. The closing lines seek redemption:

> Come, Justice, come! In glory drest,
> O come! The woe-worn negro's friend,
> The fiend-delighting trade arrest.
> The negro's chains asunder rend![13]

Amelia and Dr Alderson, were among Norwich subscribers to the eighth (1794) edition of *The Interesting Narrative of Olaudah Equiano or Gustavus Vassa, the African*, an account of the slave trade written by a former slave.† The author expressed his appreciation of the citizens' support in a notice in the *Norfolk Chronicle* on March 15th, 1794:

> Gustavus Vassa, the African to the Inhabitants of this City and its Environs
> Permit me, one of the oppressed Natives of Africa, to offer you

---

* Some feminist writers in the late 20th century suggested that women writers who took slavery as a subject were, consciously or otherwise, using their own experience in the female role as a yardstick. Moira Ferguson in her *Subject to Others: British Women Writers and Colonial Slavery 1670-1834* (New York & London: Routledge, 1992) sees the subtext of *The Negro Boy's Tale* as 'a misty picture of female suppression and sabotage'.

† First published in 1789, the book ran to nine editions in five years. Re-issued as *The Interesting Narrative & Other Writings* by Olaudah Equiano (Harmondsworth, Middlesex: Penguin Books, 1995).

the warmest thanks of a heart glowing with gratitude to you for your fellow feeling for the Africans and their cause:- Having received marks of kindness from you who have subscribed to my interesting Narrative, I heartily wish all of you every blessing that this world can afford, and all fullness of joy in the next world. NB Subscribers and others, may now have the Narrative of the Author at Mr Johnson's, Bridge St, St George's, and of Mr Stevenson, at the Norfolk Arms, in the Marketplace, price 4s.

A notice in the *Norfolk Chronicle*, March 15th, 1794, for the eighth edition of the former slave's book to which Amelia and Dr Alderson subscribed.

The list of more than 200 subscribers to this edition included dissenters, Quakers, Church of England vicars and their families, members of the Corporation – several of whom had served as sheriff or mayor – doctors, merchants, members of the Norwich Revolution Society and the United Friars, a group set up in the city in 1785 for men of an inquiring mind who were interested in literature, science and philosophy. This group had enabled Elizabeth Bentley to publish her *Poetical Compositions* and were active in distributing soup and bread to the poor. The slave trade was a recurring topic for discussion at their meetings.

Also named in the Norwich list were William Buck and Miss Buck, of Bury [St Edmunds]. William Buck was a prosperous yarn-maker and Miss [Catherine] Buck his eldest child, who was known both to Amelia Alderson and Susannah Taylor. A lively and intelligent young woman, Catherine had attached herself to the anti-slavery campaign with great dedication and enthusiasm after meeting Thomas Clarkson at the home of her uncle Joseph Hardcastle at New Cross in Surrey. There, Clarkson had shown her items from the chest he carried around the country – handcuffs, branding irons and shackles made to restrain the human cargo on slave ships. He also carried examples of woven and dyed materials and other goods made by African natives, which he used to demonstrate that they were craftsmen and women of great skill, not the ignorant savages that some people chose to believe as a way of justifying the slave trade. He had been working tirelessly for the Abolition Society, travelling the length and breadth of the country, rallying supporters and collecting information, especially at the ports of Liverpool and Bristol, from sailors who had worked on the slave trade ships. Catherine's contribution to Clarkson's work was to make copies of the mounting sheets of evidence and to write out the questions being drawn up to present to MPs. Inevitably, perhaps, the couple fell in love, and were married in January 1797. He was 37 and she was 25.

Before her marriage Catherine was part of a group of liberal-minded, non-conformist young people who met regularly, often at her father's house, to discuss the issues of the day. A near neighbour was Henry Crabb Robinson, three years younger than Catherine and a great admirer of the young Miss Buck. In later life, when he had achieved success as a German scholar, foreign correspondent for *The Times* and barrister, he recalled that she was 'the most eloquent woman I have ever known, with the exception of Madame de Staël'.[14] Catherine lent books to Henry and introduced him to new ideas and opinions. At 15, he was articled to an attorney in Colchester, where he lived until he moved to London in 1796 for his first job as a solicitor's clerk.

On a visit to his home town in the spring of 1795 Henry was invited to dinner at Mr Buck's when the party was made up of the most distinguished liberals in the neighbourhood. There he renewed his acquaintance with the 25-year-old Amelia Alderson whom he had met previously at her father's house in Norwich. Reminiscing about the occasion, he wrote: 'there came to visit Miss Buck a young lady from Norwich who had already acquired a great provincial celebrity,

Amelia Alderson…It was given to her for accomplishments and supposed literary attainments and not her beauty, but she was attractive and made much of at Bury.'[15]

Chapter Three

The 'supposed literary attainments' of the young Miss Alderson, to which Henry Crabb Robinson referred when recalling their meeting in 1795, were a novel published in 1790, a play performed in Norwich in 1791 and a short story and poems contributed to a magazine, *The Cabinet*, launched in the city in the autumn of 1794. Robinson himself had contributed a piece to the latter. 'It was in December 1794 that my vanity was delighted by the appearance in print of an essay I wrote on *Spies and Informers*. It was published in *The Cabinet*, which had been got up by the young liberals of the then aspiring town of Norwich.'[1] The first edition of the radical magazine appeared on October 11th, 1794, and it was published every fortnight for about 12 months.* Robinson's Norwich friend Thomas Amyot, articled to an attorney, was a keen but critical reader of *The Cabinet*. In a letter to their mutual friend William Pattison, articled to an attorney in Diss, he wrote on February 5th, 1795: 'It is the work of young men, perhaps more zealous than wise; it is rather a display of juvenile abilities than a repository of political knowledge.'[2]

Before becoming a regular contributor to the magazine – of which more later – Amelia achieved her first success as a published author with a novel *Dangers of Coquetry*. It was published anonymously in two volumes by William Lane, of Leadenhall Street in London in 1790,† when she was 20. Lane, the son of a Whitechapel poulterer, had set up as a bookseller in his father's shop in about 1770, moving to Aldgate in 1773 and then to Leadenhall Street in 1775. At his new premises he experimented with various types of publication but by 1785 the main focus was on fiction. He had already set up a system of circulating libraries, the first one of which was in London, which were ideally suited to accept the tales and romances being brought out by his publishing business.

In 1784 Lane had placed an advertisement in *The Correspondent* in which he offered to supply anybody who wished to set up a circulating library with a stock of books from his warehouse. In 1790 he

---

* When *The Cabinet* ceased publication its contents were re-published in three volumes by the Norwich printer J. March in 1795.
† The 1790 edition of the novel held in the British Library is marked 'rare'.

gave his business a new name, The Minerva Press, installing a figure of the goddess over the central door of his premises in Leadenhall Street – now extended with the addition of two neighbouring houses –and adopting a vignette of a seated Minerva for the logo on his customers' bills and library labels.

The anonymous novel was very much in vogue, particularly for women writers, during the latter part of the 18th century and well into the first years of the 19th.* The title page of Amelia's *Dangers of Coquetry* does not even offer the discreet 'A Lady', the most commonly used epithet for women novelists at that time. It is not known why Amelia offered her first major work of fiction to William Lane. Possibly she had borrowed and read some of the popular Lane romances from a circulating library. In Norwich, as in many other provincial cities, there were tradesmen, such as grocers, who also advertised themselves as librarians; the city had an increasing number of such libraries from 1780 onwards. There were at least 24 different circulating libraries in Norwich and Great Yarmouth during the first quarter of the 19th century. The one run by John Hunt, bookseller, ornithologist and taxidermist, was, in fact, named the Minerva Circulating Library.[3]

Although Lane attracted a great deal of criticism from his contemporaries and later reviewers – both for publishing and promoting in his libraries what was regarded as cheap fiction – there is no doubt that the genre in which he specialised was enormously popular. 'Leadenhall Street in those days would be thronged with fashionable women, with their carriages and books, on their way to and from the Minerva Press....he [Lane] made a fortune which enabled him to drive about town in a magnificent carriage accompanied by cockaded footmen complete with gold-headed canes, before he died in 1814.'[4]

Dangers of Coquetry, with its far-fetched (to modern eyes) plot and tragic heroine, was in keeping with the kind of melodramatic romantic novels which were among Lane's best sellers. Its subject matter was an interesting choice for an aspiring author and one which, it would appear, Amelia felt it her duty to present as a warning:

---

* Dorothy Blakey (*The Minerva Press 1790-1820* (London: The Bibliographical Society, 1939) offered in her *Appendix 1* (pp.127-271) the names of authors who had been identified as those responsible for some of the hitherto anonymous works. She was at pains to list the titles for which 'no conjecture as to the authorship can be offered'. One such was *Imogen*, a pastoral romance, published by Lane in 1794, which has since been identified as William Godwin's third novel, loosely based on Milton's *Comus*.

For the perusal of the thoughtless and the young, is this tale given to the world – it teaches that *indiscretions* may produce as fatal effects as *actual guilt* and that even the appearance of *impropriety* cannot be too carefully avoided.[5]

The subject of women using coquettishness to attract members of the opposite sex was explored by several writers. Mary Wollstonecraft, who was to become one of Amelia's literary friends in London, was highly critical of young women being encouraged, from an early age, to acquire 'the arts of coquetry' in order to fit into society's stereotyped gender roles. In Amelia's debut novel the coquettish behaviour of Louisa, the rich, beautiful and accomplished heroine, leads to her downfall. Henry, her upright husband, under whose firm guidance she has modified her flirtatious behaviour, is killed in a duel defending his wife's honour after she has lapsed into her old ways at a society ball. She then dies from guilt and grief. Although Louisa's father plays only a minor role in *Dangers of Coquetry*, he is defined as 'a fond and doating [sic] parent', his wife having died when their only child was 'at an early age'. He is deeply affected at having to say farewell to his daughter when she marries and leaves home for London; she, too, is distressed at their parting, weeping copiously as her new husband takes her away. *Father and Daughter*, Amelia's second novel, published 11 years later, returned to and expanded upon this theme of a deep paternal and filial affection.

From the first pages of the 1790 novel the reader is left in no doubt about the heroine's fatal flaws:

Vanity and love of admiration had possession of her heart, and tho' in her moments of reflection Louisa, listening to the dictates of self-reproach, resolved on suppressing her indiscretion, and discarding the train of admirers whom she alternately encouraged, she still remained eager for admiration, even from those whose understandings she despised: and though shrinking with anguish from the thought of being regarded as such, was at eighteen a finished coquette.

Ostensibly a moral tale pointing out the perils facing any young miss who practises coquetry, the novel also contains a message about a judgemental society. Poor Henry has fought the duel after overhearing a conversation in a London coffee house in which his wife is called 'a despicable coquette'. He knows that Louisa has many admirable qualities, not the least of which is her kindness to the poor and needy. Before hastening to his end, the distraught young husband writes a farewell letter to his wife in which he owns his dread of being killed and leaving her: 'a prey to the malice of a censorious world, which, unacquainted with your worth, and ignorant of your real goodness of heart, may extend their disapprobation of but one foible so far as to tarnish the lustre of all your other virtues and accomplishments.'

The work received a brief notice in *The Critical Review*: 'The moral to be drawn from this work is so good, that we are blind to the dulness [sic], the insipidity, and improbability of the narrative.'[6] Amelia herself recalled the novel with some pride when writing to Susannah from London a few years later:

> I am glad on reperusing *The Dangers of Coquetry* that you think so highly of it. I read it at Seething* soon after I married and felt a great respect for it; and if I ever write a collection of tales, I shall correct and re-publish that as *I originally wrote it*, not as it now is, in the shape of a *novel in chapters* – I believe I told you that Mr Hoare [artist and playwright] was so struck with it as to intend writing a play from it. I wish he would![7]

The next known work by Amelia Alderson was a five-act drama, *The Tragedy of Adelaide*, which was performed on two evenings at the home of her friends the Plumptres in the Cathedral Close in Norwich in January 1791. The 21-year-old Amelia played the title role. The event was reported in the *Norfolk Chronicle* as:

> …the production of a lady of this place, whose abilities and accomplishments have long engrossed the public admiration; and we are informed by those who had the pleasure of witnessing the performance, that few modern productions ought to be named with *Adelaide*. The powers and exertions of the different gentlemen and ladies charmed, astonished and greatly affected the polite audience.[8]

A few weeks later the newspaper added further to its interest in the young playwright's efforts with a new report:

> We are now enabled to add the following particulars of *Adelaide*,

---

* Seething Hall in Norfolk, where John Opie painted portraits of the owner, Thomas Kett, his wife Hannah (née Gurney) and two daughters in 1799. Amelia Alderson, aged 11, attended the Kett wedding in Norwich in 1780, and her father assisted at the birth of the Ketts's son George in 1783. Hannah was a cousin to John Gurney of Earlham Hall.

the choice theatrical *morceau* with which a select company were regaled [sic] at Mr Plumptre's in the Close on the 4th & 6th of January last.'⁹

It then named the *dramatis personae*, with information about each role, and a detailed outline of the plot, noting that the drama 'does great credit to the amiable hand and heart that guided it.' *Adelaide* was a melodramatic piece, typical of the kind of dramas which were popular at that time.

Vallery, the son of Count Daminville, has married the beautiful but destitute Adelaide, against his father's wishes. Estival, the Count's devious nephew, plots to oust his cousin from the inheritance; the friar Beranger steps in to tell the Count about Estival's plotting, whereupon the dastardly nephew decides to hire an assassin to kill his uncle. Vallery and Adelaide suffer greatly from their poverty-stricken state; Vallery hints that his father would forgive him if she were out of the way. Adelaide decides to kill herself but stops when she hears the cries of her helpless infant. By then Vallery is at the house of the Count, where he saves his father from the assassin's knife. Estival intervenes and Vallery kills him. In the final scene Adelaide succeeds in poisoning herself; the Count and Vallery arrive too late and the grief-stricken young husband takes his own life.

The cast list was made up of Mr[Ollyett] Woodhouse as Count Daminville and Mr J[ames] Woodhouse as the Assassin; a Mr Thomas took the role of Vallery. The remaining roles were taken by four Plumptre siblings – Mr[James] Plumptre as Estival, Miss[Anne] Plumptre as Julia, Estival's wife, Miss M[ary] Plumptre as Beranger and Miss A[nnabella] Plumptre as Teresa, an old family servant.

The Woodhouse brothers were Amelia's cousins; their mother Judith (née Alderson), wife of a Norwich draper Robert Woodhouse, was sister to Dr Alderson. The Plumptres were the offspring of Dr Robert Plumptre, a prebendary of Norwich Cathedral, and president of Queens' College, Cambridge, who had died three years earlier. Dr Plumptre and his wife Anne, daughter of his former schoolmaster Dr Henry Newcombe, who ran a public school in Hackney, had six daughters and three sons. A man of liberal opinions, Dr Plumptre had ensured that all his children were well educated, particularly in languages. Both Anne and Annabella, the two older daughters, were part of the Norwich literary scene and went on to achieve success as authors and translators.

James Plumptre, youngest of the three sons, was educated at his father's old school at Hackney and became a minister; he, too, went on to pursue a literary career as a playwright and critic. As well as performing in *The Tragedy of Adelaide*, James wrote and spoke the play's prologue, which was printed in full in the newspaper's *Poets Corner*. In 52 lines of rhyming couplets, he likened the author's fears for the reception of her play to those of an anxious mother for 'a darling son' sent out into the world. Calling upon the audience to show indulgence to her and to the 'fearful, trembling unexperienced' players, he urged them 'gently to hear, kindly to judge our play'.

The newspaper's coverage of and enthusiasm for her debut as a playwright was an encouraging start for Amelia who had set her heart on writing for the London theatre. Soon she would become acquainted with the leading lady of the Drury Lane theatre company, the celebrated Sarah Siddons (née Kemble) and some of her theatrical siblings. It is most likely that before she associated with the Kembles in London, Amelia had seen Mrs Siddons in action when she performed for eight nights at the Theatre Royal in Norwich in September, 1788. The actress specialised in tragic heroines; her portrait by Sir Joshua Reynolds, completed and hung in the Royal Academy in 1784, was known as *The Tragic Muse*. In Norwich Sarah Siddons played in seven tragedies, including *Jane Shore*, one of her early Drury Lane triumphs, and in only one non-tragic role – Rosalind in Shakespeare's *As You Like It*. The effect of her dramatic prowess was reported in the local press:

> To particularize [sic] the points of excellence which discriminate this unrivalled actress, would be only to re-echo what has been repeated a thousand times in the London papers. Suffice it to say that the faintings of some of the female part of the audience, with the many fair faces suffused with tears, added to the glistening eyes of the other sex, have borne ample testimony of her unequalled powers.[10]

With such acclaim for the great tragedienne and the impact of her work, it is hardly surprising that the ambitious Miss Alderson hoped to make a name for herself as a playwright on the London scene. For the time being, however, she concentrated on writing poems and stories. Her next success as a writer would be in 1794 as a contributor to *The Cabinet*, by which time she had established an important new friendship with the political writer and novelist William Godwin.

Amelia Alderson's friendship with Godwin – 13 years her senior – began in June, 1794, when he stayed with friends in Norwich for 12 days. He was born in 1756 in Wisbech, where his father was a dissenting minister; two years later the family moved to Debenham in Suffolk and then to Guestwick in Norfolk. When he was 11, William was sent to Norwich as a pupil of Samuel Newton, an independent minister, who preached at the Old Meeting House in Colegate. After four years in the city, where he boarded with Newton and his wife, Godwin returned to the family home and went to work as an usher (teacher) at his old school in the nearby village of Hindolveston. Following the death of his father, he left Norfolk for London to train as a minister at the Hoxton Academy. During the summer of 1777 he preached in East Anglia; the next year he was appointed as a minister at Ware in Hertfordshire. His next post was at Stowmarket in Suffolk, where his religious beliefs underwent a revolution and he fell out with his congregation.

Returning to London, Godwin was encouraged by friends to try his hand at writing for a living; his *Life of Lord Chatham* was published in the spring of 1783. Still wrestling with his religious beliefs, he had a period on trial as a minister at Beaconsfield in Buckinghamshire, but was rejected by the congregation. In the autumn he was back in London, where his writing career began in earnest, his first significant job being as a reviewer for John Murray's *English Review*. By the time he got to know the young Amelia Alderson, Godwin had written three short novels, all published anonymously in 1784. Of these, *Italian Letters* was published by George Robinson, who also traded as a bookseller.

Robinson commissioned Godwin to write the British and foreign history section of his *New Annual Register* – a post which he held for nearly seven years and which gave him some financial security. At the same time he was establishing friendships in the capital with politicians, writers, artists and theatre people. Giving up his work on the *New Annual Register* in 1791, Godwin persuaded Robinson to finance him while he worked on a treatise on political principles. The work, published under the title of *An Enquiry Concerning Political Justice* in February 1793, was an instant success and established Godwin as the philosophical spokesman for English radicalism. His next literary work was a novel *The Adventures of Caleb Williams*, the first of his six major novels and the most popular. It was published in May 1794, a few weeks before his sojourn in Norwich.

Chapter Four

Godwin left his home in Somers Town on Monday, June 23rd, 1794, reaching Norwich two days later, after stopping en route to renew old acquaintanceships at Stowmarket. In his diary, which he had started in 1788, and in which he wrote brief notes about his work, whom he called on or ate with, who visited him, what he was reading and places visited, he made many references to Dr Alderson and his daughter over the 12 days he spent in the city.[1] Amelia's father called on Godwin on the Thursday morning – his first full day in Norwich; the two men also saw each other the next day.

William Godwin was painted by several artists. This stipple engraving by Miss P Roberts, after Thomas Kearsley was published in 1821. The original portrait was painted in 1794, the year in which Godwin spent time with the Aldersons during a stay in Norwich.

On Saturday Godwin dined at the Alderson home: other guests included the banker Bartlett Gurney, who, although born into a Quaker family, attended the Octagon Chapel for many years, and the poet and dramatist Robert Merry, whose actress wife Anne was the daughter of the actor John Brunton. Born in Norwich, Brunton's career had taken him to London, Bath and Bristol, before he became manager of Norwich Theatre Royal from 1788 to 1800. Also present were William Firth, who wrote pamphlets on political and legal matters, and Charles Marsh, a member of the dissenting congregation, who went on to become a barrister and MP. Marsh dined with Godwin again the next day, when the guests included Amelia Alderson, John Brunton and his wife Elizabeth, Dr Edward Rigby and John Pitchford, the son of a Norwich doctor. Their talk, Godwin recorded, was 'of the punishment of Kings'[2]. Marsh, Rigby and Pitchford all became contributors to *The Cabinet*, which was launched in October that year.

Two days later Godwin had tea with the Aldersons after which he left the city to spend time with his mother, now living at Wood Dalling a few miles from the old family home at Guestwick. Back in Norwich on July 5th he had supper at the Alderson house with Amelia, her father, Pitchford, Firth and others; the following day he dined with the Aldersons before taking the mail coach back to London.

Within a few weeks Amelia and Godwin met again, when she went to stay in Southgate, at that time a village, a few miles north of London. The Aldersons had several friends, most of whom were of the dissenting persuasion, in the Southgate area – people who had connections with their Norwich circle or who were connected through marriage to Alderson relations. One of these was George Cadogan Morgan, a former minister at the Octagon Chapel, who had been living in Southgate, where he ran a school, since 1791. Morgan's wife Anne (née Hurry) was a cousin to Elizabeth (née Hurry), the first wife of Amelia's uncle Robert Alderson. Anne's father William and Elizabeth's father Samuel were partners with their brother Thomas in the family shipping business in Great Yarmouth and leading members of the town's dissenting community. Morgan was also great friends with the Boddington family, wealthy merchants and nonconformists, who had properties in Southgate, Hackney, Clapton, Enfield and London.

While staying so near to London it was important for Amelia to maintain and develop her friendship with Godwin. An established writer, with significant literary and theatrical contacts in the capital, he made an ideal mentor for the young woman hoping to make her own way as an author and playwright. Godwin wrote in his diary of Miss Alderson calling on him at Somers Town on Wednesday August 20th, when he was not at home, and of she and Boddington calling on him on Tuesday, August 26th. Amelia gave a full account of 'my journey to town yesterday' in a chatty letter to Susannah:

> Mr J. Boddington and I set off for Town yesterday by way of Isling-
> ton, that we might pay our first visit to Godwin at Somers' Town.
> After a most delightful ride through some of the richest country I
> ever beheld, we arrived at about one o'clock at the philosopher's
> house, whom we found with his hair *bien poudré*, and in a pair of
> new, sharp-toed, red morocco slippers, not to mention his green
> coat and crimson under-waistcoat.[3]

Although Brightwell transcribed Amelia's companion's name as Boddington with the initial 'J' it is possible that she mis-read Amelia's
handwriting in this instance. The male members of the Boddington
family with whom Amelia associated during the autumn of 1794 in
Southgate and London were Samuel and Thomas, sons of the late
Benjamin Boddington, who befriended Morgan when he moved from
Norfolk, first to Hackney and then to Southgate.* His family tree had
no 'J' Boddington.[4] In later letters from Southgate Amelia mentioned
Tom Boddington, so perhaps it was he who accompanied her on this
visit. She maintained friendships with both Samuel and Thomas well
into her middle age and recalled times spent with them in subsequent
letters to friends and family.

It is not clear from this letter, nor from the next letter which she
wrote to Susannah from Southgate, whether Amelia was staying with
the Morgans or the Boddingtons. Reading between the lines it seems
most likely that, to begin with at least, she was with George Cadogan Morgan, his wife and children; when Godwin challenged her to
justify why she was staying there, 'I told him I had not yet outlived
my affections, and that they bound me to the family at Southgate.'
She added that, after debating some time, Godwin 'promised to come
over to spend a day at Southgate, when I shall pit rational belief in
Mr M, against atheism in Mr Godwin.' What was clear in the letter,
however, was that Amelia had been away from home for two or three
weeks and was thoroughly enjoying herself.

On that first visit Godwin told her that he had been talking to
Mrs Inchbald, the actress and writer and a fellow East Anglian, who
remembered Amelia and wished to see her. She decided to call on
Elizabeth Inchbald after she had paid a visit to Sarah Siddons.

---

* It has not been possible to check the original letter. The Huntington Library
holds six letters written by Amelia to Susannah Taylor, but the letter from which
Brightwell transcribed 'J. Boddington' is not one of them.

I found Mrs Siddons in the very act of suckling her little baby,* and handsome and charming as ever. She played last Wednesday before her month was up, and is now confined to her room with a cold she caught behind the scenes. There too, I saw Charles Kemble, as I passed through his sister's dressing room, and thought him so like Kemble, Mrs Twiss, and Mrs Siddons, that it was some time before I could recollect myself enough to know whether he was a man or a woman. Sally and Maria, tell my father, are quite well, and inquired much concerning him. The baby is all a baby can be, but Mrs S laughs, and says it is a wit and a beauty already in her eyes; she leaves town today, or she would have invited me for a longer visit.[5]

Thus, in a few sentences, Amelia named several members of the celebrated theatrical Kemble family, knowing that Susannah would recognise the names and understand the references. Sarah, the oldest of the Kemble siblings, married to fellow actor William Siddons, was the country's leading actress; John Philip Kemble (Kemble, as Amelia named him), two years younger, was actor manager at London's Theatre Royal at Drury Lane. Mrs Twiss – Frances, known as Fanny, – was the fourth of the Kemble siblings and a particular friend of Amelia's. She had joined Sarah on the stage at Bath as a young actress in 1780, but was diffident by nature and left the theatre after her marriage to Francis Twiss, a theatre critic and Shakespearean scholar, whose parents were both from Norwich. His father, also called Francis, was for some time a proprietor of the city's Theatre Royal, but his main business was as a merchant at Rotterdam where he lived for many years.

Fanny and Francis Twiss spent much of their time at Catton, a village just outside Norwich, where five of their children were born and where their first daughter died and was buried.[6] Francis' sister Ann lived at Catton House with her husband Thomas Harvey, a master weaver, man of property, amateur artist and art collector. Charles, one of the younger Kembles, made his London stage debut in April 1794, playing Malcolm to his brother John Philip's Macbeth. Sally (nickname for Sarah) and Maria were Sarah Siddons's two oldest daughters, who had got to know Dr Alderson when they stayed with their Aunt Fanny and her children at Catton in the summer of 1793. The previous year 'during Passion Week, when the theatres were closed,

---

* Cecilia, her last child, born July 25th, 1794.

the Kembles [John Philip and his wife Priscilla] rusticated with the Twisses at Catton, near Norwich.'[7]

Continuing her newsy letter to her friend in Norwich, Amelia wrote:

From Marlborough Street [Mrs Siddons's home] we drove to Mrs Inchbald's, who is as pretty as ever, and much more easy and unreserved in her manner than when I last saw her. With her we passed an hour, and when I took my leave, she begged I would call on her again. She is in charming lodgings [in Leicester Square, opposite the house where Sir Joshua Reynolds lived], and has just received two hundred pounds from Sheridan, for a farce containing sixty pages only.[8]

Amelia was at that time working on a play, the first draft of which she offered to Godwin for perusal. He had kept his promise of paying a visit to Southgate, recording in his diary that on Tuesday, September 16th he dined 'at Morgan's with Battie [sic], Boddington and Amelia', when they talked 'of God and Burke' (Edmund Burke, the statesman and philosopher, author of the controversial *Reflections on the Revolution in France*, written in response to a sermon preached by Morgan's uncle Dr Richard Price espousing the philosophy of universal rights of man). Godwin slept at Southgate that night. Possibly this was the occasion when Amelia handed over her play; in a letter dated September 1794, Godwin gave his judgement:

Amelia, are you in a hurry? No. Well then, I will criticise at my leisure. I could not refrain however from a first rapid reading the morning after I saw you, and can therefore no longer withhold from you the general information that your comedy has, in my opinion, no inconsiderable merit, and that it agreeably surprised me. Why surprised me? First, because I had seen you only in tragedy. We are always backward to suppose in one individual variety of excellence. Secondly, because comedy and humour are, I believe, among the most autumnal fruits of the human understanding. Thirdly, because, reprobate and villain as you are, you will not be persuaded to cultivate the art of arts, the Art *par eminence*, the art of conversation.[9]

No record exists of the comedy which Amelia had submitted to Godwin, but as the friendship between the two ripened over the next two years she continued to seek his opinion and advice on her dramatic writings. Not one of the plays which she wrote during that period was ever performed, but years later her first best selling novel *The Father and Daughter* was adapted for the stage as an opera in two-acts called *L'Agnese*.* She also wrote an epilogue for *The Curfew*, a five-act play by John Tobin put on at the Theatre Royal, Drury Lane, in February 1807, when she was living in London with her husband John Opie.

Like the young Amelia Alderson, Tobin had made several attempts at play writing. His first success, *The Honey Moon*, was accepted for production at Drury Lane a few weeks before he died at the age of 34 in 1804. Its popularity led to the subsequent production of *The Curfew*, written in 1797 but rejected when first offered to the Theatre Royal. It is not known how or why Amelia was invited to write the epilogue for its first performance, but she was by then well established as a published poet. Her 48 lines of rhyming couplets, in which she contrasted customs of the period in which the play was set – the days of the Norman Conquest – with 'modern' practices was an accomplished tongue-in-the-cheek piece. Dr Alderson acquired a copy of the play when it was published in 1807 and lent it to Susannah Taylor for her perusal.

Although Amelia had set her heart on becoming a notable playwright she was also writing poetry and short stories during her late teens and early twenties. In the autumn of 1794, when she was still staying at Southgate, one of her poems was published in *The Cabinet*. It was the first of many contributions to the publication. Dr Alderson, a man of radical opinions and liberal principles, was associated with many of the people behind the project – ardent reformers who were influenced by events at home and abroad following the French Revolution of 1789.

The Cabinet to which Amelia Alderson contributed one short story and 17 poems was the brainchild of a group of Norwich radicals calling themselves 'A Society of Gentlemen'. The preface to collected editions of the magazine, brought out soon after it ceased publication, reported:

No work in the English language, perhaps, ever appeared to the world, under circumstances more inauspicious and depressing than *The Cabinet*. Its publication was announced at a time, when the

---

* With music by Ferdinando Paër and libretto by Luigi Buonavoglia, *L'Agnese* was performed for the first time in England at the King's Theatre in the Haymarket, London, in May 1817, following several successful productions on the Continent.

public mind seduced by the base artifices of a designing and profligate administration, rejected with a furious disdain, every attempt at rational reform. A sullen gloom, the supposed precursor of some dire event, silenced alike moderation and bigotry. The paths of science and liberal investigation were choked up: the study of morals, at once so useful and fascinating, was discouraged: the press groaned beneath the weight of the fetters it sustained, whilst the giant arm of a ferocious and unrelenting despotism threatened destruction to the defenders of liberty and truth.[10]

Furthermore, declared the preface writer, although the French Revolution had been 'sullied by many a foul deed' it still seemed to promote 'the sublime spectacle of a great and powerful nation governing itself on the principles of *liberty* and *equality*'. No wonder then that such an event should draw forth in England 'the rancorous passions' of those 'whose lives had been spent in the annihilation of those liberties'. He continued:

> Impressed with a deep sense of the awful situation of their country, and convinced that ignorance or forgetfulness of, and contempt for, the natural rights of man,* are the sole causes of the corruption of governments and of public grievances, some individuals educated in, and admirers of, the genuine principles of its constitution, came forward and laid the foundation of the present work.[11]

Some of those who wrote for the magazine were members of two debating societies which were established in the city in 1790. The youthful members of the Tusculan School met regularly in each other's houses to discuss questions of religion and politics. A group of slightly older radicals belonged to the discussion group known as the Speculative Society, which was more philosophical in character. They assembled every fortnight in the house of a member who took the chair for the evening. There they drank tea and listened to one who gave a paper which was then discussed.

Dr Alderson's nephew Ollyett Woodhouse was a member of the Tusculan School. He and three companions – Edward Rigby, George Cadogan Morgan and Samuel Boddington – were travelling in France at the time of the Revolution in July 1789, and witnessed many of

---

* After war was declared on France early in 1793, Prebendary Robert Potter, a staunch patriot, had inveighed against Norfolk-born Thomas Paine's *Rights of Man* (1791) in a sermon at St Peter Mancroft. Those who supported Paine's radical principles were seen as unpatriotic and traitorous.

the dramatic events in Paris. Firth, Marsh and Pitchford, who had dined with Godwin during his stay in Norwich, were all members of the Tusculan School. Dr Rigby, whose maternal grandfather John Taylor had laid the foundation stone for the Octagon Chapel, was a member of the Speculative Society, along with others associated with the Octagon. They included its co-pastors William Enfield and the Rev Pendlebury Houghton, who had succeeded George Cadogan Morgan and Robert Alderson, the latter having decided to leave the ministry to study law. William Taylor, the German scholar who was by then well set on his literary career, was a member of both societies. Marsh, Pitchford, Rigby and Enfield all contributed to *The Cabinet*; Amelia Alderson and her friends Anne and Annabella Plumptre were the only women known to have written for the magazine.

The new publication was a beacon for people whose zeal for the reformation of the British electoral system had been reawakened by the dramatic events in Paris and the increasing efforts of the British Government to quell any actions or behaviour which was perceived as akin to the uprising in France. On the day of the launch of *The Cabinet* in October 1794, three radicals accused of high treason – Thomas Hardy, John Horne Tooke and John Thelwall – were waiting in the Tower of London for their forthcoming trials. Amelia attended the trials at the Old Bailey and wrote lively accounts of the proceedings for her father, who 'after reading these letters to his confidential friends, thought it prudent to destroy them.'[12]

During its brief lifetime of barely one year the publication featured essays and opinion pieces in which the writers covered the important issues of the day. They called for the freedom of the Press, assessed the impact of the execution of the French monarch, advocated a free society in which the Arts and Sciences could flourish, condemned spies and informers who brought radicals to trial, upheld the rights of women and argued the case for new laws which would eliminate poverty. There was also a series called *The History of the War* which explored the rise and progress of post-Revolutionary France's war against 'almost every European power'. At the time of the magazine's first issue Great Britain had been at war with the new republic since February 1793.

The contributors were known only by letters or symbols – Amelia was N – but citizens who moved in the same intellectual circles would have had a good idea of their identities. Although she was away from home at the time of its launch, Amelia must have received the first editions, perhaps from her father or Susannah Taylor. Writing to the latter from Southgate not long before the treason trials in London, she gave her opinion:

> What a pity it is that the *Cabinet* is dangerous. I should have enjoyed it else so much. I admire what is already written. We are going tonight as usual to W. Morgan's where I shall sing as usual your husband's song. How I wish he was here to sing it instead of me.[13]

John Taylor, who also wrote poems for *The Cabinet*, had written the words and music for *The Trumpet of Liberty* to mark what he and fellow citizens saw as the dawn of liberty in France at the time of the Revolution. He sang it first at a public dinner in Norwich and it was taken up by many who shared his radical views.

Amelia had added Taylor's song to her own repertoire. The Morgan she mentioned in her letter to Susannah was William, elder brother of George Cadogan Morgan. A successful actuary, he had built one of the first houses at Stamford Hill, then a rural neighbourhood. A pleasant walk through the fields led to his brother's family home in Southgate. Morgan family gatherings were recalled many years later by William's grand-daughter Sarah Travers:

> Miss Travers remembers the precautions taken at her grandfather's house against the intrusion of an enemy on the lively gatherings which were held at Stamford Hill on Sunday evenings. The shutters were carefully closed, and Amelia Alderson (afterwards Mrs Opie), who was often present, would then sing, with great spirit, in her charming voice, the following song, the music and words of which were composed by Mr John Taylor of Norwich:– 'The trumpet of Liberty sounds through the world, And the Universe starts at the sound, Her standard Philosophy's hand hath unfurled, And the nations are thronging around. *Chorus.* Fall, Tyrants, fall, fall, fall! These are the days of liberty! Fall, Tyrants, fall!'[14]

Amelia's only piece of prose for *The Cabinet* was a short story, *The Nun*, set in 1794 at the time of the invasion of Belgium by the army of revolutionary France.[15] The nun's tale is told by an Englishman escaping from Bruges as the French reach the gates of the town. Along the road he passes a group of nuns also fleeing the French and soon afterwards he comes upon a solitary nun who has outstripped her companions and is waiting for them by the side of the road. Feeling pity for her plight, the young man dismounts from his horse and tarries long enough to hear her story. She is the daughter of a French marquis and has taken the veil rather than be forced by her father and brother into a loveless marriage to a debauched nobleman. The man she loves but cannot marry because of his 'obscure birth' is now in the republican army. In a spirited defence of her countrymen, the nun asserts her belief in 'the pure and unalterable principles of liberty', adding that although the French may be guilty of horrible crimes, their cause is a just one. As they part she urges her listener, should he ever 'be tempted to execrate the French revolution', to remember her and the miseries she has suffered under the old government of France.

Several of Amelia's poems which were accepted for publication in *The Cabinet* were later published in *Poems*, her first volume of verse which ran into six editions. When she began writing poetry she sought advice and opinions from friends and acquaintances such as Mrs Barbauld's brother, the author and physician Dr John Aikin.* After reading one offering, *The Virgin's First Love*, he wrote to his sister:

> ...[the poem] is indeed a very pretty idea, and in some parts beautifully worked up; but I want a *finished piece* from this clever lass. I want her to hold her pen awhile from her paper, and study, instead of pouring out the first thoughts or expressions that offer.[16]

A tragic ballad about a girl who dies from a broken heart when her lover proves false, this poem was published in *The Cabinet*. Possibly in the light of Dr Aikin's helpful comments Amelia re-worked the version which appeared eventually in *Poems*, changing several words and phrases and removing three of the more florid stanzas. Many of her poems in *The Cabinet* were concerned with love or loss; others were lines inspired by her feelings for the seashore, the sunset or a particular season.

However, she also penned two pieces in tune with the editorial anti-war stance, one of which, *Ode Written on the Opening of the last Campaign*,[17] calls on Spring to hold back and bid Winter 'check the War-fiend's murd'rous chace [sic]'; but if both War and Spring must come then let 'the patriot flame triumphant shine' and 'War his blood-stain'd throne resign'. It was a thoughtful reversal of a more traditional poetic theme – that of bidding welcome to the season of hope and rebirth – and more overtly political than most of her work for the magazine. It was re-published as *Ode on the Opening of a Spring Campaign* in *The Warrior's Return*, her second volume of verse which

---

* Dr Aikin was the first editor of the radical *Monthly Magazine* launched in 1796.

had two editions. The other anti-war poem *Ode on the Present Times* was dated January 1795. Again, the poet links the horrors of the battlefield with the season of Winter – a time when 'trembling Europe' was in the 'bloody grasp' of War and Britain feared an invasion.

Chapter Five

While staying just outside London in the autumn of 1794 Amelia was in regular correspondence with Susannah and her father. Her first biographer, Cecilia Lucy Brightwell, opined:

The allusions to political events, contained in these letters, render it necessary to say a few words respecting the opinions entertained by Dr Alderson, and the friends with whom he associated, on these subjects: as his daughter's views were naturally to a great degree formed after those of her father and his companions.... at the time when this country was so vehemently excited by the great changes then occurring in France, and which were regarded by many as the commencement of a new and much happier era for the nations of Europe generally; party-strife ran to a fearful height, and scarcely any, even of the weaker sex, remained passive spectators of the struggle.

Dr Alderson was among those who hailed the dawn of the French revolution with pleasure; and, though he afterwards saw cause to moderate his expectations as to the results of that movement, he seems (in common with many sincere patriots) to have held his allegiance true to the original revolutionary cause. It is well known that at this time various societies were organised, in different parts of the kingdom, for the purpose of discussing the political questions then agitating the public mind, and Norwich was among the foremost in these associations.[1]

In addition to the two debating societies set up in Norwich in 1790, comprising well-to-do radicals who supported political reform and many of whose members contributed to *The Cabinet*, there was an upsurge of political activity among citizens of a different class. During the treason trials, when much was made in court of the correspondence between provincial societies and their London equivalents, it was stated that Norwich had between 30 and 40 separate societies. For the purposes of correspondence the groups sometimes joined forces under the banner of United Political Societies.

Isaac Saint, a victualler, who ran the Weaver's Arms in the parish of

StAugustine's, was secretary of the Society for Political Information and also involved with Norwich Constitutional Society; his premises were used for meetings of the groups. Following the arrest in London of radicals who were later indicted for high treason, Saint was taken into custody by King's messengers, who searched his property, seized his papers and removed him to the capital where he was interrogated by the Privy Council. He was held in custody 'at the house of Thomas Wagstaffe, in South-street, in the parish of StGeorge, Hanoversquare'[2] and subpoenaed to appear as a witness at Hardy's trial. In the event he was not called to give evidence.

The Norwich Revolution Society – made up of intellectuals and businessmen – was also active in pressing for political reform. Its name came, not from the French Revolution of 1789, but from the centenary of what was known as the Glorious Revolution of 1688, when James II was overthrown as a result of trying to impose absolute rule by the monarchy. The centenary was celebrated throughout the city in November 1788. Among those rejoicing were many members of the dissenting fraternity whose forefathers had benefitted from the Toleration Act, which followed the overthrow of James and gave them freedom of worship. The Norwich Revolution Society had many dissenters in its ranks and, as events in France began to unfold, its name took on a new dimension.

Certainly the dissenting Aldersons, their friends and relations were keenly interested in political events at home and abroad and of a mind to discuss and debate them. In the gossipy letter to Susannah in which she related her visits to MrsSiddons and MrsInchbald, Amelia also wrote of going to Ives Hurry's 'in the City' where she and Boddington left their chair and horses before going by coach to their next destinations. Hurry, born in Great Yarmouth, was a brother of Anne, wife of George Cadogan Morgan. He worked in London as an underwriter at Lloyds; his wife Margaret wrote stories for children. It seems as if his was a familiar port of call for his Norfolk friend, who told Susannah: 'Ives Hurry, as soon as we arrive at his house, always treats us with as much ice and biscuits as we can eat.' Later in the day, as they returned to Hurry's, Amelia and her companion went to Daniel Isaac Eaton's shop.

Bookseller, printer and publisher, Eaton was an important figure in the reform movement of the time. He published a popular periodical *Politics for the People* and his bookshop in Newgate Street was a meeting place for London radicals. In the previous December he had been arrested for publishing a speech made by John Thelwall and imprisoned for three months before being brought to trial for libel. John Gurney (later the judge Sir John Gurney and a friend of Amelia's) was hired as junior counsel to defend Eaton only two months after qualifying as a barrister. When his senior failed to turn up Gurney ran the case himself so successfully he was hired as junior counsel for the treason trials of Thomas Hardy and John Horne Tooke. Eaton's acquittal was greeted with great delight among fellow radicals and one of the movement's leading groups, the London Corresponding Society (founded in 1792 by Thomas Hardy), had commemorative medals struck. With her connections to the Norwich radicals and her budding friendship with Godwin and his radical friends, Amelia's decision to call at the bookshop would not have surprised Susannah:

> …we had scarcely entered it, when a very genteel-looking young man came in. He examined us, and we him; and suspicion being the order of the day, I dare not talk to Mrs Eaton till the stranger was engaged in conversation with Boddington. I then told her that curiosity led me to her shop, and that I came from that city of sedition, Norwich. Her eyes sparkled, and she asked me if I knew Charles Marsh? 'You come from Norwich,' cried the stranger, 'allow me to ask you some questions.'[3]

Amelia and Boddington were charmed with the stranger's manners and conversation. They became 'so fraternized [sic]' that Mrs Eaton shut the shop door and gave them chairs. 'I could have talked with him all night. "Well, but who was he?" Have patience and you shall hear,' continued the letter writer. Then followed a lengthy passage in which she related snippets of information dropped by the stranger about recent proceedings in Scotland and cryptic clues about his own involvement. Amelia understood the clues – the stranger was referring to a convention in Edinburgh of Scottish and British reformers which led to the arrest and trial for sedition of five delegates – but she chose not to give details, knowing that Susannah would be au fait with the story. (Two of the men tried – a leading Scottish reformer William Skirving and a member of the London Corresponding Society Maurice Margarot – were given sentences of transportation to Botany Bay. Another member of the London Corresponding Society, Godwin's friend Joseph Gerrald, was also found guilty, but the order for his transportation was not made until the end of the year. The other two, Matthew Campbell Browne, a delegate from the Sheffield

Constitutional Society, and Charles Sinclair, a London delegate from the Society for Constitutional Information which had been set up to promote parliamentary reform, were acquitted.)

As the conversation continued, with interjections from Mrs Eaton, Amelia began to suspect who the stranger was:

> ...at last, having said that he had laid it down as a rule for his conduct; that a patriot should be without the *hope of living*, or the *fear of dying*, he took his leave, leaving our minds elevated and delighted. Mrs E told us it was Mr [Charles] Sinclair, he who was tried and acquitted.... He looks in bad health, but his countenance is fine, and his manners elegant. 'What think you of Mr Windham?' said I. 'Oh! The poor creature is out of his element; he might have done very well for a college disputant or a Greek professor, perhaps, but that's all.'[4]

William Windham, of Felbrigg, who was MP for Norwich and also Secretary at War, had first represented the city in 1784 when his liberal views made him popular with the young radicals. But by late 1792 he was dubbed 'Weathercock Windham', after making a speech in Parliament condemning those who wished to destroy 'our present form of government' and giving his blessing to proposals for putting an end to political clubs and political debates in ale houses.

Amelia stayed on with her friends at Southgate for several weeks and continued her outings to London, where she was getting to know more of Godwin's friends and enjoying new friendships in theatrical circles. At some point she was joined by her father, whose visit she mentioned in her next letter to Susannah:

> I wish my Father could have remained with us, but he was very good to stay as long as he did and I have the satisfaction of knowing he was happy while he did stay. He will tell you enough about Mrs Inchbald for he is quite smitten with her – nay I rather suspect he paid her a farewell visit. Pray tell him to write to me soon.[5]

She told her friend that 'the state of the times' pressed upon her mind continually. In particular, she had in mind the shadow hanging over the liberal thinkers and writers who were friends of Godwin. These included the novelist and playwright Thomas Holcroft, the maverick politician and writer John Horne Tooke, the lecturer and pamphleteer John Thelwall and the radical politician Thomas Hardy, who were awaiting trial on charges of high treason:

My Father will have told you a great deal, he will have told you too how much we are interested and agitated by the probable event of the approaching trials – would to God you and your husband were equally so, for then would one of my cares be removed; as you would like us perhaps turn a longing eye towards America as a place of refuge, and one of the strongest ties that bind me to Norwich would be converted into an attraction to lure me to the new world...we are *resolved* to emigrate if the events of the trial be fatal....[6]

The treason trials were an attempt by the Government, fearing an uprising akin to the French Revolution, to cripple the British radical movement of the 1790s. In the 1770s and 1780s some of the more liberal-minded Members of Parliament had tried to reform the British electoral system which at that time allowed the vote to a select few only and by which many seats were simply bought. The reformers pressed for universal suffrage (for men) and for an end to corruption and patronage. But they failed in their efforts and the reform movement stagnated. It was reinvigorated by the revolutionary events in France. Adherents of the old order were fearful of the destructive influences, as they perceived them, at work across the Channel, while the radicals saw the events in France as indicative of political change which they hoped and believed would be reflected in England.

The Aldersons' friend George Cadogan Morgan was the nephew of Dr Richard Price, a notorious dissenting minister, moral philosopher and political pamphleteer, active in radical and liberal causes. He was a mentor to his nephew and had encouraged him to study at the dissenting Hoxton Academy from where Morgan had taken up his first ministerial post in the Octagon Chapel. After leaving Norwich Morgan had been a minister in his wife's home town of Great Yarmouth. He was then invited to become his uncle's assistant at the Gravel Pit meeting place at Hackney, where Price had been morning preacher since 1770 and both morning and evening preacher since 1783.* The Morgans settled in Hackney in 1787, where the dissenters had set up an academy known as New College the previous year. Price, then 63, was one of its first tutors but his health was none too good, and when George moved to Hackney the college allowed him to give lectures

---

* Price had been a minister at Newington Green Unitarian Church since the 1750s and continued to preach there after his move to Hackney. He also preached at the Old Jewry meeting house in London.

in his uncle's place. Morgan and his family remained in Hackney till Price's death in 1791 when they moved to Southgate, where George Cadogan set up his own school.

Like many radicals, Dr Price linked the French Revolution with the Glorious Revolution in England, which had resulted in a shift away from exclusive monarchical powers to a monarchy tempered by government. In November 1789, a few months after the fall of the Bastille, he celebrated the spirit of the French Revolution in his Glorious Revolution anniversary sermon, *A Discourse on the Love of Our Country*, to the Society for Commemorating the Revolution in Great Britain. This attracted the attention of Edmund Burke, the Whig statesman and philosopher, whose response to Price, *Reflections on the Revolution in France*, published in November 1790, provoked an outpouring of criticism, abuse and counter-attack as revolutionary enthusiasts seized the opportunity to put pen to paper in support of the dramatic actions taking place in France.

Mary Wollstonecraft (later to become the wife of William Godwin), a former member of Price's Newington Green congregation, was one of the first. Her *A Vindication of the Rights of Men,* written in great haste as both a personal attack on Burke and a defence of Price, her friend and mentor, was published in December 1790. Another was the Norfolk-born radical Thomas Paine whose *Rights of Man, Part One*, was published in 1791. Anna Barbauld, now settled in Hampstead after her sojourn in France, wrote a tract in which she hailed the French Revolution as sublime evidence of human improvement. It was during this period of intense public debate over concepts of government, social order, heredity, property and rights that the societies which Brightwell referred to in her explanation of the Aldersons' viewpoint sprung up in Norwich and across the country. Two of the most significant groups were the London Corresponding Society and the Society for Constitutional Information.

The increasingly anxious British government issued a royal proclamation against seditious writings in May 1792 and went on to take even more drastic steps. Publicans were threatened with having their licenses revoked if they hosted politicised debating societies, suspected dissidents had their mail seized, radical groups were infiltrated. The number of political arrests increased as the government sought evidence which would justify it taking legal action against those suspected of subversive intentions. In May 1794 more than 30 radicals were arrested. By the time Amelia Alderson was staying with her friends in

Southgate 13 of the radicals had been indicted for high treason. She had been an enthusiastic follower of court proceedings since her teens and, despite her anxieties about the outcome, she was keen to attend the forthcoming treason trials at the Old Bailey.

Her interest in court procedures began at an early age, when she was taken by her parents to watch the time-honoured rituals which marked the arrival of the circuit judges in Norwich for the summer Assizes. The interest persisted throughout her life; by 1832, when the Assizes became a twice-yearly event, she was still not only an enthusiastic attendee of trials, but also a friend of many of the judges. The summer Assizes were marked by a week of festivities, with public dinners at the fashionable inns, performances at the Theatre Royal and Assembly Rooms, breakfasts and open-air concerts in the public gardens, a service of sacred music at Norwich Cathedral, with collections in aid of the Norfolk and Norwich Hospital, and fireworks at night.

The festivities began with a procession made up of the two city sheriffs, under-sheriffs and officers, along with the high sheriff of Norfolk and his staff, accompanied by trumpeters and flanked by people waving banners. They processed to the outer bounds of the city, where they greeted the newly-arrived judges and escorted them into Norwich. At the city's old shire house (since demolished), adjacent to the Norman Castle where the Norfolk county Assizes were held, the procession paused while the high sheriff took the judges inside to open the court commissions. Having completed the formalities, the judges re-joined the procession which accompanied them to the Guildhall, the flint-faced early 15th century building (still standing), where the city Assizes were held. Taken inside by the city sheriffs, the judges opened the commissions there, before returning to the cavalcade which escorted them to their lodgings. The following day the judges were taken in a procession to the Cathedral, where they were received by the corporation (the mayor, sheriffs, aldermen and councillors) and took part in a service at which the Assizes sermon was preached by the Norfolk high sheriff's chaplain.

In the notebook in which she wrote accounts of some of her youthful experiences the mature Amelia Opie explained:

> To a girl fond of excitement it will easily be believed that the time of the Assizes was one of great interest. As soon as I was old enough to enjoy a procession, I was taken to see the judges come in; and, as youthful pages in pretty dresses ran, at that time of day, by the side of the high sheriff's carriage in which the judges sat, while the

coaches drove slowly, and with a solemnity becoming the high and awful office of those whom they contained, it was a sight which I, the older I grew, delighted more and more to witness.[7]

Once she learned that 'ladies' were allowed to attend trials she was not satisfied until she obtained leave 'to enjoy this indulgence'. On her first day in court 'by some lucky chance' she found herself on the bench beside the judge:

The 15th century Norwich Guildhall, where the city Assizes were held when Amelia first became interested in court procedures. By L Haghe on stone, from drawing by Amelia's contemporary, the Norwich artist David Hodgson. Published by Charles Muskett, Norwich. (Norfolk County Council Library & Information Service)

Sir Henry Gould was the judge then presiding, and he was already on the verge of eighty; but the fire of his fine eye was not quenched by age, nor had his intellect as yet bowed before it....This handsome and venerable old man, surprised probably at seeing so young a listener by his side, was so kind at last as to enter into conversation with me. Never, I think, had my vanity been so gratified, and when, on my being forced to leave the court, by the arrival of my dinner hour, he said he hoped I was sufficiently pleased to come again, I went home much raised in my own estimation, and fully resolved to go into court again next day. As I was obliged to go alone, I took care to wear the same dress as I wore the preceding day, in hopes that if the judge saw me he would cause way to be made for me.[8]

However, the courtroom was so crowded she had little hope of being seen. As she was struggling in the crowd a man 'not quite in the grade of a gentleman' pushed her back rather rudely, calling her 'miss', advising her to go home and saying the court was no place for her:

> But miss was obstinate and stood her ground, turning as she did so towards the judge, who now perceived and recognised her, and instantly ordered one of the servants of the court to make way for that young lady; accordingly way was made, and at his desire I took my place again by the judge's side.

On the third day of the Assizes Amelia decided to arrive at the court in good time and managed to get a seat near to the judge's bench:

> It was expected that the court would be that day crowded to excess, for the cause coming on was one of the deepest interest. One of our richest and oldest aldermen was going to be proceeded against for usury, and the principal witness against him was a gentleman who owed him considerable obligation.
>
> The prosecutor was unknown to me: the witness named above I knew sufficiently to bow to him as he passed our house, which he did every day; and he was reckoned a worthy and honourable man. These circumstances gave me an eager desire to be a witness of the proceedings.... The cause at length began, and it was so interesting that I listened with almost breathless attention, feeling, for the first time, what deep and agitating interest a court of justice can sometimes excite, and what a fearful picture it can hold up to the young of human depravity; for, as this cause went on, the witness for the accused, and the witness for the accuser, both swore in direct opposition to each other! One of them therefore was undoubtedly perjured! And I had witnessed the commission of this awful crime.[9]

As the case proceeded young Miss Alderson realised, to her horror, that her acquaintance was the man committing perjury. 'I felt a pain wholly unknown before,' she recalled. And worse was to come. The next morning, confined to her bed with symptoms of influenza, she was roused when 'the servant ran into the room to inform me that poor _____ had been found dead in his bed, with strong suspicions of suicide by poison.'

Although Amelia forbore to name the unfortunate perjurer in her unpublished memoir, she left enough clues – such as the age of Sir Henry Gould (who was born in 1710) – for the case to be identified by a search through local newspapers covering the relevant period. The case was, indeed, as she recalled, of the deepest interest to the citizens of Norwich and it was reported fully in both the *Norwich Mercury* and the *Norfolk Chronicle*. Headlined in the papers as 'Atkinson against Harvey', the hearing was in the Guildhall on Friday 18th and Saturday, July 19th, 1788. Robert Harvey, the defendant, was a wealthy merchant in the city's textile industry, an alderman, the son and grandson of Mayors of Norwich and twice Mayor himself. In essence, the action against Harvey was brought for the recovery of £22,500 'upon the statute against usury', following complex financial transactions between him and George Mann, involving a mortgage and a loan of £7,500. In court, the defence mounted a strong case full of facts and figures which, it was claimed, proved that Harvey had done nothing illegal. Mann, the chief witness for the prosecution, denied any knowledge of documents, covenants and conversations relating to his dealings with Harvey.

According to the report in the *Norfolk Chronicle* on Saturday July 26th, 1788, 'it was clear to demonstration that Mr Mann had deviated from the truth.' The jury retired for a little time and gave a verdict exonerating Harvey. 'The verdict was received with repeated and the loudest shouts of approbation,' said the report. It went on to tell its readers that Mann had been employed as a hotpresser* in Harvey's business for nearly 30 years 'and very frequently applied to Mr H for pecuniary assistance'. Then, in the column adjoining the court report, the paper also gave this brief item of news: 'On Sunday last died suddenly, of an apoplectic fit, in the 53rd year of his age, Mr George Mann, hotpresser, in St George's, Colegate.'

The *Norwich Mercury*'s report of the same date gave an almost identical account of the court proceedings; the adjacent column carried another brief news item: 'On Monday last an inquisition was taken by Thomas Marks, gent, on the body of Mr George Mann, of this city, who died suddenly. Jury's verdict – Natural death.' Over the next four weeks both newspapers published correspondence in which the supporters and critics of both parties expressed strong opinions on the background to the case and its verdict. Clearly, there was consid-

---

* Hotpressing – also known as calendering – was a way of finishing fabrics to make them smooth and to give them a fashionable sheen. It was a highly skilled job involving the use of heated iron plates or heated rollers. The resulting glossy shine was much admired. The process also enhanced the colours but if the hotpresser made a mistake the colours changed, sometimes turning brown from the heat.

erable public interest in the events, and, for a budding author, some interesting material about human nature to store away in her mind.

When Amelia was growing up, the Aldersons lived in one of these houses in Colegate, not far from her friends the Taylors. (Norfolk County Council Library & Information Service: black & white lantern slide)

At the time of the trial, Amelia and her father were living in Colegate opposite St George's Parish Church.* In her notebook she explained how, having learned of the death of George Mann, who also lived in Colegate, she fell into painful reflections about him:

> Well do I remember the ghastly expression of the wretched man's countenance as he left the court. I saw his bright grey eyes lifted up in a sort of agony to heaven, with, as I supposed, the conviction that he was retiring in disgrace, and I had been told what his lips uttered, while his eyes so spoke. 'What! are you going?' said a friend to him. 'Yes; why not? What should I stay for now?' and his tone and manner bore such strong evidence of a desponding mind, that those words were repeated as confirming the belief that he had destroyed himself....

---

* The house in which they lived was demolished in the 1870s to make way for a shoe factory. The building – now offices and a restaurant – bears a plaque commemorating Amelia Opie.

What would I not have given to hear that the poor man who had thus rushed unbidden into the presence of his heavenly judge, urged by the convictions of having been condemned in the presence of an earthly one, was innocent of this second crime?* It had been terrible to believe him guilty of the first!

My mind was so painfully full of this subject, that it was always uppermost with me; and, to increase my suffering, the unhappy man's grave was dug immediately opposite our windows, and although I drew down the blinds all day long, I heard the murmuring voices of the people talking over the event, some saying he was an injured man, and venting curses on the heads of those who had brought him to that pass. The verdict having been that 'he was found dead in his bed', the interment took place in the usual manner;† and it did so early in the morning.‡ I took care to avoid the front of the house till all was over; and when the hour in the following morning arrived, at which I used to go to the window, and receive the bow and smile of our neighbour, I remembered with bitter regret that I should see him no more, as he lay beneath the wall before me.[10]

Judge Gould was back in Norwich for the Assizes in 1789. Having heard that he had inquired for her, Amelia returned to the courtroom: 'One of his first questions was concerning the result of the Usury cause, which he had found so interesting, and he heard with much feeling what I had to impart.' When she took her leave of him the judge gave her his London address and said if she was ever in the capital he would be pleased to see her and introduce her to his daughter Lady Cavan. 'I did go to London before he died, but I had not the courage to call on him,' she recalled.

She did, however, maintain her great interest in (some might call it an obsession with) all aspects of criminal law and court procedures and, a few years after attending the Assizes in Norwich for the first time, had the opportunity to be present at an exceptional sequence of trials. Having spent several weeks staying with her friends just outside London in the summer of 1794, she determined to remain there in

---

* Suicide (thus also attempted suicide) was illegal under English law until 1961 when the Suicide Act was passed; this Act makes it an offence to assist in a suicide.

† Until 1823 suicides were denied burial in consecrated ground.

‡ *St George Colegate Baptisms & Burials 1786-1812*: July 23, 1788: Mann, George, aged 52 years. (NRO, PD/74)

order to attend the treason trials, the outcomes of which were of such significance to all who shared her and her father's radical opinions and anxieties about the future. Towards the end of her life she attempted to write a reminiscence about those eventful days, the introduction to which was among the papers her executor Thomas Brightwell gave to his daughter Cecilia Lucy for her biography of Mrs Opie:

> The occurrences of the year 1794 have lately been pressing with such power on my remembrance, demanding from me a decided confession that it was the most interesting period of my long life, (or nearly such,) that I am inclined to give an account of what made it so, and acknowledge that it was the opportunity unexpectedly afforded me of attending the trials of Hardy, Horne Tooke, and Thelwall, at the Old Bailey, for High Treason. What a prospect of entertainment was opening before me when (while on a visit at Southgate, near London) I heard that at these approaching trials, to which I hoped to obtain admission, I should not only hear the first pleaders at the bar, but behold, and probably hear examined, the first magnates of the land; and on the event depended, not a *nisi prius* cause, or one of petty larceny, but interests of a public nature, and most nearly affecting the safety and prosperity of the nation; aye, and much personally interesting to myself; as I knew, in the secret of my heart, that my own prospects for life might probably be changed and darkened by the result. To such a height had party-spirit reached on both sides, in my native city and elsewhere, that even innocent men were accused of treasonable intentions and practices....[11]

Chapter Six

As we have seen in earlier chapters, the Aldersons' friends, relations and acquaintances in Norwich, London and Southgate were liberal-minded and radical, eager for political reform and – in the first instance – enthusiastic about revolutionary events across the Channel. For Amelia, the young writer whose work was being accepted for publication in *The Cabinet* and who was mixing with established writers and intellectuals, there was much to focus on in the political arena. In addition, there was the attraction of spending time in the capital with its theatres, galleries and fashionable shops and the chance to meet the celebrities of the day.

Writing to Susannah in the weeks preceding the 1794 treason trials Amelia had confirmed that she and her father would emigrate to America with like-minded friends, if the accused men were found guilty. That decision still weighed on her mind more than 50 years later when she wrote her memoir of the trials:

> This was, indeed, an alarming idea to me, who was only beginning to taste the pleasures of London society, and who could still say, in spite of the excitement of party feeling, and my unity of opinion with the liberals of that day, 'England! with all thy faults I love thee still'... when the trial of Thomas Hardy began at the Sessions-house in the Old Bailey, existence acquired in my eyes, a new, but painful interest; and with the pleasing anticipations of the unexpected enjoyment awaiting me, were mingled some apparently well-founded fears of evil to come.[1]

It is not known where Amelia was staying when the trial of Hardy began, but during the second trial – that of John Horne Tooke – she stayed at the house of a friend of his, Mr [Samuel] Boddington. This was the eldest surviving son of Benjamin Boddington, who had befriended George Cadogan Morgan when he took up his preaching and lecturing work in Hackney in 1787, leasing him one of his properties and then sending his youngest son Thomas to Morgan for 'preparatory education for the new Colledge [sic]...[2] Benjamin and his brother Thomas were wealthy merchants, directors of the family importing and exporting businesses established by their grandfather.

Samuel had been introduced to the family 'counting house' in Mark Lane in London in 1782.

By the time that Amelia was expanding her circle of friends in the capital and its environs, Samuel Boddington was married and working for his father in London. It is known that he had a house in Southgate but his father also owned properties in London, including a substantial house in Bedford Square – complete with stables and a coach house – which he acquired not long before his death in 1791. Samuel was married from the house in Bedford Square in 1792. It is likely that when he wanted to attend the treason trials he was staying in this or another of the Boddington London properties. Since the court proceedings began at 8am and often went on until late at night it seems likely that Boddington – and any of his friends wishing to be at the Old Bailey – would choose to be in residence at comparatively close quarters.

It is not possible to determine precisely when Amelia became friendly with the Boddingtons, but Samuel would have been known to her – either by name or in person – at least five years before she was in London for the treason trials. He was one of the group of four friends who set off on a tour of France in June 1789, arriving in Paris days before the outbreak of revolution – the others being George Cadogan Morgan, Dr Rigby and Ollyett Woodhouse, then a law student.

The revolutionary events in Paris were of great significance to the four radical Englishmen, all of whom were in favour of political reform at home and felt inspired by what they perceived to be oppressed people struggling for a fairer society and just government. Their letters home, giving eye-witness accounts of the dramatic scenes unfolding before them, were preserved by their families who shared the first-hand news from France with all who cared to hear it. Amelia and her father were among those who wanted to be kept informed of the events across the Channel.

Here is Morgan, writing to his wife from their hotel near the Palais Royal:

We went to the theatre and there on the raising of the curtain the manager came forward to say we were to have no play, and being asked why, he replied that the people at the door commanded it. All the streets leading to the Palais Royal were blocked, the cry *aux armes* resounded from thousands of throats. The Dragoons, it was said, were firing on the citizens, and the people rushed off to the scene of action, leaving the Palais Royal deserted for a time.

Alarmed by the approach of shrieking bands we returned to the citadel of our hotel. There during the whole night we surveyed the mob as they passed and repassed. The sky was red with fires, the air full of the reports of guns and of the cries of women.[3]

Morgan also wrote from Paris to his uncle and mentor Dr Richard Price. Two of these letters, expressing his gratification at being witness to the unprecedented events and sharing his enthusiasm for the principles of revolution, were published in copies of *The Gazetteer* newspaper in August and September.

Rigby's letters were kept in his family for decades and eventually published by his daughter Elizabeth (later Lady Eastlake), who was born 20 years after the events he witnessed (one of 12 children from his second marriage). In her introduction she described her father as 'ardent in all movements for reform and enlightenment'. Writing to his first wife and their two daughters on July 18th, four days after the storming of the Bastille, Rigby professed:

I have been witness to the most extraordinary revolution that perhaps ever took place in human society. A great and wise people struggled for freedom and the rights of humanity; their courage, prudence and perseverance have been rewarded by success.... The particulars of this wonderful event, which I have been witness to, have made a lasting impression on my mind....'[4]

Boddington wrote similar accounts to his father; he also noted the rejoicing they encountered after they left Paris on July 21st and headed south:

It is wonderful how much the love of liberty has diffused itself all over this Kingdom. Every town and village we have passed through have cried out *Le Tiers Etat pour toujours* and when we show them our cockades* we have always been applauded by them....[5]

He and Morgan's uncle Dr Price were stewards at a special dinner at the Crown and Anchor Tavern in London's Strand on July 14th a year later – two of 'many gentleman' who, in an advertisement in *The Times*, were said to be determined to celebrate the first anniversary of the French Revolution. They wished 'to testify their common joy at an event so important in itself, and which is likely so essentially to

---

* Presumably the tricolour cockade which was adopted as a symbol of the Revolution.

promote the general liberty and happiness of the world.'[6]

It was at this time that Edmund Burke published his *Reflections on the Revolution in France* and the British debate about the events in France began in earnest. Burke's opposition to the Revolution and defence of the *ancien régime* was an eloquent piece of writing in which he used powerful theatrical metaphors to warn of the 'monstrous tragi-comic scene'[7] he saw being enacted on French soil. The anonymous author of a pamphlet attacking the actions and opinions of dissenters, brought out at the same time as Burke's book, quoted extracts from *The Gazetteer's* copies of Morgan's letters to his uncle, adding:

> It cannot but have occurred to the observation of those who have much intercourse with the Dissenters, with what pleasure they contemplate the anarchy and confusions of France, not as tending to restore the liberties which had been infringed (which every friend of liberty must rejoice to see) but as shaking off all authority and levelling all distinctions.[8]

The controversy over the French Revolution became known as the Pamphlet Wars.

Many supporters of the basic revolutionary principles – the curtailment of the French monarchy and the introduction of a more democratic form of government – were less enthusiastic when the first French republic, established in 1792, became engaged in a series of wars with neighbouring powers. The infamous period of violence in France, following the overthrow of the monarchy, was perceived with horror. Known as the Reign of Terror and incited by conflict between rival political factions, it lasted from June 1793 to July 1794 and brought about the execution of the former King Louis XVI and his wife Marie Antoinette. Many thousands more were also sent to the guillotine, accused, often on the flimsiest of grounds of being enemies of the revolution. Such was the background to the British Government's increasingly draconian attempts to suppress revolutionary fervour at home.

For the Aldersons and their friends, who supported the original revolutionary cause (as Brightwell described it) and were in favour of electoral reform and equal rights, the Government's measures were a matter of grave concern. Amelia's growing friendship with Godwin increased her anxieties about the treason trials since two of the accused, Horne Tooke and Thelwall, were known to him. They were arrested in May 1794, along with Hardy and other radicals, and were imprisoned in the Tower. In the last week of October, indicted on capital charges of treason, they were transferred to Newgate Prison.

Horne Tooke – 20 years older than Godwin – had been ordained into the Church of England at the insistence of his devout father, but his real interest was in politics and law. A philologist and noted conversationalist, he had become increasingly active in the burgeoning reform movement of 1791 and was instrumental in getting the first part of Thomas Paine's *The Rights of Man* circulated among members of the Society for Constitutional Information. He also helped to draft the constitution of the London Corresponding Society at the invitation of its founder Thomas Hardy. His circle of friends included Dr Price, the Boddingtons and others in the dissenting fraternity.

Thelwall, only five years older than Amelia, had made short-lived attempts at several careers, including the law, before achieving some success as a writer, poet and speaker at public debating societies. By 1793, as a member of the London Corresponding Society, he was involved in the political reform movement, soon becoming one of its most eloquent campaigners, using wit and satire in speeches calling for universal suffrage.

Both Godwin and his best friend the playwright and novelist Thomas Holcroft wrote to Horne Tooke and Thelwall while they were held in the Tower. Thelwall kept a diary of his time in custody – later incorporated into a memoir edited by his widow – in which he wrote of the feelings of insecurity throughout the country:

> Numbers of persons were out upon bail, in custody, or suffering oppressively heavy penalties on conviction for libel. Hundreds were thrown into jail on *suspicion* only, and neither they, nor their families, knew one day from another that suspicion might not be ripened into accusations of High Treason. All felt that in the event of the conviction of the 12 men, no one could think himself secure in his own house, or surmise where these arbitrary measures of Government would end.[9]

Little did Godwin and Holcroft know when they were writing to the prisoners in the Tower that Holcroft himself would be in custody before long. On October 6th he learned that the Grand Jury (a jury summoned to inquire into accusations of crime and ascertain whether the evidence is adequate to found an indictment)* had substituted his name (for that of John Lovett, the chairman of the London Cor-

---

* The practice was abolished in Great Britain in 1948.

responding Society) on the list of those to be indicted. His father and friends urged him to flee the country but Holcroft presented himself in court before the Lord Chief Justice the next day. He was promptly arrested and taken to Newgate Prison, where he remained until the beginning of December.

Chapter Seven

Amelia's father destroyed the letters she wrote to him describing the events in the Old Bailey when she was attending the treason trials, but in her memoir she called it 'the most interesting period of my long life'. The first trial opened on Tuesday, October 28th, 1794, and went on for eight consecutive days (apart from the Sunday). It was the case against Thomas Hardy, a London shoemaker, whose interest in radical politics was inspired by tracts written by Dr Richard Price. In January 1792, Hardy had helped to found the London Corresponding Society, of which he was appointed treasurer and secretary. The society corresponded with similar radical societies, most notably in Norwich and Sheffield, and also developed links with the Society for Constitutional Information.

Amelia would have been aware of Hardy's correspondence with the Norwich radicals and, perhaps, concerned about her fellow citizens' possible implication in the evidence against him. On October 6th, when the Grand Jury named the men to be indicted for high treason, the list of those being called for jury service was also announced. It included Thomas Boddington of Hackney, a director of the Bank of England and the London Dock Company, the younger brother of Benjamin Boddington and uncle of Samuel. Amelia was depressed by the reactions of her Southgate friends to the news about the potential jurors, as she confided to Susannah:

> My weak spirits have been lowered this morning by hearing Mr Boddington and Mr Morgan *mark* the printed list of the jury – Every one almost is marked by them as unfit to be trusted, for almost every man is a rascal, a contractor or in the pay of government some way or another. What hope is there then for these objects of ministerial rancour? Mr B objects even to his own uncle whom he thinks *honest*, because he is so prejudiced an aristocrat that he looks upon rigour in such cases to be Justice only. What a pass are things come to when even Dissenters lick the hand that oppresses them! Hang these politicians! How they haunt me![1]

In her unfinished reminiscences Amelia wrote of being afforded the opportunity of attending all three trials, which were presided over by

Sir James Eyre, Lord Chief Justice of the Court of Common Pleas. In all three the counsel for the defence was headed by Thomas Erskine (later Lord Erskine), assisted by Vicary Gibbs (later Sir Vicary Gibbs and Lord Chief Justice). Neither Erskine nor Gibbs were paid for their services as it was considered unprofessional to take fees for defending people charged with high treason.

Erskine, 45, had served in both the navy and army before studying for the bar. As a student at Trinity College, Cambridge, he won the English declamation prize for an oration on the 'glorious revolution of 1688' – a foretaste of what was to come in his legal career. By the time he was in court for the treason trials he had achieved great acclaim for the brilliance of his speeches in a succession of notable cases. In 1791, against the advice of his friends, he chose to defend Thomas Paine, who was charged with seditious libel after publishing the second part of his *Rights of Man*. On this occasion, Erskine's eloquent argument in favour of a people's right to criticise and reform its government failed to convince the jury who found Paine guilty. The decision to defend Paine also cost Erskine his position as legal adviser to the Prince of Wales (later George IV).

Amelia Alderson, with her passion for court proceedings, was eager to be present in the Old Bailey and see for herself the distinguished lawyer in action. Since becoming acquainted with legal matters she would have known what an extraordinarily long time a day in court might take. On the opening day of Hardy's trial, once the jury had been sworn in, the chief counsel for the Crown, the Attorney General Sir John Scott, spoke for nine hours, much of his speech being a detailed analysis of the nine 'overt acts of high treason' contained in the indictment, before he began calling witnesses for the prosecution. When midnight was approaching Erskine interjected to ask 'How long can this evidence go on?' After exchanges between the Lord Chief Justice and his associates on the bench, the Attorney General and Erskine, it was decided to provide mattresses for the jury in another room in the building, rather than allow them to be dispersed, and to adjourn the proceedings until 8am the following day.

On the second day the proceedings again dragged on from 8am until nearly midnight, by which time, when another adjournment was suggested, the jury complained that they could not have 'the necessary refreshment of sleep in the Sessions House, having only one room and nothing but mattresses to lie down upon and that they had not had their clothes off for more than 40 hours'.[2] The court was told that the jury could have beds at the Hummums (a hotel in Covent Garden); they were escorted there by officers who were to stay with them. The hearing was adjourned till 11am the next day. An overnight stay at the hotel, kept watch over by officers, after anything from 12 to 16 hours in court each day, was the jury's lot until the trial concluded a week later.

The case for the prosecution consisted of detailed examinations of papers relating to the London Corresponding Society – records of meetings, persons who attended, correspondence with other societies across the kingdom – which had been seized from members' houses under warrants by the Privy Council and intense questioning of people involved in the society's activities, including booksellers and printers. The counsel for the Crown held sway until the Saturday afternoon when Sir John finally sat down. The proceedings had not started that day till noon, Erskine having the night before asked for time to look at the papers, saying he had not been getting home till two or three in the morning. He launched his defence by addressing the jury for six hours, examining in some detail many of the documents produced by the Crown and challenging the prosecution's interpretation of them. For example, referring to a letter from the Society for Political Information at Norwich to the London Corresponding Society and the society's reply – both of which had been read to the court during the Crown's case – Erskine stated:

> It is asserted, that this correspondence shows, they aimed at nothing less than the total destruction of the monarchy, and that they, therefore, veil their intention under covert and ambiguous language. I think, on the other hand, and I shall continue to think so, as long as I am capable of thought, that it was impossible for words to convey more clearly the explicit avowal of their original plan for a constitutional reform in the House of Commons.[3]

Having addressed the jury, Erskine began his examination of witnesses for Hardy. These were people prepared to vouchsafe that the prisoner was an inoffensive man whose reason for being involved with the London Corresponding Society and other groups was to try to obtain parliamentary reform by lawful and peaceful means. Shortly after midnight the court was adjourned until 8am on the Monday. Erskine concluded his witness examination on that day, after which Gibbs addressed the court on Hardy's behalf. The Crown then began its final address to the jury – another long speech which was halted in the early hours and resumed at 8am the next day. Lord Chief Justice Eyre's summing up, in which he explained, in great detail, the nine treasonable acts contained in the indictment and went on to give his résumé of the evidence, was still not finished as midnight drew near, when the court was adjourned. He resumed his speech the next morning. The jury retired at 12·30pm and were back in court just over three hours later. Their verdict was 'Not guilty.'

How many hours Amelia sat in court during Hardy's trial is not known, but it must be assumed that she was there for some considerable time. Certainly she would have relished the aftermath. Hardy's few words of thanks to the jury were almost drowned by expressions of joy throughout the court. Once outside the building he was surrounded by an exuberant crowd, some of whom insisted on pulling his coach in triumph through the streets to his house in Piccadilly. Such was their noisy enthusiasm it was some time before Hardy was able to tell them he really wanted to go to the house of his brother-in-law in the Strand:

> He was drawn thither; and having got out of the carriage, before he entered the house, he went into the church-yard of St Martin, and was shewn [sic] to the grave of his wife, from whose side he had been taken when first seized, and who had fallen under the shock. The multitude respected this feeling with a sympathy that did them credit. They kept at a distance, while his relation pointed out to him the grave. After this affecting scene he went into his brother's house, and, in a short address, thanked his fellow-countrymen for the kind interest they had shewn [sic] in his favour; and he requested them, as they valued the cause in which they had displayed their zeal, that they would separate in peace.[4]

Crowds surrounded the Old Bailey throughout the trial and every night they drew Erskine and Gibbs to their chambers 'amidst the loudest huzzas'. Once the verdict was announced:

> Mr Erskine and Mr Gibbs, whose glorious struggle upon this occasion will make them forever dear to mankind, were eager to avoid the burst of gratitude that they expected from the multitude. They continued a very considerable time in the court after the acquittal; but the vigilance and patience of gratitude were not to be wearied. They were recognised and conducted in triumph to Serjeants Inn, where that incomparable defender of national liberty admonished them in a few words, in his own impressive way, to retire to their

separate homes, confident, from the grand proof of this day, that they had the best security for the maintenance of their rights, in the love of justice, which the constitution had indelibly planted on the English heart.[5]

Eleven days later – on Monday, November 17th – the two men were back in court for the trial of John Horne Tooke, which lasted for six days. During that period, Amelia was staying at the house of Samuel Boddington. She accompanied him and his wife every day to the Old Bailey, where they sat with his friend, the banker and poet Samuel Rogers. Known for his sharp tongue and love of gossip, Rogers came from a dissenting family. His father Thomas, who had died the previous year, had been a close friend and neighbour of Dr Richard Price in Newington Green and a member of the Society for Constitutional Information, of which Tooke was a leading light and the activities of which were under intense scrutiny throughout his trial. Years later Rogers recalled that he and Boddington had paid five guineas for a loge (a small enclosure or box) at Tooke's trial:

> It was the custom in those days to place bunches of strong-smelling plants of different sorts at the bar where the criminal was to sit (I suppose, to purify the air from the contagion of his presence!). This was done at Tooke's trial; but, as soon as he was brought in, he indignantly swept them away with his handkerchief.... If Tooke had been convicted there is no doubt he would have been hanged. We lived then under a reign of terror.[6]

Hardy, said to have behaved with 'the most exemplary decorum' throughout his trial, had left cross examinations of the witnesses to his counsel and refrained from addressing the court himself. Tooke, with many years of experience as a public speaker – at first preaching sermons in church and then as an orator in the political arena pressing for reform – made an appeal to Lord Chief Justice Eyre as soon as he was 'set to the bar'. Nor did he refrain from interjecting and asking questions as and when he saw fit, as the trial proceeded. His first appeal was a request to be allowed to sit near to his counsel, which he saw not as an indulgence but as his right by law: 'My lord it is not for a small stake that I stand here – it is to deprive me of my life, to beggar my family, to make my name and memory infamous to all posterity....'[7] With his age and infirmities, he said, 'the many degrading and many humiliating circumstances' of his custody had impaired the health and the strength of his body. After consulting his fellow judges, Eyre proclaimed they felt 'extremely disposed to indulge you on the score of your health'; for the rest of the trial Tooke he sat at a table near to Erskine.

Fortunately for everyone concerned, the late night sessions which marked the Hardy trial were done away with in Tooke's case. Erskine brought up the subject of an adjournment late in the evening of the first day when the Crown was just getting into its stride examining witnesses. Judge Eyre told the court the general rule was that in these criminal proceedings there should be no adjournment. In particular, he said, the jury should not be separated and there should be no access to them till they had given their verdict, the idea being to make sure that justice was done. However, it was manifest that justice was unlikely to be done if the cause went into a length which would exhaust human faculties.

From the bench Sir Archibald Macdonald, Lord Chief Baron of the Court of the Exchequer, confessed that, after 14 hours of close attention, he was incapable of doing his duty. Tooke told the court he had a painful infirmity which required him to be up four or five hours before coming to court at 8am; late sittings would mean he would have no time for sleep. The Judge proposed that for the rest of the trial they would start at 9am and conclude at 9pm, with an interval of quarter of an hour to take refreshment. Again, once they were sworn in, the members of the jury were not allowed to go home until the trial was over; every night they were accompanied to the London Coffee-House, where they slept, attended by court officers.

As in Hardy's trial, the key players in the drama indulged in exceptionally lengthy speeches, with Tooke himself joining in on occasion. The prosecution once more focused on papers seized under warrant, this time dealing primarily with the activities and correspondence of the Society for Constitutional Information and, again, there was much evidence of dealings with radical societies in the provinces. Much was made of letters which passed between London and Norwich. A group calling themselves the Delegates of the United Constitutional Societies sent a letter giving a full report of their meeting in Norwich in March 1792, at which they had agreed to communicate with the London society. Read in full in court, the letter expressed members' wish that all societies of a similar kind were 'strongly and indissolubly united in one political body'. They added that 'the greatest care has been taken to preserve order and regularity at our meetings, to convince the world that riots and disorder are no part of our political creed....' The court also listened to the reading out of a letter from the Revolution Society in Norwich, sent in April 1792, asking if 12 of its members might be admitted as associate members of the Society for Constitutional Information. Paine's *Rights of Man* and its effect on members of these societies came under intense scrutiny and, once again, booksellers and printers were called to account for their associations with the author.

The prosecution's case continued throughout the second day and well into the third day, after which Erskine began his case for the defence with a reflection on the Hardy trial in which, he said, he had taken part 'under circumstances of distress and agitation'. Expounding upon the role he played, representing 'a poor, lowly, and obscure mechanic against a pressure with which no advocate in England ever before had to contend', he went on to explain to the jury just how powerful were the forces arraigned against Hardy and how the Court had faced a situation 'new and unparalleled in the criminal justice of the country'. And now, when he recollected that 'an humble and obscure individual was not merely acquitted, but delivered with triumph from the dangers which surrounded him', it aroused 'a whirlwind of emotions' in his mind. Turning, at last, to the case in hand, Erskine claimed that it was a little difficult, at first view, to establish the nature of the accusations against Tooke. He then pressed on with the indictment, telling the jury in great detail what he understood it to mean, before giving a résumé of the prosecution's case. By the time he had started on his defence of the prisoner, telling the jury that he had come to court that morning 'perfectly subdued with fatigue' and was now tearing himself to pieces by exertions beyond his powers it was nearly 9pm and the court was adjourned till 9am the next day.

Many distinguished witnesses were called by the defence on the fourth day. They included the radical Whig politician Charles James Fox (one of Amelia's heroes, whom she would meet in person in Paris a few years later), the playwright Richard Brinsley Sheridan, who was also an MP and ally of Fox, and Charles Earl Stanhope, brother-in-law of William Pitt, the Prime Minister, with whom he had crossed swords over Parliament's repressive measures to silence the radical reformers. Asked to recall who had attended a meeting of the Revolution Society called in London to celebrate the first anniversary of the fall of the Bastille, Stanhope – the Society's chairman – told the court 'Some hundreds of a very respectable description.'

The penultimate day of Tooke's trial saw Gibbs giving a long speech summing up the evidence for the defence after which the prisoner was told by the judge that if he wished to address the jury now was the time to do so. Tooke declared he had already spoken too much and too often. 'I do not mean to trouble you with one word,' he concluded. Lord Chief Justice Eyre began his summing-up. After speaking for several hours he declared that, although he would be glad to get through his summing up that night, he saw that the length of it would carry them beyond any reasonable hour and that he had not the strength to go through it. The court was adjourned. When it convened again on the following morning the Judge took all day to conclude his summing-up – reading out, in full, many of the letters already read in court as evidence for the prosecution and expounding in detail on the legal points relevant to the charges. The jury withdrew at 7·50pm and came back into the courtroom after eight minutes, giving the verdict: 'Not guilty'. It was received with loud acclamation in the court room, followed by shouting from the people assembled outside. Tooke thanked his lordship and the bench for their conduct towards him 'during the whole of this tedious trial' and thanked the jury for affording 'a just protection of my life'.

Outside, a huge crowd was waiting to pay tribute to the counsel for the defence:

At length Mr Erskine and Mr Gibbs came to their carriage; the horses were instantly taken out; the people collected about it in considerable numbers, and with this escort they were drawn to Serjeant's Inn.... the streets blazed with flambeaux which the people had prepared. Mr Erskine addressed the people from his window.... The jury on their return from the Old Bailey, after their verdict on the trial of Mr Tooke, had a lane formed for them all the way to the London Coffee-House. On their arrival there, the company, who amounted to about 500 gentlemen, immediately arose, took off their hats, ranged themselves on each side as they passed through, saluting them with the most animated and expressive tokens of applause.[8]

It would be surprising if Amelia had not written dramatic accounts for her father of the scenes she had witnessed. In Norwich, the *Norfolk Chronicle*, published on Saturdays, was not able to give full – or even up-to-date coverage – of the court proceedings. It gave a front page account of the first few days of Hardy's trial three days after the case had ended, regretting that: 'Of the immense mass of evidence brought forward on this important trial, we have room only to give the following short abstract...'9 Readers had to wait another week for a report on the final days of the trial and its verdict. And so it was with reports of the trial of Tooke and the subsequent appearances in court of Thomas Holcroft and John Thelwall. Amelia's friend Hudson Gurney believed her letters 'contained matters which might render Dr Alderson cautious to whom he read them. Reading them with *infinite delight* to those whom he thought to be *trusted....*'10

Amelia's first biographer made no mention of a rumour which persisted for decades about the ebullient Miss Alderson's reaction to Horne Tooke's acquittal. The alleged incident was mentioned by Sarah Isabella Sidgwick, daughter of Amelia's cousin Margaret Thompson, when she wrote a memoir of her famous relative, whom she knew only as an old lady: 'She was present at Horne Tooke's trial, and it is said that when he was acquitted she walked across the table, and gave him a kiss. This she would laugh at and never quite admit, but I never heard her deny it.'11

However, as a younger woman, Amelia was at pains to deny the story. She took great exception to an account of her behaviour at the end of the Tooke trial written by William Beloe, who had enjoyed a chequered career as a clergyman, teacher, translator, writer, editor of the *British Critic* and under-librarian at the British Museum. In his literary memoirs he claimed:

> Her [Amelia's] natural connections, her education, and the principles on which she had been brought up, gave her an unavoidable predilection in favour of those who, in the breaking out of the French Revolution, vainly imagined that a glorious opportunity was presenting itself for the melioration of the condition of mankind....
>
> On one occasion indeed, her enthusiasm got the better of both her prudence, and the natural delicacy of her sex. She attended the trial of her admired – what shall we call him? Patriot! – Well then, Patriot, if you please, Horne Tooke, for High Treason. When the verdict of 'Not Guilty' was pronounced, she scrambled over seats and benches as she could, and hastening to where he stood, kissed him in the public court.12

Beloe had known Amelia since she was a girl. Born in Norwich in 1758, he was educated at Samuel Parr's school at Stanmore (then a village 11 miles north-west of London) before graduating from Cambridge and being ordained into the Church of England. Parr, also an ordained priest and, later, a prolific writer, was appointed head of Norwich Grammar School in 1778 and curate at St George's Church in Colegate. He settled happily in the city where he lived for seven years and made many friends, including the Aldersons; in 1780 he invited his former pupil to join him as under-master at the school. Beloe spent nearly four years in his home city where he kept a watchful eye on the local literary scene and took the first steps in his own writing career. He then moved to London, where he lived for the rest of his life. His recollections – published soon after his death in 1817 – caused much controversy, particularly for what was regarded as his unfair assessment of the now elderly Parr.

Amelia was at pains to refute Beloe's story, when she wrote to her friend Archibald Constable, publisher of the *Edinburgh Review*:

I know not whether the *Edinburgh Review* will think that very amusing work, the *Sexagenarian*, by the late Mr Beloe, worthy of its notice, nor, if it should do so, am I quite sure that the editor may think it advisable to redress an individual grievance at the representation of a complainant... I wish to state, through your means, to Mr Jeffrey [Francis Jeffrey, editor], of whose good opinion I am, I trust, meritoriously ambitious, that Mr Beloe in this posthumous publication has asserted of me a positive falsehood.

I never saw Mr Horne Tooke till I saw him on his Trial, and the charge of my having scrambled over chairs and tables to get up to him on his acquittal, and then kissed him in public court, is as false as it is malignant.

Such conduct not even my youth could have been excused, and never at any period of my life could I, I trust, have been guilty of such an outrage on the delicacy of my sex, and such a violation of my respectability as a gentlewoman.[13]

She continued the letter with an account of what really passed between her and Tooke once he had been found 'Not guilty':

During his trial I was staying at the house of Mr Boddington (a friend of his), and I used to accompany them every day to the Old Bailey. Mrs Boddington (the frail and the beautiful) had never then been introduced to Mr Tooke, and after the acquittal she was very angry with her husband for not finding out whither Mr Tooke had retired, that she might be presented to him at once. This remonstrance induced Mr Boddington to go in search of Mr Tooke, and having discovered him in a small room waiting for his carriage, he took his wife and me into the apartment where he was. 'This is my wife, sir,' said Mr B. Mr Tooke saluted her and exclaimed, 'Madam, you have made me hate your husband.' 'Why, sir?' 'Because I always hate the husbands of pretty women.'

I was next presented, and having saluted me he said, 'I think, ma'am, I have seen you every day during my trial.' 'Yes, sir.' 'Then grant me one favour: when I am tried for my life again, which I daresay I shall be six months hence, promise me to attend my trial again every day.'[14]

Tooke was acquitted on Saturday, November 22nd. There was a week's respite for Erskine and Gibbs before their next appearance at the Old Bailey on Monday, December 1st for the third treason trial. On this occasion there were four prisoners at the bar: Thomas Holcroft; John Augustus Bonney, a lawyer and poet; Stewart Kydd, who later wrote several legal works; and Jeremiah Joyce, at that time private secretary to Lord Stanhope (who had been a defence witness in Tooke's trial) and tutor to his son. All four were members of the Society for Constitutional Information and Bonney was also a member of the London Corresponding Society. Once again the court was presided over by Lord Chief Justice Eyre. Brightwell reported that Amelia attended 'the famous trials of Horne Tooke, Holcroft, and others'. During the period of Tooke's trial Godwin's diary entries mentioned people he saw in court, among them Miss Alderson. As Holcroft was a friend of Godwin, it is most likely that Amelia was also present in the courtroom when his trial opened at 9.15am.

Once the jury was sworn in, the Attorney General Sir John Scott, got to his feet and, in a brief address to the court, recalled that in the two previous trials the juries had found verdicts of not guilty. Since the evidence given then was the same as that which was to be applied in this case, he submitted that the prisoners should be acquitted. The Judge agreed, telling the jury that if there was no evidence they must, of course, find the prisoners not guilty. The jury did so and all four were discharged. Bonney, Kydd and Joyce left the court but Holcroft lingered and attempted to address the jury. He was interrupted by Eyre, who told him that, having been acquitted, he had no *right* to address the jury, but that he (Eyre) would not stop him if he conducted himself properly. It soon became clear that Holcroft had a great deal

to say, whereupon the Judge interrupted him again and said he had no
right to detain the court by a long speech. Holcroft said he would not
detain the court for more than half an hour. 'Half an hour!' exclaimed
the Judge. 'Mr Holcroft you must withdraw.' Still Holcroft persisted,
claiming that having suffered an injustice it was his desire to make a
public statement in court.

> Lord Chief Justice Eyre: 'Mr Holcroft you have been dealt with most
> honourably, on the part of the attorney-general.... You brought
> yourself into custody by your own voluntary surrender. You have
> had no extraordinary hardships since that time; and you have in
> the close of it been treated most honourably, and with all possible
> attention, by the attorney-general who has consented to your be-
> ing acquitted, instead of standing at the bar upon evidence.... You
> have no right to complain of injustice, and therefore you ought not
> to be heard upon a complaint of injustice.'[15]

Holcroft responded that he did not wish to appear as a violent or
obstinate man, but he had something to say to the court which he
felt should be heard; but he saw he must now accede to the court's
opinion 'and must take some other means of publishing my sentiments upon the prosecution that has been instituted against me.' Not
long afterwards he published a pamphlet entitled *A Narrative of Facts
relating to a Prosecution for High Treason, including the Address to
the Jury which the Court refused to hear.*[16]

Once Holcroft had left the Old Bailey the case against John Thelwall
was opened, with Erskine and Gibbs as counsel for the defence. The
proceedings on each day lasted well into the evening. Although much
of the evidence produced covered similar ground to that given in the
Hardy and Horne Tooke cases, there was also additional information
about Thelwall's role in the London Corresponding Society and his
political lectures on behalf of the reform movement. On the fifth day
the jury retired just after noon to consider its verdict, returning at
1.50pm to declare Thelwall 'Not guilty'. On his acquittal the freed
man addressed the court, confessing that he had sometimes acted
with imprudence, but never with a criminal design; he could not hear
the verdict without emotions too vast for utterance and too sublime
for thought.

How well Thelwall was acquainted with Amelia at this time is un-
certain, but he may have been known to her father through his writings on scientific and medical issues and his close friendship with the

Norfolk-born surgeon Astley Cooper and other medical men. Before starting his medical training in London, Cooper had been allowed into the Norfolk and Norwich Hospital to learn about medical procedures and to watch a surgeon operating. By 1791 he was lecturing on anatomy and surgery at St Thomas's Hospital in London, where he got to know Thelwall, an enthusiastic attendee at the lectures. John Taylor, a surgeon from Norwich, called as a witness on behalf of Thelwall at his trial, said they had got to know each other at the St Thomas's Hospital lectures; they had occasionally been together at meetings of the Friends of the People (a reform group) at Southwark and he had always found Thelwall a very peaceable man. Thelwall himself dined and possibly also stayed at the Alderson home when he was in Norwich on a lecture tour of East Anglia in 1796.

Chapter Eight

It was during her extended visit to Southgate and London in 1794, that Amelia's friendship with Godwin blossomed. So, too, did her friendships with theatrical, artistic, literary and political people in the metropolis; but however tempting it was to remain in London, Amelia was always aware of her 51-year-old widowed father at home in Norwich and her need to be with him. She returned home and did not go back to London till the following spring.

Her return to London in 1795, at the age of 25, heralded three years of interest, excitement and pleasure as a single woman in search of success as a writer and, perhaps, a husband. Susannah Taylor said her young friend had 'poetical genius and taste'. Her singing voice was particularly appealing; she had created a style of singing which was her own and which had the power of 'awakening the tender sympathies and pathetic feelings of the mind'. Above all, Amelia's heart and mind were 'distinguished by frankness, probity, and the most diffusive kindness' and she 'made the happiness of her friends her own'.[1] Brightwell understood that Amelia had numerous admirers who paid her homage and courted her favour:

> Her countenance was animated, bright, and beaming; her eyes soft and expressive, yet full of ardour; her hair was abundant and beautiful, of auburn hue, and waving in long tresses; her figure was well formed; her carriage fine; her hands, arms, and feet, well shaped; and all around and about her was the spirit of youth, and joy, and love.[2]

Brightwell did not name any of the admirers, but it is likely that one was the author of 46 lines of rhyming couplets which were published in the *Norwich Mercury* on March 31st, 1787, under the heading 'By inserting the following lines in your entertaining Paper, you will much oblige A Constant Reader'. The verses were addressed to 'Miss A____ of Norwich' and attributed to 'J.B.'. Since he acclaimed her beautiful singing voice and addressed her as 'Amelia' it is not unreasonable to suppose that the 17-year-old Miss Alderson was the object of his affection.* The first part of his tribute extolled her talents and beauty:

Oh! say, thou fairest of the tuneful throng,
Who add'st to all thy charms the pow'rs of song,
Whose strains immortal ev'ry breast must move.
And melt each heart to tenderness and love,
Say – in what language shall I boldly aim
To tell thy charms or celebrate thy fame?
How shall I paint that face where sweetness smiles,
And even envy of her frown beguiles?
The beauties of thy flowing locks portray
Where thousand sportive cupids wanton play?
How paint that form where loves and graces meet?
Or praise thy heav'nly voice as seraph's sweet,
Where all the pow'rs of harmony combine
To give each soul an extasy [sic] divine?

He concluded with advice to 'fair Amelia' on how to recognise the right suitor, one who felt such love as glowed in *his* bosom, even though she had rejected him.

Brightwell made a brief reference to Amelia having owned that she had been guilty of the 'girlish imprudence' of love at 16 and concluded that this fancy of her youth was but a day-dream. She made no mention of a love affair which later biographers Jacobine Menzies-Wilson and Helen Lloyd claimed – without quoting their precise sources – had happened before she married John Opie in 1798. Suggesting that many of Amelia's friends were wondering why she had not married, despite having received many advantageous offers, they wrote:

Unfortunately, she had given her heart to a married man, discreetly referred to in her letters as B. His wife showed some feminine indignation on the subject. This was not unnatural, as Amelia was in the habit of paying the couple long visits, at the end of which there was as a rule a tearful and somewhat sordid scene between the two women. Nothing, however, could come of this affair, though the object of Amelia's affections would gladly have left his ageing and peevish wife to find a refuge in his love's pretty arms.[3]

---

* The likelihood that the lines were addressed to Amelia Alderson was suggested by David Chandler in his doctoral thesis *Norwich Literature 1788-97: A Critical Survey* (NHC, N 820.6)

Presumably Menzies-Wilson and Lloyd were the source for subsequent writers on the subject. In an essay on Amelia, V.S. Pritchett argued that she was 'the skilful heartbreaker' and that by the time she was 28 and still unmarried she was 'in her first mess. "Mr B", the married man, was only too well married and there was no way of getting him.'[4] Paula R. Feldman took the alleged affair one step further when she suggested a name for the mysterious man: 'Opie appears to have had a long and discreet affair with an older married man, possibly the J. Boddington of Southgate whose home she visited frequently during the 1790s.'[5] As explained in Chapter 4, the initial transcribed by Brightwell from Amelia's letter (and subsequently quoted in biographies not just of Amelia but also of Godwin, Mary Wollstonecraft and others) was probably not 'J'. If the letter was really 'S' for Samuel or 'T' for Thomas then the alleged affair with an 'older married man' was neither of these Boddingtons. Samuel was only three years older than Amelia; Thomas five years younger.

It seems that Amelia did fall in love with somebody she named as 'B' (possibly just the initial of his first name) in letters to Susannah. Whatever the truth of the matter, the lively Miss Alderson enjoyed her visits to London from 1794 onwards. She had first visited the capital in May 1784, when, according to the recollections of her lifelong friend Hudson Gurney, her father took her to Westminster Abbey for the Handel Commemoration.[6] The event, commemorating the 25th anniversary of the composer's death, was a series of concerts given by singers and instrumentalists. For a 15-year-old provincial girl with a beautiful singing voice and a keen interest in music the outing would have been a splendid treat. She was at that time beginning to experiment with different forms of poetry; later several of her poems were set to music and she was also invited to write lyrics for popular airs of the time. Susannah considered that song writing was Amelia's forte.

By the time she was getting to know Godwin's friends in London, Amelia was already part of the Norwich literary scene, which, in the late 18th century was a flourishing one, known and commented upon by visitors from further afield. 'Norwich was always a haven of rest to us, from the literary society with which that city abounded,' recalled Basil Montagu, circuit companion to the judge Sir James Mackintosh.[7] Many distinguished visitors spent time with the Taylor family. Mrs Barbauld's niece Lucy Aikin said that Susannah 'darned her boy's grey worsted stockings while holding her own' with intellectuals from the Octagon Chapel and distinguished guests such as the poet Robert

Southey, whose younger brother was at school in Norfolk, and Mackintosh, author of *Vindiciae Gallicae: A Defence of the French Revolution and its English Admirers* (1791). A great admirer of Mrs Taylor, Mackintosh was in regular correspondence with her:

> I know the value of your letters. They rouse my mind on subjects which interest us in common: friends, children, literature and life. Their moral tone cheers and braces me. I ought to be made permanently better by contemplating a mind like yours....[8]

Harriet Martineau, whose family were part of the Octagon dissenting congregation. Thirty years younger than Amelia, she took an (often critical) interest in the older woman's work. She herself was a distinguished journalist, essayist, novelist and social reformer. This image of her, aged 33, was used as the frontispiece in her autobiography.

But the writer Harriet Martineau, born in Norwich in 1802 when Amelia Opie was in London establishing herself as a novelist, was scathing of those who had been part of the city's literary scene:

> Norwich, which has now no claims to social superiority at all, was in my childhood a rival of Lichfield itself, in the time of the Sewards, for literary pretension and the vulgarity of pedantry.... William Taylor was then at his best, when there was something like fulfilment of his early promise.... Among the mere pedants were some who were qualified for something better. Such woman

as Mrs Opie and Mrs John Taylor ought to have been superior to the nonsense and vanity in which they participated.[9]

Miss Martineau dismissed Dr Enfield, minister at the Octagon and a contributor to *The Cabinet*, as 'a feeble and superficial man of letters' and regarded Dr Alderson as 'solemn and sententious and eccentric in manner, but not an able man in any way'. However, she recalled visits of Mrs Barbauld to the Martineau family home as having 'kept alive in us a sense of what intellectual superiority ought to be and to produce. I still think her one of the first of writers in our language.'

Mrs Barbauld was living in Hampstead when Amelia began to make regular visits to London; her expanding circle of acquaintances included many of the radicals and intellectuals known to the Barbaulds. In one letter to Susannah – undated but probably written in the early summer of 1795 – she wrote how 'month follows month in this *wilderness* of pleasure'. Only the day before she had received a visit from Mr [Francis] Wrangham, the latest winner of the Seatonian prize (awarded annually by Cambridge University for a sacred poem written by one of its MA graduates), who went on to be a prolific writer, translator and editor, while carrying out his duties as a Church of England clergyman. Wrangham had promised to send her a copy of his winning poem, wrote Amelia, adding how pleased she was with her fellow citizen William Taylor's *Ode to the ship that conveys Gerald* [sic]. The fate of Godwin's friend the political reformer Joseph Gerrald was very much in the thoughts of all his radical friends at that time. He had been in prison in Edinburgh and then London for months since being found guilty of sedition and was at last taken to Portsmouth early in May 1795, and put aboard the convict ship *Sovereign* to await transportation to New South Wales. Gerrald had been a student at Dr Parr's Stanmore school and, when he was transported, Dr Parr became the guardian of his young son.

Writing of a forthcoming engagement with Mrs Barbauld and Dr [Alexander] Geddes, the Scottish theologian and scholar, Amelia wished that she could *wish* Susannah there to enjoy 'the feast of reason and the flow of soul'. She went on to tell her friend that:

> Godwin drank tea and supt here last night; a leave-taking visit, as he goes tomorrow to spend a fortnight at Dr Parr's. It would have entertained you highly to have seen him bid me farewell. He wished to salute me, but his courage failed him…. 'Will you give me nothing to keep for your sake, and console me during my absence,' mur-

mured out the philosopher, 'not even your slipper? I had it in my possession once, and need not have returned it!' This was true; my shoe had come off, and he had put it in his pocket for some time. You have no idea how gallant he is become; but indeed, he is much more amiable than ever he was.[10]

Godwin's diary for the spring and summer of 1795 noted many occasions on which he was with 'A Alderson' – calling on her, going with her to call on Mrs Siddons, walking with her to Hampstead to dine with the Barbaulds, having supper with her and other friends, including Holcroft and Horne Tooke. Although neither he nor Amelia said precisely with whom she was staying, she was certainly with her friends the Battys for some of the time. Godwin recorded in his diary that he called on Battie [sic] and Amelia on March 17th, 1795; on that same day she wrote to the poet George Dyer from Marlborough Street:

As I am to set off for Southgate at half past 12 tomorrow, I beg to see you and Mr Frend* by eleven or half past at latest. I am very desirous of knowing Mr F; therefore I hope he will be able to come at the hour I mention if not, I shall return from S. on Friday morning and shall be in Marlbro' Street by half past two.[11]

Robert Batty, listed in London directories of the 1790s as 'surgeon, medicine' living in Marlborough Street, had trained in Edinburgh. He was probably known to Dr Alderson's colleague, Philip Meadows Martineau, who had also trained in Edinburgh.† In the final paragraph of her letter to Susannah Amelia wrote: 'Farewell! Mr Batty and I both wear you "in our heart's core" and so would Mrs B if she knew you. I love and admire them more every day.' Godwin wrote two or three times of breakfasting, supping or dining at the Batty household. His entry for Saturday, June 20th 'Sup at Batty's w[ith] A.A.' was probably the 'farewell' visit described by Amelia, for he then left London for three weeks, during which period there were references to being at Hatton (where Dr Parr lived) and to time spent

---

* William Frend, a leading light in the radical dissenters' movement. He had been ordained into the Church of England, which he left in 1787 to become a Unitarian.
† Batty's daughter Elizabeth, who was four-years-old at the time of Amelia's visit, married into the Martineau family. Her husband Philip Martineau – a nephew of Philip Meadows Martineau and cousin to Harriet Martineau – was a son of John Martineau who left Norwich to work as a brewer in London.

with his old friend. Soon after his return to the capital he was again supping at Batty's with Amelia Alderson.[12]

One of the leading woman in Godwin's circle was Elizabeth Inchbald (née Simpson), a farmer's daughter from Suffolk who had run away from home at 18 to seek a living on the stage in London. Within a few months she was married to the actor Joseph Inchbald and made her debut as Cordelia to his Lear in Bristol in September 1772. The couple spent a few years touring with theatrical companies, during which time Elizabeth met and became friends with Sarah Siddons and her brother John Philip Kemble. In 1778 the Inchbalds worked for the Dimond's company, who gave them a summer season at Canterbury, where she met and acted with Thomas Holcroft, who was then making a precarious living as an actor, theatrical journalist, essayist and budding playwright. After Joseph's death in 1779, Elizabeth continued with her career; but, although moderately successful, she really wanted to try her hand at writing. By the time she got to know Amelia Alderson she was well established as a popular dramatist, with a string of comedies, farces and sentimental dramas to her name. The first of her two novels had also been published. Attractive and sociable, Elizabeth was a well-known figure in London society; her friendship with Amelia, 16 years her junior, lasted until her death in 1821.

Holcroft was also becoming an important friend to Amelia. Since getting to know Elizabeth Inchbald, he had continued with his various theatrical and writing jobs – minor acting roles in Drury Lane and in the provinces, writing pieces for the London stage, publishing a book of poems and an epistolary novel, writing a column entitled *The Actor* for the *Westminster Magazine*, and, following a brief spell in Paris as a newspaper correspondent, embarking on a new role as a translator of French works. He began to align himself with those seeking political reform and attend clubs where philosophical issues were debated. In 1786 he met Godwin; the two men became close friends, spending time with each other almost on a daily basis. When Godwin's new friend Amelia Alderson appeared on the scene, Holcroft, widowed for the third time and approaching his 50th birthday, found her an appealing companion. She was entertained by rumours about possible relationships in her new circle of London friends and reported them to Susannah:

Mrs Inchbald says, the report of the world is that Mr Holcroft is in love with her, *she* with Mr Godwin, Mr Godwin with *me*, and I am in love with Mr Holcroft! A pretty story indeed! This report

Godwin brings to me, and he says Mrs I always tells him that when she praises *him* I praise Holcroft. This is not fair in Mrs I. She appears to me jealous of G's attention to me, so she makes him believe I prefer H to him. She often says to me, 'Now you are come, Mr Godwin does not come near me.' Is not this very womanish?[13]

Both Inchbald and Holcroft were to have their portraits painted by John Opie. The artist had been launched into the London art world in 1781, at the age of 20, as 'the Cornish Wonder', by the entrepreneurial art connoisseur and writer Dr John Wolcot. By the time Amelia started spending time in London Opie had achieved great success in his chosen career, enjoying the patronage of the royal family, exhibiting at the Royal Academy and associating with some of the artistic, theatrical and literary people known to Godwin.

There is some uncertainty about when and where Amelia Alderson met John Opie. Brightwell understood that Opie first saw Amelia at an evening party at the house of 'one of her early friends', but named neither the friends nor the location of the party. She implied that the account she was giving about the occasion came from a family, personally known to her, who were among the guests. She named a 'Mr F' as having been sitting next to Opie when Amelia arrived and, presumably it was from this mysterious Mr F or his family that Brightwell was given this anecdote:

Some of those present, were rather eagerly expecting the arrival of Miss Alderson; but the evening was wearing away, and still she did not appear; at length the door was flung open, and she entered, bright and smiling, dressed in a robe of blue, her neck and arms bare; and on her head a small bonnet, placed in somewhat coquettish style sideways, and surmounted by a plume of three white feathers. Her beautiful hair hung in rich waving tresses over her shoulders; her face was kindling with pleasure at sight of her old friends; and her whole appearance was animated and glowing. At the time she came in, Opie was sitting on a sofa, beside Mr F, who had been saying, from time to time, 'Amelia is coming; Amelia will surely come. Why is she not here?' and whose eyes were turned in her direction. He was interrupted by his companion eagerly exclaiming, 'Who is that? Who is that?' and hastily rising, he pressed forward, to be introduced to the fair object whose sudden appearance had so impressed him. He was evidently smitten; charmed, at first sight....[14]

With no other reliable evidence about the couple's first meeting – and no clues as to the identity of 'Mr F' – it is not possible to identify the 'early friends' at whose house the alleged encounter took place. A.M.W. Stirling, biographer of Thomas Coke, First Earl of Leicester, decided that the meeting took place in Norwich because Opie was on a visit to Holkham, the Norfolk seat of the Coke family, in connection with his work. Coke, she wrote:

> ...gave Opie commissions to paint portraits of Dr Parr, Fox and other of his friends. Opie therefore visited Holkham several times in connection with this work; and it was on one of these occasions that he was beguiled into attending a party at Norwich, under promise of an introduction to the fascinating and gifted Amelia Alderson, whom he had a great curiosity to see. He described afterwards how he awaited her arrival with impatience....[15]

Then followed a direct quote from Brightwell's account, attributed by Stirling to Opie himself, rather than to Mr F. Certainly, Opie's portrait of the politician Charles James Fox was commissioned by Coke, but the actual painting of it did not take place until the Opies had been married for a few years; Opie's portrait of Parr was also painted after Opie and Amelia were married. Opie's biographer Ada Earland was more cautious about the Brightwell anecdote. She suggested that if the meeting occurred in Norwich, as related by Stirling, it must have been in the spring of 1797; 'if in London, for some accounts place the scene of the party there, it might have been a little later.'[16] However, Amelia herself, in a letter written in December 1796, to Mary Wollstonecraft, teasing her about rumours that she (Mary) might marry Opie referred to the artist in a way which suggested she had got to know him that year.

According to the Godwin diaries, both Amelia and John Opie were in London at corresponding periods in the summer and autumn of 1796 and the spring and summer of 1797. In 1796 Opie was going through the lengthy process of divorcing his first wife Mary (née Bunn), who had eloped in May of the previous year with a Major Edwards. He was finally made a free man on December 23rd that year.

Godwin first recorded Opie's name in his diary as a fellow diner at King's in December 1795; 12 days later Godwin called on Opie at his house in Berners Street, when they talked of 'sincerity and painters'. In January 1796, he dined at the artist's home; by March Miss Alderson was back in London and associating once more with Godwin and his friends, as, indeed, was Opie. Godwin was a reliable recorder of the names of people present at events he attended, but, clearly, he was not keeping notes of those who attended get-togethers in which he did not participate. However, it seems more than likely that the couple met each other once Amelia was back in the capital or, at the very least, were aware of the other's presence in the same social circles. The first diary entry in which Godwin mentioned the two together was in August 1796: he had called on Opie in the morning, Amelia had called on him later in the day; in the evening, after supper at another friend's house, the diarist recorded he had overtaken Opie and Amelia. At that time Opie was still married, although separated from his wife. The next diary entry in which they appeared together was in April 1797, when Amelia accompanied Godwin as he called on the artist Fuseli and on Opie. By then both Opie and Godwin were in changed circumstances; Opie was divorced and Godwin was married to Mary Wollstonecraft, who was expecting his child.

Chapter Nine

During the period in which Godwin and Opie were undergoing changes in their marital statuses, Amelia was busy with her own concerns. After spending the spring and summer in London in 1795, Amelia returned to Norwich, from where she wrote Godwin a chatty letter. She had read the first volume of the *Memoires*, written in prison while awaiting her death on the guillotine by Madame Roland, a leading supporter of the French Revolution. 'I long for the others. She interests, delights and makes me unhappy,' wrote Amelia. She asked Godwin to say 'everything that's friendly and affectionate' to Holcroft and 'tell Fanny [Holcroft's daughter] to write to me'. She had just returned from a visit to Mrs Sothren (née Godwin), whom she found 'of sound health and unimpaired intellect in her conversation'. A deeply religious woman, who had lived with his family when William was a boy, the then Miss Godwin had persuaded him to read didactic religious books and moral tales.

> Annabella Plumptre accompanied me to Mrs Sothren; we think her a sensible woman and I dare say our acquaintance with this cousin of yours will not end with this day's meeting. Miss Plumptre has made an effort to continue it by lending her Mr Holcroft's narrative and letter and my servant is to be the bearer of them.
>
> Here I am again in this world of *stillness* not to say *dullness* – but it gives me an opportunity of entering into myself; of thinking over à tête reposé the scenes and persons I have left, of marshalling the new ideas I have gained and of acting in consequence of them.[1]

Amelia's ambition was to have a play accepted for the London stage and she was encouraged by the support of both Holcroft and Godwin. She had shown Holcroft the manuscript of her first drama *The Tragedy of Adelaide*, on which he wrote:

> At seventeen, when scenes like this occurred
> You promis'd much. Remember! Keep your word. T.H.*

---

* Macgregor had access to the *Adelaide* ms, which was then in the possession of a descendant of one of Amelia's cousins. She reported in a footnote that underneath these lines Mrs Opie had written: 'The above couplet was written in pencil by Mr Holcroft.' (Macgregor, *Amelia Alderson Opie*, p.13)

Godwin had been complimentary about the comedy which she showed him in September 1794. During the winter months of 1795-6, she tried her hand at another comedy and also a tragedy, which she was adapting from a Gothic novel. She continued to keep in touch with the political scene and take an interest in what was happening in literary and theatrical worlds, but correspondence with friends was reduced while she pressed on with her writing. In February she wrote twice to Godwin, apologising for the delay but assuring him he was often in her thoughts, then noting she was sending two letters in a fortnight after months of neglect: 'But you will know that there is no accounting for the caprice of woman – and that I, alas, have a great deal of the woman still hanging about me you know too well.'[2]

Much of her first letter was concerned with Godwin's most recent work which, she told him, she had read 'with delight'. Following the treason trial acquittals the reform campaigners had become increasingly strident, with radicals such as Thelwall – now a hero of the movement – organising mass public meetings and promoting radical pamphlets. In October 1795, King George III was jeered at and his carriage window broken by a mob as he made his way to the opening of Parliament. The government used the incident as an excuse speedily to introduce two bills – one making it a treasonable offence to incite people, by speech, to hatred or contempt of the monarch, constitution or government; the other ruling that meetings of more than 50 persons must be authorised by magistrates who could dissolve such gatherings if they considered them 'seditious'. Godwin's response was to take up his pen and write an 86-page pamphlet *Considerations on Lord Grenville's and Mr Pitt's Bills*. Examining the vexed question of freedom of speech, from an historical, legal and philosophical standpoint, the work addressed both the government's wish to curtail it and the reformers' increasingly aggressive exhortations.

Amelia feared her admiration of the work deprived her of all claims to the title of Democrat. 'I am afraid I must never show my face at certain political lectures again, unless I chuse [sic] to run the risk of being pointed out as a spy.'[3] In her next letter she asked Godwin if Thelwall resented the pamphlet and if their acquaintance had ceased. She had amused herself fancying a dialogue amongst members of the corresponding societies upon reading the first part of *Considerations*; and she had sent the pamphlet to Mrs Sothren. 'Heigh ho! There had need be pleasure and profit in the acquaintance of eminent characters for there is infinite trouble attending it.'

A few days later she was writing to Godwin again about her own work. Her latest attempt at writing for the stage was from *The Sorcerer*,* which she had read and admired:

> I resolved to present the piece to Mrs Twiss and thro' her to Mr Kemble. In rather better than a fortnight my tragedy was in reading order, I mean tho' the language was not publish'd the scenes and the situations were so arranged that I knew it would be easy for Mr H [Thomas Harris, manager of Covent Garden] to decide whether the general dramatic effect would be good, after time and application had polished the tale into some degree of excellence – accordingly I sent the *Sorcerer* to Mrs T. She gave it to her brother but learnt from him that the *proprietors* were the readers of plays now, but he said he could give it to them, and very civilly assured me of his good wishes. But I taking fright at my tale's being referred to the awful proprietors wrote again, entreating Mr K to read and give me *his* opinion. This at first he positively refused but at last to oblige his sister he complied and I received yesterday his opinion – which is that it is full of repetitions and in short he sees 'no use in giving it to the proprietors as it is', nor does he see how it could be altered....
>
> I am now finishing a *second* comedy and when I tell you it is the first wish of my heart to write a good play and have it performed at either house I hope you will suppose that with application and advice of good judges I may in time succeed... pray let your letter be kind – do not *chill* me. I am sooner depressed than encouraged.[4]

Telling Godwin she was also 'desirous' of putting herself under Holcroft's tuition, Amelia ended her letter 'Farewell! In about five weeks I shall see you.' From Godwin's diary it would appear that she did complete the comedy and hand him the manuscript soon after her arrival in London at the end of March 1796. Godwin called on her on March 25th, supped with Holcroft and her at Batty's three days later and had tea with her and other friends at Holcroft's on March 29th. A meticulous recorder of what he was reading or working on, he noted 'A.A's comedy' on March 30th and again on April 9th. Amelia called on Godwin on April 1st and later in the day wrote him a grateful note:

---

* Probably *The Sorcerer* by Veit Weber (pseudonym of Georg Philipp Ludwig Leonhard Wächter), translated from the German by Robert Huish (London: J. Johnson, 1795).

I did not expect anything so civil from you relative to my play and am myself 'agreeably surprised'. I look forward to many a severe criticism from you when you read it over à tête reposé, but I long for them – as I wish to be employed and sigh already for the leisure of my own study at Norwich.[5]

Godwin was consulted again later in the year when she wrote entreating him to read another play she was working on. She was then back in Norwich, after five months in the capital, during which time she had added Mary Wollstonecraft and the writer Mary Hays to her circle of literary friends.

Hays, ten years older than Amelia, was born into a family of rational dissenters in Southwark. The death of her father, when she was 15, was followed four years later by the death of her fiancé a few weeks before their wedding. She started corresponding with Robert Robinson, a dissenting minister based at Cambridge, attending lectures at the newly established academy for dissenters at Hackney and writing poetry and essays. Her pamphlet *Cursory Remarks on an Enquiry into the Expediency and Propriety of Public Worship*, published in 1791 under the pseudonym Eusebia, brought her to the notice of the radical group connected to the publisher Joseph Johnson. Hays met Wollstonecraft at Johnson's home in St.Paul's Churchyard and the two became friends. Her next work, *Letters and Essays, Moral and Miscellaneous*, covered religion, philosophy and politics, and argued for the better education of women. Soon after its publication in 1793, Hays moved into lodgings in Hatton Garden intending to support herself by writing. After reading Godwin's novel *Caleb Williams*, she wrote him an admiring letter; their correspondence developed into friendship. When the *Monthly Magazine*, a periodical for liberal dissenters was launched in February 1796, Hays became one of its regular contributors.

Godwin had first met Wollstonecraft at a dinner party held at Johnson's for Thomas Paine in November 1791. He particularly wanted to meet and talk to Paine and was thoroughly irritated by the opinionated Wollstonecraft dominating the conversation. At that time she had been earning her living as a writer for five years but Godwin had read none of her works; nor was he interested in getting to know her better. Wollstonecraft, also ten years older than Amelia, came from a reasonably well-off family in Spitalfields, where her paternal grandfather owned a silk weaving business. But she endured an unsettled childhood with a feckless, alcoholic father and a mother who doted on her first-born and ensured he was given the education of a gentleman. Mary, the second-born, and her younger siblings received little schooling, as the family moved across the country, accompanied by a decline in their financial state.

With determination, Wollstonecraft snatched at whatever educational chances came her way. In 1784, with her close friend Fanny Blood, she and her sisters set up a school for girls in Newington Green, where she became acquainted with the flourishing circle of rational dissenters, including Dr Price. The school failed when Wollstonecraft went to Lisbon to nurse the newly married but ailing Fanny, who subsequently died in childbirth. Her next job as a governess to an aristocratic family in Ireland lasted only a year, after which she returned to London and decided to try to make her living as a writer. She was introduced to Johnson, who found her somewhere to live, lent her money and gave her regular work on his *Analytical Review*. In 1787 he published her first book, *Thoughts on the Education of Daughters*, a rigorously didactic piece; her first novel, *Mary: A Fiction*, and a book for children, *Original Stories from Real Life*, followed a year later. She also applied herself to learning French, German, Italian and Dutch, becoming proficient enough to do some translation work for Johnson.

The publisher's confidence in Wollstonecraft was fully justified. When Burke's notorious *Reflections on the Revolution in France*, came out in 1790, causing outrage to all English radicals, Johnson encouraged his protégée to express her antagonism in writing. Her *A Vindication of the Rights of Man*, published only a few weeks after Burke's *Reflections*, brought her instant fame; pursuing her passion for equal rights, she focused on the particular wrongs against women, as she perceived them, to write *A Vindication of the Rights of Women*. Published in 1792, the book was a forceful polemic against a culture in which women were not encouraged to be their true selves but were expected to adopt a submissive female role in order to please and gratify the tastes of men – a process which she described as 'the system of dissimulation'. It was an immediate best-seller. But Wollstonecraft's professional success was not repeated in her private life. She met the writer and painter Henry Fuseli at Johnson's home and fell desperately in love with him. Although married – to one of his models – the self-important artist encouraged the infatuation, but the relationship foundered when she approached his wife and suggested the three of them should live together. The outraged Sophia Fuseli sent her packing.

After the dramatic ending of her affair with the artist, the unhappy Wollstonecraft decided to travel alone to Paris in December 1792. She soon became associated with a lively group of British and American radicals and within a few months was passionately in love with and pregnant by an American revolutionary soldier, Gilbert Imlay. By then the complex and intense conflict between political parties in France had made Paris a dangerous place, especially for English visitors – Britain having been at war with France since February 1793. As a protection, Imlay registered Wollstonecraft as his wife; she followed him to Le Havre, where her daughter Fanny was born in May 1794, and then to London. Realising that her lover was seeing other women and had no intention of settling down with her, she attempted suicide by overdosing on laudanum. In a last-ditch effort to please Imlay she agreed to travel to Scandinavia, accompanied by her infant daughter and a maid, to sort out problems connected with his business dealings. She was away for four months. On her return to London she found that Imlay had a new woman in his life, whereupon she made another suicide attempt, throwing herself into the Thames off Putney Bridge. But she was rescued by two passing watermen.

Although still hoping for a reunion with her former lover, Wollstonecraft, calling herself Mrs Imlay, began to associate once more with friends in the Johnson circle. In January 1796, Mary Hays invited her to tea, along with Godwin and Holcroft. She and Godwin met again a few days later when they were guests at a dinner party. Johnson had just published her *A Short Residence in Sweden, Norway and Denmark*, which Godwin found completely captivating. By the end of February, recognising at last that she and Imlay would not make a life together, Wollstonecraft wrote him a farewell letter in which she said 'I part with you in peace'[6], left her lodgings and went to stay with a friend in Berkshire. Within a few weeks she was back in London. So, too, was Amelia Alderson.

Chapter Ten

Amelia returned to London in March 1796. She stayed with the Batty family, resuming her social contacts in the capital and neighbouring villages. Since her first encounter with John Horne Tooke after his acquittal at the treason trial she had added him to her list of acquaintances, possibly meeting him at Holcroft's home, where he was a frequent visitor. Holcroft's eldest daughter Ann was to marry a widowed Norfolk friend of Godwin's, William Tooke Harwood, who was the nephew of John Horne Tooke's wealthy benefactor William Tooke.* Amelia's friendships with Holcroft, Inchbald and Fanny Twiss continued to flourish and in June Godwin introduced her first to Mary Hays and then to Mary Wollstonecraft. The latter, on her return to London from Berkshire, had moved into lodgings in Cumming Street, off the Pentonville Road, not too far from Godwin's lodgings at Chalton Street in Somers Town. On an April morning, soon after her return, she decided to call on Godwin, uninvited; he returned her call a few days later and their friendship began in earnest.

Amelia was delighted to meet the two Marys, especially Wollstonecraft. In response to a postscript which Wollstonecraft had added to a letter Amelia received from Godwin in August, after she had gone home to Norwich, she wrote a letter addressed to 'Mrs Imlay', in which she enthused:

> I derive so much pleasure from thinking of you that I was delighted to find you *wish* to claim a place in my remembrance. Will you help me to account for the strong desire I always feel when with you to say affectionate things to you? Perhaps it is because you, like Julie [heroine of Jean-Jacques Rousseau's *Julie or the New Héloïse*], appear so capable of feeling affection that you cannot fail to excite it. I remember the time when my desire of seeing you was repress'd

---

* John Horne Tooke was born John Horne; he added 'Tooke' in 1782 in the belief that he was to be the bachelor William Tooke's heir. Tooke, the son of a Norwich weaver, owned estates and properties in Norfolk, Purley and London. He left the bulk of his fortune to his nephew William Tooke Harwood, son of his sister Elizabeth and her husband Thomas Harwood, and to Elizabeth's grandson John Baseley. Part of Harwood's bequest was a substantial estate at Thompson, near Hingham in Norfolk.

by fear – but as soon as I read your letters from Norway, the cold awe which the philosopher had excited, was lost in the tender sympathy call'd forth by the *woman*. I saw nothing but the interesting creature of feeling and imagination and I resolved if possible, to become acquainted with one who had alternately awakened my sensibility and gratified my judgement. I *saw* you and you are one of the few objects of my curiosity who in gratifying – have not disappointed it also....

I write for my *maiden aunt* – your critique on my other play appears to me very just in all places except on the scene between Lady [illegible name] and her old lover – I do not think it overdone – however it will certainly undergo with the rest, great alteration.[1]

Godwin, in his methodical way, had recorded in his diary reading '*Maiden Aunt*, Acts 1, 2 & 3' on July 29th and '*Maiden Aunt* Acts 4 & 5' two days later. During the next few weeks his relationship with Wollstonecraft was ripening into a sexual affair and they were spending a great deal of time with each other. Unaware of this development, Amelia concluded her letter on a light-hearted, gossipy note:

Weaver Browne* has been two or three times of our parties here. He talk'd in a very *warm* manner of you to a *Mr Rigby* who repeated his conversation to me – one of his expressions was 'she is a very voluptuous looking woman'. I *stared*! not that I dispute the propriety of the epithet as applied to *you*, but that I was surprised to find *him capable* of applying it.

... upon my word I can see you blush at this distance, n'importe – a blush is very becoming. What would Miss Hays say? Would you believe it the false hearted man calls her old, ugly and ill dressed – he is no philosopher.

Pray write to me soon. The fascinating society of London is still but too present to my mind – now my *first feelings* are over the society *here* seems 'flat, stale and unprofitable'.[2]

Although, in the first instance, Amelia spent time with Wollstonecraft and Hays at gatherings at which Godwin was present, the philosopher was away from the capital in July, spending his days in Norfolk, visiting his family and friends. While he was away the women

---

* The Rev Stephen Weaver Browne. Born in Norwich, he was ordained at Cambridge into the Church of England but later became a Nonconformist. He worked as a minister in Norwich, Birmingham and London. His literary friends included William Taylor.

continued to further their friendships. Wollstonecraft also moved to new lodgings in Judd Place West, close to Godwin's Somers Town address. Hays was about to publish her first novel *Memoirs of Emma Courtney*, based on her failed relationship with William Frend, whom Amelia had been so keen to meet while in London the previous year. He had become involved with Hays after reading her 1791 pamphlet and writing her an admiring letter. A close friendship developed. Hays fell deeply in love with Frend and hoped to marry him, but he claimed that he lacked the means to support a wife. Much of her passion for Frend and her distress at his rejection was poured out in letters to him and Godwin, versions of which were incorporated into the novel, which brought her considerable notoriety. The heroine's passionate approach to love and her aversion to rules of society which kept women dependent on men, was regarded as shocking by some readers. But it did receive some positive reviews and Amelia, writing to Wollstonecraft later that year, said she was delighted with the novel and would have given a great deal to have written it.

Amelia would have been interested in hearing news from Norwich when Godwin returned to London and, indeed, he called on her straightaway. While in her home city he had spent time with Susannah and John Taylor, Anne and Annabella Plumptre, William Taylor, Edward Rigby, John and Elizabeth Brunton, Amelia's old teacher Mrs Beecroft, Bartlett Gurney, Hudson Gurney, William Enfield, John Pitchford and her Woodhouse cousins Ollyett and Robert. Dr Alderson was often present on these occasions; Godwin also paid several calls on Amelia's father and spent one night in the Alderson house. In his diary entry for Sunday July 10th he recorded that he and the doctor had spent the day together, dining at Thomas Harvey's, taking tea at William Taylor's and supping at Anne Plumptre's. The entry concluded: 'Propose to Alderson.' This intriguing statement has been interpreted by some Godwin scholars to mean that he was seeking Dr Alderson's permission to ask Amelia to marry him; others argue that since he was, by then, seriously involved with Wollstonecraft, the proposal was nothing to do with young Miss Alderson. She herself returned home a few weeks later and continued corresponding with Godwin in her usual flirty manner, which, probably, she would have deemed inappropriate had she thought he had asked for her hand in marriage.

Whatever the proposal was, the two men spent time together over the next two days before Godwin drove out to the country to visit family and friends, including Tooke Harwood. A week later he was back in the city in time for the Norwich Assizes, possibly to give moral support to Dr Alderson who was being prosecuted for assault. He walked with Alderson in the public gardens before the trial and supped with him once the case was over and done with – the doctor having been found not guilty.* When Godwin called on Amelia as soon as he returned to London he was able to give her a full account of the proceedings, at which her father had been represented by Robert Plumptre, the barrister brother of Anne and Annabella.

It is possible that Godwin's 'proposal' to Dr Alderson was to do with their friend Robert Merry who was in severely straitened financial circumstances. Before his marriage to Anne Brunton, whom he met when she was acting in his tragedy *Lorenzo* at Covent Garden in 1791, he had travelled widely on the Continent. In Florence for three years he was part of a literary group with whom he collaborated to produce collections of poetry, writing himself under the pseudonym Della Crusca to indicate his devotion to the city's Accadamia Della Crusca. Merry visited Paris after the storming of the Bastille, which inspired him to write *The Laurel of Liberty* which went down well with French Revolution sympathisers.

Anne Brunton, 14 years younger than her husband, was an immediate success when launched on the stage by her father John in 1785. She continued as an actress under the name of Mrs Merry for only one season after her marriage, as her husband's family disapproved of such a career.† Unfortunately, Merry's literary efforts were bringing in little money. The couple were falling on harder and harder times and needing support from friends and relations. In 1796 Anne spent some time in Norwich with her family; her husband was with her early in the year, returning to London in late March, possibly in connection with the publication of his latest poem *The Pains of Memory*. Amelia, in a note to Godwin on April 1st, told him that Merry had

---

* The *Norwich Mercury*, 23 July, 1796, gave a brief report of the case: 'Traverse for an assault – Robert Ives Browne against J. Alderson MD. The prosecutor's case was opened by Charles Harvey Esq and when Mr Serjeant Le Blanc had addressed the jury Lord Chief Justice Eyre interposed, and in a dispute of so much delicacy earnestly recommended a mediation. In deference to such high authority, a consultation ensued between the parties of their respective counsels, and an ample apology on the part of Dr Alderson under the direction and sanction of the Judge was read in the Court by Counsellor Wilson, which being accepted by Mr Browne, the Jurors were directed to find the defendant not guilty.'

† Merry's father was governor of the Hudson's Bay Company and his mother was a daughter of Sir John Willes.

called on her that morning bringing her letters from Norwich.

Three months later Merry and Godwin travelled together on the London to Norwich mail coach. On July 8th Merry was arrested for debt. That night Godwin slept at Dr Alderson's; he also saw Amelia's father over the next four days, along with many of the city's intellectuals and radicals. Perhaps Godwin was enlisting support to aid Merry, for on July 12th the poet was discharged, and he and his wife dined with Godwin at a city hostelry. Merry returned to London, while Godwin remained in Norfolk; he and Dr Alderson called on Mrs Merry before Godwin caught the mail coach back to London on July 23rd. He saw Amelia a few times before she went home to Norwich, but by then the main woman in his life was Wollstonecraft, whom he was seeing almost every day. Despite – or perhaps because of – this, she chose to tease him about other women, including Inchbald, whom she referred to as 'Mrs Perfection'. Of Amelia she wrote to Godwin on August 4th: I spent the evening with Mademoiselle Alderson – you, I'm told, were ready to devour her – in your little parlour. Elle est trés jolie – n'est pas?[3]

Although so occupied with his developing relationship, Godwin did find time to write to Amelia, whom he had missed on her last day in London. She replied, reprimanding him for not meeting her at Frances Twiss's (unknown to her, he was having tea with Wollstonecraft), but declaring that, although he had inflicted pain on her, she forgave him. She said she valued his friendship and assistance, adding that Mrs Imlay was 'a more rigid critic'; but she hoped that the fruit of her efforts and application would entitle her to the praise of both of them.

By the time she wrote to Godwin again Robert Merry and his wife had left England and were sailing to America where Anne Merry had been offered an engagement at the New Theatre, Philadelphia. Merry consented to his wife returning to the stage because of their mounting debts. They arrived in New York on October 10th and she went on to achieve great success on the American stage.* Amelia wanted to know if Godwin was privy to Merry's design of leaving England and, if so, she much wished to know how he looked and talked when he bade Godwin adieu, whether he was most full of hope or dejection.

---

* After Merry died in December, 1798, aged 43, his widow married Thomas Wignell, manager of the theatre in Philadelphia where she had made her American debut. They had one child. When Wignell died, Anne married another theatre manager, William Warren. She died in childbirth in 1808.

My heart felt very heavy when I heard he was really gone and gone too where I fear the charms of his conversation and his talents will not be relished as they deserve to be. On Mrs Merry's account I rejoice – here, from a variety of causes she could not be happy. She was in a state of anxiety concerning him. She also felt the consciousness of having great powers which were perishing from want of being called forth into action – now, she will be stimulated to action and be rewarded for her labours by the delightful consequence of supporting by her talent, the man she loves. But are his prospects so bright? I fear not.[4]

She added a postscript telling Godwin that Merry had 'transmitted to his friends here' the sum of £100; presumably these were the Norwich people who had helped to bail him out when he was arrested for debt in the city that summer.

Amelia also brought Godwin up to date with news of John Thelwall and his recent escapades in East Anglia:

Have you seen your friend Mr King [probably John King, the moneylender and radical writer] lately? While Thelwall was with us [in Norwich] he received a letter from him… desiring him to set his name down for £10 to defray the expense of the prosecution on account of ye outrage at Yarmouth.[5]

Since being found not guilty of treason, Thelwall had resumed his literary and public speaking careers. After the government had introduced its two 'Gagging Acts', as they were called by radicals, in December 1795, he continued his political career under the guise of lectures on history. In the spring and summer of 1796 he gave a series of 22 lectures in Norwich, where he had many friends and supporters. He had supped with Godwin and Dr Alderson at Anne Plumptre's in July. Thelwall's reception in Norwich encouraged him to accept an invitation to give a series of six lectures in Great Yarmouth in August. Samuel Hurry, the wealthy merchant and shipping agent, whose daughter had married Dr Alderson's brother Robert, offered his warehouse for the lectures and he himself attended the events with his young grandson Edward Hall Alderson.

The first two lectures were delivered without incident but the third was broken up by a gang of sailors armed with bludgeons and cutlasses. Thelwall managed to escape, aided by townspeople who grappled with the attackers. In his own account of the incident – a 52-page pamphlet written and published less than three weeks later 'to be circulated in the town where this unprecedented outrage was committed,[6] – Thelwall claimed he was the victim of a plot devised by 'the infamous commander' of one of the ships of war anchored off the port to carry him off to be murdered or transported to Siberia. Despite the uproar, he went ahead with all three of the second week's lectures, the last being on Friday, August 26th. 'I quitted Yarmouth the next day, and returned to the friendly, the intelligent, the beloved society of Norwich....'[7]

Having dealt with Merry and Thelwall, Amelia informed Godwin that she hoped to have her play ready for his inspection in a fortnight, if he would have leisure to 're-peruse and re-criticize it'. Apparently, he agreed, for she wrote next entreating him to read the manuscript as soon as it reached him, opening her letter in flirtatious mode:

> What a sweet creature I am! I declare I have already forgiven you all the anxiety which you occasioned me by your silence and even all the sarcasms which your letter contains....
>
> I hate you for always throwing *coquette* in my teeth – it is a bad habit and you have lately acquired a worse – you called me a bitch[*] the last time I saw you but no matter....
>
> Will you deign to enter into the feelings of an impatient girlish parent whose whole soul is wrapt up in the babe she has brought forth and who, unlike the owl in the fable, does not think her offspring a beauty herself but is very desirous others should think it so? Will you assist her at her bantling's [archaic: young child] toilette with all possible expedition? and let the anxious Mamma know whether you do not think Miss may grow up handsomer when her features are more formed? O that I could but transport myself to Somers Town for one half an hour! Then would you read in my wild looks, frantic gestures and incoherent conversation, my wishes, fears and tormenting uncertainties about your opinion in the first place.[8]

Godwin responded to the young playwright's request, noting in his diary three days on which he read the five acts of the 'A.A.' manuscript. She wrote back immediately thanking him for the parcel which he had dispatched on November 11th and telling him that his opinion

---

[*] According to the Rev Robert Forby's *The Vocabulary of East Anglia*, the word bitch in late 18th century Norfolk meant a trull, the female companion of a vagrant – a coarse term suggesting loose morals.

of her play gave her 'most heartfelt pleasure'. She went on to ask for more advice on the problems she was having with some of the characters, adding: 'When I have heard from you I shall shut myself up till my task is ended.'[9] Towards the end of the year, having followed Godwin's advice, she wrote thanking him for his 'judicious criticism'. Her play she informed him was now 'in Richardson's hands' [probably Joseph Richardson, one of the three managerial proprietors of Drury Lane Theatre] and she was starting to rewrite her 'other comedy'. Despite all her efforts, none of Amelia's plays were accepted for the London stage; instead she was to make her name as a novel writer and poet, but which time she was no longer Miss Alderson, but Mrs Opie.

Chapter Eleven

While corresponding with Godwin and Wollstonecraft during the autumn of 1796 Amelia was unaware of the couple's now well established intimate relationship. Writing to Wollstonecraft in December, and still addressing her as Mrs Imlay, she passed on the latest gossip:

> I hear from a letter just received from Town that you are to marry Opie, I mean *Law willing*. That he would be most happy to marry you, I firmly believe, but I doubt your willingness to marry *him*. I wish I did *not* for many reasons, all of which, if I expressed them, you would find affectionate towards you.[1]

Presumably Amelia's '*Law willing*' was a reference to Opie's impending divorce or perhaps she believed that 'Mrs Imlay' was still married. Her assumption that Opie would be happy to marry Wollstonecraft suggests that she had formed her own impression of the man who, less than two years later, would become own husband.

The rumour about Opie and Wollstonecraft was certainly being circulated among friends and acquaintances in London. The landscape painter Joseph Farington, whose portrait by Opie had been exhibited at the Royal Academy two years earlier, noted in his diary:

> I told Opie it had been reputed that he was going to be married to Mrs Wolstencroft [sic] but that could not be as she is already married to Mr Imlay, an American. He replied that would not have been an obstacle if he had had any such intention as Mrs Wolstencroft had herself informed him that she never was married to Mr Imlay, though she lived at Paris under his protection as an American to avoid a prison and had a Child by him.[2]...'

Wollstonecraft had got to know Opie in the early 1790s, when he was living with his first wife, about whom she wrote to her sister Everina:

> Mr Opie, who frequently calls upon me has introduced me to his wife. She is really a pretty easy woman, too much of a flirt to be a proper companion for him, yet though they do not appear to see *many* things in the same light they concur in shewing me uncommon civility.[3]

In 1796 John Opie had been earning his living as an artist in London for 15 years. Born in May 1761, in the village of Mithian, near St Agnes, in Cornwall, he was the youngest son of Edward Opie, a carpenter. Mary Opie, his mother, was 48 when John was born, his three brothers were grown up and his only sister Elizabeth (known as Betty) was in her teens. Educated at the village school, he was a bright pupil and showed skill at drawing and painting from an early age; but his father, wanting the boy to follow in his footsteps, bound him first as his own apprentice and then to a local sawyer. Opie persisted with his sketching, rising early and going to bed late in order to spend any spare time on his art work.

When he was 14, some of his drawings were seen by a Dr John Wolcot, a man in his late 30s, who was in practice in Truro and who had ridden over to Mithian to see a patient. A keen amateur artist, he detected Opie's potential and decided to take charge of his future development. Within a matter of weeks Wolcot had bought the boy out of his apprenticeship and taken him to live in his own house, Edward Opie having at last realised the futility of trying to block his son's artistic ambitions. In addition to art lessons, the doctor felt it was necessary to give the rough lad instruction in manners and etiquette. 'I want to polish him,' he wrote to a friend. 'He is an unlicked cub yet.'[4]

Wolcot understood that portraiture was the most promising route for a young man hoping to make a living as a painter. His long-term ambition was to launch his protégé onto the London art scene, but for the next few years he kept Opie busy working as an itinerant portrait painter in Cornwall, armed at first with letters of recommendation to the doctor's friends and patients. The first major public recognition of Opie's work was in 1780, when one of his portraits was accepted for the Society of Artists' exhibition at the Great Room in London's Spring Gardens (later the Vauxhall Gardens), south of the river. It was listed in the catalogue as 'A Boy's Head, an instance of Genius, not having seen a picture' by 'Master Oppey,* Penryn, Cornwall'. The writer and art historian Horace Walpole described it as 'an exceeding good picture both as to colouring and expression'.[5]

In order to foster Opie's burgeoning career, Wolcot decided they must move to London. He resigned from the medical profession and set himself up as a writer under the nom-de-plume of Peter Pindar; in the autumn of 1781 the two men moved into lodgings in Orange

---

* Earland accounts for the spelling 'Oppey' by confirming that this was the Cornish pronunciation of the name Opie.

Court, Leicester Fields (behind what is now the site of the National Gallery). Although Wolcot had taken the trouble to instil socially acceptable behaviour and manners into his pupil, he chose to introduce him to London society as 'the Cornish wonder', an untaught genius whom he had plucked from a simple peasant background. The strategy worked and, before long, their lodgings were besieged by fashionable people seeking to have their portrait painted by the 'new' artist. When the engraver Thomas Hearne described Opie as 'a rude, clownish boy, with lank, dark hair' and suggested to Wolcot that he ought to be more polished in his appearance now that he was mixing with smart people, he was told:

> 'No, no! you may depend on it, in this wonder-gaping town, that all curiosity would cease if his hair were dressed, and he looked like any other man; I shall keep him in this state for the next two years, at least.'[6]

Wolcot lost no time in introducing Opie to the celebrated portraitist Sir Joshua Reynolds, first president and founder member of the Royal Academy of Arts, who showed a kindly interest in the newcomer. When Reynolds's former pupil James Northcote returned to London, after three years studying art in Italy and achieving some success as a portrait painter in his native Devon, he called on his old master to tell him of his wish to succeed in the capital:

> 'Ah!' said Reynolds, 'you may go back now, you have no chance here. There is such a young man come out of Cornwall.' 'Good! Sir Joshua, what is he like?' 'Like? Like Caravaggio, but finer.'[7]

Through an influential acquaintance, Wolcot succeeded in getting Opie presented to King George III and Queen Charlotte. He took with him four or five pictures and spent nearly an hour and a half at the Queen's House (Buckingham House, now Palace). Writing to tell his mother of the meeting, he said:

> I have been with the King and Queen, who were highly pleased with my works, and took two of my pictures, and they are hung up in the King's collection at the Queen's Palace.[8]

Wolcot continued to promote Opie's name in all the right quarters, but the partnership was entering its final phase. In December 1782, the 21-year-old Opie married Mary Bunn at the Church of St Martin-in-the-Fields and took her back to his Orange Court lodgings. She was the daughter of Benjamin Bunn, a solicitor and money-lender whom the bridegroom had met through the sale of some of his paintings. Wolcot and Opie were known to indulge in frequent, but good-natured, verbal spats, but the introduction of a wife on the scene led to serious friction. Opie's father-in-law contributed to the tension, by pointing out that the contract between them – pooling their incomes and sharing expenses – was unequal now that the artist had a wife to provide for. After a serious falling out, the two men parted. The rift was not final. A year or two later Opie and his wife accompanied Wolcot to Wales. Moving in the same social circles, they dined together at friends' houses and Wolcot, although lampooning other artists while writing satirical pieces as Peter Pindar, continued to extol the superior talent of his former pupil.

In 1782, his first full year in London, Opie had five paintings accepted for the Royal Academy's exhibition. He was to exhibit there every year (with the exception of 1793) for the rest of his life. For Opie work was everything. His instant celebrity was beginning to subside a little, so he used any time not devoted to commissions to learn as much as he could about painting techniques and to make up for the gaps in his education by reading the best authors and seeking the company of clever, educated men with whom to converse. Northcote, with whom he spent most evenings, became a great admirer of the man and his work.

According to William Hazlitt, who made notes of his conversations with Northcote for publication in *The New Monthly Magazine*, the artist told him:

> You did not know Opie? you would have admired him greatly. I do not speak of him as an artist, but as a man of sense and observation. He paid me the compliment of saying that we should have been the best friends in the world if we had not been rivals. I think he had more of this feeling than I had; perhaps, because I had most vanity. We sometimes got into foolish altercations. I recollect once in particular, at a banker's in the City, we took up the whole of a dinner-time with a ridiculous controversy about Milton and Shakespeare; I am sure we neither of us had the least notion which was right.[9]

Northcote also had strong views on his friend's early marriage:

> Opie ought never to have married, for he was no more fit to be married than a log of wood. He ought to have known this, as Sir

Joshua did. ... he had none of the softness fit for married life. Now, had I had a daughter, I would as soon have married her to an American savage.[10]

How the new Mrs Opie felt about being left alone most evenings while her husband was fraternising with Northcote and others cannot be known. No doubt she would have wanted him to do well in his career and would have understood his wish to better himself and move in the right circles. He painted his first portrait of Mary before they were married. She was the subject of at least five more paintings, one of which depicting her as a nymph, was shown at the Royal Academy in 1786.* After a brief lull in the first few months of his marriage, his work was picking up again under the patronage of a wealthy landowner, Richard Wyatt, of Egham Manor in Surrey. He removed the newly-weds from their modest lodgings to a house in Great Queen Street near Covent Garden. It was a favourite area for artistic, literary and theatrical people. Opie did portraits of Sarah Siddons, Elizabeth Inchbald and Dr Johnson and, thanks to his new patron, began to resume his place as a portrait painter of minor royals, members of the aristocracy and upper classes. He also branched out into the then popular genre of scenes from history.

In the summer of 1786 Opie went on a tour of art galleries in the Low Countries, with his father-in-law and a friend. His first major historical painting, *The Assassination of James the First of Scotland*, shown that year in the Royal Academy exhibition, led to him being elected an Associate of the Academy and brought him to the attention of John Boydell. An engraver, publisher and print dealer, Boydell was also a London alderman (sheriff in 1785 and Mayor in 1790) and a member of the Stationers' Company. He was an important figure in the art world, often donating paintings from his own collection to London Corporation to be hung in the Guildhall, and using his numerous contacts to promote public and private patronage of the arts. He bought Opie's *Assassination* (and also the picture of Mary Opie as a nymph) and signed him up to be a contributor to his newly-launched Shakespeare project. Boydell planned to open a Shakespeare Gallery for the display of paintings depicting scenes from the plays and to publish an illustrated edition of Shakespeare and a folio of

---

* The painting, called *The Sleeping Nymph and Cupid stealing a kiss*, shows Mary, as the nymph, clad in a diaphanous gown with one bare breast. (Heinz Archive & Library sitters folder: National Portrait Gallery)

prints based on the paintings. For this ambitious scheme, he commissioned the most eminent painters and engravers of the day. After
Opie's next historical work, *The Murder of David Rizzio*, was hung
in the 1787 exhibition he was made a Royal Academician. The painting was bought by Boydell.*

The alderman was known to be a generous employer and paid his
artists handsomely. Opie painted seven Shakespeare scenes for Boydell's gallery, which opened in Pall Mall in May 1789. It was an immediate success. The first volume of the illustrated *Dramatick Works*
– paid for by subscribers and Boydell himself – was published in the
same year and the ninth and last volume in 1805. Meanwhile, sales
of the print folios were also doing well. In 1791 the Opies moved
to Berners Street. The high-profile work for Boydell brought Opie
more commissions; he continued to specialise in portraits and in
1792 he was invited to paint more historical scenes for a new edition
of Hume's *History of England* by the publisher Robert Bowyer. He
worked on the 11 paintings over several years.

Not only was the artist very busy with his own paintings and
fraternising with fellow artists, he also took pupils. Although very
little has been recorded about his relationship with his first wife, the
general impression seems to have been that the couple were not well
suited. Amelia, writing her memoir of John, was decidedly circumspect about Mary. She neither mentioned her predecessor by name,
nor related any anecdotal evidence about her. In fairness to the second
Mrs Opie, addressing her memoir to Prince Hoare, the editor of *The
Artist*, who had prevailed upon her to write it, she did make it clear
that her account was concerned with her own observations on 'the
character of Mr Opie during an union with him of nine years'. She
said it was impossible for her to write the biographical account which
had been requested 'as there are circumstances in his life on which it
would be improper and indelicate for me to expiate'. She did, however, when writing about her husband's love of wit and repartee, recall
one incident in which he mentioned his first marriage:

> As we were coming from your [Mr Hoare's] apartments one eve-
> ning, and were passing St Giles's church, in company with a gen-
> tleman of avowedly *sceptical opinions*, Mr Opie said, 'I was *mar-
> ried* at that church' (alluding to his first marriage, dissolved by act
> of parliament). 'And *I*,' replied our companion, 'was *christened*

---

* Boydell gave both Opie historical paintings to the Guildhall. *The Assassination*
was lost in a fire caused by an air-raid attack in the Second World War.

there.' 'Indeed!' answered Mr Opie: 'It seems they do not do their work well at that church then, for it does not *hold*.'[11]

Since Opie was married at St Martin-in-the-Fields, perhaps he was making a point about the Church of England in general; or perhaps Amelia had forgotten which church triggered his memory. Her anecdote was picked up by subsequent writers and went on to acquire further alterations and additions. Earland opted for a version given in *Recollections of John Adolphus* (1871) in which a similar exchange was said to have taken place between Opie and Godwin when walking past St Martin-in-the-Fields. As Godwin was born into the family of a dissenting minister at Wisbech, it is scarcely possible that he was the man claiming to have been christened there.

As for writing about Mary Opie, Earland expressed it thus: 'In truth, there is not much to tell.' Brightwell claimed merely that Opie had 'unhappily married a woman wholly unworthy of him'. Trying to be fair, Earland dismissed gossip about Mary's wanton behaviour (passed on by a man who had never met her) and opted for the more likely credibility of an account from the oculist and writer John Taylor:

I knew her well, and am disposed to speak more with regret than severity on the cause which deprived her of her husband. Opie was devoted to his art, to which he chiefly and almost solely seemed to direct his attention.... She was a pretty little woman, with pleasing and unaffected manners. Being left much to herself, and at liberty to go abroad when and where she pleased, it was not wonderful that, comparing the unavoidable neglect of her husband with the persevering attention of a gallant, she should manifest the frailty of human nature.[12]

Wrapped up in his own concerns, Opie knew nothing of Mary's affair with Major John Edwards, an Irishman in his 50s. On May 20th, 1795, she left the house in Berners Street, telling the housemaid she was going to dine with her father. In fact she was running off to Bristol with Edwards. The couple lived in lodgings there as man and wife – which was useful evidence for Opie when suing for a divorce – and, once the tortuous procedures were finally completed on December 23rd, 1796, when their divorce bill was granted the Royal Assent, Mary was free to make a fresh start as Mrs Edwards. Opie, too, was free. He had already found the woman he wanted to be his second wife – Elizabeth Booth, one of his pupils. She was the daughter of Benjamin Booth, a director of the East India Company and a serious art collector, who lived in a splendid Robert Adam house in the Adelphi. According to Farington, Opie called on him on November 29th to speak of 'an engagement he has entered into with Miss Booth to marry'. Both Opie and his intended bride foresaw some difficulties with her wealthy father:

> ...but it is necessary to break the matter to him and Miss Booth concurred with Opie in thinking I should be a proper person to do it. I suggested to him that it might appear indelicate to speak to Mr Booth before the Divorce Bill has actually passed.'[13]

Opie told Farington he wished to delay notifying Mr Booth, but Elizabeth had confided in her sister, Mrs Ford, about her marriage plans. He feared that the well-connected Ford family would intervene, as indeed they did. Although Farington wanted to help his friend, the marriage proposal was doomed. Once he was aware of the situation, Booth packed his daughter off to stay with friends. He also enlisted the help of a solicitor to put pressure on Opie and by mid-January, 1797, the relationship was over. Elizabeth had no more painting lessons with the man she loved and she died, unmarried, in 1819.

Opie, however, had another prospective wife in mind – his pupil Jane Beetham. She was the daughter of Edward Beetham (also known as Betham), a versatile and resourceful man who had worked in the theatre, devised a new method of painting onto glass, invented a new piece of laundry equipment – the mangle – and was then running a publishing business in Fleet Street, where he lived with his family. His wife was well known for her skill in making profile and silhouette pictures which were very popular at the time – Amelia had called on Mrs Betham to have her profile taken on her visit to London with Mr Boddington in August 1794. Jane, the eldest of three daughters, was a talented artist who first exhibited at the Royal Academy in 1794, when she was 20. Opie painted all three sisters and gave Jane one of his self-portraits. Not long after the failure of his attempt to wed Miss Booth, he asked Edward Beetham for his daughter's hand in marriage. He was refused. Almost immediately, Beetham married Jane off to an elderly rich solicitor called John Reed.

During those winter months when Opie was released from one marriage and attempting to start another, Amelia was at home in Norwich with her father. She continued to correspond with Godwin about her play writing, sending him, on one occasion, a gift 'meant in simple courtesy as a mark of affection merely' – a local speciality which she frequently sent to friends further afield:

> I think I see your wonder on opening the basket and seeing what it contains. Perhaps you do not know that beefins* are a sort of apple cultivated almost entirely in Norfolk and that when dried they are reckoned a dainty and are sent in large quantities abroad, as well as over England from Norwich, where and where only, the process of drying them is understood. This will account for my sending you what might otherwise appear an odd gift; but now worthy perhaps of adorning the dessert of one or two of your smart friends.[14]

Amelia, like Opie, was also thinking about marriage. It was certainly on her mind, when she penned the letter to 'Mrs Imlay', passing on the gossips about *her* possible impending marriage. Having just returned from a few days' visit to friends in the country, where the master of the house read aloud to the company from Mrs Radcliffe's novel *The Italian*, she added – in the form of a memo to herself:

> When I marry to have it inserted in the marriage articles that my husband shall read to me in an evening while I work – God grant he may also be able to converse well on the merits of the work he has just read, for at least two hours after supper – then my greatest idea of domestic happiness will be realised![15]

After spending the winter in Norwich Amelia was back in London in the last week of March 1797. She dined at Holcroft's with Godwin and others on Sunday 26th; he called on her two days later. On Wednesday 29th he and Wollstonecraft, now four months pregnant with his child, were married at St Pancras parish church, with only Godwin's friend James Marshall, who had been a fellow student at Hoxton Academy, in attendance. A week later they moved into a new house, No 29, The Polygon, in Somers Town. Godwin also took rooms at Evesham Buildings in Chalton Street, about 20 doors away, where he would work and sometimes sleep. At first the newly-weds

---

* Beefins [also known as Biffins], the dried version of the apple known as the Norfolk Beefing, were a popular dessert item throughout the 18th and 19th centuries. They were sold by bakers who placed weights on the fruit, dried them overnight in their cooling bread ovens and then coated them with melted sugar. Throughout her life Amelia sent them to friends and relations at home and abroad: several were dispatched to Paris by the diligence (the French stagecoach) which she was assured was the safest means of transport.

kept the news to themselves, but within a week or two it had seeped out. For those who knew of Godwin's well documented aversion – in theory – to the state of marriage as practised in European countries, the news was a shock. Most of the couple's friends rallied and wished them well: Holcroft wrote 'from my very heart I wish you joy'; Anna Barbauld called it 'a very suitable match'; Mary Hays was pleased for her feminist friend, but urged her to retain the name Wollstonecraft.

Before the wedding, arrangements had been made for a group of friends, including Inchbald, to attend the theatre one Wednesday evening. Amelia, one of the party, had been spending time with the newly-weds over dinner at Holcroft's. A day or two before the theatre outing, she wrote to the new Mrs Godwin, calling her 'My dear Madam' and asking if she could spare a place in her box for 'an aristocratic friend'. Having addressed her note to 'Mrs or Mr Godwin, 29 The Polygon', she added a postscript: 'The direction will make you laugh, but I wrote it on the presumption that you, as Mrs Godwin were not known yet....'[16] Inchbald, already somewhat hostile to Wollstonecraft and ignorant of her relationship with Godwin, was aghast when she heard they were married. She wrote, ostensibly wishing them well:

> But, assured that your joyfulness would obliterate from your memory every trifling engagement, I have entreated another person to supply your place, and perform your office in securing a box....If I have done wrong, when you next marry, I will act differently.[17]

The good-natured Amelia was dragged into the developing conflict between Inchbald and the Godwins when Wollstonecraft appealed to her 'to set the matter right', even though she believed Mrs Inchbald's conduct had been 'very rude'. Who made the final arrangements for the evening is not clear, but when Godwin turned up at the theatre with his new wife, she and Inchbald exchanged hostile remarks. It was the end of any further contact between them. In a letter to Amelia, Wollstonecraft explained the kind of marriage she was hoping for and shared the reasons for having committed herself to a husband. Addressing Amelia as 'My Dear Girl' and signing the letter 'Mary Wollstonecraft femme Godwin', she mentioned the possibility of having more children, without admitting she was already pregnant.

> ...my conduct in life must be directed by my own judgment and moral principles; it is my wish that Mr Godwin should visit and dine out as formerly, and I shall do the same; in short, I still mean

to be independent, even to the cultivating sentiments and principles in my children's minds (should I have more) which he disavows.... I found my evenings solitary, and I wished, while fulfilling the duty of a mother, to have some person with similar pursuits, bound to me by affection; and beside, I earnestly desired to resign a name which seemed to disgrace me.[18]

Brightwell decided not to dwell on the Godwin/Wollstonecraft relationship. Godwin she wrote, had 'proved that his heart was not so wise as his head', while his wife was 'a strange incomprehensible woman, whose unhappy existence terminated shortly after this marriage'. From London Amelia wrote to Susannah, the much loved friend of and correspondent to so many literary people:

Mr Godwin was much gratified by your letter, and he avowed that it made him love you better than he did before, and Mrs Godwin was not surprised at it; bye the bye, he never told me whether you congratulated him on his marriage or not; but now I remember, it was written before that wonder-creating event was known. Heigho! what charming things would sublime theories be, if one could make one's practice keep up with them; but I am convinced it is impossible, and am resolved to make the best of every-day nature. I shall have much to tell you in a *tête à tête* of the Godwins, &c. – so much that a letter could not contain or do it justice; but this will be *entre nous*.[19]

Susannah had expressed 'kind fears' for her young friend when they parted and shed tears when bidding her adieu. Amelia wrote to assure her that she was enjoying everything and 'if my head be not turned by the large draughts which my vanity is daily quaffing' she would return to Norwich much happier than when she left it. Her letter was undated, but was probably penned some time in the spring or early summer. Godwin's diary indicated that Amelia and Opie were visitors or guests at mutual friends' houses during the spring months of 1797; he himself was making regular calls on both. By the beginning of August she and Opie were supping together at Godwin's house. Apparently Opie had recovered from his unsuccessful wooing of Elizabeth Booth and Jane Beetham and was turning his attention to Miss Alderson, as she confided to Susannah:

Mr Opie, has (but *mum*) been my declared lover, almost ever since I came. I was ingenuous with him upon principle, and I told him my situation, and the state of my heart. He said he should still persist, and would risk all consequences to his own peace, and so he did and does; and I have not resolution to forbid his visits. Is not this abominable? Nay more, were I not certain my father would disapprove such, or indeed *any* connexion for me, there are moments, when, ambitious of being a wife and mother, and of securing to myself a companion for life, capable of entering into all my pursuits, and of amusing me by his, – I could almost resolve to break all fetters, and relinquish too, the wide, and often aristocratic circle, in which I now move, and become the wife of a man, whose genius has raised him from obscurity, into fame and comparative affluence.... But I had forgotten to tell you the attraction Mr O held out, that staggered me beyond anything else; it was, that, if I was averse to leaving my father, he would joyfully consent to his living with us. What a temptation to me, who am every moment sensible, that the claims of my father will always be, with me, superior to any charms that a lover can hold out! Often do I rationally and soberly state to Opie the reasons that might urge me to marry him, in time, and the reasons why I could never be happy with him, nor he with me; but it always ends in his persisting in his suit, and protesting his willingness to wait for my decision; even when I am seriously rejecting him and telling him I *have* decided.[20]

Menzies-Wilson and Lloyd, indicated that Brightwell had 'carefully edited' some of the letters and omitted 'incidents of doubtful propriety'. They managed to gain access to this particular letter (then in private hands) and inserted some of the deleted phrases into their transcription:

Mr Opie, whose head and heart are so excellent as to make me forget the coarseness of his voice and manners and the ugliness of his face, has (but *mum*) been my declared lover almost ever since I came. I was ingenuous with him upon principle and I told him my situation relative to B* and the state of my heart but all in vain. He said he was sure I did not actually love the gentleman whoever he was, and he should still persist and would risk all consequences to his own peace.[21]

Opie's pursuit of Amelia continued. In mid-August she was at the

---

* The unidentified – and possibly married – man Amelia had fallen in love with. See Chapter 8.

village of Englefield Green, some 26 miles from the city of London, from where she wrote a brief letter to Susannah indicating she would have much to tell her when she returned to Norwich. Within a few days she was back at home with Dr Alderson.

Chapter Twelve

In London the Godwins were awaiting the birth of their child. Mary had found giving birth to Fanny a trouble-free experience and she fully expected her second child's arrival to be straightforward. Her daughter Mary was born late at night on August 30th after a long and extremely painful labour, but there were complications when the placenta failed to come away. In the early hours of the next day, the midwife from the Westminster Lying-In Hospital who attended the birth, called for Godwin to fetch a doctor, a 'man midwife' from the same hospital, who extracted the placenta manually and, undoubtedly, introduced infection. Within three days Mary was desperately ill. Godwin summoned help and advice from all his medical acquaintances, in the frantic hope that something could be done to save his beloved wife. Women friends took care of the household and men friends, including Opie, called to offer support to the stricken husband. But Mary grew steadily worse, as septicaemia took hold, and she died on the morning of September 10th. She was 38.

Elizabeth Inchbald was one of many friends to whom Godwin wrote immediately, telling of his loss: 'My wife died at eight this morning. I always thought you used her ill, but I forgive you.'[1] Inchbald replied straightaway, saying she was 'shocked beyond expression', but had not 'the smallest portion of remorse'. Further letters between the two were exchanged over the next few days before Inchbald, while expressing sincere sympathy for all he had suffered, said there must be 'an end to our acquaintance *for ever*'. Godwin's friend Marshall took charge of the funeral arrangements and made sure that friends knew the time, date and place – St Pancras parish church where the couple had been married five months earlier. Opie responded to the invitation in a note to Marshall: 'Sincerely lamenting the melancholy occasion, I will not fail to attend on Friday at the time and place you have mentioned.'[2] The widower was too distressed to attend the service which was followed by his wife's burial in St Pancras churchyard.

Amelia was in Norwich with her father at this time. No doubt several of her London friends wrote to inform her of Mary's death; her letter of condolence to Godwin indicated that that he had given her a lock of his wife's hair, so it seems likely that he, too, wrote to tell her of his loss. She was in correspondence with Holcroft before taking up her pen to her bereaved friend:

> Before I obtained leave to write to you a sense of propriety could scarcely restrain me from writing; but as soon as I learnt from Mr Holcroft that I might address you without being thought an intruder on your sorrows, my desire of writing vanish'd before my conception of the difficulty of the task. To endeavour to express my sympathy in your distress would be absurd, because your's [sic] is one of those distresses which sympathy cannot soften; to deplore the loss I myself have sustained in one so justly dear to you, would be still more absurd, as my loss is nothing when compared to your's [sic]....
>
> But I must write to you, as I could not bear the idea of appearing regardless of you at a time which has, I doubt not, called forth the active tenderness of your other friends – and I wish to tell you that till I heard of your affliction, I knew not how truly and warmly I esteemed you. I will not attempt to describe what I felt when the melancholy news arrived – the *bitterness* of regret is past, and the *tenderness* alone remains – perhaps even amidst the acuteness of your grief you derive some comfort from the consciousness of having for some time past, cheered with your tenderness and society, the lonely hours of one whose life was but too much chequered by misfortune, and of having ensured to the fondly anxious mother a tender protecter [sic] for her orphan. I return you many thanks for the hair – should I ever be the mother of a daughter, I shall have a pride in shewing [sic] it to her as a memorial of a woman, who nobly, and *incomparably* fought for the violated rights of her sex, but died alas! before she could see the victory which she so well deserved to obtain.[3]

Godwin responded to Amelia's condolences with a frank account of the pain of his bereavement and his anxieties concerning the upbringing of Mary's two daughters:

> If you are impressed with the difficulty of writing a letter of condolence, how much greater must be my difficulty in answering it! I could easily let loose a whole torrent of regrets, but this would be contrary to my present ideas of propriety and right; it would be of little benefit to you and exquisitely painful to me. I am by no means of the opinion of those persons who are for instantly banishing the memory of a beloved object when the loss of it is irreparable. I am

gratified on the contrary by having the idea constantly present to my mind; I hope to be made wise and more humane by the contemplation; I find a pleasure, difficult to be described, in the cultivation of melancholy....

Be sure I feel it. Be sure I am not the fool to look for that happiness in any further vicissitude of life, that I was beginning to enjoy, when I was thus dreadfully deprived of it. My understanding was enlarged, my heart was improved, as well as the most invaluable sensations of admiration and delight produced in me by her society.[4]

Having dealt with the death of his much loved wife, Godwin concluded his letter to Amelia with what amounted to a lecture. This was in response to the final paragraph of her letter of condolence in which she had claimed, 'I have been told that you say I have *no heart* – the severest of all assertions perhaps – but I shall not plead *not guilty* to the charge.' The subject of coquetry had been a bone of contention between Amelia and Godwin in previous correspondence. Grieving the loss of Mary, herself a stern critic of women adopting coquettish roles, the widower, while denying he had accused Amelia of having no heart, chose to expand upon the subject:

> To the best of my recollection I never said any such thing. I said indeed, you were a flirt. But that is no secret; everybody knows that. I might say that a flirt and flirtation has no heart. But I know several admirable women who put on and off the flirt, and consequently, according to my interpretation, put in and out a heart, as easily as they put on and take off their clothes....
>
> In a word, I do, from my heart and soul, abjure and detest coquetry. If by rivers of tears I could wash it out of your character, I would shed them. But it lies too deep for that. You must get rid of much vanity and much restlessness, or rather perhaps direct these useful propensities to noble objects, before you can effect this change.

Obituaries in the literary journals were sympathetic over the tragic circumstances of Wollstonecraft's death and complimentary about her writing. Her friend and publisher Joseph Johnson was keen to bring out an edition of her most recent work, which included an unfinished novel, *Maria, or the Wrongs of Woman*. He also suggested that Godwin might contribute a short memorial essay. John Opie had completed his second portrait of Mary only a few weeks before her death. Godwin took over Mary's study at The Polygon as his own, hung the Opie portrait above his desk and channelled his grief and distress into an intense period of work. He immersed himself in re-reading his wife's published works, sorting out her unpublished manuscripts, interviewing her friends and family and collating all the letters which he and she had exchanged. The brief essay became a biography.

Godwin had decided it was right and proper for him to tell the story of Mary's life and work as truthfully as possible. Published by Johnson in January 1798, the book, with its frank accounts of Mary's passion for the married Fuseli, her sexual liaison with Gilbert Imlay, the birth of her illegitimate daughter and her suicide attempt, caused outrage and fierce criticism of both the author and his subject. However, the memoir sold so well that a second edition was brought out a few months later; but it would be many decades before a third edition was published in 1927. Despite his heavy work load Godwin continued to spend time with his literary and artistic friends, including Opie and Holcroft.

Meanwhile, Amelia was in Norwich, where, during her adolescence, she had been an enthusiastic participant in the social scene. Dancing, singing and playing a musical instrument were essential accomplishments for young women of her class. Susannah's judgement was that her young friend 'never arrived at superiority as a player' but that her singing had 'very seldom been equalled', particularly when she performed one of her own ballads.

> She may fairly be said to have created a style of singing of her own, which, though polished and improved by art and cultivation, was founded in that power, which she appears so pre-eminently to possess of awakening the tender sympathies and pathetic feelings of the mind.[5]

The impact of Amelia's singing was also remembered by Harriet Martineau in an essay for the *Daily News*, later published in a collection of brief biographies:

> She sang finely – ballads sung with heartfelt impulse and pathos, and without accompaniment. Those who, as children, heard her sing *Lord Ullin's Daughter*, will never forget it. They cannot now read the 'Come back' of that ballad, without feeling again the anguish conveyed in those heart-rending tones.[6]

William Beloe recalled:

> From a child she gave indications of talents above the ordinary level, but her earliest propensity was for music, in which she soon became proficient; and in the provincial town where she resided frequently entertained and enlivened numerous parties with her concerts. From music to poetry, the transition is natural and easy; she wrote, when very young, many elegant and beautiful things.... she was a most affectionate and dutiful daughter, warm and animated in her attachments, lively and agreeable in conversation, steady and consistent in her principles.[7]

Through her father, the young Amelia had been introduced to the Quaker Gurney family then living in a house in Magdalen Street, not far from the Alderson home. John Gurney, a successful wool merchant, had acquired Gurney Court (as it became known) in 1754 and by the time Dr Alderson had set up in practice in Norwich there were three generations of Gurneys living there. Dr Alderson became the family doctor* and continued in this role for several decades, attending all three of John's sons – Richard, John and Joseph – after they married and moved out of the city. Rachel, the only daughter, left Norfolk when she married Robert Barclay of Bury Hill in Surrey. John, senior, died in 1770; his widow Elizabeth remained at the Magdalen Street house until her death in 1788. Richard, the eldest son, left Gurney Court after the death of his first wife Agatha (née Barclay) in 1776, when he moved with his young son Hudson and daughter Agatha to Keswick Hall, another Gurney family property two miles from the city centre.

By then, John, the second son, also in the wool business, was married to Catherine (née Bell). They lived at Gurney Court but spent their summers in the Norfolk village of Bramerton, where they rented a cottage. Over the next 12 years Catherine gave birth to nine children: seven girls – Catherine, Rachel, Elizabeth, Richenda, Hannah, Louisa and Priscilla- and two boys, both named John (the first died in infancy); three more sons – Samuel, Joseph John and Daniel – were

---

* Two of Dr Alderson's bills for his services to the Gurneys were preserved in the family papers: Mrs E. Gurney's bill from J. Alderson for 1772 came to £14.4s.7d and included pectoral drops, purging powder, draughts. volatile drops, lavender drops, liniment, pills, liquorice, hartshorn, peppermint water. She also paid him £6.9s.0d for treatment to her room maid, cook, footman, and her daughter Miss Rachel Gurney's maid. (SoF, Gurney MSS, 2/76A)

born after they moved to Earlham Hall,* a substantial manor house set in parkland three miles from the city centre, in 1786. When John Gurney first took over the hall he invited the 16-year-old Amelia and her father to go and have a look round before the family moved in. They rode out from the city, she on a pony, her father on horseback, and drank tea with Mr Gurney. John and Catherine were hospitable and charitable and the friendships which Amelia forged with the flock of siblings were strong and binding. She greatly admired the third daughter, known to the family as Betsy, who became famous as the prison reformer Elizabeth Fry. Joseph John Gurney, born at Earlham in 1788, grew up to be one of the most influential people in Amelia's life.

Richenda Gurney's drawing of Earlham Hall, as it was when she and her siblings were growing up. Photographed by Richard Dykes Alexander, a Quaker banker at Ipswich, related by marriage to the Gurneys and an enthusiastic and very able amateur photographer. (Reproduced with the permission of Suffolk Record Office, Ipswich Branch: Ref: K420/1)

The Gurneys of Earlham, as they became known, were linked by blood, marriage and business ties to a complex network of relations with whom they maintained regular contact through frequent visits and correspondence. John Gurney's brother Richard, of Keswick Hall, married a second wife Rachel (née Hanbury) by whom he had a son, Richard Hanbury and two daughters, Elizabeth and Anna, who would become one of Amelia's most important women friends.

---

* The building is now owned by the University of East Anglia and houses its Law School.

Joseph, the youngest of the brothers, set up home at The Grove, a country house with lawns and trees, not far from the new Norfolk and Norwich Hospital on the outskirts of the city. Amelia was close to 'Uncle Joseph' as he was known to the Earlham siblings and his wife Jane (née Chapman), who were the parents of nine children. In 1799 Richard and Joseph became partners in Gurneys Bank in Norwich with their second cousin Bartlett Gurney, whose father and uncle had founded the bank in 1775. John Gurney of Earlham joined his brothers as a partner in the bank in 1803. Robert and Rachel Barclay, who lived at Bury Hill, also had a house in London; they had 15 children.

To Amelia Alderson the large family at Earlham offered the companionship and affection she might have enjoyed from siblings of her own. She also benefited from frequent contact with the numerous Gurney uncles, aunts and cousins, who welcomed her into their homes and shared with her their ups and downs. As she grew older she embraced younger generations of Gurneys as members of her own family. Harriet Martineau, recalling her childhood, wrote of her admiration for the Gurneys of Earlham:

> The remarkable family from which issued Mrs Fry... were then a set of dashing young people – dressing in gay riding habits and scarlet boots, as Mrs Fry told us afterwards, and riding about the country to balls and gaieties of all sorts. Accomplished and charming young ladies they were....[8]

During her last few months in Norwich as a single woman Amelia was a frequent guest at Earlham Hall. Recording one such visit in September 1797, 13-year-old Louisa Gurney (who later married Samuel Hoare and made her name as a writer of educational books) wrote:

> Amelia Alderson came to dinner – I say this because it has given me so much pleasure – I never liked her half so much – I have always admired her *character* as every body must do – She is so good – but I never admired and liked her so much as a *person* as I have done today. I am much too apt to take violent prejudices *for* people – I have taken the greatest one *for* Amelia Alderson – I think this disposition is *most foolish* ....However there *is every reason* to admire and *like* Amelia Alderson she is such a truly virtuous and good character.[9]

Louisa also noted that December 29th was 'a brilliant day' when Amelia was a guest of the family at a dinner attended by Prince William Frederick, of Gloucester (who later would be painted by Opie), and his three aide-de-camps 'all agreeable and elegant and clever and pleasing'. Everybody was 'in full dress' and after dinner they all sang.[10]

Amelia acted as hostess when her father entertained guests. The 15-year-old Richenda Gurney (later the wife of a Church of England vicar) recorded in her journal in January 1798:

> …on Saturday we went to Dr Alderson's and had a most pleasant evening indeed. We danced from seven to twelve. I don't know when I enjoyed dancing so much, there were such beaux, so superior to the bank boys. What a surprising difference rank and high life make in a person's whole way and manner: it is most pleasant being with people who have been brought up in that way. I am very glad to have seen a little of what high life is, for I think everybody who can should be acquainted with all ranks in society. We had a most merry time, I really did enjoy it.[11]

In that same month John Gurney had appointed a drawing master for his daughters – the young Norwich artist John Crome, who later founded the Norwich School of Painting. He remained in the post for several years and accompanied his young pupils on two Gurney family trips to the Lake District and Scotland. The son of a journeyman weaver, Crome had received little formal education and worked as an errand boy (one of his employers being Dr Alderson's colleague Dr Rigby), before being apprenticed to a sign painter. His real ambition was to be an artist. In his spare time he went on sketching trips and began to sell his sketches to Norwich print sellers. Either through Dr Rigby or the print sellers Smith and Jaggers, Crome met the wealthy Thomas Harvey of Catton Hall. Harvey encouraged the young man to pursue a career as a drawing teacher and allowed him access to his own art collection where he might develop his own artistic skills by copying works by established artists.

Competition among portrait painters was intense; however skilful an artist might be it was always helpful to have contacts in the right social circles. The Gurneys' close friendship with the Aldersons proved useful to John Opie. Once married to Amelia, he received several commissions to paint members of the family; further Norwich and Norfolk connections made him a popular choice for local people seeking a skilled portraitist. But in the early months of 1798, while Amelia was enjoying farewell social visits in her home city, Opie was completing paintings for the annual Royal Academy summer exhibition. He exhibited five pieces that year, one of them a portrait of Thomas Holcroft, – 'a most admirable painting and likeness', according to the sitter.[12]

Having confided in Susannah (before she left London the previous August) that she had much to tell her, it would appear that Amelia was either on the verge of accepting or had already accepted Opie's proposal. They were in correspondence during the winter months and he was eagerly awaiting her return. Writing to tell her of the preparations he was making at his house for her reception there as his bride, he concluded:

> To love thee much better than I did, is, I think, impossible; but my heart springs forward at the thought of thy near approach. God bless thee ever, my dearest love, and guard thee up safe to thy fond, anxious, devoted, J.O.[13]

Amelia was back in London in mid-March. With only a few weeks to go before her wedding it may be assumed that much of her trousseau was created during her winter months in Norwich. The city had enjoyed a thriving textile industry since the 14th century, with flourishing markets for its output at home and abroad. But the outbreak of war with France in 1793 badly affected the export of materials to markets on the continent. At about the same time the advent of steam-powered mills in Yorkshire began to provide cheaper textiles with which the Norwich manufacturers found it hard to compete. For the hand loom weavers, used to regular employment, the situation caused great distress. By December 1794 the local press was urging

> ...the ladies of this city to wear nothing but Norwich manufactures this winter, and to promote the wearing of them amongst their servants and dependants as the most effectual method of relief.[14]

Amelia was proud of the Norwich textile business, sending gifts of Norwich shawls to cousins and promoting the excellence of their design and craftsmanship to her aristocratic friends. As a fashionable young woman, about to become the wife of a fashionable painter, she put together a trousseau, which included satin slips and gowns, muslin gowns, cambric gowns, bonnets and caps, lengths of figured lace, feathers and ribbons. In London she spent a few weeks re-acquainting herself with old friends including Godwin and Holcroft.

Then, on Tuesday, May 8th, 1798, she and John Opie were married at St Marylebone Church* by the curate Benjamin Lawrence – the second of five marriages at which he officiated that day. The witnesses were Dr Alderson and Amelia's Norwich friend Anne Plumptre.

---

* The church was a small building, erected in 1740 to replace the original 15th century St Marylebone Church. The poet Lord Byron was baptised there in 1788. In 1817 the church became a chapel of ease when a larger parish church was built next door. After the chapel was bombed in 1940, the site was laid out as a memorial garden.

Chapter Thirteen

Amelia, 28, and John Opie, 37, set up home together at the house in Berners Street, where he had lived since 1791. Dr Alderson spent a few days in town before and after the wedding – he called on Godwin the day after the service – but, despite his new son-in-law's expressed willingness to share his home with the older man, the arrangement was not necessary. The doctor was committed to his patients in Norwich and, however painful the parting from her father, the new Mrs Opie knew her place was by her husband's side. Little is known about how her friends regarded the match but the redoubtable William Beloe had views on the matter:

> Her union with a celebrated artist could not, as one should think, be entirely congenial to her natural habits and propensities. Those who knew her from her childhood held up their hands in astonishment, but Venus delights in these vagaries.[1]

Beloe was probably correct in stating that many of her friends were astonished when the cultured Miss Alderson agreed to marry Opie, who was regarded by some as a rough diamond. After two encounters with the artist in 1797, Robert Southey, who later sat for Opie at the request of his Norwich friend, William Taylor, said:

> Opie is indeed a very extraordinary man.... Without anything of politeness, his manners are pleasing, though their freedom is out of the common; and his conversation, though in a half-uttered, half Cornish, half croak, is interesting. There is a strange contrast between his genius, which is not confined to painting, and the vulgarity of his appearance, his manners, and sometimes of his language.[2]

Amelia was aware of his lack of polish, but, whatever she thought in private, she was far too loyal a wife to draw attention to her husband's shortcomings. After he died, she sprang to his defence and strove to explain what Mrs Inchbald, in a tribute to the artist, called his 'ruggedness of address, stigmatised by the courtly observer with the appellation of ill-breeding'.[3] As his widow, she claimed: 'Though Mr Opie had never learnt those habitual restraints which are the result of early good breeding' he had 'a well principled contempt and aversion' for those who spoke their minds and caused offence to others.[4] Hudson Gurney was of the opinion that Opie was

> ... a man of *strong* natural sense, expressed himself *strikingly and forceably*[sic] in few words. I believe they lived in the most perfect harmony and if in his manner there might have been occasionally a degree of abruptness I know no reason for accusing him of 'roughness'.[5]

The eccentric sculptor Joseph Nollekens, whose portrait was painted by Opie in 1782, believed that Amelia's influence on and support of her husband was excellent. One of the founders of the Royal Academy, he himself had befriended Opie soon after his arrival in London. The young artist's appearance then, he recalled, was:

> uncouth in the extreme, and the manner in which he sometimes conveyed his remarks to elegant females was vulgar and coarse.... His first wife was in no respect like his second in whom he found an elegant friend, who took great pleasure in his improvement, and in whatever delighted or comforted him.[6]

Northcote, too, believed Amelia was good for John: '... she left no stone unturned for him; she drove all before her into his painting room; she had a woman's power and would take no denial....'[7]

Not only did the new Mrs Opie seek sitters for her husband, she also encouraged regular get-togethers with friends. She loved being part of the social scene and had many aristocratic friends, but John had no particular interest in smart society. However, he was willing to accompany Amelia to the theatre or to dine with valued friends, with whom he might converse on subjects which interested him and when he would not have to make small talk. Above all, he preferred to work; as Northcote said of him: 'Other artists paint to live. Opie lives to paint.' Fortunately, he was also very much in favour of his wife pursuing her literary endeavours:

> On no subject did Mr Opie evince more generosity, and liberality of mind, than in his opinions respecting women of talents, especially those who had dared to cultivate the powers which their Maker had bestowed on them, and to become candidates for the pleasures, the pangs, the rewards, and the penalties of authorship. This class of women never had a more zealous defender than my husband against the attacks of those less liberal than himself.... When our marriage took place, he knew that my most favourite amusement

was writing; and he always encouraged, instead of checking, my ambition to become an acknowledged author.[8]

During her nine years as Opie's wife, she wrote her second novel *The Father and Daughter* (1801), published a book of verses, *Poems* (1802), wrote the novel *Adeline Mowbray* (1804) and a collection of stories, *Simple Tales* (1806). Amelia had an allowance of £200 a year from her father, but no doubt the income from her writing would have been a welcome addition to the family finances. Opie was known to be careful with money – a sensible attitude for one in his profession.

Soon after their May wedding the couple went to Bath, where John was to do a portrait of Amelia's friend Lady Dickson (née Frances Willins), a celebrated beauty, who had been raised in Norwich where her father, the Rev James Willins, was the rector of St Michael's Coslany, not far from the Alderson home. They were back in London by mid-June. They visited the Morgans in Southgate, probably the last time they would see George Cadogan Morgan, who died in November that year,* then were out of town from mid-July for several weeks. In October, when Holcroft called on Opie, he noticed in his studio:

> ...his view of St Michael's mount, a moon-light, the manner hard, but the scenery and effects grand, and the composition good. A well painted portrait likewise of Dr Alderson.[9]

Opie painted two portraits of his father-in-law; probably the one noted by Holcroft was his first and was painted that summer. The time spent in Norwich gave Amelia the chance to introduce her new husband to her many friends and acquaintances. She wrote to Inchbald, telling her that they were 'feasting and frolicking' and that 'Mr Opie finds employment here', adding that they were dining at Catton (the home of Thomas Harvey), later that day.[10] This was the year in which Opie did his portrait of John Crome and started his portrait of John Gurney of Earlham, which was shown at the Royal Academy in 1799. His presence in the city also attracted the attention of a Norwich hairdresser seeking advice about his son's ambitions:

At about this time Edmund Cotman was hesitating whether he

---

* Morgan's portrait by Opie (undated) is mentioned in his family history as 'unfortunately not in the possession of his descendants'. (Williams, *A Welsh Family*, p.81) Earland was unable to locate the painting when she compiled her comprehensive list of Opie works in 1911.

should yield to his son's instinctive urge to become an artist. He consulted John Opie, the portrait painter, who was spending the summer of 1798 in Norwich. This painter, after obtaining a spectacular success in London, had suffered a temporary eclipse of fortune. During this lull in his career he had married in May.... Some of Cotman's sketches were shown to him.... Opie's verdict was unambiguous 'Let him rather black boots,' he said 'than follow the profession of an artist.'[11]

The son, John Sell Cotman, chose to ignore the advice and went on to become a leading figure in the Norwich School of Painting. Both he and Crome were employed by Dawson Turner of Great Yarmouth, a wealthy banker and patron of the arts, as drawing masters for his six daughters. He and his wife Mary, a talented etcher and water colour artist, became friends of Amelia. Many years later she was asked by Turner, who was writing a biographical memoir of the Norwich artist, for her memories of Crome:

> My husband was not acquainted with our friend John Crome before the year 1798 when we first visited Norwich after our marriage. Crome used frequently to come to my husband's painting room in N[orwich] and I have often seen *him*, Crome and our dear friend T[homas] Harvey *painting together* in the painting room of the *latter*.
>
> I have also seen my husband painting *for* Crome – that is, Crome looking on while the former painted a landscape or figures and occasionally I have seen him at work on C's own canvass[sic] while the latter amused us by his droll stories and humorous[sic] conversation and observations.
>
> But this is, to the best of my belief, the *extent* of the 'assistance' which he received from my husband – this, however, Henry Briggs [Amelia's cousin, the artist Henry Perronet Briggs] says, was 'assistance' – and as he highly admired Crome's talents I am sure that he would be eager to do him all the good in his power....
>
> Crome used always (I think) to call on us when he came to London and was, no doubt, a welcome guest in the painting room.[12]

Once Opie's connection with Norwich and Norfolk was established he received more commissions for portraits. Over the next few years he completed more than 50 portraits of local people, of which eight were exhibited at the Royal Academy. One of these (in 1802) was a portrait of Amelia's cousin, Isabella Alderson, daughter of Robert Alderson and his first wife Elizabeth, who died in 1807 at the age of 20. He did a portrait of the elderly Sarah Martineau (grandmother of Harriet) for her eldest son Dr Philip Meadows Martineau. For the Gurneys Opie painted three of the Earlham youngsters in a fanciful piece called *A Fortune Teller*, in which they were depicted listening spellbound to an old woman. He also did portraits of Hudson Gurney and his sister Agatha Hanbury, the son and daughter of Richard Gurney of Keswick by his first wife, and of the family of the banker Thomas Kett of Seething Hall, whose wife Hannah was a second cousin to the Earlham and Keswick Gurneys.

Soon after his marriage Opie was commissioned by the Common Council of Norwich to do a portrait of their speaker Samuel Harmer, 'as a mark of their approbation of his uniform conduct in supporting the rights of his fellow citizens'.[13]

Two years later a portrait of a Mayor of Norwich was financed by public subscription:

> ...as a tribute of respect for the vigilance, fidelity and impartiality with which John Herring Esq executed the important office of Chief Magistrate of this city in the year 1799.... In October 1799, some 2,000 troops, who had landed at Yarmouth from Holland, marched into Norwich by torchlight and through the indefatigable exertions of Mr Herring, the innkeepers, and inhabitants, the troops received every accommodation. The Mayor was presented at Court, and declined an offered Knighthood.[14]

Opie's painting of Herring featured some of the troops in the background; it was shown at the Royal Academy in 1801 before being hung in the city's St Andrew's Hall (the main public hall). Herring, a near neighbour of Dr Alderson, had also introduced a scheme for workhouse children to be taught how to spin wool, for which they were paid.

Opie was back in Norwich again when he was asked by William Taylor to do a portrait of his friend Dr Frank Sayers, the poet and philosopher. The two men had met and become firm friends in the 1770s when they were pupils at the Barbaulds' boarding school at Palgrave. Sayers went on to study medicine in Edinburgh; by then his widowed mother was living in Norwich and attending the Octagon Chapel. After abandoning his medical studies, Sayers decided on a literary career and spent several months travelling in Europe before settling in Norwich. By the time he met Opie, Sayers had moved into a house in the Cathedral Close (thanks to a legacy from a rich aunt), published two books, converted to the Church of England and become a generous contributor to charities in the city. In his memoir of his friend Taylor recalled:

> In 1800 Mr & Mrs Opie came to Norwich on a visit to her father, Dr Alderson, when, at my request, Dr Sayers sat to this celebrated painter for the portrait which has been engraved as a frontispiece to this edition of his collected works.... Dr Sayers conversed much with Mr Opie on art, listened to his native strength of talent and originality of judgment, and has happily applied to him a Greek distich in his *Essay on Beauty*.[15]

During this visit to Norwich John and Amelia attended the wedding of Elizabeth Gurney to Joseph Fry at the Friends Meeting House in Goat Lane on August 19th. Two years earlier Elizabeth had decided to become a Plain Quaker, renouncing her fashionable social life and choosing a new path dedicated to upholding the ideals of Christianity. (Much later she was to lead Amelia towards her decision to become a Quaker.) Elizabeth's decision was inspired by listening to a charismatic itinerant American preacher, William Savery, when he visited the Norwich Friends. Following his visit, she opted to go and stay with relations in London, where she might sample the 'folly' of worldly pleasures and confirm that her decision to abandon them was the right one. During her seven weeks in the capital she spent time with Amelia at the theatre and on visits to Elizabeth Inchbald, Sarah Siddons and Frances Twiss:

> Mrs Twiss gave me some paint for the evening. I was painted a little. I had my hair dressed and did look pretty for me. Mr Opie, Amelia and I went to the Opera concert. I own, I do love grand company. The Prince of Wales was there.... I had a very pleasant evening indeed.[16]

Returning home to Earlham, the 18-year-old Betsy, as she was known to her family and friends, went through agonies of doubt as she turned her back on the social scene. Her sisters refused to take her decision seriously; but Joseph Fry, who wooed and won his bride during her months of soul-searching, felt himself ready to support her in every way. He was from a wealthy Quaker family with business interests in the tea trade; the newly-weds set up home in London – at first living

Elizabeth Gurney (known as Betsy to her family and friends), aged 19, drawn by Amelia. (© Religious Society of Friends in Britain, 2014)

with Joseph's family in their city house at the centre of the Fry business empire. Amelia did not return to London until mid-November. A few weeks later, writing to Susannah, she reported on the newly-wed Frys and on Susannah's second son Richard who was apprenticed to the Unitarian printer Jonas Davis in Chancery Lane:[*]

Betsy Fry is settled down as a married woman with every thing requisite to domestic happiness about her. I wish her sisters were as well settled. Mr Fry pleases me very much and Bell [Annabella] Plumptre who accompanied us was equally pleased with him. Richard and I have frequent meetings now – I have been twice to his house. ...On Sunday he is to breakfast with me, squire me to the Catholic chapel in King Street where French Bishops (or sometimes the Archbishop of Narbonne) officiates and then eat his beef with us. Tomorrow if Anne Plumptre returns I shall go with her into the pit at Drury Lane to see a new tragedy, the author nameless to me....

I shall have left Norwich a month only next Sunday and it seems to me *three* at least so much have I done since my return. Mr Opie too has been constantly employ'd. The Twiss's will be here in a month. That is a great joy to me.[17]

In conclusion, Amelia supposed that Susannah had attended 'poor Mrs [Sarah] Martineau's deathbed', adding that she herself was uneasy about Mr Opie's mother who last winter had a 'long struggle with death' and had again taken to her bed. 'I did so ardently wish to see her.' That wish was not to be fulfilled; Mary Opie died in 1805, many years before Amelia set foot in Cornwall for the first time.

Although busy with her social life, Amelia also made a point of welcoming those who came to the house in Berners Street for sittings with her husband. Her hospitality was recalled by the author Mary

---

[*] Davis printed the transactions of the Linnean Society, which was founded by the Norwich-born botanist James Smith, in 1788. Smith recommended Taylor as Davis's apprentice.

Russell Mitford in a letter to Cecilia Brightwell a few weeks after Mrs Opie's death:

I first saw our late dear and lamented friend 54 or 55 years ago when a little girl of 12 or 13, I was taken by my father to Mr Opie's to whom he was sitting for a portrait. He took me, I believe, to have somebody to talk to, Mr Opie being very deficient in the agreeableness usually so remarkable in portrait painters. The picture being intended as a birthday present for my mother, a surprise, the artist positively refused to complete his work until she had seen and approved it, thus radically frustrating my father's intention. I need not tell you in what contrast the kind and charming wife appeared to the poor little schoolgirl, nor how great was the good natured indulgence displayed towards her by that gifted woman.[18]

Since the early days of their marriage Amelia had been trying to write another novel, no doubt struggling, sometimes, to find time for herself away from the demands of husband or father or friends. By 1800 she was ready to offer her completed manuscript to the well-established publishers Longman & Rees (other partners were added or subtracted over the decades). They accepted *The Father and Daughter* and published it under her married name, Mrs Opie, early in 1801. It was the beginning of a long and fruitful association for both parties.

The novel was dedicated not to the husband who encouraged her literary endeavours, but to 'Dr Alderson of Norwich', an apt enough dedication, perhaps, given the subject matter and title:

...having endeavoured in *The Father and Daughter* to exhibit a picture of the most perfect parental affection, to whom could I dedicate it with so much propriety as to you, since, in describing a good father, I had only to delineate my own? Allow me to add, full of gratitude for years of tenderness and indulgence on your part, but feebly repaid even by every possible sentiment of filial regard on mine, that the satisfaction I shall experience if my publication be favourably received by the world, will not proceed from the mere gratification of my self-love, but from the conviction I shall feel that my success as an Author is productive of pleasure to you.

The Father and Daughter was sent forth by its author as 'a simple moral tale'.

The daughter, Agnes Fitzhenry, is devoted to her widowed father, a respectable merchant in a country town, which had an army barracks (as did Norwich at that time). Along comes Clifford, a charming but profligate guards officer. Flattered by his attentions and blind to his faults, Agnes is distraught when her father disapproves of the young man and agrees to elope with him. The anticipated (by Agnes) marriage does not take place immediately and she finds herself stranded in lodgings in London;

> Agnes passed the night in sleepless agitation; now forming and now rejecting schemes to obviate the danger which must accrue to her character, if not to her honour, by remaining for a whole month exposed to the seductions of a man whom she had but too fatally convinced of his power over her heart; and the result of her reflections was, that she should insist on his leaving town, and not returning till he came to lead her to the altar. Happy would it have been for Agnes had she adhered to this resolution.[19]

John Opie's frontispiece for Amelia's first best-seller, *The Father and Daughter*, published in 1801. It shows the heroine Agnes and her father in his asylum cell, where he has drawn a coffin with her name on it.

Before the month is up Clifford has 'triumphed over the virtue of Agnes'. He is called away on active service and by the time he returns she has given birth to their illegitimate son. During a rare visit to the theatre, she overhears gossip about Clifford's forthcoming marriage to an heiress and about herself being his 'favourite mistress'. Agnes determines to return home with her child and beg her father's forgiveness, only to find that he has gone mad because of her desertion and disgrace and is being cared for in a local bedlam. There are many more traumas for the penitent daughter to endure before the death of her father, closely followed by hers. They are buried together. The novel ends with a résumé of Clifford's part in the drama and a warning from the author about the far-reaching consequences of succumbing to temptation.

John Opie, finely attuned to the powerful father-daughter bond, designed the novel's frontispiece, an extraordinary scene depicting the desperate daughter visiting her father in his cell at the bedlam, where he is drawing a coffin with the name 'Agnes' on the lid. Just before its publication Amelia confided in her friend Susannah that she was worrying about its reception:

> As usual, all the good I saw in my work before it was printed is now vanish'd from my sight and I remember only its faults. All the authors of both sexes, and artists too, that are not too ignorant or full of conceit to be capable of alarm, tell me they have had the same feeling when about to receive judgment from the publick [sic]. Besides, whatever I read appears to me so superior to my own productions that I am in a state of most unenviable humility. Mr Opie has no patience with me but he consoles me by averring that fear makes me overrate others and underrate myself.[20]

The first edition also appended one of Amelia's poems *The Maid of Corinth* and some smaller pieces, which were later included in her first book of poems and thereafter omitted from subsequent editions of the novel. She wrote to Susannah about some of the initial responses to her work:

> Anne P[lumptre]* has just been here but not a word did she say to me about my *book*, nor ever will I dare say, but she was very friendly, pitying me I dare say for having exposed myself so egregiously and quite sure now that I am *nobody*....
>
> I am going today to carry Mrs Inchbald my book to read. She has promised me her *opinion* of it and I long to receive it. She is a judge of y *tale only*. Poetry is to her an undiscovered country....
>
> I am very glad you like my tale – The Hoares† called today and expressed themselves much pleased and affected by it. Mr H could not sleep all night after it – it made him so wretched.[21]

---

* Anne Plumptre had already had two novels published; her third came out in the same year as *The Father & Daughter*.
† Banker Samuel Hoare and his second wife Hannah. As a boy he was apprenticed to Henry Gurney, of Norwich, one of the founders of Gurneys Bank. His first wife, Sarah Gurney, was a cousin of John Gurney, of Earlham. His eldest son Samuel married Louisa Gurney of Earlham, in 1806.

The tale was very well received by the public. There were reviews in *The Monthly Review* and *The Critical Review*, both of which appreciated the pathos of the story. 'The moral inculcated by this tale is seriously impressive,' said the latter, adding that the style of the authoress was 'elegant and correct'. The first number of *The Edinburgh Review* in 1802, also drew attention to the novel in its review of Amelia's book of poems published that year, noting that it was one which 'excites a very high interest'. By 1844 the book had run to ten editions, with translations into French. A total of 750 copies of the first edition were published early in 1801; a second edition, brought out later in the year, advised readers: 'A volume of poems by Mrs Opie is in the press and will speedily be published.'

A selection of her poetic writings over several years were gathered together for *Poems*. Opie did the frontispiece – a mournful young woman dressed in black standing by the grave of Henry, her lover, to illustrate a brief poem about loss. Amelia included her first anti-slavery poem, *The Negro Boy's Tale*, which she had penned in 1790, and several pieces which had been published in *The Cabinet*. There were narrative verses, love poems and odes addressed to a variety of topics such as *Winter* or *Twilight*. Her interest in charitable work was exemplified in *Lines respectfully inscribed to the Society for the Relief of Persons imprisoned for Small Debts* (a Norwich charity supported by some of the Gurneys) in which she extolled:

> ...all who others' sufferings feel,
> And ills they pity nobly strive to heal

The collection also brought to the attention of the public Amelia's interest in song writing. Not only was she possessed of a beautiful singing voice, she also enjoyed writing lyrics for well known airs. By the time she was putting together works for her first book of poems she had begun a mutually beneficial association with Edward Biggs, a pianist and composer who specialised in setting verses to music. *Song* and *A Mad-Song*, for which he had composed the music, were published in the book, along with *Song of a Hindustani Girl*. With the latter, the author wrote an accompanying note explaining that she had written the words for 'a plaintive melody', given to her by Biggs, and said to have been 'composed and sung by a Hindustani girl on being separated from the man whom she loved'. She added that the piece had been already 'given to the public' in a second set of *Hindoo Airs* arranged and harmonised by Biggs. One of her early pieces, known originally as *Elegiac* Song (to be sung to the Welsh *Ar hyd y nos*) was also included in her book. Later re-named *Poor Mary Anne*, the piece was harmonised by Biggs and published with his other arrangements of Welsh airs.[22] He continued to adapt and arrange further poems by Amelia; sheets of the music and lyrics were sold at Robert Birchall's music circulating library in New Bond Street and were immensely popular.

The Italian tenor and singing teacher Guiseppe Viganoni, who was a regular performer in opera at the King's Theatre (now Her Majesty's Theatre), gave singing lessons to Amelia. 'Viganoni was with me from 12 to 3 today alternately singing with me and talking,' she reported to Susannah. 'He has with all his genius a great deal of what the French call *bonhommie*.' From Norwich Susannah sent him a gift of fowls, for which Amelia wrote to thank her: 'The basket arrived safe and its contents were excellent V. told me yesterday.' She went on to tell her friend that the Italian 'with great readiness and great humility' had granted her request to set a little song she had written 'the other day'. Opie, she added, had been at Chatham.

> I expect my husband home in half an hour. He went to *please me* and after he was gone I repented of my persuading him to go – but I thought the air and exercise would do him good. *Do not laugh* but tho' only two days absent the house seems so strange without its master that I have learnt to *excuse,* nay to commend women for *marrying again.* How dreadfully forlorn must be the situation of a widow! I think I shall write an essay recommending second marriages....[23]

In July the Opies were back in Norwich, where John had another civic commission. Amelia recalled:

> Whenever he came to Norwich while I was on a visit to my father, I had no chance of detaining him there unless he found business awaiting him. But no society, and no situation, however honourable and however pleasant, could long keep him from his painting-room.[24]

Joseph Stannard, a builder living in St George's Plain, just round the corner from Dr Alderson who had moved back into Snailgate, let the artist use a room adjoining his house. Entrance to the makeshift studio was reached up a flight of steps. Opie was working on his portrait of the Mayor, John Harvey, who had raised and commanded the Norwich Light Horse Volunteers in 1797. During the years of war with France, Norwich citizens, fearing an invasion, had prepared themselves for the defence of their homeland by forming the Norwich Loyal Military Association (an infantry corps) and then the Norwich Light Horse Volunteers. Members of the latter had subscribed to the Opie portrait of their commander 'in testimony of their attachment, esteem and regard'. Harvey posed in front of a horse, which had to be led up the steps for sittings. In lieu of rent for the studio Opie did a portrait of Stannard's wife Mary (née Cubitt), which was cherished by her descendants.

As the year 1801 drew to a close, not many commissions for Opie were forthcoming, but, with his dislike of idleness, he kept himself busy:

He was always in his painting room by half past eight in winter and by eight o'clock in summer; and there he generally remained, closely engaged in painting, till half past four in winter, and till five in summer. Nor did he ever allow himself to be idle even when he had no pictures bespoken: and as he never let his execution rust for want of practice, he, in that case, either sketched out designs for historical or fancy pieces, or endeavoured, by working on an unfinished picture of *me*, to improve himself by incessant practice in that difficult branch of his art, female portraiture.[25]

Opie painted several portraits of his attractive second wife. The first, now owned by the National Portrait Gallery, shows Amelia, looking pensive, in a white muslin dress with a frilled neckline, holding a hat wreathed in black muslin, on her lap. She was flattered when Dawson Turner approached her in 1821 asking if his wife Mary might do an etching from the portrait:

The picture to which you and Mrs Turner have done so much honor [sic] was painted soon after I married, that is in the year 1798. It was begun in May and finished, I think, in July.[26]

In a subsequent letter she added that she approved Mrs Turner's 'taste and judgement' in cutting her drawing off at the shoulders, as the dress in the original picture was '*slovenly* and *bedgownish*, according to the mode of the day'.

Chapter Fourteen

The dearth of commissions for Opie continued into early 1802, causing Amelia to worry about reducing their already small expenditure:

Not that I allowed myself to own that I desponded; on the contrary, I was forced to talk to him of hopes, and to bid him look forward to brighter prospects, as his temper, naturally desponding, required all the support possible. But gloomy and painful indeed were those three alarming months; and I consider them as the severest trial that I experienced during my married life. However, even despondence did not make him indolent; he continued to paint regularly as usual, and no doubt by that means increased his ability to do justice to the torrent of business which soon after set in towards him, and never ceased to flow until the day of his death.[1]

Once her husband's work began to pick up and her first poetry book was published, Amelia began to think of travelling abroad, but John did not believe they could afford it. For years she had longed to visit France, but the French Revolution and its violent aftermath, followed by the outbreak of war between France and England in 1793 had put paid to any such hopes. The ending of the war and the signing of the 'Definitive Treaty of Peace' at Amiens in March 1802, brought great rejoicing throughout the land. Amelia was not alone in hoping to venture across the Channel.

But before making plans to travel anywhere Amelia had another writing project to attend to. This was a poetic tribute to Francis Russell, the Fifth Duke of Bedford, following his death on March 2nd at the age of 36. Published in pamphlet form and said to have been composed on the evening of his funeral,[2] the 280 lines of rhyming couplets expressed her thoughts on the solemn occasion and acknowledged 'the great day' when she first saw the Duke. Apparently, this had been at Holkham Hall, the Norfolk seat of the Coke family. Although she omitted factual information per se, her poetic references indicated that both she and Russell, a particular friend of Thomas Coke, were there on November 5th, 1788, for celebrations to mark the centenary of the Glorious Revolution of 1688, when William of

Orange had arrived in England to take over the throne. Amelia was one of the specially invited guests from across the county to the event, which involved a ball, a spectacular firework display and supper in the house. Coke also laid on refreshments in booths on the lawn for members of the public who had turned up to watch the fireworks. In her elegy to the Duke Amelia also paid tribute to Coke's first wife Jane, who had died in 1800, calling her 'the loved Mistress of the proud domain... [who] now fills an early grave....'

An unknown admirer of the elegy, who signed himself 'J.W.H.', wrote her a letter of praise, saying the work 'contains many exquisite touches of true taste, genius and virtuous emotion' and appending a poem he himself had written. The writer posted the letter to Amelia's London address, from where it was forwarded by John to his wife at 'Dr Alderson's, Norwich'. The affectionate husband added his own message to the last page of the admirer's epistle:

> This came to me in a cover on Monday so I thought it too delicious not to be sent immediately. Who is J.W.H.? Your letter is arrived and I am very sorry to find this cursed election's lasting so long and I wish you would not appear so prominent in it. Dr Haweis [the Rev Thomas Haweis, a fellow Cornishman] has been sitting two or three times and makes a good head. I shall write you tomorrow or next day, so God bless you. Yours ever. J.O.
>
> Let me hear again Friday or Saturday at *farthest*. I feel desirous enough of seeing you but I have not much more to say at present unless I begin scolding you about the election. What business had you to get mounted up somewhere so conspicuously? But there is no more room.[3]

The Norwich election to which Opie referred took place on July 5th and Amelia was drawn into the campaign which was in full swing for weeks beforehand. Windham was standing for re-election, together with his fellow Tory MP John Frere; their Whig opponents were Robert Fellowes and William Smith. In the wake of the peace treaty, which had been greeted with great enthusiasm and a round of celebrations in the city, the election aroused strong feelings, particularly against Windham, whose opposition to the terms of the treaty had made him extremely unpopular. Fellowes, who was the treasurer for the Norfolk and Norwich Hospital, and Smith, a dissenter and reformer, campaigned vigorously on the benefits of peace, which, already, were having a positive effect. The Guardians of the Poor, who ran the city's workhouses, for which Dr Alderson acted as surgeon, noticed that the price of bread was half what it had been the previous year. Windham and Frere were defeated; the triumph of Fellowes and Smith was celebrated at the city's Assembly House, when 180 friends gathered for a victory dinner; it seems likely that Dr Alderson, a friend of both candidates, was there and maybe Amelia stayed on for the celebrations before returning to her impatient husband.

Despite John's earlier misgivings about financing a trip to France, they were about to set off for Paris. They travelled with a group of friends, arriving in France on August 14th, 1802. After staying overnight in Calais, they set off for Paris and their chosen accommodation, the Hôtel de la Rue des Étrangers – the street, according to Brightwell, being at that time 'the best in Paris', opening at one end on the Place de la Concorde where 'the perpetual guillotine' stood.

Opie's main aim was to spend time at the Louvre. The building – originally a fortress – had been a royal palace before the monarch and his family moved to Versailles. In 1793 the Louvre opened as a public museum, with 537 paintings on display, including works by Raphael, Titian, Rembrandt and Van Dyck. It closed three years later for structural repair work and re-opened in the summer of 1801. As soon as the English party reached their hotel, John set off immediately for the Louvre, returning in great distress because it was closed for the day. Subsequently, he spent many hours in the gallery. Recalling their time together in Paris, Amelia wrote of the importance of these visits:

> Why should I dwell on emotions which every one probably has felt on entering the Louvre gallery? My own pleasure, my ignorant pleasure, was nothing to the more scientific delight of my husband: and I recall with melancholy satisfaction, the enjoyment which he derived from this visit to the French metropolis; an enjoyment purchased and deserved by many years of the most assiduous labours in his difficult profession.[4]

For her, there was the tantalising prospect of catching a glimpse of Napoleon Bonaparte, who had been created First Consul (head of the Consulate, the French government) following his military achievements as commander of the French republican forces in the wake of the Revolution:

> I was in the Louvre gallery and standing alone...when I heard some one say that the First Consul was just going to enter his carriage, on his way to the Conservative Senate. 'Oh that I could but see him!'

exclaimed I aloud, and in French; on which, one of the guardians of the gallery said, 'Eh bien! mademoiselle, suivez moi et vous le verrez.' Without daring to lose a moment in order to seek for my companions, I followed rapidly whither he led.... Another door led us into an apartment, which looked immediately on the Place du Carousel. Ladies were sitting at the window, who, at my guide's request that they would make room for an English stranger, kindly allowed me a seat beside them.

I arrived just in time to see the procession form. The carriage of Buonaparte, drawn by eight bays, was already at the palace gates, and was soon followed by that of the other consuls.... At length an increased noise at the door announced that he was coming, and I gazed to an almost painful degree of intensity, in order to catch one glimpse of this extraordinary man; but he sprang into his carriage with such rapidity that not one of us could see him![5]

A few days later Amelia had another chance to see Napoleon. Opie's acquaintance John Masquerier, a young artist born in England to French parents, had studied at the Royal Academy which offered him a travelling allowance to study painting in Paris, where he had lived during the Revolution, before returning to England to complete his studies. He was in Paris during the Opies' visit and offered them a window seat in a ground-floor apartment at the Tuileries (the former royal palace, now the official residence of the First Consul) on a day when there was to be a review of the troops:

The door which opened into the hall of the palace was shut, but, after some persuasion, I prevailed on the attendant to open it; and he said he would keep it open till the First Consul had mounted his horse.... Just before the review was expected to begin, we saw several officers in gorgeous uniforms ascend the stairs.... A few minutes afterwards there was a rush of officers down the stairs, and amongst them I saw a short pale man, with his hat in his hand, who, as I thought, resembled Lord Erskine in profile; but though my friend said in a whisper, 'C'est lui,' I did not comprehend that I beheld Buonaparte, till I saw him stand alone at the gate. In another moment he was on his horse, and rode slowly past the window; while I, with every nerve trembling with strong emotion, gazed on him intently; endeavouring to commit each expressive, sharply chiselled feature to memory.... At length the review ended; too soon for me. The Consul sprang from his horse – we threw open our door again, and, as he slowly re-ascended the stairs, we saw him very near us, and in full face again, while his bright, restless, expressive, and as we fancied, dark blue eyes, beaming from under long black eyelashes, glanced over us with a scrutinising but complacent look; and thus ended, and was completed, the pleasure of the spectacle.[6]

The other members of their party had also watched the review from a window overlooking the Place du Carousel, thanks to Count de Lasteyrie, another friend of the Opies. Samuel Favell and Elizabeth, his wife, were among those who travelled with John and Amelia from England. Favell, whose portrait was painted by Opie, had been a leading member of the Friends of the People, a reform group based in Southwark, which had connections with the radical societies whose activities were so thoroughly investigated in the 1794 treason trials. A member of the Clothworkers' Company, he was also a campaigner for the abolition of slavery, and went on to co-found the Mill Hill School for protestant dissenters. Both Earland and Brightwell understood that the party from England included Anne Plumptre; in fact she had been living in France for a few months, having accompanied two French émigrés back to their home country. Before Anne left for France Amelia had written about the sisters in a letter to Susannah:

> Of the Plumptres I see but little. Bell [Annabella] is laudably attentive to her studies and stays at home; while Anne, a *little in love* as usual, is more at Ham with Mr and Mrs Barthelemi than in Caroline Street, even Drury Lane and Kemble are deserted for this interesting émigré as she tells me he is....
>
> She and Mr Barthelemi* have had (entre nous) a literary concern together and this gentleman is about 36, very clever, and in Anne's eyes very like her two old flames Mr Lambert and Merry, and Mrs Barthelemi is, Anne says, *in a consumption*. Here is a situation for *fair hopes* and *young desires*! All this I learn from Bell, who, you know, piques herself on her penetration, and chuckles at Anne's *entanglement*. But Bell says Mr B is not to *her* taste at all.
>
> I have not seen him yet – Ham is 8 miles from Town, yet y fair pedestrian walks thither and back, untired.[7]

Anne Plumptre had been an enthusiastic supporter of the French Revolution; by the time of her stay in France she had developed a passion

---

* He was related to the French writer Jean-Jacques Barthélemy.

for Napoleon. Already a published author, she remained in France for three years, eventually writing a book about her experiences in the country and her thoughts on Napoleon who became Emperor in 1804.* Amelia certainly spent some time with her old Norwich friend in Paris; possibly it was Anne who introduced her to Helen Maria Williams, the English novelist, poet and translator. Williams, another staunch supporter of the Revolution, had first travelled to France in 1790. She returned to England for brief visits over the next two years before settling in Paris in 1792, where she allied herself with the Girondists, republican enthusiasts who had played a prominent role in the Revolution. Williams was imprisoned for a few months during the Reign of Terror, one of her fellow prisoners being Masquerier's mother, who had made her home in Paris when her son was studying there. After her release and a tour of Switzerland with a married man (a liaison which many saw as scandalous), Williams settled in Paris and resumed her writing career. By the time of Amelia's visit she had published five volumes of poetry, one novel and two non-fiction works including *Letters on the French Revolution* (1791).

The Williams salon was a gathering place for French liberals and a magnet for English intellectuals and radicals. Brightwell, who took her account of the Opies' visit to France from a lengthy piece put together by Amelia in 1831, chose not to quote the details of the visits, merely stating 'Mrs Opie gives some pleasant recollections of the evenings she spent…in the house of Helen Maria Williams'. Earland was more forthcoming:

> Mrs Opie took a strange and violent fancy for that queer woman Helen Maria Williams. It must have been her revolutionary principles, and the glamour surrounding a friend of Madame Roland and a prisoner of Robespierre, that made this perverter of history attractive to Mrs Opie. 'Miss Jane Bull', as Wolfe Tone called her, one of the most aggressive emancipated women of her time – credited with two liaisons: one with fickle Imlay, Mary Wollstonecraft's first lover – does not seem to have had much in common with Amelia Opie, whose Bohemianism was all on the surface and who was singularly pure-minded.[8]

In a letter written during her stay in Paris to Thomas Coke, Amelia confided how much she had enjoyed Williams's society:

---

* Anne Plumptre, *A Narrative of a Three Years' Residence in France* (London: J.Mawman; J.Ridgway; J.Clarke; B.Crosby & Co.; Constable & Co., 1810)

We leave this motley scene on Tuesday next, and *I* shall leave it with *reluctance*. My *nationality decreases* every day, but during ye first week I was surprised at its *magnitude*....

Yet, I must repeat, I depart with reluctance. The society I leave with regret; but chiefly I regret General Kosciusko and Miss Williams.[9]

The Polish war hero Thaddeus Kosciusko had fought with distinction in the American War of Independence before returning to his homeland where he led uprisings against Russia and Prussia. He was seriously wounded and taken prisoner by the Russians; on his release he returned to America before settling at Breville near Paris where he was active in Polish émigré circles. One of Amelia's fellow contributors to *The Cabinet* had written a poem paying tribute to his heroism and she herself was an ardent admirer. Kosciusko was a guest at a party which the Opies attended. She was – with the help of an interpreter – having a conversation with the Turkish ambassador:

...when I was interrupted by my husband, who, with a glowing cheek and sparkling eyes, exclaimed 'Come hither, look, there is General Kosciusko!' Yes, we did see Kosciusko; 'Warsaw's last Champion!' he who had been wounded almost to death in defending his country against her merciless invaders....

Instantly forgetting the ambassador, and, I fear, the proper restraints of politeness, I took my husband's arm, and accompanied him to get a view of the Polish patriot, so long the object to me of interest and admiration. I had so often contemplated a print of him in his Polish dress, which hung in my own room*.... His forehead was covered by a curled auburn wig, much to my vexation, as I should like to have seen its honourable scar...we were very glad when our obliging hostess, by introducing us, gave us an opportunity of entering into conversation with him. He spoke English as well as we did.[10]

Later in the evening Kosciusko approached Amelia saying he had a favour:

'I am told that you are a writer, pray do write some verses on me, a quatrain will be sufficient, will you oblige me?' I told him I could rarely write extempore verses, and certainly not on such a subject,

---

* Amelia kept the print of Kosciusko until she died, listing it in her will as a bequest to her cousin, Col Thomas Perronet Thompson.

as I would wish to do it all the justice possible. 'Well then,' said he, 'I will await your pleasure.' I saw him again only once before I returned to England; but the next time that his birthday was commemorated at Paris, I wrote some verses on the occasion, and sent them to him by a private hand.[11]

Another of Amelia's heroes was the radical Whig politician Charles James Fox, who had supported the American War of Independence and the French Revolution. An eloquent and forceful speaker, he favoured religious tolerance and individual liberty and was a notable figure in the anti-slavery campaign. Thomas Coke, knowing that Fox would be in Paris at the same time as the Opies, had given them a letter of introduction to the statesman. Possibly the tribute to his late wife in Amelia's elegy to the Duke of Bedford's memory had endeared her to him and he sought to promote the couple's interests. In her letter to Coke she devoted a substantial paragraph to her poetic tribute to Jane Coke, claiming that the death of Bedford had given her the opportunity to 'pay my slender but just tribute to such departed excellence'.

On the day of her first glimpse of Bonaparte from a window at the Louvre, Amelia had returned to her friends in the picture gallery, where she and John were talking with Timothy Brown (a partner of the brewer and politician Samuel Whitbread who sat for Opie twice), when Fox and his wife walked in. Brown introduced them and Opie took the opportunity to present Coke's letter to Fox, who invited them to accompany him on his tour of the art works and spent time conversing with Opie about some of the pictures. Thanking Coke for his introduction letter, Amelia assured him his kindness had not been in vain; she and her husband had been invited to dine with Fox and his wife a few nights later.

Farington, who arrived in Paris with a party of friends at that time, noted several meetings with his fellow artist in the metropolis:

Sept 1. Opie dined with us. He dined with Mr Fox a few days ago and in the evening went with him to a conversatione at Miss Helen Maria Williams, where many French were assembled to see so extraordinary a man.... Opie said that he had seen more handsome women in walking from Berners Street to the end of Oxford Street than in all Paris....

Sept 3. Opie called and talked about the play of last night. He said the acting was so extravagant as to be to him ridiculous, most furious and unnatural.... Opie described Madam Zavier, one of the actresses, as being one of the most beautiful figures he ever saw. Her neck and shoulders were formed like that part of a fine statue....

Sept 4. Opie came to tea with us. I went to the Frascati [a fashionable resort in Boulevard Montmartre] with him and Mrs Opie.... It is a prettily fancied light building calculated for amusement.[12]

The Opies also went on a 'round of picture seeing' in a group, which included the artist Benjamin West (president of the Royal Academy) and which was led by Maria Cosway, the artist, composer and society hostess. Separated from her husband the artist Richard Cosway, Maria was living in Paris, where she took groups of English tourists to view art collections. Amelia had no idea to whom Maria was referring when she said they were to see the fine collection belonging to 'Fesch'. She was entranced when she learned that the gentleman 'in the garb of an ecclesiastic' who met them at the top of a magnificent flight of stairs was Joseph Fesch, the Archbishop of Lyons (later Cardinal Fesch) and an uncle of Bonaparte; even more delightful was Maria's announcement that the splendid building in which he lived and kept his art works was the home of Napoleon's mother, who had apologised for being unable to receive them, as she was unwell. As the party left the house, Amelia lingered behind to take a look at a colossal bust of Bonaparte:

I contemplated it with great pleasure, and was passing my hand admiringly over the salient chin, when I heard a sort of suppressed laugh, and, turning round, saw the Archbishop observing me, and instantly, covered with confusion, I ran out of the house.[13]

Her almost obsessive interest in Napoleon persisted until he crowned himself Emperor in December, 1804:

How many years of my life was I a Republican, till Napoleon made himself an Emperor! Then the bubble burst, and I thought a Republic there, and perhaps elsewhere, would always end in being a sanguinary humbug.[14]

But in 1802, as an enthusiastic believer in liberty and the rights of man, she was still idealistic and had no qualms about publicly declaiming her beliefs. Brightwell reported that those who were with the Opies in Paris used to relate how she sat on the boulevards and sang, with heart and voice, 'Fall, tyrants fall!' – the song written by Susannah's husband John which had become part of her repertoire. The same friends also recalled with what ardour and intense delight Amelia greeted each new experience during the four weeks in Paris. However, as she wrote to Coke, 'my husband is more wild than ever to get home to work again – indeed nothing else could be expected from the effect of ye gallery.'

At home in Berners Street the Opies picked up the threads of the pattern they had established for their marriage: Amelia writing, socialising and supporting her husband in every way – he fraternising with fellow artists, but, primarily, spending as much time as he could in his studio.

Chapter Fifteen

Before marrying John Opie Amelia had told Susannah She hoped one day to become a mother. The hope was unfulfilled,* but the marriage, although childless, was productive in other ways and Amelia, in particular, took a great interest in the children of cousins and friends. Her husband painted several portraits of children; in Norwich he painted Augustin and Harriet Noverre, whose mother Harriet was the third daughter of the actor and theatre manager John Brunton, and sister-in-law to the unfortunate Robert Merry. Unlike most of her siblings, Harriet Brunton had not taken to the stage but married and remained in Norwich. Her husband, Francis Noverre, was the son of a dancing master, the Swiss-born Augustin Noverre, who was a witness to their wedding at St Stephen's Church, Norwich, in 1797. He first worked in England in 1755, with his brother Jean-Georges Noverre, when David Garrick, the great theatre producer, actor and manager, invited them to perform with their French ballet troupe at Drury Lane. Jean-Georges was dancing master to Marie-Antoinette. Augustin had connections with Norfolk through his engagement as dancing master to children of landed gentry when they were in London 'for the season'. He retired to Norwich, where he set up Francis in the same profession. His grandchildren Augustin and Harriet – Francis and Harriet's first two children† – were aged about three and two when Opie painted their portrait.

During the first year of their marriage the Opies often spent time with Holcroft. The artist had done his first portrait of Holcroft in 1782 and a second, which, according to Holcroft's diary, belonged to Godwin and was exhibited in 1798. In January, 1799, Opie started on another, for which the sittings continued until mid-March, by which time Holcroft had married his fourth wife Louisa Mercier, daughter of his friend, the French writer Louis-Sébastien Mercier; he was

---

* John and his first wife Mary were also childless, but the Royal Academician Robert Smirke discovered, many years later, that she had given birth to two illegitimate children before she married Opie. A full account of his revelation is reported in Viv Hendra's *The Cornish Wonder*.

† Augustin became a dancing master in London before emigrating to Canada. Harriet died aged 15 and was buried in the Noverre family vault at St Stephen's Church. There were seven more siblings, five of whom survived to adulthood.

pleased when the Opies paid an evening call on his new wife.

Holcroft, facing insolvency, was planning to move to the Continent where he believed he could live more cheaply. Before leaving England in May he arranged for an auction of his books, prints and pictures. The couple settled in Hamburg. During the major conflicts in Europe following the French Revolution, many art works from important galleries had been looted and dispersed. With little or no provenance for many paintings, the art market was awash with a mixture of genuine and spurious old masters. Holcroft decided he could make money by buying some of these pictures at a bargain price and sending them for sale in England. Despite a warning from Opie to be careful, he sent back 57 pictures, which were entrusted into the care of Godwin, who was to prevail upon artistic friends to assess the works before they were put up for auction. Holcroft was anxious to know what Opie thought and sent an impatient letter to him. But Opie was in Norwich with Amelia at the time and, as he explained to Holcroft when he did respond, he had waited till he returned to town and could see the pictures before he wrote. Having given his opinion of the works, in which he expressed some doubts about their authenticity, he added:

> You will do great injustice to the sentiments of esteem and friendship, which both Mrs Opie and myself feel for you, if you do not rest assured that to hear of your health and welfare will at all times give us pleasure; and we have only to beg that in your next, you will make no other use of your bridle, than to lay its reins on the neck of your affection, in the utmost confidence that all that comes from you will be received with a most hearty welcome.[1]

Holcroft was disappointed with the sale results and thought Opie had approached the matter with a prejudiced mind. Nor did he approve of the auctioneer chosen. The Holcrofts were in Hamburg for a year, after which they moved to Paris, where they were living when the Opies were in France. Amelia made no mention of spending time with them in Paris, but John may have seen Holcroft and passed on news about him to Farington, who noted in his diary for September 4th:

> Opie informed me that Holcroft, the author, who went abroad with strong prejudices founded upon political notions is become quite national to England. In painting, in acting &c. he will admit of no comparison on the part of France; in short after having taken leave of his Country he is preparing to return to it.[2]

Holcroft's finances improved during his years away and, on his return to England in October 1802, he achieved some success with stage plays and two volumes of essays on his travels. Anne Plumptre, in her narrative of her three years in France, was highly critical of his observations, saying she had expected accuracy and impartiality from 'the great Apostle of truth and justice' and found none.

After the Opies' stimulating visit to France John was soon back in his painting room. He had exhibited seven paintings at the Royal Academy in 1802, including the portrait of Amelia's cousin Isabella Alderson and the Norwich Mayor John Harvey. In April he started work on a portrait of Coke of Norfolk, who later commissioned him to paint Charles James Fox. He had other portrait commissions and was also working on paintings which depicted scenes from the Bible, Shakespeare or British history. He had first attempted sacred subjects at the request of the publisher Thomas Macklin, who wanted them for a new edition of the Bible which he brought out in the early 1790s. Opie also produced seven paintings which were published as engravings in Macklin's series *English Poets*, which became better known as *The Poets' Gallery*. It was published at monthly intervals between 1790 and 1795 and the King and Queen headed the list of subscribers.

It was just as well that the Opies had visited France in 1802, as the peace between the French and English was short-lived. Since the Treaty of Amiens, Bonaparte had been consolidating his power in France and its dependent states. His appetite for conquest was watched with alarm by the English, who failed to remove their naval presence in Malta, as agreed in the terms of the peace treaty. Tension mounted and on May 18th, 1803, England declared war. More than 1,000 British travellers in France were arrested, on the orders of the First Consul; in England many feared an invasion.

The war was on everyone's mind. Farington, a regular visitor to the Berners Street household recorded calling on Opie on June 1st, when he had 'some talk on politicks [sic] with him and Mrs Opie.' He added:

Mr Coke said to Opie that he hoped he should die before the period of our subjugation arrives. Mackintosh says that Mr Coke is the truest John Bull mind, the most of strong attachment to his country of anyone he knows.[3]

John Gurney, of Earlham, alarmed by the mustering of volunteer

Amelia's friend Thomas Coke, of Holkham Hall, Norfolk, who was created Earl of Leicester in 1837. Line engraving (with facsimile autograph) by Edward Smith, after Thomas Lawrence, published by Charles Muskett, of Norwich. (Norfolk County Council Library & Information Service)

forces in Norwich, made plans to remove his family should French troops land on the Norfolk coast. His daughter Priscilla wrote to tell her married sister Elizabeth Fry about it:

> It is now finally settled that as soon as ever we hear the news of their arrival, we six [the sisters], Danny [the youngest brother], and Nurse...are immediately to set off in the coach-and-four for Ely, where we are to take up our abode, as my father thinks it is a very safe place, being so completely surrounded by marshes.[4]

Two of Opie's 1803 commissions were for portraits of women from Norfolk families known to Amelia. They were Agatha Hanbury (née Gurney) and Lady Charlotte Bedingfield (née Jerningham). Agatha was the wife of Sampson Hanbury, of the London brewers Truman, Hanbury & Buxton; Gatty (as she was known to her family) was said by her brother Hudson to have been 'the best and most beautiful woman' he had ever known. Charlotte was the wife of Sir Richard

Bedingfield of Oxburgh Hall, Norfolk, and the daughter of Sir William and Lady Frances Jerningham of Cossey Hall*, near Norwich, where Amelia was sometimes a house guest. Just before her marriage in 1794 Charlotte had become friendly with Matilda Beetham, daughter of the Rev William Beetham, a Suffolk parson. She was a cousin to Jane Beetham, the young woman courted by Opie after his divorce, and was herself acquainted with the artist from her visits to her cousins in London. Charlotte wrote to Matilda in the summer to tell her she was having her portrait painted:

> My father desired I would sit for my picture which I did to Opie. I believe it is like, as a picture I like it very well, the costume was according to my fancy. We talked (Opie and I) of you and your cousin....[5]

Opie's portraits in the 1803 Royal Academy exhibition included Earl Stanhope, who had appeared for the defence in Tooke's trial. According to Farington, Opie enjoyed his conversations with Stanhope, who was a fellow of the Royal Society, and gave the artist news about the latest scientific inventions. Also on show in 1803 was Opie's portrait of James Mackintosh, who was knighted in December before leaving England to take up a new post as Recorder of Bombay in May, 1804. The sociable Mackintosh had helped to set up the King of Clubs for the purpose of literary debates and had a wide circle of friends. Amelia enjoyed the presence in her house of some of the sitters; she certainly paid attention to the way in which people behaved when her husband was painting them:

> Sitters themselves Mr Opie rarely found troublesome, except when they were not punctual, or when they exhibited impatience to be gone; and the restlessness consequent on that feeling: but not so, sometimes, were their companions and friends. *Persons of worship*, as Mr Opie used to call them, that is, persons of great consequence, either from talent, rank, or widely spreading connections, are sometimes attended by others, whose aim is to endeavour to please the great man or woman by flattery, wholly at the expense of the poor artist.... Hence arise an eulogy on the beauties and perfections of the person painted, and regrets that they are so inadequately rendered by the person painting.... I have known, indeed, several honourable exceptions to this general rule, but I have only too frequently witnessed its truth, and *my* temper and patience

*Later known as Costessey Hall

have often been on the point of deserting me, even when Mr Opie's had not, apparently, undergone the slightest alteration.[6]

In the summer Amelia returned to Norwich to spend several weeks with her father; although busy with commissions in London, including a portrait of John Horne Tooke,* John joined her for some of the time. Godwin was also visiting friends in Norfolk in the late summer; on his first day in Norwich he supped with Dr Alderson and the Opies and went on to spend time with all three of them – together or individually – during his time in the city. Staying with her father gave Amelia the chance to spend time with old friends; she also had the opportunity to peruse a new, but short-lived, weekly newspaper called *The Iris* which was being published in the city. The first edition came out on February 5th, 1803; the last on December 29th, 1804. It was founded by city radicals, in the wake of the previous year's elections. They promoted their new venture thus:

> During the late elections, both the Norwich Papers, with a consentaneity [sic] formerly unusual, joined their influence to thwart the success of the County and City Candidates supported by the Whig Party. This coalition, however inefficient, was vexatious; and many supporters of the present Members [the two successful Whig candidates], in consequence, expressed a wish, that some Newspaper were undertaken, in which the sentiments of their friends would find not only admittance, but welcome....
>
> What will distinguish *The Iris* from other similar publications? But little – the wish, rather than the power, to inculcate anew those principles of liberty, which, before the intrusion of an intolerant sect into the leading literature and active politics of Britain, had lifted this nation to an eminence and felicity now, alas! of doubtful return....[7]

A leading figure in the project was William Taylor, who tried to persuade Robert Southey to be its editor. Taylor and Southey had met in 1798, when the poet took his younger brother Henry to Norfolk to be a pupil of George Burnett, a Unitarian minister at Great Yarmouth. Three years later Henry took his first steps towards what would become a distinguished career in medicine, when he moved to

---

* Tooke's portrait was commissioned by Lieut Col William Tooke Harwood, nephew of his benefactor William Tooke. Harwood provided a carriage to convey the sitter from his home in Wimbledon to Opie's studio in Berners Street.

Norwich to become a student of Philip Meadows Martineau. Taylor took young Henry under his wing and hoped that Robert would agree to edit the new paper and settle in Norwich. But, although tempted by the job itself and by the prospect of being Taylor's neighbour, he declined. However, he did ask his friend to send him copies of the newspaper; Taylor then undertook to 'supervise' *The Iris* for two years.

Very little is known about contributors; Taylor told Southey that Edward Taylor (one of Susannah's sons) was to abridge parliamentary debates and that his friend Stephen Weaver Browne, the former Norwich clergyman, might also be involved. It is unlikely that Amelia wrote for the newspaper as she was busy with so many other matters, including work on her new novel, *Adeline Mowbray*, but Dr Alderson would certainly have been a subscriber. In the previous year Opie had completed a portrait of Henry Hobart,* who had been an MP for Norwich in three successive Parliaments. *The Iris* carried a report about the forthcoming hanging of the portrait in St Andrew's Hall, using the story to indulge in a burst of civic outrage about the placing of a portrait of the unpopular Windham in the building. Suggesting that permission to hang that portrait had neither been obtained nor asked, the writer urged the Corporation to take it down, saying its hanging was a direct insult to the majority of citizens, who thought Windham unfit to be their representative. He went on:

> Mr Hobart's picture, by Opie, will be placed in the Hall after an Engraving, by Mr Bell, has been taken from it. However we might have differed from Mr Hobart's politics, we always considered him as a friend to the local interests of the City, and think the Corporation do well in granting permission for it to be placed among our other representatives....[8]

A week later (May 5th, 1804) *The Iris* 'rejoiced' in being able to report on 'a warm debate' in the Corporation's general assembly about permission not having been granted to hang Windham's portrait. It was resolved, eventually, that the picture should remain, but that in future 'no picture or portrait whatsoever' should be placed in the hall without the Corporation's full consent.

As John's wife, Amelia had persuaded him to introduce some order into the house in Berners Street and to create a gallery where his work might be seen to its best advantage. Years later when her artist cousin

---

* Hobart died in 1799. There is no available record of when the portrait was started, nor of any sittings.

Henry Perronet Briggs was moving from his rented house in Charles Street, London, to larger premises in Bruton Street – formerly occupied by the artist William Owen – she wrote to his wife Eliza giving her approval and recalling her own experiences:

I shall always believe that if my poor husband would have made years before a proper gallery and cleared out his pig stye sooner his employment and his gains would have been comfortably increased. *He* thought so *too late*.... I must own that a fine gallery does give an artist a great advantage. How imposing was [William] Beechey's gallery! A painter might make his gallery a pretty lounge – I have forgotten how poor Owen's was lighted but I know there was ample verge and room enough to shew [sic] the pictures to advantage.[9]

She expanded upon her theme, when writing to wish Henry joy in his new abode:

... but neither of you can feel the delight *I* did when I saw *our* gallery finished and the pictures removed into it! Because your house is anything but a *pig stye* and ours was one. Oh! The secrets of that prison house! Our back parlour, a large room, which we never used but the *cats did*, was filled with very large unframed pictures standing in series, one before the other and making vallies [sic] behind and *between* them. In these *glens* our three cats had their soirées and as I had only two servants (one maid and a man) and *they*, the cats, had no servants of their own to sweep out after their revels were over, thou will suppose that *pig stye* was not too strong an expression, only *cat stye* would have been better still. So thou may judge what a deliverance to me was the making that room into a gallery with the yard adjoining laid into it![10]

In May 1804, Opie gave a lecture on painting at the Royal Institution. *The Iris* covered the lecture, reporting that it was attended by 'a very fashionable and, in many respects, a critical audience', adding that the artist was 'highly flattered by the approbation he had met with that night'.[11] It may be assumed that Dr Alderson sent a copy of the paper to his daughter, who would also have enjoyed reading its lengthy feature on William Wilberforce's intention of once again 'submitting to the consideration of Parliament a motion for the abolition of the Slave Trade'.

May was also the month in which Opie started work on his portrait of Fox.

Nollekens had carved two busts of Fox and the portrait painter believed it would be helpful to borrow one:

> Dear Sir. Can you (I am sure you will if you can) lend me your last bust of Mr Fox for a day or two? He has been with me once and if I could have the bust I could make myself quite master of the markings of the head before he comes again which would facilitate very much the progress of the picture.[12]

By June 3rd, according to Farington, the statesman had sat for Opie seven times:

> He was much pleased with the liberal feelings which Mr Fox expressed about artists, for when he disapproved certain works, he would still mention what the merits of the artists were.... Opie thought Lord Lauderdale [former MP and staunch supporter of Fox] the most cute and just in his observations of any of those who came while Mr Fox was sitting. Mrs Fox always came with Mr Fox.[13]

Amelia never forgot how John dealt with his commission to paint the statesman:

> Of all persons of worship, he was most eager to paint Mr Fox, whose character he loved, and whose talents he venerated: but it was with fear and anxiety that he began a task so arduous and so interesting; because he knew that to the result of his labours many an eager and expecting eye would be turned, and because he felt a grateful desire to execute his task so as to satisfy his generous employer.... Mr Fox saw and felt for the uneasiness that Mr Opie experienced, and with his usual kindness and good sense he said to him one day, 'Mr Opie, don't mind what these people say, for after all you must know better than they do.' The picture under all these disadvantages was, however, finished; and pleased, at least, the many; and what was of most consequence, it satisfied Mr Coke... when exhibited [in 1805], the portrait was an object of interest and approbation; and Mr Fox, who sat opposite to Mr Opie at the Academy dinner, and overheard the general tribute paid to the strength of the resemblance, said to him across the table, 'There, Mr Opie, you see I was right; everybody thinks it could not be better.'[14]

In the summer and autumn Amelia was away from home for much of the time. John had a commission to do a portrait of the Rev Samuel Foster, headmaster of the city's Free School, so he may have joined his wife in Norwich for two or three weeks. He was certainly back in London in the autumn. Farington recorded that Fuseli and he had called on Opie to discuss changes at the Royal Academy. Fuseli had been Professor of Painting since 1799, Opie had offered himself for the post but withdrew in favour of Fuseli, who was now in line for the office of Keeper (the Academician responsible for running the schools). Farington said they told Opie that if Fuseli was made Keeper he would resign the Professorship and Opie would fill the post.

News of the possible appointment would have been pleasing to Amelia, who had great faith in her husband's abilities. She did not return to Berners Street until December, having been away from home for four months. In London, she found that the talk of the town was a new star of the theatre, 13-year-old William Henry West Betty, who had made his debut in Belfast two years previously. After hugely successful tours in Ireland, Scotland and the north of England the young actor, who was given the epithet the Young Roscius (after the celebrated Roman actor Roscius), was invited to perform in London. He made his first appearance at Covent Garden on December 1st in John Brown's tragedy *Barbarossa*; he also acted in another tragedy, John Home's *Douglas*. There were 12 performances at Covent Garden, for which he was paid 50 guineas a night; on intervening nights he acted at Drury Lane.

All those with an interest in the theatre flocked to see the young prodigy and troops were called out to control the crowds. Godwin recorded attending the theatre three Saturdays running to see *Barbarossa*, *Douglas* and *Barbarossa* again. It is certain that Amelia and John would have been in the audience for one or both of the plays. The demands of the work and the pressures of publicity took their toll on Betty and from December 18th until the new year he had a break from acting. Perhaps this was when Opie painted what was to become one of his most celebrated portraits of the day – the boy actor as 'Young Norval' in *Douglas*. It was shown at the Royal Academy the following April, when Betty was back on the stage in London and 'Bettymania' was at its height.

By the time Amelia was back in London she was achieving celebrity of her own with the publication of *Adeline Mowbray or The Mother and Daughter*, which would become her most talked-about and controversial piece of fiction. Unlike *The Father and Daughter*, which she had introduced as 'a simple moral tale', her new novel was a complex exploration of relationships, codes of conduct and the upbringing of children. Believed to have been inspired by the relationship of her friends Godwin and Wollstonecraft – he the radical philosopher with theories on the irrelevance of marriage, she the committed feminist with views on the rights of women and the maternal role – the novel was brought out in three volumes.

Its heroine, Adeline Mowbray, is brought up by her mother Editha, to be a radical free thinker. Editha's mother plays a conventional wifely role but, believing her daughter to be intellectually superior, has neglected to train her in the accepted feminine duties. Thus Editha is assertive and egotistical, personifying what the conservative members of society believed to be the disagreeable aspects of educated women. Adeline is a more balanced character, but, wishing to escape the sexual advances of the man who marries her widowed mother, she starts a relationship with Glenmurray, a philosopher with radical views on wedlock. Choosing to co-habit with him exposes Adeline to the opprobrium of both sexes. She learns, to her cost, that progressive views are all right in theory but almost impossible in practice. Regarded by society as no better than she should be and the object of unwelcome attention from other men, coupled with hostility and some jealousy from other women, Adeline is also estranged from Editha who takes her husband's side against her daughter. Becoming pregnant, she begins to reconsider her views on marriage; but she miscarries and Glenmurray dies, urging her to marry one of his kinsmen. Adeline agrees and gives birth to a daughter, but her husband is unfaithful and leaves her for another woman. Fortunately, Adeline has attracted the compassion of a kind doctor who appreciates intellect in woman, the support of a wise and sensible Quaker who becomes her surrogate mother and the uncritical love of a young mulatto woman called Savanna* whose family she has saved from destitution. The story ends with Adeline on her deathbed, re-united with her repentant mother, and reviewing what she has learned from her life experiences.

The novel was well received by the main reviewers, who applauded the author's ability to evoke pathos. But while commending characters and events, *The Critical Review* expressed unease about the portrayal of Adeline's and Glenmurray's co-habitation as being happy,

---

* Possibly the name was inspired by family stories of Savannah, the black nurse who brought Amelia's mother to England from India following the death of her parents.

and Adeline's marriage as miserable, the implication being it gave vice 'an air of respectability'. Her publishers promoted the second edition of *Adeline Mowbray* with appropriate quotes from reviews: 'Upon the whole this work must be allowed to rank considerably higher than the ordinary productions of the same kind (*Literary Journal*) and 'The Language is simple and appropriate...and the characters indicate much acute observation of the human mind (*General Review*).'[15]

An un-named writer on Mrs Opie in 1805 described Adeline thus:

Educated in the principles of the new jargon, mis-named '*philosophy*', and exemplifying in her own life the miseries attendant upon reducing its wild theories to practice, the heroine of this tale, after a series of trial, discovers that an adherence to the old '*prejudices*' of society are at once the safest, and indeed the only rule for the government of human contact. She expiates her errors by death; and, dying repentant, exhibits an awful and instructive lesson to youth....

In the publication of *Adeline Mowbray*, Mrs Opie has rendered an essential service to society; it is a present which every mother ought to make to her daughter, and cannot fail of producing the most salutary effect.[16]

Apparently few (if any) of the contemporary reviewers linked the leading characters with Godwin and Wollstonecraft. Soon after its publication, Godwin, who by then had been married to his second wife Mary Jane Clairmont for two years, noted in his diary of February 9th, 1805, that he had started to read Volume 1; two days later he was on to Volume 2 and he finished Volume 3 on February 15th. His reaction was not recorded. Several of Godwin's biographers believed him to have been hurt by his old friend's 'attack', but quite how the attack was perceived is unclear. The novel's philosopher is depicted as a thoughtful and caring man, his and the heroine's radical views on marriage are explored with sympathy; it is, rather, that society and its prejudices are under attack. Amelia herself, although impressed by the radical views of others, was perhaps not as radical as she wished to be when it came to nailing her own colours to the mast. Primarily, she was interested in ideas and in relationships. The main theme of the novel – as its title suggests – is the mother and daughter relationship. She had been impressed by the way Fanny [Imlay's daughter] was being raised and in a letter to Wollstonecraft, referring to what she called 'my testimony as eye witness to the success of your plan', had sought advice on some aspects of child-rearing to pass on to a friend who was about to become a mother.[17] Wollstonecraft's views on mothers and daughters, expressed cogently in her *A Vindication of the Rights of Women*, were also a significant influence.

The Irish writer Julia Kavanagh, who spent many years in France, where translations of the Opie novels were very popular, was particularly interested in the contributions made by women to the development of the novel and in the way they handled sexual and social differences. Writing a few years after Amelia's death, she believed that the author 'by a masterpiece of delicacy and grace' had created a heroine whose errors neither seduced nor offended the reader and that the work contained 'some of the most pathetic passages of any tale written in Mrs Opie's generation'. Kavanagh also perceived a connection between the heroine and Godwin's first wife:

> Mrs Opie knew Godwin before he married Mary Wolstonecraft [sic], and if she did not know that generous and noble-minded though erring woman, she was well acquainted with her history. It suggested the chief incidents in the tale of *Adeline Mowbray*, and it is well for Mrs Opie's credit that she did not invent them herself, for they are so remote from the common realities of life that, had not the whole world known them to be true, few would have tolerated them. Their truth, though still a matter of fact, is no longer a matter of feeling at this distance of time....[18]

In 1883 Anne Ritchie (née Thackeray) wrote a tribute to Mrs Opie in *The Cornhill Magazine* – later reproduced in *A Book of Sybils* – in which she, too, made the Wollstonecraft connection:

> It is a melancholy and curious story, which seems to have been partly suggested by that of poor Mary Wollstonecraft, whose prejudices the heroine shares and expiates by a fate hardly less pathetic than that of Mary herself. The book reminds one of a very touching letter from Godwin's wife to Amelia Alderson, written a few weeks before her death, in which she speaks of her 'contempt for the forms of a world she should have bade a long good-night to had she not been a mother'. Justice has at length been done to this mistaken but noble and devoted woman, and her story has lately been written from a wider point of view than Mrs Opie's, though she indeed was no ungenerous advocate.[19]

Amelia's contemporaries, however, were more interested in the issues presented in the novel. Sir James Mackintosh, writing home from Bombay to a friend in England, thought:

Mrs Opie has pathetic scenes, but the object is not attained; for the distress is not made to arise from the *un*nuptial union itself, but from the opinions of the world against it; so that it may as well be taken to be a satire on our prejudices in favour of marriage, as on the paradoxes of sophists against it.[20]

The literary Porter sisters, Jane and Anna Maria, were in the habit of exchanging their views on current novels in letters to each other. Anna Maria described *Adeline Mowbray* as 'the history of a Faux Madam Philosopher' who refused marriage 'for all the sapient reasons broached by the new school' and suggested it might well stand as a beacon for the unwary.[21] Some years later, William Johnson Fox, a Unitarian minister who was raised in Norwich, recommended the novel to his fiancée Eliza Florance. Choosing to call it *Mother and Daughter*, he told her she could easily get the book 'at the circulating libraries'. Having done so, Eliza wrote, in January 1819, to tell William:

Tis a sweet tale, and a delicate and beautiful exposition of that fallacious and absurd system, miscalled *moral* philosophy; better had this *nouvelle* philosophy never been broached, or published only among the Gonoquais* than it should ever have played havoc with a mind pure and exalted as that of the lovely Adeline. My Godwinanism, that you used to laugh at, and which I never fully explained, is a modification of their scheme; ridiculous enough, 'tis true, but I once mused over my theory with great pleasure, though I never was so far gone as to anticipate its practice; the theory I still think not so bad.[22]

Towards the end of the 19th century the Opie tales were out of fashion. In 1884, her cousin's daughter Sarah Isabella noted:

It would be vain to expect any modern novel reader to attempt any one of Mrs Opie's stories…Her pathos seems to us long out of date, but Sir Walter Scott and Sir James Mackintosh shed tears over it, or said they did.[23]

---

* A primitive African tribe described in an 18th century French travel writer's work and taken up by the author Elizabeth Hamilton in her 1800 satirical novel *Memoirs of Modern Philosophers*.

But, more than 100 years after its publication, *Adeline Mowbray* began to enjoy serious attention from academics. Allene Gregory, in his 1915 exploration of how Revolutionary principles and ethics were incorporated in novels of the period, chose to include Mrs Opie and the work in his chapter on *Some Typical Lady Novelists of the Revolution*, suggesting that:

> As an interpretation of Mary Wollstonecraft, if such were intended, it is not unjust, but merely absurdly inadequate. Amelia Opie was one of those simple, kindly souls to whom the real power and originality of a mind like that of Mary Wollstonecraft must remain forever a closed book.[24]

Since 1986 there have been three separate paperback editions of *Adeline Mowbray* and the novel has been analysed in numerous serious academic works about the sexual and social politics of women writers in Opie's heyday.

Chapter Sixteen

The month of May 1805 brought sad news to John Opie – the death of his beloved mother at the age of 92. Mary Opie died in Harmony Cottage, her home for more than 60 years and where, in her widowhood, she had been cared for by her only daughter Elizabeth. John had supported his mother and unmarried sister financially. Amelia, who never met her mother-in-law, understood that John was devoted to her:

> Mr Opie used to speak of his mother with the most touching enthusiasm. He described her as the most perfect of human beings; as the most mild, most just, and most disinterested of women: and I believe that scarcely any one who knew her would have thought this description an exaggerated one. He loved to relate little instances of the sacred love of justice which led her regardless of the partialities of a parent to decide even against her own children, when as criminals they appeared before her, and were in the slightest degree culpable; and these stories always ended in recollections of her tender care of him during his feeble childhood, of the gloves and great coat warmed at the winter's fire against he went to school....[1]

Sadly, Mary died before her son was made Professor of Painting at the Royal Academy in August, Fuseli having resigned the office on being elected Keeper. Opie was elected unanimously. Among the letters of congratulation was one from a fellow Cornishman, the MP Davies Giddy, whose portrait by the new professor would be exhibited at the Academy in 1806. Opie replied:

> Nothing surely gives us more pleasure than the approbation of those whose abilities and conduct we admire and respect. I therefore take the first moment of my return to Town, to tell you how much I was gratified and how much I thank you for your kind and friendly congratulation on my being elected professor of painting to the R.A.
>
> Whether similar feelings towards me spread to any great extent amongst my countrymen I shall not at present enquire. Quality in these cases I hold to be infinitely preferable to number and whilst I possess the countenance of yourself and a very few more, I cer-

tainly can have no right to complain.[2]

Amelia spent the summer in Norwich, where, to her delight, Thomas Erskine was appearing for the plaintiff in a right-of-way cause. Since falling under his spell at the treason trials, she had become acquainted with the famous lawyer. Erskine had appeared for her friend Samuel Boddington, when he sued his cousin Benjamin Boddington for damages on the grounds of his adultery with his (Samuel's) wife Grace. The couple had married in 1792, when she was 17 and a minor, needing her father's permission. It was significant that Amelia referred to Mrs Boddington's as 'the frail and the beautiful', when writing to Constable about the aftermath of Tooke's trial. Benjamin had joined Samuel in the family business in the year of the treason trials. After she eloped with Benjamin, Grace's distraught husband sued his cousin for damages in a notorious court case in which much was made of Mrs Boddington's exceptional beauty.

A contemporary pamphlet, giving a full report of the trial before the Sheriff of London in September 1797,[3] claimed that it 'engaged the particular attention of a very crowded audience'. Erskine was in fine form, arguing that the defendant's crime was of 'the greatest magnitude of depravity' – seducing a beautiful, virtuous and devoted wife, depriving two innocent children of a tender mother's care and bringing sorrow and disgrace to 'a large and truly honourable family'. Samuel was awarded damages of £10,000. His son and daughter remained with him; the following year he divorced Grace and she married Benjamin. Recalling the Boddingtons many years later, Amelia wrote that Samuel was 'a man I greatly esteemed and was once intimate with – aye – and with his *beautiful* but faithless wife'.[4]

She also valued her friendship with the lawyer, writing a full account of his appearance in Norwich in 1805, the year before he was made Lord Erskine. She believed herself fortunate to have heard him that day, as all the lawyers present in the court declared they had never before heard him 'so great in reply'. Amelia arrived early at the court and obtained a seat by the side of the judge.

In that place I remained the whole day, except when, on being assured that my seat should be kept for me, I went home to tea, but soon returned to the scene of action, where I staid [sic] all night; as I could not bear to go away without hearing the great orator's reply to the defendant's counsel.

But the defence was by no means finished. The case dragged on and on; more and more onlookers left the court; members of the jury began to nod.

> ...and it seemed likely, that, except the judge, the high sheriff, the barristers, the officers of the court, and myself, there would soon be no hearers left awake, and the beams of rising day were forcing themselves through the windows! The observant Erskine took the hint, so palpably given, and coming up to me, he kindly said, 'Go home! Go home! I shall not reply tonight; but you had better be here by eight in the morning,' and soon after the court adjourned to that hour.
>
> I was in court again by half-past seven, but too late to obtain a seat, and I stood many hours, in a painful position, but I was soon made unconscious of it by the eloquence of Erskine; for during those hours he spoke, and hushed a court, crowded even to suffocation, into the most perfect stillness....The plaintiff gained her cause, and her advocate new laurels....
>
> A few months afterwards he was made Lord Chancellor, and when, while talking to him at a party in London, I told him I was every day intending to go into the Court of Chancery, in hope of hearing him speak in his new capacity – his reply was 'Pray do not come! You will not hear anything worth the trouble. I am nothing now; you heard the last and best of me at Norwich last year!'[5]

John joined Amelia later in the summer. One of his commissions was to do a portrait of a seven-year-old boy, William Buckle Frost, who, according to Earland, was allowed to play around in the painting room. The boy's mother, a contemporary of Amelia's, was brought up in Norwich where her father, the Rev Stephen Buckle, was Rector of All Saints Church. However, as Opie wrote in to Davies Giddy, he also enjoyed some leisure activities:

> I have been spending five weeks at Norwich and parts adjacent, where through the medium of beef dumplings, wine, riding, swimming, walking and laughing, I have endeavored [sic] (I hope not unsuccessfully) to lay in a stock of vigour against winter and my time I must say has passed pleasantly enough, as in addition to the above mentioned substantial and capital enjoyments, I have had occasionally some agreeable conversation with several not unclever people.[6]

Having been appointed to the professorship, Opie was required by the Academy to give a course of lectures on painting, within three years of his election. Already well-established as a portrait painter of some distinction, he was even more in demand following the appointment. Returning to London in good health, he was soon hard at work; in 1806 eight of his portraits were selected for the Academy exhibition. In April that year he started work on a portrait of Southey, at the request of the poet's friend William Taylor. Staying with Taylor, Southey had admired the Opie portrait of Dr Sayers, which was displayed prominently in his host's library, whereupon Taylor persuaded him to sit for Opie.

Southey was well acquainted with the Opies, having met John in London in 1797; a year later he had got to know Dr Alderson in Norwich. On visits to London he usually called on the Opies, being pleased on one visit to find Amelia's father staying with the couple. Once the work on his portrait was begun he kept Taylor informed of its progress:

Had I begun to write to you sooner I could not have told you that your picture was begun this morning, that I had sat two hours in a very fine velvet chair, and that there my portrait is, looking, Mrs Opie says, quite alive; and, if it does, looking very unlike the original, which is but half alive. London has always affected my spirits, but it never before affected my health. I breathe with difficulty and positively hunger and thirst for fresh air.[7]

In reply, Taylor thanked his friend for 'submitting to the ennui of Mr Opie's velvet chair', adding that he hoped Mrs Opie herself now and then handed him chocolate and talked to him pleasantly. Towards the end of May, Southey was able to report:

I sate [sic] five times in the velvet chair, and each time little less than three hours, though the law is satisfied with one hour in the pillory and at the gallows. Opie will perhaps complain; if he does, put him in the 30th chapter of the Book of Proverbs, as the fifth of those things which are never satisfied. You, I hope, will like the picture, as every person who has seen it is much pleased.[8]

Indeed, Taylor did like the portrait,* which he put up alongside that of Dr Sayers. According to Robberds, his biographer:

The possession of these two portraits was always a source of com-

---

* He bequeathed the portrait to the sitter's brother Dr Henry Southey.

placent gratification to William Taylor; the literary eminence of the two individuals, his friendly regard for them, and the fidelity and skill with which the painter had traced their features, were the standards by which he appreciated the intrinsic value of these efforts of art.[9]

Although willing and able to assist John at Berners Street, Amelia was also busy with her own work and enjoying social life in the capital. In February she had the opportunity to meet the writer Jane Porter, whose novel *Thaddeus of Warsaw*, published in 1803, had been highly acclaimed. It was inspired by Jane's hero-worship of the Polish patriot Kosciusko and the stories told by Polish refugees living in London following their doomed struggle for independence in the 1790s. Jane was said to have based the accounts of the title character Thaddeus Sobieski's efforts to make a living as an artist on the early struggles of the Norwich-born Cotman, who was a friend of her artist brother Robert Ker Porter. Her book was praised by the great Kosciusko himself. The two women met at a party attended by literary and theatrical people. Jane wrote to tell her sister Anna Maria about the guests, who included the celebrated 'young Betty' and 'Miss Duncan the actress', who was making a name for herself as a leading lady at Drury Lane, where she had she created the role of Juliana in Tobin's *The Honey Moon*.

> ...and Mrs Opie, who desired to be introduced to poor me, styling me 'that great creature'. I could have shrugged my shoulders, and smiled. Alas! All is not great that we think so! – I at least am a case in point.
>
> These nights are entertaining, but they are very empty....[10]

Amelia's next publication was four volumes of short stories which came out under the title *Simple Tales* in the spring of 1806. Her publishers, advertising the new work, informed readers that *The Father and Daughter* and *Poems* were now in their fourth editions and *Adeline Mowbray* its second. Substantial quotations from reviews of all three works were added, the author being described by one reviewer as 'a Lady whose uncommon Talents do Honour to her Sex and Country'.[11] All the review excerpts stressed the author's ability to affect the reader's emotions – 'her Power of working upon the Passions', as one called it. As with *The Father and Daughter* and *Adeline Mowbray*, Amelia focused on relationships in her new stories. The titles of five of the 12 which made up the collection give some indication of her fascination with such matters: *The Fashionable Wife and Unfashionable Husband*; *The Mother and Son*; *The Brother and Sister*; *The Uncle and Nephew*; *The Orphan*. Frequently in her correspondence she chose to pass on anecdotes about the behaviour of others, with her opinion on the issues involved. This interest was explored in her story writing. The new short stories were mentioned in *The Edinburgh Review*, whose critic suggested that, although the author lacked the ability to reason well, she had a talent for perceiving truth and there was something 'delightfully feminine' in all her writing.

Many authors, taking a didactic stance on duty or piety, might choose to write something on the lines of the parable of *The Prodigal Son*, when the errant offspring is restored and forgiven by a loving father. But Amelia created several instances in which a feckless or transgressive parent is redeemed by filial devotion. In *The Black Velvet Pelisse* the heroine is a beautiful, kind and selfless young woman, who behaves with perfect discretion and courtesy towards her parsimonious and disagreeable father, bringing about his repentance and, in the process, attracting the love of a baronet, when she saves a poor family from the workhouse. *The Mother and Son* features an adulterous wife who abandons her only child to elope with her lover; many years later, when she is alone and rejected by polite society, the son believes it his filial duty to take her into his home, even though his decision to house a fallen woman threatens his forthcoming marriage. *The Death Bed* also concerns a guilty wife, whose love of clothes and finery leads her into debt and the arms of a lover; she, too, leaves husband, home and child.

The stories, almost without exception, are replete with highly-charged emotional scenes in which characters of both sexes *in extremis*, swoon, faint and fall unconscious. To modern eyes such reactions seem absurd; they are more likely to arouse amusement than sympathy. However, as a writer in the *Monthly Review* (quoted in the catalogue) stated there were many with 'a sympathetic taste for distress' for whom Mrs Opie's works possessed 'pathos enough to affect the Heart of the most callow of Critical Readers'.

One such reader was the young Mary Russell Mitford – later to become a distinguished author and dramatist in her own right – who reported to her father in May 1806: 'We have been reading Mrs Opie's *Simple Tales* and are greatly pleased with them.'[12] Having first met Amelia, when John Opie was painting the portrait of her father, she got to know her better once she herself had become part of the literary scene, as she explained to Cecilia Lucy Brightwell:

> ...when I myself was a poetical aspirant, I saw her often – for though she was perhaps in a gayer world than I, we were yet often brought together and besides visiting at each other's houses met frequently at the parties of friends...she was one of the most brilliant adornments of London society. To hear her sing her own songs and especially without music was a treat never to be forgotten so perfect was her articulation and so consummate her sentences, her expression and her looks. It was poetry. [13]

Mitford had found Opie unwilling to indulge in small talk with his sitters, but he seemed to have been happy to converse with fellow artists. One such was the young David Wilkie, son of a Scots clergyman, who arrived in London in May 1805, living in abject poverty while trying to establish himself in the art world. By November, at the age of 21, he was formally enrolled as a student at the Royal Academy; a few months later his picture *Village Politicians* was accepted for the annual Academy exhibition. That summer he accompanied the Opies on a visit to Southill in Bedfordshire, the country seat of the MP and brewer Samuel Whitbread, who had sat for Opie. A keen supporter of Charles James Fox and a leading campaigner for parliamentary reform, religious toleration and the abolition of the slave trade, the politician and his wife became dear friends of Amelia. The visit was a break from work – 'and never did I see him so happy, when absent from London, as he was there' – recalled his wife. It was the last holiday they were to spend together.

The first of Opie's portraits of Samuel Whitbread was executed six or seven years before he and Amelia went to stay at Southill in 1806; the second was exhibited at the Academy in 1804, when it was described by the *Monthly Mirror* as 'a very fine portrait, possessing every quality of excellence'. Whitbread's great friend Tom Adkin, whom he had met when they were both students at Cambridge in the 1780s, and who now lived and worked at Southill, was also been painted by Opie. Adkin, the son of a curate at Downham Market in Norfolk, was said to be witty, open-handed and a good conversationalist.

Whitbread had inherited some significant art works from his father and added more to the family collection. He was a patron of several young artists, including Samuel William Reynolds (usually referred to as S. W. Reynolds), a mezzotint engraver and landscape painter. His engravings of portraits were highly regarded – he engraved both Opie portraits of Whitbread – and he was a frequent visitor to Southill. He was a guest there when the Opies and Wilkie paid their summer visit. Whitbread's interest in the young Scot was prompted by the acclaim which his *Village Politicians* had received when it was hung at the Academy exhibition. In June Wilkie wrote to tell his father of the eminent people who were seeking him out:

> I had the honour of a call from that mirror of patriotism, Mr Whitbread, a man who, although, in his public character, he has professed an antipathy to all my countrymen, has nevertheless in private professed a great friendship for me.[14]

The friendship ripened when Wilkie called at the MP's London home to show some of his works to Whitbread's wife and was then engaged by Whitbread to do a painting for him. Soon after this meeting Wilkie was invited to accompany the Opies on their August visit to Southill. Opie wrote to the young artist at his new lodgings in Sol's Row, explaining their plans:

> I have just received a letter from Mr Whitbread saying that they are out on an excursion and will not be at home till the middle of next week. They therefore wish us to come to Southill tomorrow se'nnight instead of tomorrow. I hope this will not prevent our going together at the time he appoints.[15]

The guests arrived at Southill on Saturday, August 16th; soon Amelia was busy writing to her father. She told him about their 'pleasant journey' of 42 miles from London, followed by a description of the house and grounds:

> On entering the house, the true use and enjoyment of unbounded opulence force themselves at once on one's conviction....The family not expecting us till near six, were out when we arrived; so the groom of the chambers led us to our apartments....As soon as we had had sandwiches &c., the barouche and the family arrived, and we had the sorrow to find Lady Elizabeth [Whitbread's wife] very unwell...she immediately went to lie down. Mr Opie accompanied Mr Whitbread &c. in the barouche, in a drive which he was going to take, four-in-hand; and Mr Wilkie and I took a walk. At six we all met at dinner.[16]

Resuming her letter on Wednesday, she told Dr Alderson about the delicious dinner which was 'French enough to delight me' and the 'delightful day' the Whitbreads and their guests had spent at Woburn Abbey, home of the Duke of Bedford. Always happy to meet and make friends with titled people, she was pleased that Lady Rosslyn and her young children were house guests. The meeting with Lady Rosslyn made quite an impression. Amelia made notes about her stay at Southill, which she drew upon for a tribute to her titled friend which was published many years later:

Our dear host drove us out together more than once in his phaeton, and as we could not conveniently have the pleasure of conversing with him, we were obliged to converse with one another; consequently, we did not long remain on distant terms. We visited the new jail at Bedford, in which we found but one inmate, a man, of whom we bought some pincushions, the fruits of his industry and his solitude. We drove also to some gentlemen's seats in the neighbourhood. At one of these, where our host left us while he transacted some business, Lady Rosslyn asked the woman in whose care the house had been left, and who was then basting a leg of mutton, to fetch her a draught of new milk. Accordingly she laid down the basting-spoon, and eagerly ran to get it. 'What a pity it would be,' said the considerate Lady Rosslyn, 'if the mutton should burn while the good woman is employed in my service! I will baste the meat till she returns.' So said, so done – and the graceful countess, seizing the ladle, commenced operations.[17]

According to his wife, John Opie also enjoyed their time with the Whitbreads:

Never did I see him so happy, when absent from London, as he was there; for he felt towards his host and hostess every sentiment of respect and admiration which it is pleasant to feel and honourable to inspire. But though he was the object of the kindest and most flattering attention, he sighed to return to London and his pursuits – and when we had been at Southill only eight days, he said to me, on expressing my unwillingness to go away, 'Though I shall be even anxious to come hither again, recollect that I have been idle *eight days*.'[18]

At Southill, Lady Rosslyn received letters from her mother, Mrs Bouverie, with news of Fox's state of health. He had been ill for months and died on September 13th. By then Amelia was in Norwich with her father and John was back at work in London. When he first started courting Miss Alderson, he had recognised that her attachment to her father was paramount; keeping it in mind enabled him to deal kindly with her absences but there were times when he was desperate for her to return home. In the autumn of 1806 he was unusually anxious, having started work on the lectures on painting which he was required to give at the Royal Academy. In response to a letter from Norwich, apparently informing him of Amelia's plans, he wrote:

My dearest life, I cannot be sorry that you do not stay longer, though, as I said, on your father's account, I would consent to it. Pray love forgive me, and make yourself easy, for I did not suspect, till my last letter was gone, that it might be too strong; I had been counting almost the hours till your arrival for some time, and have been unwell and unable to sleep these last three weeks, so that I could not make up my mind to the disappointment. As to coming down again, I cannot think of it; for though I could, perhaps, better spare the time at present from painting, than I could at any part of last month, I find I must now go hard to work to finish my lectures, as the law says they must be delivered the second year after the election.... I have shut myself up in the evenings, and I doubt not, shall be ready with three or four of them at least.... Pray love be easy, and as I suppose you will not stay; come up as soon as possible, for I long to see you as much as ever I did in my life.*

---

* Brightwell suggested (pp.76-7) that this undated letter was written in 1800, but the reference to the lectures indicates it must have been 1806. Furthermore, in a paragraph not quoted here, Opie mentions a meeting at which [Augustus Wall] Callcot was elected an associate of the Academy. Records show this appointment took place in 1806.

Chapter Seventeen

From September 1806 to February 1807, Opie spent every evening working on his lectures, taking little exercise and seeing no friends. Many years later, when Amelia's cousin Henry Perronet Briggs, was in line for the professorship she wrote to his wife expressing her relief that he was not appointed to the job:

> I have always attributed the death of my poor husband to his election to the post of Professor. The *extra* labour of mind was incessant and was too much for him. When I returned from Norwich the 11th month I found him painting from 9 to 4 and writing from half-past to bed time. Nor was the labour too much to do the thing as he did it admirably – but he *sunk* under it....[1]

In January Opie worked on another commission from Coke of Norfolk – a portrait of the Aldersons' old friend Dr Samuel Parr, which was shown at the Academy that summer. Writing to Sir James Mackintosh, who, as Recorder of Bombay had been in India for nearly three years, Amelia told him that the Parr portrait was 'a fine likeness'. Her letter was full of news about mutual friends at home and abroad, including Boddington, whose ex-wife Grace (née Ashburner) had been born in India, where her father William was employed by the East India Company as Governor of Poona. Amelia herself was in touch with Grace's brother Luke Ashburner, a former pupil of George Cadogan Morgan, who had returned to India, where he became Sheriff of Bombay and edited the *Bombay Courier*. As a widower, Luke, on a visit to England in 1804, fell in love with Morgan's only daughter Sarah, married her and took her back with him to Bombay. Amelia's cousin Ollyett Woodhouse was also in Bombay, where he had been appointed Advocate-General. His wife was about to join him:

> Mrs Woodhouse will be the bearer of this and I should rejoice at Olyett's [sic] being re-united to a woman whom he loves did I not fear that his expenses will be doubled by her residence in India and consequently his necessary savings terribly diminished.[2]

A few days later she wrote a chatty letter to Lady Mackintosh,* in which she reported on 'the blue-stocking set which Lady Cork† assembles at her conversationes', explaining that 'all that is most recherché in ye world of talents, all that has *talent* or a *love* for it in ye world of rank and fashion meets at her house'. She hoped Lady Mackintosh, when she returned to London, would join her at one of these gatherings, adding:

> Were my spouse as fond of having parties as I am I would have an open conversatione once a fortnight – my rooms are now smarted [sic] up and open out of each other with folding doors of a large size which being thrown back make a room 45 feet long so my house would do for any sized party, but my husband loves not the trouble even of a small one. I am at home every Sunday morning after church and find that very pleasant, as some of my visiters [sic] are regular in their attendance and I am sure of two, or three hours of pleasant society.[3]

Amelia also updated her correspondent with news about their friend, the Rev Sydney Smith, whom she described as 'the divine Sydney (as my husband calls him to ridicule my passion for him)'. The clergyman and writer – he was the first editor of *The Edinburgh Review* – had moved to London with his wife and children in 1803. In the capital he became well known as a preacher, lecturer and sought-after figure in the social scene. From 1804 to 1806 he gave three series of lectures on moral philosophy at the Royal Institution, which were so highly regarded that the nearby streets became impassable because of the number of carriages assembled there. When possible, Amelia attended the lectures; one evening Smith made particular reference to a poem which he admired – an incident described by his daughter in a memoir of her father:

> These verses alluded to were a beautiful little song of Mrs Opie's, *Go, youth beloved, in distant glades*, and, in a letter to my mother, she gives an amusing account of my father suddenly telling her, as she met him at the entrance of the lecture-room, that he was going

---

* Catherine (née Allen) was Mackintosh's second wife. She was sister to Caroline, wife of Edward Drewe, whose daughter Georgiana would later marry Amelia's cousin Edward Hall Alderson.
† A leader of fashion, known for her eccentricities. Her portrait was painted by Reynolds.

to quote it. She describes the struggle between her timidity and her vanity, whether she should enter; and the new light in which both she and her poem seemed to shine in the eyes of her friends, after this notice of its beauty in his lecture.[4]

In conclusion, Amelia told Lady Mackintosh of her husband's lectures which were due to start 'next month', adding that Mr Coleridge [the poet] was to lecture at the Royal Institution on the relationship between the different fine arts with each other:

...and he has *bargained* with ye management to be allowed in his disquisitions on *painting* to attack the principles of Sir Joshua Reynolds on ye art. I expect much amusement from hearing him....[5]

Opie was expected to give six lectures on painting at Somerset House, the home of the Royal Academy: four were to be delivered in February and March. Although Amelia did not attend the lectures, she took an interest in his work. She had glanced at some parts of his previous lectures before he delivered them at the Royal Institution and later read them herself to her friend the Bishop of Durham [Shute Barrington], who declared Opie was 'a great writer'. As for the Academy lectures, John read each one to her when he had finished it. In order to scotch any suggestion that she had helped him in their writing she asserted:

...let me declare in the most solemn and unequivocal manner, that to my certain knowledge, Mr Opie never received from any human being the slightest assistance whatever in the composition of his lectures.[6]

The first lecture was delivered on Monday, February 16th. He was congratulated by his fellow artists, then escorted home to his proud wife by Sir William Beechey. The next three lectures – on successive Mondays – were also very well received. Prince Hoare, editor of *The Artist*, had asked Opie to write a piece for publication once he had completed the first four lectures, but he had refused, saying he was tired of writing and intended 'to be a gentleman' during the spring months, keep a horse and ride out every day. Amelia felt that that their improved financial circumstances were at last allowing them to have 'more of the comforts and elegancies of life'.

So, although worn out by his work on the lectures and busy with commissions for further portraits, Opie was looking forward to taking some time off. There was no pressure to work on the last two lectures – they were not due to be given until the next season. Amelia was happily basking in his success, enjoying her social contacts and keeping an eye on national and local news. On the day of her husband's fourth lecture she wrote to Coke congratulating him on being returned as MP for Norfolk, and also as a member for Derby. She also gave her opinion of a newly-published print of Opie's portrait of Coke:

> I wonder I can feel at all disposed to be cheerful while writing to you, as I am broken-hearted at the ill success of the print [an engraving by Reynolds – one of her fellow guests at Southill], but I expected it – a colourless, grave and black and white representation of you, could never please the Norfolk farmers. I have much to say on the subject, but I dare not say it.[7]

Within a few days Mrs Opie was faced with something much more serious than an unappealing print to cause her heartbreak – John Opie's sudden and inexplicable illness. When he was taken ill a few days after his fourth lecture, there was no hint that he was suffering from anything serious. His friend and former pupil Henry Thomson, now a Royal Academician, told Farington that Opie caught cold after attending an Irish Society dinner held in a badly-heated room, followed by a walk home through the snow. After a few days in bed he got up to work on a portrait of a 16-year-old boy, Peter Wilson,* but after two days had to abandon the project, as his symptoms, including severe back pain, worsened. Leading medical men were summoned to his bedside, but they were unable to determine the precise nature of the illness, which progressed at an alarming rate, leaving the patient delirious for much of the time. Amelia never forgot how solicitous they were, calling two or three times a day to attend to the desperately sick man. She longed for the comfort and medical skills of Dr Alderson, but he was in Norwich at what was believed to be the death bed of his 85-year-old mother. (She pulled through and lived another five years.) He managed to get to London on April 2nd. Thomson reported to Farington that Dr Alderson told him Opie would never recover. What he told his daughter was not recorded, but Thomson was under the impression that neither her father, nor any of the other

---

* The portrait, which had been commissioned by the boy's father, was retained, unfinished, by the family, according to John Jope Rogers in *Opie and His Works*.

medical men told her of their worst fears.

Opie's unmarried sister Elizabeth (known as Betty) made the journey from Cornwall. She had been a second mother to her dearly loved young brother and had visited London only once before, when she stayed with John during his early days in the capital. On that visit she had enjoyed seeing all the sights, returning home full of anecdotes about her adventures. Now, full of fear and dread, she was confined to the house in Berners Street, where her presence was a 'blessing' to her sister-in-law:

> ...that sister so dear to my husband, who, by sharing with me the painful yet precious tasks of affection, enabled me to keep from his bed all hired nurses, all attendants but our deeply interested selves – that was indeed a consolation.[8]

Before Dr Alderson arrived in London, Amelia's cousin Dr Robert Woodhouse – now a distinguished mathematician and fellow of the Royal Society – was also present. He and Thomson, she recalled, 'shared with affectionate solicitude our exertions and our anxieties'. Amelia also appreciated the number of friends and acquaintances who 'thronged our door with inquiries'. From Norwich William Taylor wrote to Southey:

> Mr Opie, who has been at the point of death from abdominal paralysis which Dr Sayers thinks may reasonably be classed with the Devonshire colic, and ascribed to the absorption of the lead vapours to which plumbers and painters often fall victim, begins to amend. Dr Alderson went to London, thought him in danger, advised a change of treatment, from cathartic to strongly stimulant, and has, we hope, given a good turn to the disorder.[9]

Thomson was at the Berners Street house when the 45-year-old Opie died at 4 o'clock in the morning on April 9th. Within a few hours, 'pale and distressed', he was calling on Farington, to whom he gave an account of the artist's last few days, complete with graphic details of his distressing and painful symptoms. The following day [Anthony] Carlisle, the main physician in attendance on Opie, having 'opened the body' that morning, called on Farington to report his findings. He confirmed the condition was an inflammation of the spine which had spread to the bowels and brain. Recalling her husband's decline, Amelia wrote of the early stages of his illness, when fellow artists were asking – should he recover – for Opie to be given time to complete his pictures at Somerset House before the opening of the annual exhibition. Northcote was one visitor. She was delighted to hear the two men in conversation, hoping that John's mental powers 'remaining so vigorous and unimpaired' meant he might also recover his physical strength:

> But in a very few hours more, I saw than fine mind completely overthrown, and learned to feel in all its acuteness the bitterness of disappointed hope.[10]

She described the visits from Thomson and his offer to complete any pictures which her husband wished to submit for the exhibition. Thomson, in his account to Farington of these events, said Opie wanted him to apply some finishing touches to his portrait of [Prince William Frederick] the Duke of Gloucester. When he took the portrait into the dying man's bedroom, Opie was delirious and Thomson could make no sense of what he was saying; he completed the picture and took it to the Academy, believing it to be one of Opie's best. Amelia, with her novelist's eye, gave this account of the Thomson episode:

> On Saturday morning (the day on which the pictures were to be delivered at Somerset House) Mr Thomson brought the portrait of the Duke to the foot of the bed; and though the delirium attending Mr Opie's complaint was then begun, 'the ruling passion strong in death' conquered it awhile, and he made his remarks on what his friend had done for him, as clearly and as justly as if he had been in perfect health. 'I think,' said he, 'there is not colour enough in the background.' Mr Thomson owned the justice of the remark, and having added more colour brought it again to the room. Mr Opie then looked at it with the greatest satisfaction, and said, with a smile, 'It will do now. Take it away. It will do now. Indeed, if you can't do it, nobody can.'[11]

Much of the gossip among the Opies' friends in the days following his death concerned the fact that he was to be buried at St Paul's. Farington was of the opinion that the decision was a result of 'the *vanity* of Mrs Opie'. She said she was influenced by Betty's recollection that at the time of Sir Joshua Reynolds's funeral at the Cathedral her brother had declared he, too, would be buried there. Amelia believed that the bereaved should hold such wishes as sacred. John Penwarne, the eldest son of one of Opie's earliest Cornish patrons, undertook to make the arrangements, sending out black-edged invitation cards:

The honor [sic] of your Attendance is requested on Monday next, the 20th instant, at twelve o'clock, to Assist at the Funeral of the late John Opie, Esq., Professor in Painting to the Royal Academy. You are desired to be at eleven o'clock, at 8, Berners-Street, from whence the Funeral will proceed to St Paul's. *

The funeral guests were treated to wine and cake at the Opie house before proceeding to the Cathedral. According to Earland, 'mutes' took up positions at the front door of the house and stood there in attitudes of dejection. Mutes was the term used for men hired by undertakers to act as official mourners. Six of them, carrying black staves, and walking two by two, headed the Opie funeral procession to St Paul's from Berners Street – a distance of well over two miles. They were followed by the undertaker on horseback and then eight more horsemen, riding two by two. Then came another mute holding a funeral banner, with a page walking on either side of him. The hearse, pulled by six black horses was next, followed by three mourning coaches, each also pulled by six horses. The first two held the pall-bearers, who included Samuel Whitbread and William Smith, the Norwich MP, whose portrait Opie had painted a few years earlier. The third coach was occupied by Dr Alderson, Dr Woodhouse, Thomson and Penwarne. Then came 27 mourning coaches, each pulled by two horses, and carrying eminent artists and other friends of Opie. The rear of the procession consisted of 30 private carriages belonging to noblemen and gentlemen who had chosen to pay their respects. Among these was the Duke of Gloucester, whose portrait had just been accepted for the Academy summer exhibition. Years later Amelia recalled that she had looked on Gloucester as 'a kind friend':

> He dictated to me such a pretty note when I lost my husband saying he was sorry for his early removal, but was glad to have known a man whose talents he so much admired and whose character he respected, and that he was pleased to find that Royal etiquette would allow of his letting his carriage follow in ye procession to his funeral. The duke's carriage brought up ye rear.[12]

Two London city marshals on horseback, in full uniform with black sashes, met the procession at Temple Bar gate, from where they rode to the Cathedral in front of the mute carrying the banner. The six pall-

---

* Card with the name *Rev'd Mr Giddy* handwritten on the back. (BL, Opie, John, RP 3144)

bearers carried the coffin into the building. After the service Opie was laid to rest in the crypt next to the remains of Reynolds. The stone marking the spot names him as 'John Opie, Esq. Member of and Professor of Painting to The Royal Academy of Painting Sculpture and Architecture'.* His fellow Academician Benjamin West was buried in the same crypt thirteen years later. The funeral expenses were borne by the widow who found the occasion all she could wish for:

> *I bless God* that *I* was *able* to bury him there! – Nor shall I ever cease to remember with gratitude and satisfaction the long and honourable procession which attended him thither! So general seemed the wish to do his memory honour by such an attendance, that, of those who were invited to attend, scarcely any sent a refusal.[13]

A few days later Amelia's pride in her husband's status was gratified by *The Artist*, published on Saturday, April 25th, and inscribed to John Opie's memory 'amidst the united sorrow, affection, and respect, of those who were his associates'. Prince Hoare opened his biographical account by stating that few men had attained eminence by a more irregular course of study, by stronger native endowments or by more determined industry than 'the great painter whose name at this moment inspires public regret'. Benjamin West, the Academy President, contributed a piece on Opie's merits in painting; Northcote praised the late artist's intellectual powers and indefatigable industry, saying 'he did not so much paint to live, as live to paint'; there was a tribute poem from M[artin] A[rcher] Shee, a fellow Academician and aspiring poet, a brief memoir by Elizabeth Inchbald and a letter from the biographer and playwright James Boaden, praising Opie's 'frank, open conduct' and 'noble simplicity'.

Inchbald wrote in her diary[14] that she had spent 'all day' [Sunday April 19th] trying to write her piece on Opie. She completed it the next morning. The day was 'gloomy and very cold' and at two o'clock, she noted, 'his grand funeral passed'. (Inchbald was at that time living in an attic above a milliner's shop in the Strand.) She was relieved that Hoare sent her a note of 'high praise of my character of Opie'. She kept in close contact with Amelia over the next few weeks, exchanging notes and paying calls.

Farington and his friends continued to gossip quite unkindly about Opie, the general opinion being that the artist had been parsimonious and had never revealed to his wife the extent of his income. After his

---

* The stone gives the incorrect date of April 29 for Opie's death.

death, according to Thomson, a £50 note and a £10 note were found in 'a dirty cupboard' and 195 guineas in gold were found in an old rag among lumber in a closet. (Whatever Opie's estate was worth, he died intestate and Amelia was obliged to apply for letters of administration,[15] which eventually saw his personal estate of cash and stock accounts shared between his widow, sister, nephews and nieces.) Disposing of John's works and effects was a time-consuming business, but she had the support of Betty Opie who stayed on at Berners Street until everything was concluded. Amelia enlisted the help of Thomson, who was, where possible, to complete unfinished works, while she herself dealt with other matters:

> Mr Coxe has been requested by Mr Thomson to call on me...to consult with me about the disposal of the house &c. About y pictures which Mr Thomson is to finish we cannot, you know, write yet. Tomorrow I hope to make out a list of those to be written to as debters [sic] and to take away their pictures.[16]

The sale of Opie pictures, which took place on June 6th, attracted substantial crowds. Farington believed it made £1386, with the top price of £136 10s paid for *Clothing the Naked*. Earland traced many of the items sold on that day, three of which had been exhibited at the Academy and fetched up to 65 guineas. The most modest sum, £1 6s, was paid for a picture entitled *Old Man and Child*. A portrait of Elizabeth Inchbald went for 5½ guineas. The sitter recorded in her diary that 'Mrs Opie called to tell me Mr Harris* had bought my Picture.' At the sale of Opie's effects 'everything went for high prices', according to Farington. The lease on the house in Berners Street was sold to James Lonsdale, another portrait painter. Betty Opie went home to Cornwall and Amelia left London to make her home once more with her father in Norwich.

---

* Probably Thomas Harris, the manager of Covent Garden theatre, with whom Inchbald had worked as an actress.

Chapter Eighteen

W hile Amelia was dealing with the aftermath of John's death, Susannah Taylor was penning a piece on her friend for the June edition of *The Cabinet* (subtitled *Monthly Report of Polite Literature*), a new periodical which was launched in February that year (1807). Previously there had been articles on Amelia in the *Ladies Monthly Magazine* (1801) and the *European Magazine* (1803). Susannah's *Mrs Opie* was headed with an engraving from one of Opie's portraits:

This engraving by R.Cooper, from a painting by John Opie, was published in February, 1821, for *La Belle Assemblée*, a fashionable women's magazine, which had an article on Mrs Opie. The location of the original painting is not recorded by Jope Rogers or Earland.

The portrait which we here present to the public, is peculiarly valuable, as it exhibits a characteristic resemblance of a lady who is no less admired as a writer, than beloved as a friend and companion. Seldom have the graces of person, mind, and manner, been more happily united, or their attractive influence more generally felt and acknowledged. How much are the feelings with which we view a likeness so interesting in itself, increased from the recollection that

it was traced by a hand eminently calculated to do justice to the
subject, both by nature and by circumstances, and that this hand,
alas! can trace no more....

In her own house, where Mr Opie's incomparable talents drew a
constant succession of the learned, the gay, and the fashionable, she
delighted all by the sweetness of her manners, and the unstudied
and benevolent politeness with which she adapted herself to the
taste of each individual.*

Following an assessment of her friend's character and accomplishments, Susannah affirmed that those who knew Mrs Opie well were
confident that the conduct which had preserved her character 'un-
spoiled' through the brilliant periods of her life, would dignify and
support her in her 'hour of trial'. This belief in her friend's resilience
and good nature was confirmed in a letter she received from Sir James
Mackintosh, commenting on the news of Opie's death which had
reached him in Bombay:

> Assure Mrs Opie of our sympathy. Her grief will be deprived of its
> bitterness by her mild and cheerful nature; and she will find the
> most powerful resource in her charming talents; but I do not expect
> that she should ever cease to think with tenderness of such a mind,
> as that to which she was associated.[1]

Amelia herself was busy writing to friends and colleagues of her late
husband. Before returning to Norwich she wrote to Northcote, thanking him for his condolences, sharing her sense of loss and ruminating
upon her future path.

> You, I am sure, can readily enter into the feelings which have made
> me at this most trying moment of my life cling more to those who
> loved and esteemed *him*, than my own particular friends, and which
> urge me to set a value on their goodwill and approbation beyond
> that of all the world beside. He always regarded you as his sincere
> friend, and your conduct has always proved you so.... I agree with
> you that *occupation* is the best cure for grief... and when I reach
> my father's house (the only proper place for me for some months
> to come) I shall endeavour to comfort myself in my usual pursuits
> though in so doing I shall feel more than ever the loss I have sus-
> tained, as I had implicit reliance on his judgment and submitted

---

* *The Cabinet*, 2 June, 1807, pp.217-19. The writer was not named but Brightwell credited Mrs Taylor (*Memorials*, p.33)

what I wrote to his observations only.... Do not suppose that I can ever exist long out of London. It was always *dear* to me and is now dearer than ever perhaps from associations *never to be destroyed* and which, though now painful, will in time become pleasant. In the spring months, therefore, I shall always be in Town, and happy to see you. Forgive me for having intruded so long on your time, but I am alone, driven from my own house by the crowd collected to view the pictures, and writing to one who sympathizes with me has relieved my mind.[2]

The new widow did not resume fiction writing for the time being, but worked instead on her second book of poems, *The Warrior's Return*, which was brought out in the spring of 1808. It was widely reviewed by leading literary journals and a second edition appeared later in the year. Opinions were a mixture of praise and censure, as in the *Eclectic Review* of March 1809: expressing disappointment that the new collection was not up to the standard of the 1802 *Poems*, the writer decided that the principal merits of Mrs Opie's poetry were 'elegance and tenderness' and its principal faults 'feebleness and insipidity'. However, the reviewer was very taken by the 'exquisitely delicate and touching' love poems.

Amelia explained in an introduction that the verses, with two or three exceptions, had been written several years ago 'and to arrange and fit them for publication has been the amusement of many hours of retirement'. The new volume contained several songs written to specific 'airs' in association with her composer friend Edmund Biggs; the title piece, *The Warrior's Return*, one of three narrative poems, told of the fate awaiting a Crusader on his homecoming, The frontispiece, drawn by the faithful Thomson and engraved by Reynolds, depicted a death scene from the ballad *Julia*, which told the tragic story of a lovesick girl confined to a convent. There was also one poem about slavery, *The Lucayan's Song*. Having read an account of the history of the West Indies by Bryan Edwards, a politician who supported the slave trade, Amelia focused on the plight of the Lucayans who were lured by the Spanish from their settlements in the Bahamas to Hispaniola in the Caribbean – said to be the homeland of their ancestors – where they were put to work as slaves. By the time this anti-slavery poem was published the British Government's Abolition Bill was taking effect. Passed on March 25th, 1807, it decreed that from January 1st, 1808, it would be unlawful for any British ship to participate in the Atlantic slave trade. Amelia would have applauded the bill, but when it was announced she was fully preoccupied with the terminal illness of her husband.

Three of the poems in the new volume were first published in a 1799 anthology which was set up and edited by Southey, at the suggestion of William Taylor.[3] One of these bore the title *To Mr Opie, on his having painted for me the picture of Mrs Twiss* – a tribute to the artist for his portrait of Amelia's friend Fanny. In *The Warrior's Return* the poem appeared under the title *Lines written in 1799*, with no naming of either artist or sitter. Extolling the 'glowing art' of the painter and rejoicing in the 'semblance' of 'the friend I love', it concludes with a neat summary of the conflicting emotions which the portrait inspires:

> Now, pleased I mark the painter's skilful line,
> And now, rejoice the skill I mark is *thine*:
> And while I prize the gift by thee bestow'd,
> My heart proclaims, I'm of the giver proud.
> Thus pride and friendship war with equal strife,
> And now the friend exults, and now the wife.[4]

Amelia retained the much-loved portrait for the rest of her life, bequeathing it to Fanny's eldest daughter Frances, also known as Fanny. According to Inchbald's diary, Amelia was in London during February and March – possibly to be near at hand when the final touches were made to her book of poems. Back home in Norwich she wrote to Inchbald with the news that Caroline Twiss, the third of Fanny's four daughters, was said to be dying. As close friends of Fanny, both women were deeply distressed when the 15-year-old Caroline died a few weeks later.

Amelia spent much of 1808 working on a memoir of her husband, at the request of Prince Hoare who was putting together John Opie's four Academy lectures for publication. She struggled to do justice to her subject, aware that critics might think her over-prejudiced in his favour. As reached the end of the task she received a letter from an old friend of John's, expressing his thoughts on her husband's life and character. She wrote back asking if she might quote some of his words in her memoir, adding:

> The greater part of my little work is nearly ready for the press and I am now copying out and correcting the *remainder*. But for *days* I have been incapable of writing, or doing anything, as I am sub-

A bronze portrait medallion of Amelia, made by David d'Angers when he befriended her in Paris in the summer of 1829. At that time at least four foundries were casting his medallions. (Private collection)

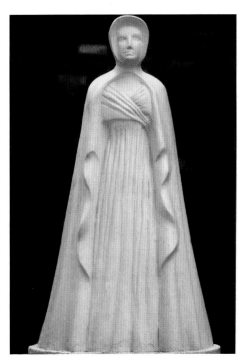

A statue of Amelia Opie on top of business premises in the Norwich street which bears her name. It was commissioned and erected by the Leicester Permanent Building Society which occupied the premises in 1956. J.P.Chaplin, a city architect, designed the figure; Z.Leon carved it in wood from which a mould was taken to cast the statue in artificial stone.

Amelia in her Quaker dress and bonnet, painted by her cousin Henry Perronet Briggs. It was shown in the Royal Academy summer exhibition of 1832. (Private collection. Photograph by Alan Howard.)

A double portrait of Amelia – two versions of which were painted by her husband. Earland listed both in her appendix and used one – at that time (1911) owned by Elizabeth Amelia Carr (née Briggs) and in poor condition – as an illustration. Both Earland and Jope Rogers understood that the two women in the portrait were Amelia, the information having come from Mrs Carr, who received the painting from her uncle Tom Alderson. That painting is now owned by the National Trust and captioned – erroneously it would seem – as being portraits of Amelia and her sister-in-law Elizabeth Opie. (Lander Gallery, Truro)

John Opie's portrait of Amelia. She told Dawson Turner it was painted soon after they were married – begun in May and finished in July, 1798. (National Portrait Gallery)

A plaster copy of the bronze medallion of Amelia made by David d'Angers, who was known to give plaster or wax copies of his bronze medallions to friends. It is thought that this one was owned by Amelia. (Private collection)

A silhouette of Amelia, when she was Miss Alderson. It is probably the one she mentions in a letter from London to Susannah Taylor in August, 1794, in which she says she had been to Mrs.Betham's 'to have my profile taken'. Isabella Betham (also known as Beetham) was regarded as the finest women profilist (silhouette maker) of the 18th century. She painted the faces all black, but did the hair and dress in exquisitely fine brushwork, as seen here. (Norfolk Record Office: MC 2784/G/1)

The bust of Amelia in white marble by the French sculptor and medallist David d'Angers. When the bust was delivered to her Norwich home in a crate from Paris in 1836, she dared not open it for three weeks fearing it would be 'frightful'. (Norwich Castle Museum and Art Gallery)

The petition for abolishing the slave trade. An illustration in Amelia's didactic poem for children, *The Black Man's Lament*, published in 1826.

Portrait of Amelia's distinguished ancestor Augustine Briggs (1617-1684), who was Mayor of Norwich in 1670 and MP for the city four times. In his will he made bequests to several charities which helped the poor and needy. (Norwich Castle Museum and Art Gallery: Civic Portrait)

The second John Opie portrait of Dr Alderson. Amelia bequeathed it to her cousin Sir Edward Hall Alderson. It was acquired in 1871 by Charles Williams, a surgeon at the Norfolk & Norwich Hospital (1869-1906), who was making a collection to celebrate the hospital's centenary. The portrait used to hang in the boardroom of the old hospital. (Norfolk & Norwich University Hospital Archive. Photograph by Alan Howard)

The statue of Amelia's uncle Dr John Alderson, which inspired a poem published in *Lays for the Dead*. Its first site was the old Hull General Infirmary where Alderson was a physician for many years; it now stands in the grounds of Hull Royal Infirmary.

John Opie's portrait of his only sister Elizabeth, who bequeathed it to a nephew. She helped Amelia to care for John during his terminal illness. (Lander Gallery, Truro)

One of the many John Opie self-portraits held in galleries and private collections. (Lander Gallery, Truro)

Amelia's cousin Margaret Thompson (née Alderson) with her first daughter Philothea in a portrait by Henry Perronet Briggs. (Private ownership. Photograph by Richard Alderson Scott)

A John Opie portrait of Amelia's cousin Ollyett Woodhouse, the eldest son of her aunt Judith (née Alderson) and Robert Woodhouse. Born in the same year and brought up in Norwich, the two were good friends. Opie did two portraits and several sketches of Ollyett. (Photograph by A. C. Cooper (Colour) Ltd)

Painted by T.J.W. MD.   Engraved by Robt Cooper, Historical & Portrait Engraver, Union Place Norwich.

Robert Alderson, Esqre

RECORDER OF IPSWICH, YARMOUTH & NORWICH.

Published 1828 by William Freeman, London Lane, Norwich.

Amelia's uncle Robert Alderson, who was ordained as a nonconformist minister, but re-signed at the age of 34 to train for the legal profession. He became Recorder of Ipswich, Yarmouth and Norwich. Line & stipple engraving by Robert Cooper, after T.J.W(oodhouse), published by William Freeman, Norwich, 1828. (Norfolk County Council Library & Information Service)

Amelia's cousin, Edward Hall Alderson, eldest son of Robert Alderson and his first wife Elizabeth (née Hurry). He and Amelia enjoyed a life-long friendship. Line engraving by William Skelton, after Henry Perronet Briggs, published by William Johnstone White, 1832.

Benjamin Haydon's painting of the Anti-Slavery Society Convention in London in 1840. The standing figure is Thomas Clarkson, who presided, giving his blessing on the opening day. Amelia Opie is seen on the right (second in on the second row) in her distinctive high Quaker bonnet. The white-haired gentleman, first left on the front row, is Samuel Gurney. Thomas Fowell Buxton is first left on the second row from the top left back row. (National Portrait Gallery)

Bust of Dr Edward Rigby by Pellegrino Mazzotti. It used to stand in the library of the old Norfolk & Norwich Hospital. (Norfolk & Norwich University Hospital Archive. Photograph by Alan Howard)

John Opie's second portrait of Mary Wollstonecraft, painted when she was pregnant with her daughter Mary, whose birth cost her mother her life. William Godwin, the grieving husband, kept the portrait in his study. (National Portrait Gallery)

Mezzotint by S.W.Reynolds, after John Opie's first portrait of Samuel Whitbread, the brewer and politician. Reynolds was a house guest when the Opies stayed with the Whit-breads at Southill in 1806. (National Portrait Gallery)

Daguerreotype of Joseph John Gurney, his third wife Eliza, son John Henry and daughter Anna, taken on a visit to Paris, where they met Jean-Gabriel Eynard, a Swiss-born banker, who joined them for religious meetings. He was one of the first exponents of the early photographic process from its development in 1839. J.J.Gurney noted the taking of the daguerreotype in his journal of 15 May, 1843. (Special Collections, Haverford College, Haverford, Pennsylvania)

Anna Gurney, who lived at Northrepps Cottage with her cousin Sarah Buxton. Both women were dear friends of Amelia, who stayed with them at least once or twice a year. (Private collection)

Portrait of Hudson Gurney in 1838, when he was 63, by Amelia's cousin Henry Perronet Briggs, who also painted Hudson's wife Margaret. (Private collection. Photograph by Alan Howard)

John Opie's 1799 portrait of Hudson Gurney, aged 24. He also painted Hudson's sister Agatha Hanbury. (Private collection. Photograph by Alan Howard)

Portrait of Joseph John Gurney. Artist unknown. The backing bears a pencil-written note: 'painted by an Italian who came to Norwich when JJG was a young man'. (Private collection. Photograph by Alan Howard)

Hand coloured photograph of Sir Thomas Fowell Buxton by T.R.Williams. (Private collection)

The Octagon Chapel in Colegate where Amelia Alderson was baptised. It was opened in 1756 by the Society of Protestant Dissenters and later became the Octagon Unitarian Church.

The Quaker burial ground, where Amelia was interred in her father's grave in 1853. The adjacent Gildencroft Meeting House was destroyed in the Norwich Blitz of 1942.

The house in the parish of St Clement, Colegate, where the widowed Amelia lived with her father. Later it was taken over as St Clement's Rectory; now it is used as offices.

ject to violent depressions *now* which my cheerful mind and happy temper had hitherto exempted me from, which are long, severe and only too frequent.[5]

She asked her correspondent if she might include the epitaph he had written on Opie. Her letter was addressed to 'Dear Sir' – and the envelope has not survived – but the recipient can be identified as John Taylor. Their friendship had cooled after Opie's divorce – Taylor was critical of his neglect of his first wife – but the two men were reconciled before the artist died, much to Amelia's satisfaction:

> I cannot sufficiently express to you how gratified I was by your letter – nor are you at all aware of the *service* which it is capable of rendering me. I certainly do not want to have the *various* merits of my husband pointed out to me, as no one *could*, no one *did* appreciate them more fully, or more truly: therefore, so far, your observations, just and well expressed as they are, were unnecessary, but think how valuable they must be to me if given to the public (part of them I mean) in *corroboration* of what *I* have already said on y same subject! *Mine*, you know, must be considered as a *partial* eye – how satisfactory then, would it be to me, to insert with your name to them, testimonials to Mr Opie's worth and powers all tending to prove what I myself have asserted.[6]

Her approach was successful. Amelia added the 'remarks' – attributed to 'Mr John Taylor' as a substantial footnote in the *Memoir*, describing him as 'a gentleman who possesses great powers of discrimination and had a long and intimate acquaintance with Mr Opie's character'.[7]

She chose to write her memoir as a letter to Hoare in which she explained she had undertaken the task out of sense of duty and in response to the desire of her friends:

> When you first urged me to do, what perhaps I alone am able to do, namely, to give a full and accurate character of a man neither correctly known, nor justly appreciated but by myself, and those who saw him in his most domestic hours, I shrunk with terror from your proposal....
>
> But all selfish considerations were soon annihilated by my wish to fulfil the dearest and the last duty in my power to the husband whom I have lost....[8]

She insisted that it was not possible for her to write 'a biographical

An engraving by S.W. Reynolds of the Opie self-portrait which was used as the preface to Amelia's *Memoir* of her husband.

account'; she was only able to give her observations on the character of Mr Opie. In conclusion she expressed the hope that:

> this public testimony to his virtues, borne by her who knew him and who loved him best, will live, I trust, as a memorial of my gratitude to him for nine years of nearly uninterrupted happiness.[9]

Hoare also decided to include the complete April 1807 tribute edition of *The Artist* in the book. The project attracted an impressive list of more than 200 subscribers, headed by the Duke and Duchess of Gloucester. Bearing the title, *Opie's Lectures on Painting*, it came out in 1809, with a preface to the lectures by Hoare, who assured readers that the manuscripts were entrusted into his care immediately after the artist's decease and that he had reproduced them faithfully. In Bombay, a year later, Mackintosh borrowed a copy of the book from Amelia's cousin Ollyett Woodhouse, and decided that the memoir was 'a pleasing sketch, in one or two parts very elegant; it breathes esteem, admiration and pride'. However, he was more interested in the lectures themselves, declaring:

> I suppose that no nation can produce two painters who have written so well on their art as [Sir Joshua] Reynolds and Opie, whom,

before I have heard the opinion of anyone else, I boldly or rashly venture to class together.[10]

In the spring of 1809 Amelia accepted an invitation to stay with her uncle Dr John Alderson in Hull. Her father's youngest brother, John's initial medical training was in Norwich under James's supervision. As a lieutenant and medical officer to the West Norfolk Militia, he moved to Hull in 1780, later continuing his training in medicine in Edinburgh and Aberdeen. Having married a Yorkshire girl, he settled in Hull where he became physician to Hull General Infirmary and a leading figure in many of the town's educational and literary organisations. The visit in March and April established solid friendships between Amelia and the Alderson cousins, particularly Margaret, the only daughter and her widowed uncle's youngest child. (His wife, Sarah, had given birth to 11 children, of whom only five survived infancy, she herself dying of consumption in 1805.)

John was a generous host to his widowed niece, as Amelia recounted to Opie's fellow Academician Thomas Phillips:

> ...if the most flattering attention and constant enjoyments and the society of an uncle who never thinks he can do too much to shew [sic] that he takes both pleasure, and pride in me can endear a residence, Hull ought to be very dear to me....
>
> On y 6th or 7th of April my uncle gives a grand ball at y public rooms to y Hull and Beverley people. I have been at one assembly here and one at Beverley last Wednesday. I danced till 1 o'clock then set off for York with my uncle who was subpoenaed on a trial, got there at five, went to bed till eight, was in court by *nine* and remained there till eight at night!!! Such a day of fatigue and after a night of exertion! However, I am now recovered from it. On Friday we go to a ball at Beverley given by one of y first families there on the coming of age of an only son, heir to three fortunes and on his safe return from Corunna.[11]

The group of literary and theatrical friends with whom Amelia had associated during her visits to London in the 1790s had long since broken up, as people moved on and lifestyles changed. While she was staying in Hull she learned of the death of Thomas Holcroft. His wealthy Norfolk son-in-law, William Tooke Harwood, was in attendance during the writer's terminal illness, about which he wrote to Amelia. He said he knew her 'kind hearted feelings' would make her anxious to be informed of all the circumstances surrounding the last days. Holcroft, he said, had wished to see Godwin, from whom he had been estranged for four years, and 'all his friends that could be sent to'. Godwin did call on the dying man, but Amelia was far from London:

> The short farewell* that he desired might be delivered to you I inclose [sic] herewith – I am sure it would have been a great consolation to him if he could have seen you.[12]

Harwood said that plans were in hand for the upbringing and education of Holcroft's children and he knew the family could depend on Amelia's 'kind and benevolent interference' should it be needed in this context. He added he would be sending Carlisle's notes on the postmortem examination to 'your worthy father Dr Alderson'.

From Hull Amelia went north to Durham to meet her cousins Thomas, Sarah and Elizabeth Alderson. They were the offspring of her father's brother Thomas, a merchant, who had settled first in Newcastle; in 1789, at the age of 44, he married Sarah Boulby, a young woman from North Shields, but died nine years later. The couple had moved to County Durham and lived near to Sarah's sister Elizabeth, who was married to the Rev Dickens Hazlewood, a minor canon of Durham Cathedral. As the widowed Sarah developed mental health problems and became increasingly unstable the Hazlewoods became surrogate parents to the young Aldersons. Amelia enjoyed the visit to Durham, where she established lasting relationships with the cousins, as she had done in Hull.

Before returning home, she went to London for a few weeks, where, at one gathering, she was introduced to Lady Charleville, a well read and sociable woman who was to become a friend. Catherine Maria (née Dawson) – only seven years older than Amelia – was first married to a Lincolnshire landowner by whom she had two children; after his death she married Charles William Bury, Lord Tullamore, who became the 1st Earl of Charleville in 1798. She met Amelia while staying at her London residence; returning to her husband's estate in Ireland in August, she responded with enthusiasm to a letter from her new friend:

> I did not expect that you could find leisure to write to me before your return to Norwich, and I feel more obliged by your not delaying it long after, than I can easily express. Your amiable, mod-

---

* The 'short farewell' has not survived.

est manners, joined to talents far beyond the pretensions of most women, attracted me immediately; and all I have seen of you, permit me to say, has so confirmed this first bias, that I do feel a sincere wish to continue to cultivate the acquaintance I have so happily begun.[13]

Saying she was awaiting with impatience the arrival of Amelia's 'latest publication' (presumably the Opie memoir), Lady Charleville urged her to begin a good, long novel, as she had the 'principles and fancy to compose an elevating and interesting work'. Her hopes were realised. The next Opie novel, *Temper, or Domestic Scenes*, was published in three volumes in 1812, by which time she had settled happily with her father in Norwich. When she decided to live with him permanently he took over a substantial house in Colegate, opposite St Clement's Church, from where he continued his medical practice until he was well into his seventies.

Chapter Nineteen

Amelia's long widowhood was dismissed by one writer as 'a plain life of such conspicuous virtue that it was written up as a religious tract'.[1] Perhaps the so-called 'religious tract' was Brightwell's second biography[2]. According to its preface, it was 'the record of Mrs Opie's religious history' and, indeed, it focused on the period following John's death.

An 1803 engraving by William Ridley, after an Opie portrait of Amelia, for the *European Magazine*. It was used as the frontispiece for Brightwell's *Memoir of Amelia Opie*, published by the Religious Tract Society in 1857. The original portrait is on display at Trerice, a National Trust property in Cornwall.

However, it was some time before Amelia – after much soul searching – chose to join the Religious Society of Friends (Quakers) and attempted to forgo worldly pleasures. She took to spending several weeks in London each summer and visiting friends further afield. Letters to her father abounded with the names of aristocrats, politicians, writers, artists, academics, theatre people, lawyers and preachers with whom she socialised at soirées, balls, assemblies, receptions, lectures and parties. Amelia's reminiscences of the period, written years later, listed names of departed friends and associates which, she said, induced 'an involuntary sadness'. Many of those friends were long forgotten by the time Brightwell produced her first Opie biography.

Whether or not she hoped to marry again is a moot point. Brightwell was circumspect on the matter, referring briefly to a letter to Amelia 'which seems to intimate that it was not *faute de solicitations* that she remained a widow'.[3] Her cousin Margaret's daughter believed she had not turned her back on romance and 'must have been wooed again and again', basing this assumption on several letters to her mother in which the elderly Amelia would refer to the death of an acquaintance, adding 'he was my lover once'. She also recounted what the family knew of a serious suitor: 'She was engaged to a young nobleman of whom we heard with awe that he was deformed like Lord Byron, and like him was something of a rake.[4] Sarah Isabella was told that the young man had stabbed a woman in a fit of temper and left the country, believing he had killed her. The first person he saw on his return to England was the very woman he thought he had murdered.

The young nobleman was Lord Herbert Stuart, a son of John Stuart, first Marquess of Bute. Amelia met him in London in the summer of 1810, when she was 40, and wrote about him at length to Lady Charleville, describing him as a new acquaintance* who 'stays a long time' and who had spent many years in India:

> Errors in early youth, as I have been told, occasioned his being sent to India and his return to England five years ago without y approbation of his father caused him to be *discarded* by this *very relentless* parent as I have heard him called. When parents and children quarrel there are usually faults on both sides, and I dare say my new friend was partly to blame. But I love not y parent that knows not to forgive, and y way in which Lord Herbert Stuart *alludes* to the cruel particulars of his fate and y pernicious effects the circumstances of his life have had on his happiness and character make me listen to, and regard him with pity as well as respect for his talents. He is Lord Bute's second son and *club-footed*.[5]

The friendship developed and became known to Amelia's acquain-

---

* A note, in an unknown hand, attached to the letter reads: 'Mrs Opie 1810, when she first became acquainted with Lord Stuart whom she would have married if her father had not refused his consent.'

tances in Norwich, where the young Harriet Martineau was taking in all the local gossip:

> [she] was very nearly marrying a younger brother of Lord Bute. Lord Herbert Stewart's [sic] carriage appeared, and made a great clatter in the narrow streets of Norwich; and the old gentleman was watched into Dr Alderson's house; and the hours were counted which he spent, it was supposed, at Mrs Opie's feet. But it came to nothing.[6]

Mary Russell Mitford was au fait with the circumstances of the engagement and its ending, as she wrote to her friend the Rev William Harness. She had just read Brightwell's biography of Mrs Opie and was highly critical of many aspects of the work, in particular the omission of the Stuart episode:

> I doubt if it be permissible to ignore so entirely the absolute engagement she was under to marry Lord Herbert Stuart (I forget names, but surely it was Lord Herbert, a lame man). My good old friend Sir William Elford was invited by her to meet him at dinner; at that time all was arranged and the time fixed for the wedding. It went off on agreement, because each had enough to live on – he as a bachelor in lodgings, passing eight months of the year in the country houses of kinsfolk and friends, and she as a poor authoress without the encumbrance of rank; but they could not muster enough to keep house and preserve a certain appearance in days when broughams and pages were not, and horses and men were, essential to an establishment, however modest.[7]

Despite the end of any marriage plans, Amelia kept in touch with Lord Herbert, who wrote to her in November 1814 with news of his father's death in Geneva. The letter, she told her new friend, the poet William Hayley, was:

> ...so full of misery, and torturing suspense as *the contents of the will*, which, as he died abroad, cannot be known of [for] weeks, that I have not been myself since – tho' I feel a degree of *thankfulness*, which I cannot utter in *words* that this event did not happen when my fate would have hung upon it, or when my peace of mind would have been utterly destroyed by the consciousness of the misery of one I loved, pitied, but could not *relieve*. As it is, my pity, and my friendship make me feel for poor Lord H, in a painful degree, especially as I cannot speak one word of comfort to him or save

him in any way. My society would do him good certainly – but that I *cannot* give him – however – he can unload his burthened mind by writing and that I have begged him to do regularly.[8]

In the autumn of 1810 Amelia spent several weeks at Cromer – a favourite place which she associated with memories of her mother. The Gurneys of Earlham Hall often took lodgings there and their cousins also spent time in the area – their uncle Richard being the owner of nearby Northrepps Hall and Northrepps Cottage and their uncle Joseph the owner of a house in Cromer known as The Grove (as was his Norwich home). During her nine years in London as John's wife, Amelia had maintained her association with the Gurneys. By the time she returned to Norwich three more of the Earlham Gurney siblings were married: John Gurney, the eldest brother, to his cousin Elizabeth Gurney of Keswick Old Hall; Hannah Gurney to Thomas Fowell Buxton, who would become a leading figure in the anti-slavery campaign; Louisa to Samuel Hoare, a banker, whose mother was a Gurney. The Hoares also owned a property at Cromer called Cliff House. Dr Alderson's old friend John Gurney died in 1809, leaving his son Joseph John, at 21, the male head of the Earlham household – John and Samuel, the older sons, both having left home.

On her deathbed, Joseph John's mother had spoken of the four-year-old boy as her 'bright morning star'. He was educated at home until he was 15, when he was sent to a tutor at Oxford. Although a conscientious student, with a particular interest in the study of Latin, Greek and Hebrew, as a member of a non-conformist religious group he was not able to take a university degree. Prone to rigorous self-examination, he was a deeply committed Christian and close to his sister Elizabeth Fry, eight years his senior. When he returned home he went to work in the family bank. In 1811 he was one of the co-founders of the Norwich Bible Society, which held its first meeting in St Andrew's Hall. Amelia's solicitor Thomas Brightwell, who had settled in the city on his marriage to Mary Wilkin, was at the meeting, according to his daughter Cecilia:

> ... then were seen for the first time, united for one great object in the spirit of Christian union – Churchmen and Dissenters, Bishop [Henry] Bathurst presided; and co-religionists of various shades of opinion joined hand in hand. Earlham Hall was made the head-quarters of the deputation; and Mr Joseph John Gurney, the be-loved and honoured host, gathered around him a numerous circle

of friends to share in the pleasures of holy intercourse and Christian fellowship. Of his favoured company, my dear father was one.... Mr Gurney showed my father much kindness from the first of their intercourse. They frequently met at the house of Mrs Opie.[9]

Signed pencil drawing of Joseph John Gurney by Amelia Opie. She made several copies of her drawing of him; this one was a gift to her friend Mary Margaret Fisk (née Eaton). (Norfolk Record Office: ACC 2002/229 Box 9, Album M.M Fisk)

After writing the memoir of her husband, Amelia turned her attention once more to fiction. *Temper, or Domestic Scenes*[10] explored the damage caused by uncontrollable temper and was more didactic than anything she had previously written. Its heroine, Emma, does not take centre stage until the reader has been given the story of the life and early death of her wretched mother – victim of a childhood in which her bad temper was not corrected. By then Emma has been received into the care of her repentant grandmother and exposed to the worthy example of Mr Egerton, a good Christian man who becomes her mentor. Young Emma struggles to behave well; she is helped by Henry St Aubyn, her fellow pupil, an exemplary young man whose filial duty to his feckless mother is unbelievably virtuous. The ups and downs of their relationship are told in a series of 'domestic scenes' which feature a succession of characters and incidents designed to show the importance of cultivating a good temper. Egerton's role in the narrative appears to be that of the moral watchdog, repeatedly adopting a preaching tone to expiate on the author's theme. Much of the action takes place in and around Paris, with descriptions of places which Amelia had visited with her husband.

Most reviewers, although commending some aspects of the work, such as her powers of observation, were more critical than enthusiastic and some found much of the plot absurd. Nevertheless, the novel sold well and ran to three editions within a matter of months. It was also translated and published in French under the title *Emma et St Aubin*. Amelia spent much of 1812 away from home, describing herself as 'a great wanderer' in a letter to her Durham cousin Thomas Alderson, whom she always called Tom. She journeyed to Malvern, Cheltenham and the Wye Valley 'with companions who suited me'. Returning to Malvern, she received news of the death of her 90-year-old paternal grandmother, who lived with her unmarried daughter Elizabeth. She set off immediately for home, where, she told Tom: 'I had the pleasure to find my father and aunt much better than I expected.[11] How sad it was, she continued, that Tom and his sister Sarah, apart from Amelia herself, were the only of the aunt's nephews and nieces who thought it 'proper' to write to her on this occasion. It was important to be 'alive to these attentions'; Amelia chose to go on paying attention – in both practical and emotional ways – to this difficult spinster aunt (only 14 years her senior) until her death in 1848, at the age of 93.

Amelia had no idea that her new novel was to be the means of establishing a fascinating friendship with William Hayley, who lived in the coastal village of Felpham in Sussex. Born into a wealthy family, Hayley hoped to make a career as a playwright, but failing distinction in that field he turned to poetry and then biography, his works on the poets Milton and Cowper being well received. He became a generous patron of William Blake and friends with the artists George Romney and Joseph Wright. His childless marriage was an unhappy one and ended acrimoniously in 1795. He was devoted to his illegitimate son, born in 1780, to the daughter of his former nurse, and suffered intense grief when the boy died at the age of 19. In 1809, 12 years after the death of his first wife, Hayley married again – a woman 36 years his junior – but they separated after three years.

In the closing scenes of *Temper*, the grandmother quotes lines from Hayley's poem *The Triumphs of Temper* which stress the importance of good temper. First published in 1781, it was the poet's most popular work and was already in its 13th edition. In six cantos it tells how Serena, the heroine, triumphs over all setbacks and dangers by mastering her temper. Amelia's reference to his work was made known to the poet, who was at that time revising it for a new edition. He decided to insert some new lines into his poem, in which Serena, a voracious reader, extolls the glory of the female pen:

And with this glory, in her fond esteem,
Her friend, the graceful Opie, shone supreme.

In January 1813, Hayley ordered that a copy of the new (14th) edition should be sent to Mrs Opie. In a fulsome acknowledgement of his gift, Amelia told the 67-year-old that his was one of the first books of poetry she had read aloud to her mother, who held up its heroine as a model for imitation:

Every succeeding year has confirmed the judgment of my childhood, and my youth relative to this immortal work; and though I am well acquainted with *all* your writings, and feel for them the admiration which they deserve, still, owing perhaps to many affectionate and grateful associations *The Triumph of Temper* retains the *first* place in my regard and I read it through every year.

Judge then, Sir, what pleasure I must have felt on receiving 'from the author' the new edition of this poem containing not only an elegant, but a most flattering and *well-imagined* compliment to myself![12]

The poet lost no time in replying, telling Amelia that her letter was 'cordial to my heart' and had induced in him a wish that their sentiments of 'reciprocal literary esteem' might ripen into confidential friendship. He believed that they had both experienced 'mighty joy and mighty woe' but he hoped her afflictions had been tempered by the kindness of providence:

It would be a high Gratification to me to be informed by your own Hand that you are now as free from oppressive troubles of every Kind as I most heartily wish you to be and I confess from an interested Motive namely that your admirable Faculties may continue to exercise and unfold themselves in new Volumes, which will interest, improve and delight the Heart like your novel entitled *Temper*.

Signing himself her 'friend and admirer', Hayley added a postscript, saying he was a confirmed hermit and seldom roved out of his cell and garden:

> I shall therefore pray that my good Stars may in some propitious Season lead you to our Sussex Coast that I may have the Gratification of giving you a personal Benediction before I vanish from the Earth.[13]

Although delighted with Hayley's prompt response, Amelia delayed writing to him again for 13 months. When at last she put pen to paper early in 1814, she explained, rather cryptically, that she had been unable to reply immediately:

> I *could* not, *dared* not answer one question in it, and therefore I forbore to write at all, looking forward however every day with sure and certain hope to the hour when, without any conscious or conscientious misgivings, I could sit down to write to you, and repay your kind anxiety, by saying 'Yes, dear Sir, I *am* happy'.[14]

However, she told him that her three months in London that summer had been happy. In June, her collection of short stories, *Tales of Real Life*,[15] was published in three volumes. Mary Russell Mitford, also staying in town, wrote to a friend that she had seen Mrs Opie: 'She looks, I think, very ill – thinner, paler, and much older, but was, as she always is, very kind and pleasant'.[16] Later, Mitford wrote to the same friend saying she had just read the first volume of the Opie stories and found it 'much better than *Temper*'. Reviewers, too, approved of the new tales, which dealt with lives blighted by deceit, lies and immoral behaviour. *Austin and his Wife* – almost a companion piece to *Temper* – told of the fatal consequences of a doting mother's failure to discipline her son. The writer in *Critical Review* (August, 1813) singled it out as 'a melancholy tale' but 'fraught with so many important truths', that it required him to give a full account of the narrative. This he did over several pages, complete with substantial excerpts from the story, concluding that 'the necessity of bringing up children in a strict adherence to truth could not well be more forcibly exemplified than in the above tale'.

It was during her time in London that Amelia met Madame de Staël, the writer, opponent of Bonaparte and society hostess, whom she found 'a woman of excelling genius and winning manners'. In one of many recollections of that period she wrote of attending a soirée given by the Frenchwoman at which the guests were 'the *elite* of London society', a brilliant group whose wit 'called forth the ever-ready repartees, and almost unrivalled eloquence of our hostess'.[17] From London Amelia hoped to go 'on a pilgrimage to the shrine of Mr Hayley at Felpham', as she explained when she eventually got round to writing to the poet. But the sudden death of a friend – not named in her letter – caused a change of plan.

Later, Amelia applied herself to editing and completing for publication the manuscript of *Duty*, an unfinished novel by the woman whose death in the summer she acknowledged as having grieved her deeply. The wife of a clergyman who ran a boys' preparatory school at Mitcham, Surrey, where she helped with nursing and practical care, Margaret Roberts had published one novel and some works for children. Amelia wrote a preface in which she outlined her friend's many virtues:

> To have known a woman so amiable and so admirable, will always be amongst the most pleasing recollections of my life, and to have lost her so soon, one of my most lasting regrets. Similarity of pursuits endeared us to each other, and did for our intimacy what is usually effected only by the slow hand of time. When we first met, we soon forgot that we had not met before, and a few years gave to our friendship a solidity and a truth, commonly the result of long acquaintance alone.

She concluded that her regret for the loss of her friend had been solaced in some measure by the widower's 'earnest desire' for her to pay this tribute to her memory and give the manuscript to the world.

> The latter task is one which I seemed peculiarly fitted to undertake, because my lamented friend read the ms aloud to me during the last moments which I passed in her society and she confided to me her intentions with respect to the principal characters.[18]

Before returning home to Norwich in the autumn, Amelia spent a month with friends in Leamington, where, she told Hayley:

> ... again and again I said to myself 'I must write to Mr Hayley', however *there* I had scarcely time allowed me to write even to my father on the days in each week allotted to him – and since then I know not what feeling exactly has still kept me silent, but silent I have been. Still, I have thought of you often, *very* often, and I send a proof that I have done so, in a purse which I beg you will do me

the honor [sic] to accept – but I am sure you will not have as much pleasure in wearing it, as I had in making it for you.[19]

The purse was undoubtedly a stocking purse – an elongated tube knitted in silk with a central opening slit and a pair of rings which were used to secure the coins held within it. The craze for making them was at its height in the early 1800s. They were considered suitable gifts for gentlemen, who tended to wear them tucked over a belt. Hayley responded straightaway with a poem addressed to the purse, which he saw as a precious token of her regard and friendship. He hoped when she next went on an excursion she would do the honour of visiting 'an old rhyming hermit' in his marine cell.

Once the correspondence with Hayley was resumed in February 1814, the postal friendship between the two grew apace, becoming an exchange not just of ideas and opinions, but of feelings and problems. Amelia wrote to thank him for his verses about her gift of the purse, adding some verses of her own to the letter; he replied promptly and in March she wrote a lengthy response. Hayley had sent her three sonnets, which prompted her to write that he was the only modern writer who *could* write sonnets and to express her pleasure at reading them. But first, she acknowledged his frankness:

> There is something to me so binding and sacred in the word 'confidential' written where you wrote it, that I could not have left home easy in mind had I not destroyed the letter so designated that, in case of my sudden death it might run no risk of meeting uninterested eyes. Having therefore well digested its contents which I did not think myself authorized [sic] to mention even to my father, I, a minute ago, committed it to the flames. Tomorrow I go into the country for a few days in hopes that change of air will restore me to health, for I am really tired of being unwell.
>
> This letter I do not mean as an answer to yours for I *intend* I *think* to let you know a little more of my secret history than my *last* contained, in return for your most flattering confidential communications. But at present I have neither time nor nerve for it....
>
> I must tell you that you are so intimately associated in my mind with my first literary ambition and literary tastes and studies and I used to feel so *envious* of the complimentary effusions of your Muse to Miss [Anna] Seward [the poet] that I have a strange bewildering sensation come over me when I read your verses to me and I ask myself if I am not in *a dream* and then I also think how pleased

my poor mother would be if she could look from her grave and hear her favourite bard singing the praises of her child!...

I published *Tales of Real Life* in June last and therefore *dare* not publish again till 1815 – but I am at work on a tale in verse and one in prose in three volumes. O! I am easily discouraged and you know not how cheering and how *efficacious* the voice of praise from such *a man* as you has been to me! On your domestic troubles I will not now touch. But I feel that when a wife has forfeited the *confidence* of her husband all hope of connubial happiness *must be at an end.*

Would I could have opportunities of free discussion with you on that and other subjects. Eh bien! nous verrons.[20]

One of the sonnets which Hayley sent to Amelia was in Italian. She told him she feared he was *deceived* into thinking her a good Italian scholar after reading her dirge to the memory of a relation – later published in *Lays for the* Dead – in which she wrote of his reciting Dante with great effect. He was Charles William Thompson, a grandson of her great-uncle William Briggs. Born in 1888 and raised in Hull, Thompson was a Cambridge scholar and soldier; he was killed in the Basque country in November, 1813, fighting with the British Army in the Peninsular Campaign. It was the campaign in which Arthur Wellesley rose to prominence and for which he was awarded the title 1st Duke of Wellington. The Napoleonic Wars had been going on since 1803, but in April 1814 Napoleon, forced to abdicate, was exiled to the island of Elba in the Mediterranean.

Peace was heralded with great joy throughout the land, but nowhere more so than in London. Amelia was in the capital from May to July, during which time the Russian Emperor (Alexander I) and the King of Prussia (Frederick William III) arrived to take part in the celebrations. She told her father: 'We are all Emperor mad, and from morn till eve the streets are thronged with people and carriages, waiting patiently for hours, to see him pass.' It was one of the busiest and most exciting times she had ever spent in London; she wrote long letters to her father full of anecdotes about her social life and descriptions of celebrities who crossed her path. Brightwell reproduced many of these letters in full – a challenge to anyone reading them 200 years later, since so many of the names are given as initials only. For clarity and economy of space, only sample excerpts and references are quoted here.

Always happy to share news of Norfolk friends, Amelia reported to her father a gathering at the London home of Hudson Gurney in St James's Square. Hudson's wife Margaret was the daughter of a Scottish MP, descended from the Barclays who were Lairds of Ury.* In 1809, the year of their marriage, Hudson inherited a fortune from his maternal grandfather David Barclay; two years later he gained another sizeable inheritance on the death of his father Richard Gurney. A major partner in the Gurney family banking business, Hudson was a staunch supporter of many Norfolk archaeological, historical and literary institutions. Amelia told her father that 'the company' at the Gurneys' house included the Norfolk MP Edmund Wodehouse, the Norwich merchant and brewer M[ichael] Bland whose father was a partner in the Gurneys' textile business, Mr Maltby (Edward Maltby, who, like Amelia, had been baptised at the Octagon Chapel but converted to Anglicanism and later became Bishop of Durham) and Lady Nelson, widow of Norfolk's Trafalgar hero.

Amelia was pleased with her drawing of Hudson Gurney which she did in 1819. Both her husband and cousin did portraits in oils of Hudson. (New York Public Library: Pforzheimer Collection)

She wrote of balls attended by royalty, adding gossip about the Prince Regent and his unsatisfactory marriage to Caroline of Brunswick whom he tried to exclude from accompanying him to social events. Summing up her account of stories she had heard of the royal

---

* The Barclay banking family were descended from Robert Barclay (1648-90), the 2nd Laird of Ury

couple's mutual and public hostility, Amelia concluded that the Princess was 'a weak vixen' violating her duty, however great her wrongs. She renewed her friendships with Sir James and Lady Mackintosh, now returned from Bombay; she went to hear Sydney Smith preach; she took a coach to Mitcham, the home of her late friend Margaret Roberts, where she felt 'the freshness of grief' but rallied herself enough to spend time with the widowed clergyman's pupils – 'the *nicest* set of children' with whom she 'played at magical music' and made herself hoarse 'singing though a comb'.

At a dinner party she met and talked to [Johann] Spurzheim, the German physician who was in England giving lectures on the 'new' and popular subject of phrenology, but while listening to his ideas about the brain, her own brain was 'rendered wool-gathering', as she told her father, by the arrival of Dr [Thomas] Brown. He was, she explained, '*the* Dr Brown', who reviewed her work in the first number of *The Edinburgh Review*. Having been told that he fancied himself as a lady's man, she was not surprised to find him 'a flattering Scotchman' and was annoyed to feel 'fluttered' while talking to him. The next day Brown called on her, 'uninvited and self-introduced'. She offered to take him to a party at Lady Cork's.

Amelia's cousin Tom Alderson was then living in London and she saw him often. It is clear from letters she wrote to his sisters over the years that she had a soft spot for their attractive brother, even though he was always getting into money troubles. Also living within walking distance, south of the river in Walworth, were more Briggs relatives – her great-uncle William's eldest son John Hobart Briggs and his family. In mid-June her cousin, Margaret Alderson, came from Hull to stay with Amelia, having been given permission by her father to experience 'the season' with her sophisticated relation. 'She is a very fine creature, and has the most dignified carriage possible,' reported Amelia to her father, 'and I assure you I like much to have to *shew* (sic) her.' The young girl never forgot the time spent with Mrs Opie, as her daughter reported:

So forth from her quiet school this shy girl of 16 came, and many were the stories she would tell of that time in after years to her children – how she was scandalised and frightened, because Mrs Opie would walk home at midnight, or after, from routs and supper parties, escorted by Lord This and Lord That, and singing catches with them by the way.[21]

Amelia and Margaret waited for hours with a party of friends in Pall Mall, hoping to witness the Russian Emperor on the day of his arrival, but were unlucky. A few days later, they came across a crowd gathered near the Pulteney Hotel in Piccadilly, where the royal visitors were staying, and managed to catch a glimpse of the Emperor and his sister in the Prince's state coach and the King of Prussia whom Amelia thought 'a most interesting looking man'. In her next letter to her father she gave a full report of the occasion on which she persuaded the porter at the hotel (by pressing coins into his hand) to let her into the hall, where she waited with about ten other ladies for the arrival of the Emperor from Carlton House, the home of the Prince Regent:

> ...we formed a *line,* and I, simple soul, meant to *keep* it, but not so my companions; for they all closed round him, and one took one hand, one the other, and really I did not know how far they meant to presume; for my part, I dared not, for some time, even think of touching him, but 'evil communications corrupt good manners', and at last, when he was nearly past, I grasped his wrist, but the grasp would not have crushed a fly.[22]

Two or three days later she returned to the hotel with Margaret and in the crowded hall they both saw the Emperor and his sister. Amelia also renewed her acquaintance with Lady Charleville and others, including Lord Erskine, the Boddingtons, the Whitbreads and Elizabeth Inchbald. Although it was midsummer, she wrote to her father, begging him to get her two pairs of black boots made as soon as possible, as she could not wear her light boots in the 'filthy weather'. Invited to dine with the Mackintoshes she was an early arrival and found 'no fire, alas!' whereupon a fellow guest said 'in all civilised houses there must be one in such weather'. Nevertheless, the dinner was 'almost worth coming up to town on purpose to be at'. The guests included Dr Brown, the classical scholar and archaeologist Richard Payne Knight, who was newly appointed as a trustee of the British Museum, and Baron de Humboldt, 'the great traveller', as Amelia called him. The Prussian-born Humboldt, explorer, naturalist and geographer, had travelled widely in Europe and Latin America and was then living in Paris. He and his brother Wilhelm were in London to join in the peace celebrations:

> I certainly never saw so many first rate men together.... Politics, science, literature, Greek, morals, church government, infidelity, sects, philosophy, characters of the Emperor of Russia, King of Prussia,

of Blücher [Prussian field marshal], of Platov [Russian general] given in a clear and simple manner by the Baron, and commented on by others, formed the never flagging discourse throughout the dinner. I did not talk much, as you may guess, for I had scarcely ears enough to listen with.[23]

The next day Humboldt called on Amelia to breakfast with her; he spent more than two hours telling her about his travels. A few days later she took her cousin to meet Mrs Siddons; after two hours with the famous actress Margaret 'came home raving all the way, saying she was the most beautiful, delightful, agreeable, woman she ever saw'. The highlight of the season was a masked ball at Devonshire House, the London home of the Duke of Devonshire, in honour of the Duke of Wellington. Amelia told her father she had been offered a ticket:

I go full dressed, but no train, and high feathers: with a pink domino of calico, made high and long, to give me height and disguise me, thrown over all, that I may be *incognita*, and be masked till I am tired, and then appear as myself.[24]

Her cousin Margaret also attended the ball, dressed as a flower girl, as she told her children when recalling the event:

Lady Caroline Lamb was there, slightly attired as the Goddess of the Silver Bow. Lord Byron, seated ('of course', my mother said), and in full Albanian costume. At last Mrs Opie was found in a corner of one of the rooms singing to an august audience, which included the First Gentleman in Europe.[25]

Chapter Twenty

Although absorbed in the pleasures of the London season, Amelia found time to keep in touch with her friends elsewhere. Her ability to empathise was appreciated by the Earlham Gurneys, who were anxious about the declining health of John, the oldest brother. Against parental opposition, he had married his cousin Elizabeth (Hudson's half-sister) in January 1807. When she died barely 16 months later, John, who worked in the family bank at King's Lynn, was devastated. He turned to religion for comfort, but, as his mental and physical health declined, he was unable to work. His unmarried sisters cared for him at Earlham from where Joseph John wrote in June to Amelia, thanking her for the 'affectionate conduct to us all'. He perceived that her mind was 'particularly alive to the duties of Christian charity' and warned her of the evils of 'the fashionable world', quoting Biblical texts to make his point.[1]

In her reply, Amelia told him his letter had arrived at a propitious moment, when she had retired to the solitude of her own chamber because 'feelings of a most bitter and painful nature' had 'deluged' her in tears, which were still streaming when her maid knocked at the door and brought in his letter. She had been thinking, in her distress, that he was one with whom she would like to talk as a means of comfort:

> In proportion to this pain therefore was the pleasure which the contents of your letter gave me, breathing as they did the true spirit of friendship, and meeting by their serious and religious nature the sentiments and wishes then more than usually uppermost in my mind. Shall I own to you that the nature of my tears became instantly changed – I wept but it was with pleasure, and thankfulness, and in a few hours my mind recovered its usual tone – nor have I had any *relapses*.[2]

Unlike the letters Amelia wrote to her father, with their entertaining accounts of the social scene, the epistle to Joseph John was an attempt to assure him of how seriously she took the matters he referred to. She read the Scriptures every day, to the amazement of a clergyman who called on her early one morning, expecting 'the slight and amusing gossip of fashionable chit chat', and found her at breakfast, reading the Bible, with a book of sermons lying beside her, whereupon they had a serious and religious discourse. She believed she was in 'no danger' from the 'real evil' which existed in the fashionable world.

Amelia continued to write to young Gurney before she left town on August 5th, 1814, to pay her first visit to Hayley at Felpham. She was also writing to Hayley. She told Joseph John that she had 'mentioned' him in her letters to the poet; Hayley, writing to confirm Amelia's forthcoming visit, calling her 'my poetical daughter' and himself 'a cripple on crutches', assured her that he was 'not less anxious for the welfare of your body and your soul than your beloved filial Quaker to whom, rivals as we are in the Sublimest of Passions Evangelic Love, I send my Benediction'.[3] She stayed up late on the night before her departure to write a long letter to the Quaker, who was concerned about some aspects of her behaviour, such as her enjoyment of being 'liked, admired and flattered'.

She began her letter by telling him of 'a droll coincidence' that on her return from Sheen [Richmond] at 11pm she had found a letter from him and a note from Hayley:

Yours of *course* I read first and I perused his afterwards with involuntary bursts of laughter. He had been alarmed at my *silence* and fancied something had happened to annoy my susceptible mind or my 'tender frame'! The tender frame of a woman who had just been walking full seven miles by moonlight! Now to answer thy letter of *friendly fears*. Mr Hayley *does* deal in flattery and so largely that it is impossible *all* his doses should fail of effect and I own I am flattered by his additional page to the last editions of the *Triumphs of Temper* published a year ago, and written on purpose to *praise* me. *This* I call *praise* not 'flattery' ...[4]

Amelia was under the impression – erroneous as it transpired – that Hayley, having admired her memoir of her husband, wished her to write his memoirs. She knew that Joseph John was not happy about this:

But you will say that the very way in which he has flattered me is y very one to make me undertake the task you are so averse to, and you say aright. Therefore I thank you dear and faithful *moniter* [sic] for having put me on my guard and I *promise you* that I will make *no such promises to Mr Hayley* but pause *long* and consider seriously before I resolve to undertake so difficult and perhaps so *improper* a task. I understand his papers and writings will be very valuable and if left to me the *lure* of gain might *tempt* me to benefit by them, but *not* I hope at the risk of any loss of reputation to myself or infringement of decorum or surrender of any *moral* feeling. Therefore kindly apprehensive friend, set thy heart at rest on the subject and *trust* me that I will do nothing *rashly*.[5]

Hayley's home at Felpham, known as The Turret,* had been built for him. It was a two-storey house, with a square turret over the entrance above which was a circular look-out giving coastal views. The principal room was his first-floor library, which ran the whole length of the eastern side of the house and in which he received his visitors. It contained busts and pictures which he had commissioned from his artist friends and his huge collection of books, prints, drawings and Chinese porcelain. Lame since childhood, Hayley had ridden, fenced and swum until past middle age, but by the time Amelia became his guest he was less active. Staying with her host was a Miss Godfrey, daughter of Hayley's cousin Captain John Godfrey, who acted as hostess.

Amelia stayed for a month at The Turret and it made such an impression on her that she was able to give an account of it to John Johnson, the Norfolk clergyman and kinsman of Cowper, when he began work on editing Hayley's memoirs for publication in 1823. 'Nothing could exceed the regularity and temperance of Mr Hayley's habits,' she recalled. He rose early and walked in the garden before breakfast; he read aloud to her during breakfast at which he drank cocoa only. Days were spent reading alone or reading aloud to each other and walking in the garden; in the evenings they conversed or Amelia sang to him, either one of her own songs or something by Handel. At nine o'clock the servants came in for prayers which Hayley read 'in a very impressive manner'.

It was all quite proper, but in a letter to Joseph John she felt it necessary to reveal, in a slightly provocative manner: 'I am here alone, *tête-à-tête* with Mr Hayley!' She supposed that some might misconstrue the situation, but '*I* feel and see no harm in a woman like me being alone with a lame man of 69, and upwards.' She was writing, she told her young friend, to set his mind at rest on the subject of Hayley's biography. She had been mistaken to believe she was being considered for the task – the poet had already written his own life. Finally, she added: 'I find my Host very well bred, very warm-hearted,

---

* The house was demolished in 1961.

and affectionate, and full of Christian belief of the most firm and supporting nature.'[6]

On her return home – after spending time in London – Amelia sent Hayley, whom she called her 'caro padre', a gold watch-chain and a silk gown for his housekeeper, to which he responded with some verses. She replied:

> Thanks for ye lines on ye chain – but I aspire to binding you in a better chain than a golden one. Your lines composed on your pillow, I read, with pleasure, at Earlham, and a copy was eagerly demanded. Rachel wanted to steal Joseph's copy of ye hymns, but he carefully locked them up as *his own* possession. He desires me to say how much he feels obliged to you, and that he truly wishes it were possible for him to see you at Earlham as his guest. I must tell you that my poor father is gone *raving mad* about your Milton! 'It is ye most beautiful life that ever was written!' and you are so clever! and so *candid*, and so everything! Doubt not but I am pleased to hear one of my papas speak thus of ye other.[7]

While she was in London her father was attending the dying John Gurney at Earlham, where his siblings were gathering. Betsy Fry wrote to her husband and children of her brother's last few hours: 'Dr Alderson called in the morning and Dr [William] Dalrymple, each much affected; he expressed himself so kindly to them, he desired his love to Amelia Opie....'[8] In a handwritten memoir, made up of extracts from her own journal and family notes, Rachel, the second of the seven sisters, quoted Priscilla's account of the deathbed scene: 'When Dr Alderson came to see him dear Betsy knelt down in supplication for Dr A – afterwards John said to him "Doctor! That prayer could not hurt anybody."'[9]

When news of John's death reached her, Amelia travelled overnight to be in Norwich in time for his funeral at the Friends burial ground at the Gildencroft. Inspired by the family's Christian acceptance of the untimely death of 33-year-old John, she wrote a poem addressed to her 'Friend long belov'd'. She had come, she said, to drop 'a tributary tear' and join the train of weeping relatives only to find their 'firm faith' had triumphed over their suffering. Her poem – an acknowledgement of how touched she had been by the sisters' 'tribute to their God' – was copied out many times for circulation throughout the Gurney family; later, an edited version was published in *Lays for the Dead*.

Growing up in Norwich, Amelia had attended the Octagon Chapel (a Unitarian chapel after 1820) with her parents; in London she was more inclined to attend church services with her friends there. Brightwell, in her record of Amelia's 'religious history' stated: 'It seems most likely that in her youth she had no settled opinions on religious subjects; and that the mere circumstances of her birth and education associated her with the Unitarians.'[10] From about 1814 she started to attend Friends' meetings when she was in Norwich, probably because of the growing love and friendship between her and Joseph John, the value she placed on his faith and the fact that he was taking a deep interest in her spiritual well-being, Priscilla, the youngest Gurney sister and a most devout Quaker, joined her brother in his struggle to woo the attractive widow away from Vanity Fair. There was also the example of Elizabeth Fry, actively involved in preaching and prison reform.

Deciding which path she wanted to take was difficult for Amelia. She enjoyed social gatherings of all kinds and was pleased with the ongoing exchanges with Hayley whom she was planning to visit again. She kept him informed of her contact with the Gurneys: 'You would be amused to see Joseph's rapture at my attending meetings,' she declared in one letter.[11] In another she shared with Hayley a prayer which Priscilla had intoned at a private meeting she and her brother had conducted for Amelia. In December she stayed at Earlham for a week; Joseph John recorded in his journal that he had read the *Epistle to the Hebrews* to Amelia and his sister Richenda before breakfast one morning.

Having spent the autumn and winter with her father, Amelia stayed for two weeks with Daniel, the youngest Earlham Gurney, who lived at King's Lynn, where he was a partner in the family bank. She paid a spring visit to her cousins in Durham and returned to London for the summer. Joseph John was also in the capital. Amelia felt able to express to the worldly poet her thoughts on the attractions of the London social scene and the contrasting pull of the Quaker way of life:

One day I am at a Countess's assembly, then at a Quaker's meeting and Quaker's yearly feast – now hearing sermons from public friends, now seeing plays, now walking along y streets on y arm of a plain Quaker, now leaning on that of a volatile viscount – and what a strange thing it is.... On Saturday I *refused* Lady Cork's party full of rank and talent to go down with Joseph to Plashet [Elizabeth Fry's home] and my Sunday was passed between *meet-*

ings at Tottenham and Plaistow and we dined at a public preacher's house (his father's at least) whom I knew at Norwich some weeks ago and who told Joseph he thought of nothing but me all meeting – y consequence was that he *preached at me*, as I and Joseph felt. How well y phrases of religious zeal resemble those of love. Joseph, with all y gravity possible, told me William Forster* told him between meetings that I woke a very tender string in his heart. I did not laugh but if W.F. had not been who he is, I should have been much flattered and not fluttered, yet flattered I ought to be at having awakened interest for my soul's welfare in y breast of one of y kindest and best of men. Joseph breakfasts with me tomorrow.... He desires his kind and respectful regard to you.

By ye by, I delivered your message to W. Scott† and he spoke of you as he *ought* and as I love to hear. Naughty calumniation! Because I do not like all he writes must it follow that I do not like him as well as you do. *Guy Mannering* I dote upon and so I *might* perhaps Walter Scott himself were it *fitting* – for I like him as well as his books.

Wordsworth also is here but he is not as *talking* as W. Scott.[12]

Amelia and her father had shared their concerns about Napoleon's escape from Elba in February, 1815, and the resumption of hostilities with France. The campaign was short-lived and in June Amelia joined in the national rejoicing on the news of Wellington's victory over Napoleon at Waterloo, followed by reports of the Emperor's abdication and the signing of a cease-fire. But her delight at the cessation of hostilities was marred by learning of the death of Samuel Whitbread whose hospitality at Southill she and John Opie had so enjoyed in the summer of 1806. Since then she had maintained good friendships with Whitbread and his wife, meeting them at social events when they were in London. The MP had been in failing health for some time, suffering mental disturbance which made his parliamentary speeches increasingly vehement. In March he had protested against renewing

* Born into a Tottenham Quaker family, Forster became a preacher at an early age and was a close friend of the Gurneys. In 1816 he married Thomas Fowell Buxton's sister Anna, who was involved with Elizabeth Fry's campaign to help women prisoners at Newgate.
† The fleeting reference to Scott, gives the impression that the meeting was not particularly significant. Amelia's notebook, written many years later, gave detailed 'recollections' of her one and only meeting with Scott in 1816 when she sat next to him at a breakfast party and he told her he had cried over her *Father and Daughter* 'more than he ever cried over such things'. (Brightwell, pp.176-7)

hostilities with France and continued to deplore the war in almost hysterical terms. He made his last speech in the house on July 4th; two days later he killed himself by cutting his throat at his London home.

Amelia shared her grief over his death with Joseph John, who had returned to Earlham. She said she had seen Whitbread and his wife at a party three days before he died. Reading the report of his inquest she felt his death, although by his own hand, 'a mercy' which saved him from years of suffering'. It was, she wrote:

a comfort to me to see the fact of his insanity established beyond a doubt – and the dreadful act which closed so valuable a life not attributable to any degree (spite of vile reports) to any other cause than a visitation from Heaven.

I can hardly bear to dwell on the grief of his *devoted*, helpless, adored and spoiled wife. He was to *her* what it is desirable a husband *should* be to his wife.... He was at once her pride and her blessing and so much her *support* also that I believe she will *sink* under the blow.[13]

Two weeks later Amelia set off for Felpham to stay with Hayley. Recalling the visit for her contribution to Johnson's *Memoirs* of the poet she chose to focus on naming people known to her who were staying in the area and who wished to be introduced to Hayley, causing him to comment: 'I think, my dear, you had better *shew* me, at a shilling a head.' To Joseph John her letters from The Turret expressed misgivings about her host. But first she responded to the earnest Quaker's inquiries about her time in London, admitting she had gone 'from dinner to assembly, and from ball to concert'. She understood Joseph John's concerns, but she had derived pleasure from some:

...namely from the dinners and the concerts – for at the former I had often good conversation and at the latter good musick [sic]. Now musick and conversation being in my eyes, two of the innocent pleasures of life, two of the many cordial drops infused into our cups by the great giver of every good, I have no scruple in enjoying them, and do it with a thankful heart.

Musing on whether she should turn her back on her past, she concluded she did not feel it a *duty* to separate herself from worldly people, 'however, it may become my *inclination*.[14]

In that first letter from Felpham she told her friend she had kept to her bed after arriving there, fatigued and with throbbing pains in her head: 'Poor Mr Hayley came to my bedside with the tenderness of a parent and prescribed for me with the skill of a physician.' But by the time she wrote again she was beginning to see her host in a different light – no doubt influenced by the Gurney scruples and warnings. 'He takes the Lord's name in vain, *incessantly*, *profanely*,' she complained. However, she attempted to make the old reprobate aware of his shortcomings and believed she was succeeding, until he began to talk 'as *usual*' about his past conduct:

> O! how shocked I felt! For I found he *still* defended to his *con-science*, his having thought proper as he had no child by his wife, to have one by his servant – his wife being *privy* to the connection. *I was silent* – as I always *am* – tho' I *flatter* myself it was a silence that *speaks* and *reproves*....

Hayley's cousin Captain Godfrey, whom Amelia described to Joseph John as 'unaffectedly and truly pious' was also staying at The Turret. 'He says if Mr H had always had such a truth-telling person as myself about him he would have been a different man....'[15]

Amelia read to Hayley and Godfrey from the manuscript of her new novel *Valentine's Eve*, which would be published early in 1816. Both admired it greatly and her visit ended on a happy note. When she left the ms behind at his house, Hayley was inspired to write 30 lines of verse in which he named the novel's heroine Catherine, paying tribute to the author and her new work, before returning it as: 'Epistle to Amelia Opie with her new novel in Manuscript which she had left accidentally in the house of a Friend'. Dated September 8th, 1815, the poem began:

> Thy Catherine follows Thee – How just her Claim
> To share, and to encrease, Amelia's Fame!
> Thou, on whose Fictions Truth & Nature smil'd!
> Thou, who I fondly call'd 'my Fancy's Child!'
> In every Scene, inventive Powers inspire,
> Thou has surpassed thy visionary Sire.[16]

The correspondence between the poet and novelist continued, going through a difficult patch when Hayley, distracted by a lawsuit brought by the family of his estranged young wife, took umbrage when Amelia, having written sympathetically about his situation, asked for details of the case. He refused. After her last visit, he said, his housekeeper had found a letter to Amelia lying about and had told him that her maid read all her mistress's letters. In vain she protested she always burnt her letters or locked them up. He responded coolly in the third person; she next addressed him as 'My Dear Sir'. Apologies and explanations followed and before long the mutual affection was restored. But she did not visit Hayley again until the summer of 1817.

Throughout the year of her second visit to Felpham, Amelia was paying attention to the prospect of Joseph John getting married; the Gurney siblings were also speculating about a possible wife for the master of Earlham Hall and discussing his apparent reluctance. Writing to Hayley during her stay at Daniel Gurney's in the spring, she reported on what was being said in the family about a prospective wife, adding that she was 'the *only* woman for whom he feels any *fondness*'.[17] Daniel, who had left the Society of Friends, told her he would not be sorry to see her turn Quaker if that meant she could marry Joseph John.

> He is no religionist and *almost hates* Quakers... being very jealous of Joseph's fine gift to me (Scott's Bible) he has *insisted* on giving me a black *sattin* [sic] gown. At Earlham I dare not wear even a *brooch* – but at Lynn I put on all *my finery* and Dan was in *ecstasies* at it. How different are the two brothers.[18]

Richenda, the fourth Gurney sister, was keeping house for Daniel at the time. She had left the Quakers in 1808 and joined the Church of England, along with Catherine, the eldest, who had been a surrogate mother to her younger siblings after their mother died. Richenda was to marry a clergyman, the Rev Francis Cunningham, in 1816. Meanwhile, she was keen to introduce Amelia into the church and persuaded her to rise at seven most mornings to accompany her to the early service.

At this time Amelia was becoming friends with Dawson Turner, who inherited his father's position as a partner at the Gurneys bank in Great Yarmouth. The wealthy Turner amassed a fine collection of paintings and books and became a patron to the Norwich artists Crome and Cotman, employing them as drawing masters to his six daughters and two sons. Amelia got to know him through his friendship with Hudson Gurney, who worked at the Great Yarmouth bank for a few years. Writing to Turner in November 1815, Amelia gave news of Hudson's sick wife, whom Dr Alderson was attending. She hoped very much to have the opportunity of seeing more of Turner and his wife Mary, who was an etcher of some distinction. Her work included etchings after Opie portraits, including that of Hudson painted in 1797: a few years later she would etch his best known portrait of Amelia. Meanwhile, Mrs Opie expressed her thanks for:

> the excellent specimens of Mrs Turner's skill in etching which you have already sent – but also for the offer of *more* and I shall probably, some time or other, presume on your voluntary kindness. I can assure you that I value those now before me for the sake of the original artist, the etcher and the giver.[19]

On New Year's Eve – always a significant date for Amelia, as it was the anniversary of her mother's death – she sat down and wrote a letter to Joseph John, asking him to consider it as 'my *new year's gift to thee*'. She began by acknowledging 'the perturbed state' of his mind that morning. Then followed an assessment of the anxieties which he had shared with her, namely the expense of maintaining the estate at Earlham and keeping the house open to entertain his siblings, their children and other relations whose presence gave him such delight. Should his 'well-principled economy' force him to give up the home he loved, she felt such a move would be '*a joyless burden*'. Rather, she believed, he should become a husband himself and fill the place of those dear relatives with children of his own.

> ...to be frank with you, I believe that *your ideas* on this subject are *the same as mine* – and that your present uncomfortableness proceeds from your inability to feel for any one (and narrow indeed is the choice in an exclusive religion) that degree of *ardent* and *determined* preference which *perhaps* ought *alone* to determine a conscientious and well-principled man to marry... I feel encouraged to hope that the man of all my acquaintance whom I think the most likely to make a good, nay, a most *excellent* husband, namely your own dear self, will ere long possess that domestic happiness he so well deserves....
>
> And now let me *brag* of my disinterested affection for you, and my surrender of self – for whenever you marry you must be, as it were, lost to me. No woman that marries ought to have, or *can* have any intimate friend but her husband – especially of the other sex and if she loves her husband, she loses the *wish* to have one....
>
> It is not in nature for any wife to approve her husband's being as intimate with a female friend as you are with me – even were she

20 years older than I am. Therefore, when you marry, I must try to console myself for the loss of the friend *almost* the most dear to me, by the consciousness that my loss is his gain, and that he is enjoying and conferring the greatest happiness this world can bestow.[20]

It would be another 18 months before Joseph John did marry, taking for his wife Jane Birkbeck, whom he had known from childhood. Her father John was one of the first partners at Gurneys Bank in King's Lynn. As with so many of the Gurney marriages the couple were distantly related: Jane's mother Martha was sister to Bartlett Gurney. (Joseph John's older brother Samuel, now a banker in London, had married in 1808 Elizabeth Sheppard, whose mother Sarah was also sister to Bartlett.)

Whether or not Amelia knew of his leanings in the direction of Jane Birkbeck, she continued associating with him in person and in correspondence throughout much of 1816. In January she visited Coke and his family at Holkham; on her return home she spent time at Earlham. Her novel *Valentine's Eve* was newly published and Joseph John read the first of the three volumes out loud to the author. As she told Hayley, the serious Quaker had laid aside 'an excellent and learned work on the deity of Christ' to do so and had been pleased with the work as 'a *proof* of talent'.[21] After she left Earlham he read the second and third volumes, his unexpectedly hostile reaction prompting an immediate letter from Amelia to Hayley:

> Joseph took me into his study, and after some preamble, said he had been employed from his intimacy with me, to venture to express to me the pain my *late* new work had given some of my best and most respectable friends from its *impurity*... one gentleman (a *notorious* profligate bye the bye) had found it impossible to read parts aloud to ladies – that I alluded to adultery, seduction &c and a house of ill fame, things not to be named, especially by a woman....
>
> I have not time dear friend to tell *you my* replies and my defence, but I mentioned having read my MS to you and to Capt G – both men of the world, and the latter, the father of *daughters* ... and that he approved the MS as a moral work – and so on – Joseph could only say that the moral standard of you and Capt G was a very low one...I was almost distracted – as Lemaistre [probably the author J.G. Lemaistre] had been worrying me with long letters against the *religion* of my work and here, my intimate friends were abusing me for my impurity and immorality!! Well – I could however lift up my

torn soul with confidence to my *creator*, that my *motives* were not only *pure* but *good*.[22]

Hayley's enthusiasm for *Valentine's Eve* helped to ease the distress and outrage she experienced when lectured by Joseph John about the work, but there was little comfort from reviews in literary magazines: critics were not impressed, the *British Lady's Magazine*, declaring it 'in every way unworthy of Mrs Opie'. Written during the months of her soul-searching about religion and her questioning of the pleasures of the social scene, Amelia made her heroine Catherine Shirley an exceptionally virtuous woman whose Christian beliefs withstand a malicious campaign against her good name. The chief perpetrators – a manipulative society woman whose unseemly advances have been rejected by Catherine's husband and a villainous society man whose jealousy of the husband knows no bounds – devise a series of situations to blacken the heroine's name. These attempts are increasingly far-fetched and implausible, but succeed in alienating her husband. Catherine's faith and honour are upheld to the end, when, re-united with her repentant spouse, she dies in his arms.

The friendship with Joseph John survived the painful encounter, but Amelia was disappointed when he did not call on her when they were both in London in June:

> I doubt not that you fancied it was next to impossible to call on me, and so I believe it was – though, as it is a maxim with me, that a strong inclination always makes opportunities to do whatever it wishes, I think I should have seen you had your desire to see me been sufficiently powerful....

She was pleased he took the trouble to give her two letters of explanation as it proved:

> ...still continuing interest and affection – and I can now write to you *again*. Before I *could not* – you had shut up my heart towards you and when my heart is shut it is a long time before it opens again....[23]

A few weeks later she wrote to Hayley, assuring him she thought of him, his kindness and his 'warm and welcome hospitality' every day. She would not be able to visit him in the autumn because she was going north to see her cousins in Durham and then on to Edinburgh.

En attendant I shall send you a *sketch* of myself painted in February 1807 by my poor husband which, tho' unfinished is reckoned, and I reckon it also more like me than any thing he ever did – except that it is younger and better looking – and I should be proud and pleased to see it hung up amongst your other *sketches* of female writers.[24]

Hayley accepted the Opie portrait with pleasure. In his will he left it to his good friend Henrietta Poole, whom Amelia had met on her first visit to Felpham, with instructions that she would bequeath it to Amelia's cousin Tom Alderson.

Amelia enjoyed her visit to Scotland in August, calling first on her cousins in Durham before going with Tom Alderson to Edinburgh, where they stayed at the home of the publisher Archibald Constable. She made an impression on Constable's young son Thomas who recalled:

In 1816, on the occasion of her first visit to Scotland, Mrs Opie was my father's guest at Craigleith House, and although I was only at the time in my fifth year, I have a distinct remembrance of her bright and cheerful presence, and of the delight her singing seemed to give to others.[25]

In October she wrote to Constable, telling him she had returned home, only to be 'seduced again from the paternal roof' by the opportunity to spend some time with William Wilberforce and his wife who were guests at Earlham. The MP had headed the anti-slavery parliamentary campaign which brought about the 1807 Abolition Bill banning British ships from participating in the Atlantic slave trade. Amelia, reporting to Constable that she stayed 'some days' in his company, added:

I must think that a fortunate chance which led me to associate with Mr Wilberforce, as his various powers of conversation, his great animation, and his winning manners make him a very delightful companion....

If my father knew I was writing to you he would desire to be most cordially remembered to you, for taking such pains to spoil his only child, whom, though she always was an only child, he flatters himself *he* never spoiled, but, poor soul, he is sadly mistaken.[26]

William Smith, the Norwich MP whose election in 1802 had caused great rejoicing in the city's radical households, stayed with Amelia and her father when she returned from Earlham. A leading member of the anti-slavery campaign and staunch supporter of Wilberforce, Smith had lost his seat in 1806 but was returned a year later and again in 1812. Time spent with Wilberforce and Smith detracted Amelia from her work, but she assured Constable that she planned soon to be 'seriously employed in writing'. During the last few months of the year she was busy writing gossipy letters to Sarah and Elizabeth (known as Eliza to her family – and named thus in subsequent chapters), her two Alderson cousins from Durham, who were being introduced to the delights of the capital by their brother Tom. They were then expected in Norwich where Amelia promised they would be received by Alderson and Woodhouse relations with such kindness as would 'render bold' even their timid natures. For herself:

> The influence of Earlham and its beloved master, with the company of my dear friend [Thomas] Fowell Buxton and Sam Hoare have restored my mind to itself and I wrote more of my poem and better yesterday than I have done for weeks.[27]

Chapter Twenty-one

Amelia believed that family ties were important and developed significant relationships with her cousins. In the wake of her widowhood she turned increasingly towards these younger relations, bringing them together and keeping up regular correspondence with them in which she offered advice, shared opinions, passed on family news and reminisced about her younger days. Once they were married and had families of their own she maintained her interest into the next generation. The correspondence with just one group – the Durham Aldersons (the bulk of it preserved at the Huntington Library in San Marino, California) – runs into many thousands of words.

For the sake of clarity and simplicity it seems appropriate at this point in the narrative – as Amelia was preparing to welcome the sisters from Durham to her father's house and to introduce them to the Norwich Aldersons and Woodhouses – to offer a *Who's Who* of the kinships and outline the salient points of their friendships and connections over the years.

The friendship between Amelia and Edward Hall Alderson, 18 years her junior, began in earnest when he went to London to read law after graduating with prizes and honours from Cambridge. He was one of four children of Amelia's uncle Robert by his first wife Elizabeth (née Hurry), who died in 1791, whereupon the youngsters went into the care of their grandfather Samuel Hurry at Great Yarmouth. Robert left the ministry to study law and practised in Ipswich for a while; he brought the family together again in Norwich, after marrying his second wife Henrietta (née Mannock) in 1800. They made their home in St Helen's House, Bishopsgate,* an elegant and spacious building near the Cathedral, where Amelia was a frequent visitor. Robert was made steward of Norwich Corporation and later became Recorder of Norwich, Ipswich and Great Yarmouth.

Edward, his eldest son, was called to the bar in 1811 and went on to have a very successful career, being knighted in 1830 when he was made a judge. He shared Amelia's enthusiasm for the theatre,

---

* A plaque on the house says it was built and lived in by Thomas Ivory, the architect who designed the Octagon Chapel.

which they sometimes attended together in London; on one occasion they went to a masked ball at Almack's Assembly Rooms, acting as a deaf old gentleman and his elderly companion. They carried on a lively correspondence, exchanging witticisms and elegant stanzas; as Edward's career progressed Amelia used him as a sounding board for her views on penal reform, court cases and other legal matters. In 1823 he married Georgina Drewe, daughter of a Devonshire rector, and they had eight children, one of whom died young. They lived in London, but made frequent visits to Norwich and to Lowestoft in Suffolk where they rented a house every summer for many years and invited family and friends to stay. Edward's and Amelia's relationship was important to them both.

Edward's older sister Isabella, who had been painted by Opie, died in 1807, at the age of 21. His younger brother Samuel Hurry also a Cambridge graduate, was ordained into the Church of England and had livings in Suffolk. He married Jane Bennett, of Rougham in Suffolk, and they had 10 children. Edward's younger sister Elizabeth, born in 1791, became Lady Milman when she married Sir William George Milman; they lived in Pinner (at that time a village in Middlesex) and had nine children. Amelia kept in touch with both Samuel and Elizabeth, visiting them when she could and taking a keen interest in all their activities.

She was in London when her uncle Robert's three children by his second wife were born. The eldest, Robert Jervis Coke, born in 1802, also went into the church; his first appointment was as stipendiary curate at St.Peter Mancroft, Norwich. In 1832, he married Sophia Mott, of Barningham Winter in Norfolk, who died seven years later, leaving him with four children, after which he moved to Suffolk. Robert's sister Susan died in 1808 at the age of four; his younger brother James died, aged 18, in 1823.* The deaths of family members grieved Amelia deeply; throughout her life she was supportive of relations when they suffered bereavements, writing thoughtful letters expressing her sorrow and, once she had become a Quaker, using the occasion to express her belief in heaven and the life everlasting.

The Norwich Aldersons also included Amelia's unmarried aunt Elizabeth, who had moved to Norwich from Lowestoft with her widowed mother Judith Alderson.† Amelia paid regular visits to Miss

---

* There is a memorial to Susan and James in St Helen's Church, Bishopsgate.
† The Octagon Chapel has a memorial to Judith 'relict of the Rev James Alderson of Lowestoft' and their daughter Elizabeth.

Alderson, who was inclined to be 'irritable' and 'querulous', and kept her informed of the comings and goings of her nephews and nieces. As a young woman, Elizabeth had tried to earn her own living 'in business' with little success, whereupon her favourite brother Thomas, the merchant, decided to give her an allowance of £300 a year, which should have continued after his death in 1798. But, due to the negligence of his executors, the annuity was discontinued, leaving Elizabeth 'heartstricken'. Her brothers James and Robert then began contributing to her upkeep – a practice which Amelia took over from her father when he died. When the whole sorry business came to light 40 years after the death of Thomas, in the context of bequests to his grandchildren, Amelia took it upon herself to seek legal advice from Thomas Brightwell and to help her aunt gain some recompense. Later she wrote several letters to her cousin Henry Perronet Briggs, giving an account of the background to the affair, her suspicions about the devious role played by her cousin Tom Alderson and the subsequent unravelling of the legal complications.[1]

Amelia's aunt Judith (née Alderson) was the second wife of Robert Woodhouse, a Norwich draper. As a young man he was apprenticed to a wool and worsted merchant named John Ollyett, whose daughter became his first wife. There were no children by the marriage. Ollyett left Woodhouse his estates in Norwich and Norfolk, entailing them on to Robert and Judith's eldest son who had been named Ollyett. The family lived in Muspole Street, off Colegate, not far from Amelia's childhood home; she and Ollyett – born in the same year – were close from an early age. As related in earlier chapters, Ollyett had radical views and was in Paris at the time of the Revolution; he graduated from Pembroke College, Oxford, and went into the legal profession, his last job being as Advocate General in Bombay. He married Harriet Atkinson, the daughter of a Yorkshire mill owner, and they set up home at Southrepps, two miles inland from the Norfolk coast near Cromer, where their first four children were born; six more were born in Bombay. As with the children of her Norwich Alderson cousins, Amelia maintained an interest in Ollyett's offspring and kept in contact with them; his eldest daughter Harriet, who married Lechmere Russell, an army officer, was a particular favourite. Opie did two portraits and also some sketches of Ollyett. When he died in 1822 Amelia wrote two poems in memory of the cousin 'belov'd from childhood's hour', recalling him as a young man 'with graceful form and manly brow' and wit which shone 'like summer lightning'. Both poems were published in her *Lays for the Dead*.

Robert, the second Woodhouse son, was four years younger than Amelia. He pursued an academic career at Gonville and Caius College, Cambridge, where he had graduated and was awarded a fellowship. He became Lucasian professor of mathematics and then Plumian professor of astronomy and experimental philosophy. Amelia never forgot Robert's kindness and support during her husband's terminal illness. In 1823, at the age of 50, he married Harriet Wilkins, daughter of a Norwich architect; he died four years later, leaving her with their two-year-old son Robert. James, the third Woodhouse son, was 16 when he acted in Amelia's drama *The Tragedy of Adelaide* at the home of the Plumptre family in 1791. It is likely that he died as a young man, as there is little record of his adult life, other than a document indicating that Ollyett released the title deeds of one of his Norfolk messuages to his brothers Robert and James in 1805, presumably before he left England for Bombay.[2]

The fourth son, John Thomas, born in 1780, became a physician. When he applied for a scholarship to Caius College, Amelia begged her friend Elizabeth Inchbald, to put in a good word for the young man with a physician who was one of the electors:

John Thomas Woodhouse is my first cousin and is *highly* esteemed by me and all his family...I am anxious for his succeeding in his application for the scholarship, and you are acquainted with Dr Gisborne![3]

The application – with two or three electors enlisted by his older brother Robert – was successful. John Thomas became a fellow of Caius and qualified as a doctor in 1810; he was in practice in Cambridge and worked as a physician at Addenbrooke's Hospital. He never married and was said to be a man of eccentric habits, with a taste for cockfighting. A keen amateur painter, as a young man he had some lessons with Opie, when the artist was staying in Norwich. John Thomas died in 1845.

Richard Woodhouse, the fifth son, born in 1782, became a merchant in London, trading with the East India Company, after having spent a few years with his brother Ollyett in Bombay, where he worked as a clerk and registrar to the Supreme Court. While in India he married Harriet Urquhart (née Williams), the widow of a colonel in the military service of the East India Company in Bombay. The first two of their five children were born in Bombay before the couple returned to England and set up home in London. They named their fourth child Amelia. Robert and Judith Woodhouse's sixth son, George Morgan, born in 1788 and named after George Cadogan Morgan, who had left Norfolk the year before, died at the age of four years. Their last child – and only daughter – Judith Maria was born in 1790; after marrying Robert Sutcliffe, an Essex clergyman, by whom she had two daughters, she wrote regularly to and occasionally received visits from her cousin Amelia.

As related in earlier chapters, Amelia's contact with two sets of Alderson cousins – the offspring of Dr John Alderson in Hull and of Thomas Alderson in Durham – began in her 40th year. When her uncle John died in 1829 it was estimated that some 15,000 people turned out to pay their respects along his funeral route. His distinguished medical career was marked with the erection of his statue by Richard Westmacott outside Hull General Infirmary in 1833. Amelia was moved to write a poem *On Seeing the Statue of my late uncle, Dr Alderson of Hull* – published in *Lays for the Dead* – in which she extolled his kindness as a physician, father and friend. Of his five children who survived infancy, she made a lasting friendship with Margaret, the youngest. Of the four brothers who reached adulthood Christopher, Ralph and James joined the medical profession and John became a solicitor. Amelia was closest to James, who, like his father, became a physician at Hull Infirmary and later worked in London, where he was president of the Royal College of Physicians.

Having taken the young Margaret Alderson under her wing in 1814, Amelia's relationship with her attractive young cousin thrived; the family connection was boosted when Margaret married John Vincent Thompson, a barrister, whose maternal grandfather William Briggs was a brother of Amelia's maternal grandfather Joseph Briggs. John Vincent's younger brother Charles William was killed in the Peninsular Campaign; his older brother Thomas Perronet, also a soldier and later an MP, was an associate of Wilberforce. His mother Philothea Perronet (née Briggs) and his only sister Philothea, died within a few weeks of each other when staying in Penzance where, it was hoped, the milder climate would ease the daughter's consumption. Their loss inspired a poem, *Epitaph on a Mother and Daughter*, for Amelia's *Lays for the Dead*. Margaret and John Thompson had eight children; Amelia was in her 70s by the time the last was born, her visits to the family home in London over the years were much enjoyed by the youngsters. Sarah Isabella, the second daughter, recalled:

She was a delightful play-fellow, as we children knew right well... the elder children were never so happy as when their 'Dear Opie', as we always called her, came to the house. She would often bring us toys and dear little sugar-plums, artfully twisted in co-loured papers. But it was not for this that we loved her, but for her sweet kindliness and merriment.[4]

Amelia's drawing of her cousin Tom Alderson. She told his sister Sarah about her 'new drawing book', and the relations she had been sketching, adding 'and thou looks so pretty in it!', but neither in that album nor another surviving one (totalling more than 130 sitters) are more than a handful of them named. (New York Public Library: Pforzheimer Collection)

Also descended from Amelia's great-uncle William Briggs was Henry Perronet Briggs, whose father John Hobart Briggs was the oldest brother of Philothea Perronet Thompson (mother of John Vincent). Henry, 22 years younger than Amelia, shared her interest in their family history; he was a student at the Royal Academy from 1811 and went on to become well known as an historical and portrait painter. Through Briggs, Amelia enjoyed a renewal of her association with the London art world and took great pains to further his career, introducing him to the great and the good in her social circle as prospective sitters. She also befriended Henry's two sisters, Catherine and Irene, neither of whom married. Henry married Elizabeth (Eliza) Alderson, of Durham – another link between cousins from both branches of Amelia's family tree – and they had two children. Sarah, the older sister, married a Frenchman, Lenon De Barbot; they lived in Paris; but

Sarah was in London when she died after only four years of marriage. Although Amelia was very fond of their older brother Thomas John (Tom), who never married and flitted in and out of jobs, there were times when his irresponsibility and downright fraudulent behaviour caused her distress and embarrassment.

But over the days of Christmas and the New Year in 1816 and 1817, when Sarah, 21, and Eliza, 19, stayed with Amelia and her father in Norwich, there were few anxieties about the future. She delighted in showing her young guests the buildings for which her home city was renowned and introducing them to the Norwich relations and her friends at Earlham. From that time onwards, the Alderson sisters divided their time between their home in Durham and their brother's house in London. Encouraged by Mrs Opie, they also began developing their own relationships with the assorted cousins.

Chapter Twenty-two

After entertaining her cousins, Amelia's first engagement in 1817 was a visit to Holkham, where Coke's two married daughters, their husbands and children were staying, along with other relations and house guests. His youngest unmarried daughter Elizabeth begged her 'to stay on' for she could not bear to hear of her leaving them too soon. 'If I were to stay here, I should be *ruined* – I am made so much of!' she wrote to Eliza, adding a full report of what she teasingly called 'a specimen' of one day there – singing and reading aloud to the family and guests, romping with the children, playing quadrille, drinking punch and staying up till 2am. She wrote 12 lines to Mr Coke and read them to the family; their 'admiration of my scribble' had given her 'fresh spirits about it'.[1]

The important friendship with the still unmarried Joseph John Gurney continued. After one visit to Earlham in March, she wrote a poem, entitled: *To J.J. Gurney on his inviting me to see his spring flowers which were suddenly hidden by a great fall of snow.*[2] Having lamented the fact that 'chill winter wears his robes of snow' and has cast his mantle over spring's 'sweet flowers', the poet uses the occasion to assure her friend that the scene is 'fraught with charm' for her because she is with him. Aware of the young man's unhappy state of mind at that time, she wanted him to know how much she valued his friendship.

According to his first biographer, Joseph John was suffering 'the deepest depression' and earnestly praying 'that the hand of discipline may bring me into a state of greater holiness and nearness to God'.[3] He confided in his journal that he wished his life might be 'to Christ, and not to the world'. In April he went to stay with his brother Daniel at his new home at North Runcton for two weeks, his mind 'deeply absorbed by the subject of marriage'. At the widowed Martha Birkbeck's house at Hunstanton, he proposed to her daughter Jane, whom he described as 'a decided Friend from conviction', and was accepted.

In Norwich Amelia was planning a visit to her cousins in London. But her thoughts were with the Gurneys. She was close to Joseph John's aunt and uncle, who lived at The Grove. Having already lost two daughters, one in infancy and another at the age of 11, they were grieving for the loss of their two sons, Henry, aged 17, in February 1815, and Joseph, aged 20, in November 1816. Amelia's distress at the deaths of the two Gurney sons led to her writing a poem in blank verse for the parents. A version entitled *Lines on the death of two brothers, the only sons of friends very dear to me* was published in *Lays for the Dead*.

A few weeks before Joseph's death, his ailing sister Rachel, aged 22 (a patient of Dr Alderson), had been sent to Nice in the hope that the milder climate would be beneficial. Her travelling companions included her cousin Priscilla Gurney, of Earlham, who remained in Nice until March, when Rachel's parents arrived to be with their daughter, who died two months later.

Amelia hoped to see Priscilla at Plashett where she stopped en route to London, The night before she left home, Catherine Gurney dined with her and Dr Alderson, she told Eliza, 'and would you believe it, *my pa* drank a *bumper* of wine on dear Cilla's safe return!' She thought that Joseph John would be home in a few days' time. Perhaps, with him in mind, she had been composing music for a psalm:

> The maids believe me to be little better than out of my mind for last night I *sung* after I got to bed and made *vocal* the midnight air! I had composed a *psalm* tune and was afraid of *forgetting* it. It is two stanzas of the 119th psalm and if no one else likes it I am sure Catherine and Joseph will.[4]

At that time she was unaware of his marriage plans and there is no record of her reaction to the news. Joseph John wrote a poem to Amelia, noting her sympathetic character, her genial temper, her kindness and willingness to please, before concluding with a heartfelt appeal that she will renounce the lure of fashion and worldly pleasures:

> Though in sweet chime its gilded fetters ring,
> Thou know'st its sorrows, *thou* hast felt its sting.
> Ah! think again! And from the busy strife,
> The gay delusion and the pride of life,
> Let Israel's God thy pliant footstep lead
> By the still waters in the verdant mead!*

The Gurney-Birkbeck wedding took place in September 1817, at the Friends Meeting House at Wells in Norfolk. From Gurney letters and

---

* Braithwaite does not identify his source, but says the stanzas were addressed to Amelia 'in the year 1817'. (*Memoirs*, Vol.1, p.241)

journals the evidence suggests it was very much a family and Friends event. Joseph John's sisters rejoiced at the union, Betsy writing in her journal that her dearest brother uttered a few words in supplication:

> to my great comfort and refreshment, not doubting that the holy anointing was poured upon him. I believe that he will be a great instrument in his heavenly father's hand if he only keep very near to his guide.[5]

Within a few months he was acknowledged as a minister for the Friends – a decision reached unanimously by the Norwich Meeting.

In the late summer Amelia went to Felpham. As the worldly Hayley was her chief confidant in the matter of her relationship with Joseph John, no doubt he was more than willing to hear whatever she needed to disclose about her feelings on the subject of the marriage. Since her visit to The Turret two years earlier, they had corresponded and exchanged significant gifts – she sending him 'the sketch' of herself by her husband and he, in return, sending her a painting of Virgil's Tomb by his friend Joseph Wright of Derby. Hayley expressed his appreciation of her visit in a letter to his friend 'Johnny' (John Johnson, who would edit his *Memoirs*):

> I may thank Heaven for having enjoyed much very kind, and delectable society this summer; particularly a social visit of several weeks from our admirable Amelia Opie, who, after having kindly devoted some pleasant months to various friends in her excursion, is just settling herself at home again, with a mind well prepared to exert its powers in several projected works.[6]

Indeed, Amelia was working on her next literary project, telling Eliza she was very busy writing *tales*, tiring her hand so much she did not know how to write letters. The result was a set of stories published as *New Tales* in four volumes in 1818. In the autumn her uncle John came to Norwich with his daughter, stayed a few days and then returned to Hull, leaving Margaret behind to spend the next six months with her relations. Amelia took her young cousin to all the important social events. They stayed for three days at Stanfield Hall (30 years later the scene of a double murder) and later Amelia introduced Margaret to the Fountaine family, whose Briggs ancestors were related to her own Briggs ancestors. They occupied the family seat at Narford Hall, built by Sir Andrew Fountaine in 1733 and containing his excellent collection of art works and ceramics. It was, said Amelia in a letter to Eliza 'one of the shew [sic] houses of Norfolk' and she and Margaret spent nearly three weeks there, enjoying balls, musical evenings, playing cards and meeting other house guests. Having done her duty to the visitor, whom she found 'pert' and expectant of 'universal conquest', she was relieved to hand her over to the Aldersons at St Helen's House in mid-December and to resume her literary work. Still musing on the value of her friendships with Quakers and their way of life, she attended the funeral of Sophia Bland, the young daughter of a business associate of the Gurneys. The occasion inspired a heartfelt poem in which she described the grief of other bereaved parents who attended the funeral at the Friends burial ground and the soothing words spoken at the graveside.*

Amelia was also enjoying contact with Dawson Turner and his wife Mary. He approached her with requests for 'the handwriting' of her theatrical and literary friends, including Sarah Siddons and Helen Maria Williams (for his autograph and letter collection). She hesitated about sending him one of her letters from the poet George Crabbe, 'because they are so very flattering', but she asked Hayley to send a letter from his late friend Anna Seward. For herself, she sought from the Turners copies of etchings of people she knew and admired, such as Mrs Siddons, Wilberforce and Coke, in order that she might frame them and hang them in her room, along with a miniature of Hayley which the poet himself had given her. She was thrilled when Mary Turner agreed to do an etching from one of the portraits which Opie had painted of Dr Alderson:

> I *admire* the etchings excessively and am truly thankful both for the skill displayed and for the bounty which has enabled me to bestow a good likeness of my beloved father on those who are, in my opinion, really likely to value it.[7]

Meanwhile, *New Tales* was attracting favourable attention. Hayley, writing to 'Amelia Carissima!' said he hoped her father continued to enjoy 'the talents and renown of his dear admirable tale-telling daughter', he himself enjoyed the new tales, his favourites being *White Lies* and 'the concluding story of Marian Trelawney' (*The Welcome Home*).[8] Hayley was not alone in his opinion; the majority

---

* The poem *Lines to the memory of Sophia Bland jun. who was interred in the burying ground in Norwich belonging to the Friends in the December of 1818* in Amelia's handwriting has asterisks with footnotes indicating that the grieving parents were Joseph and Jane Gurney and the soothing words were spoken by Priscilla Gurney. (SoF, Port 31/125)

Etching by Mrs Dawson Turner, after John Opie, of Amelia's father. She received several copies; keeping one herself, despatching others to her cousins and writing a fulsome letter of thanks to Turner for the 'precious parcel'. The original portrait which Mrs.Turner worked on was one of two which Opie painted of his father-in-law. Amelia bequeathed it to her cousin Samuel Hurry Alderson. (Norwich Castle Museum And and Art Gallery)

of reviewers were complimentary, *The Scots Magazine* claiming that while Mrs Opie could not vie with her distinguished contemporaries in all aspects of fiction writing 'she excels all of them, perhaps, in the natural and impressive delineation of *female affection*, displayed in its best and most endearing forms'.[9]

Most of the stories focus on the themes of love and duty, the value of loyalty and steadfastness, the retribution acted upon those who commit cruel and dastardly deeds. The author's great interest in court procedures prompted the story of *Henry Woodville*. In a substantial footnote, she owns it was inspired by a case at the Norwich assizes in 1684 in which an innocent man was found guilty of murder and executed, the true villain having fled to France where he confessed the crime on his deathbed. In *The Quaker and the Young Man of the World*, she personifies the beliefs of her friend Joseph John in the shape of a wise older man, who acts as a mentor to a young man whose faults he attributes to his association with worldlings. In *The*

Ruffian Boy the heroine Ethelind, reflecting on a former prisoner who is seeking to destroy her, comes to the conclusion:

that a *well-regulated* prison – a prison in which religious and moral truths were inculcated, and habits of industry enforced, might have reformed the heart and ameliorated the temper of the culprit; and that when taught that, after having reconciled himself by penitence to his God, he might reconcile the world to him by a life of active virtue and benevolence, he might have been restored to society, penitent and reformed.[10]

In a lengthy footnote at this point in the story, Amelia states she must 'indulge' herself with an extract from 'Mr Buxton's admirable book on *Prison Discipline*'. Thomas Fowell Buxton had joined the newly-formed Society for the Reformation of Prison Discipline in 1816; two year later he became an MP which gave him the chance to pursue his reform projects.

The Ruffian Boy, probably the most melodramatic of all the tales, was adapted for the stage several times over the next two decades. It was first dramatised in 1819 for a production at Norwich Theatre Royal by an up-and-coming playwright, Edward Fitzball,* the son of a farmer in Cambridgeshire. Articled to a Norwich printer in 1809, he made his home in the city, married a local girl and began writing for the theatre. His version of *The Ruffian Boy* brought him to Amelia's attention. He was at a concert in the city on the evening before his new play's first night, when she came into the concert room:

Every eye turned towards her; she was worshipped in society, not only for her great talent and her polished manners, but for her peculiar beauty, which could not fail to strike even a stranger.... Judge of my confusion when, in an instant, I saw her eye directed through her glass† at me.

In the interval, having approached the young man, she wished him 'all possible success' with his new play, adding that she was assured he had already displayed 'remarkable dramatic skill' in his previous productions:

---

* His original surname was Ball. He added his mother's maiden name of Fitz when he began his writing career.
† The 'glass' was a lorgnette; it was not common for ladies to wear spectacles at that time. In a letter to Lady Charleville (1847) Amelia admitted she was always short-sighted.

The Ruffian Boy was produced with an unusual *éclat* and Mrs Opie, being with a large party of gentry in the stage box, was amongst the first to witness and applaud its performance.[11]

A year later Fitzball had a play accepted for the London stage by Tom Dibdin, the actor and playwright, who was managing the Surrey Theatre on Blackfriars Road. Encouraged by Amelia, he decided to move to the capital. By then another play based on *The Ruffian Boy* by Sarah Scudgell Wilkinson – known for her prolific outpourings of romances and melodramas adapted from other works – was being presented in London. Later Dibdin himself adapted the Opie tale for the stage.

Early in 1819 Amelia and her father renewed their friendship with Henry Crabb Robinson. After several years abroad, studying, exploring cultural pursuits and working as a foreign correspondent for *The Times*, Robinson had enrolled at the Middle Temple. He was admitted to the bar in 1819 and joined the Norwich circuit, soon becoming its leader. He wrote in his diary of spending an evening with the Aldersons at her uncle Robert's house, when 'Mrs Opie sang, told good stories, was in spirits, and at her ease.'[12] She spent a few weeks in London in the summer, hastening down to Felpham in September in great alarm, having heard that Hayley was dying. She had promised him she would visit him on his deathbed; in the event he recovered and lived for another 14 months.

In the autumn the Aldersons entertained Charles Stothard, an art historian, and his wife Anna, who were in Norfolk to visit the Dawson Turners. Anna (neé Kempe) had met her husband when taking painting lessons with his father, Thomas Stothard RA and they had been married only a year. She accompanied him on his art projects; while he sketched monuments and memorials in parish churches, she researched local histories and customs. After she was widowed, Anna married the Rev Edward Bray; as Anna Eliza Bray she became a full-time writer of fiction, memoirs and historical accounts. But in 1819 her writing career was in its infancy and she was preoccupied with assisting her first husband. Years later she recalled stopping at Norwich to see the Cathedral, but 'above all' to visit Mrs Opie:

Charles was well acquainted with Mr & Mrs Opie in his boyhood: the elder Stothard was the fellow Academician and great friend of Mr Opie. We passed an evening with them. Mrs Opie was so animated, so full of anecdote, so agreeable that the hours seemed to speed away on wings.

A woman of such fascinating powers of conversation I have rarely met with; she had seen much of the world and had known intimately many of the most celebrated persons. She was evidently a shrewd and attentive observer and though not satirical, yet her remarks were acute and full of point. I lament that I cannot recollect clearly enough to repeat several of her anecdotes ....

We next chatted on music, and she insisted on my playing to her on the pianoforte. I found she had a great taste for music; on my begging her to let me hear her sing, she complied with her accustomed grace, and taking up her harp lute accompanied herself and sang with much sweetness.... As we had to be up and ready by 4 o'clock in the morning to set off for London, we would have retired early, but neither Mrs Opie nor Dr Alderson would allow us to go. They insisted we should stay to supper.[13]

The sociable Mrs Opie relished such occasions, both at home and in London. Her annual visit to the capital in 1820 was to be the last of its kind for some time. Elizabeth Inchbald, then living almost as a recluse at Kensington, was pleased to receive visits from Amelia that summer; the two women continued to correspond with each other until Inchbald's death in August, 1821. By then Amelia's aging father had become very dependent on her and, devoted daughter that she was, she chose to stay with him.

While taking care of her ailing father, she tried to continue with her writing. She told Eliza that she woke early and wrote for hours before she got up: one night she lay awake 'and composed a whole new tale' in her head. She was also resuming lessons on her harp lute and enlisting the help of Dr Crotch's brother* to help her 'note down' her hymns. 'This was a *bright* thought of mine and the old man seems so pleased.' It was also a time of reflection and deepening interest in the Quaker way of life.

In the spring of 1820 she, and all the Gurneys, were grief-stricken by the deaths of four of the nine children of Thomas Fowell and Han-

---

* Probably Michael Beales Crotch, an older half-brother of William Crotch, whose career as a composer and organist had begun at the age of three, when, as a child prodigy, he toured the country giving recitals on the organ. He was later appointed the first principal of the Royal Academy of Music. The Crotch family home was in the parish of St George's, Colegate. Michael Beales Crotch was a trumpeter and a founder member of the Hall Concert Society – a group of musicians who played regularly in the city's St Andrew's Hall.

nah Buxton – Thomas Fowell, aged 10, Hannah, two, Rachel, five and the infant Louisa – within five weeks of each other. In the wake of this unbearable tragedy Fowell (as he was called by his family and friends) was not able to focus on his business and Parliamentary concerns for some time. In the summer he moved what he called 'the fragments of the family' from their home in Hampstead to Norfolk where he rented the old Cromer Hall from the Wyndham family. Although unwilling to leave her father at home on his own for long, Amelia did spend a few days in Cromer in the autumn, visiting her 'dear friends'.

Her new collection of stories, *Tales of the Heart,*[14] was published that year. As in her earlier works, Amelia explored relationships, but her tone was increasingly didactic, as she attempted to prove that ill temper, unkindness and arrogance cause grief to those who possess these traits of character, while tolerance, kindness and patience bring their own reward. It seems likely that some of the tales were written in haste and she did not have time to review and remove passages which hindered the narrative flow. The longest tale, *A Woman's Love and A Wife's Duty* is told in two parts. In part one, the female narrator tells the story of her abiding love for her cousin, which starts in childhood and leads to marriage; in part two she becomes a dutiful wife who stands by her man despite his gambling away of her inheritance and leaving her for another woman. The first part goes into rather too much detail about the couple's ancestors and their involvement in the American War for Independence; the second introduces far too many unlikely circumstances, as the heroine pursues her errant husband into post-Revolutionary France. In another tale, *The Two Sons,* Amelia's hero spends many years in India before returning to England to woo and win the daughter of the couple who have chosen to rescue him from his humble background. Again, the 'co-incidences' stretch the reader's credibility, as they do in *Love, Mystery and Superstition,* a convoluted tale of illicit passion, and *The Opposite Neighbour* in which a suspicious husband tests his young wife's fidelity by taking residence in a nearby house from which, having disguised his appearance and assumed another name, he can spy on her movements.

Reviewers were disappointed with the tales. *The Monthly Review* (August 1820) while admitting the 'predicament' of exercising a cool judgment when reviewing the work of 'a female writer', explained:

> We cannot speak harshly or judge austerely, of authors in muslin or sarsanet: gallantry, or sometimes a tenderer sentiment, interposes, and blots out an ungracious criticism....We make these confessions

that justice may be done to us, when we are absolutely *impelled* to pronounce an unfavourable opinion on a production of that amiable sex.

Blackwood's Edinburgh Magazine (August 1820) opined:

This lady does not improve in her manufacture of tales as she proceeds – her great staple was her *pathos*, and that she seems, pretty nearly, to have exhausted – nor has she much talent for incident or character to make up for it.

However, the tales caught the attention of the infamous Lady Caroline Lamb, wife of the Hon. William Lamb, and a novelist herself, but known primarily for her open infidelities, including a brief affair with Byron, of whom her first impression that he was 'mad, bad and dangerous to know' has become part of literary folklore. Born into the aristocracy – her father was the third Earl of Bessborough, her mother a daughter of the first Earl of Spencer, her aunt Georgiana Cavendish, Duchess of Devonshire – she had a chaotic upbringing and always regretted her lack of formal education. Fearless and impulsive, she liked dressing as a page-boy, associating with literary people and attending parties, where she shone as a brilliant conversationalist.

The impact of Amelia's tales led to her putting pen to paper. Addressing 'My dear Mrs Opie', she asked her to do her 'the favour' of going to see her. Amelia had encountered Lady Caroline at social events in London but here was letter of a more personal nature. She kept the letter, writing across it: 'First letter I ever received from Lady C. She heard I was coming up and wrote to Norwich for my address.' Having ascertained where in London Amelia would be staying, Lady Caroline wrote:

'I have been reading for the first time two of your Tales and am delighted with them. They not only amuse and interest and affect extremely but they amend – and it must be a delightful reflection for a person who has written for others to feel that they have done good instead of harm. You must tell me when I see you whether you will refuse to give me some of your unpublished poetry. I will not allow you to answer this in a letter – refusals are more easy on paper than in person.[15]

Presumably Amelia responded positively for the two women continued to correspond; whether or not she ever told her Gurney friends of her contact with the notorious Lady Caroline is not recorded.

The poor reviews of her new work may have upset Amelia but by the time they were published she had matters nearer home to concern her. Her aging father was suffering from bouts of depression and her friend Priscilla Gurney, a devoted Quaker whose charitable work included prison visiting, overseeing education for workhouse children and aiding the 'sick poor', was seriously ill.

On November 12th (Amelia's 51st birthday) Hayley died at his home in Felpham. Mourning his loss, she wrote an epitaph in rhyming couplets to the friend whose company and support she had so much appreciated, extolling not only his poetic prowess, but his charity and 'zeal for all mankind'; it was inscribed on a memorial tablet to the poet in Felpham Church. At the end of the year Dr Alderson decided to leave his post as physician to the Norfolk and Norwich Hospital; his letter of resignation was presented to the board on January 20th, when the governors:

> ...resolved that the thanks of this General Board be given to Dr Alderson for his very long and able professional services and unremitted attention paid at all times by him to the general welfare of this Hospital from its first Institution and that the chairman of this Board and the Rev Mr Stracey and Dr Rigby be appointed a committee for the purpose of transmitting this Resolution to Dr Alderson.[16]

Writing to Alexander Dyce, one of her literary friends in London, Amelia confirmed she was remaining with her father:

> I shall not revisit London (except business may carry me thither for two or three days), not for many years, I trust, as my dear father, hitherto so young for his years and so independent of me, is now old and ailing for the *first time* at 78 and dependent on me for amusement in a great measure. I therefore shall never leave home again unless he accompanies me which is very unlikely and I do not even drink tea out except, which is a nice occurrence, that he goes with me. However time flies away fast. My morning hours are my own and I rise very early – nor does he want me till he comes in from his rounds – for he still visits his patients and, except that he is very thin and occasionally feeble, and is *always suffering* more or less from that painful disorder *Hypochondria* he is much the same as ever he was and retains his appetite and his healthy complexion. Therefore I have much to be thankful for and a quiet life agrees

with both my body and my mind.[17]

Hudson Gurney recalled that during the doctor's final years 'Mrs Opie most assiduously attended him.... She read to him much in the Bible and other religious books and his views on religious subjects *entirely changed*.'[18] Amelia was thinking seriously about her own beliefs and whether or not she should apply for membership of the Society of Friends. She still enjoyed what Joseph John called 'worldly pleasures' and continued taking an interest in clothes and fashion. Sometimes she sent fabrics woven in Norwich to her cousins Sarah and Eliza, who had moved to London to live with their brother Tom; sometimes she asked the sisters to buy items not available to her in Norwich, such as whale bone 'to put into high collars of gowns' and told them, in some detail, what she herself was wearing. But much of her correspondence over the next four years contained soul-searching passages about religion.

During visits to London she had become acquainted with the Rev William Harness, a friend of many literary people including Mary Russell Mitford. It appears that he was a sympathetic correspondent, who was prepared to offer advice about reading materials and to whom she could pour out her thoughts and feelings. The new year brought another Gurney bereavement when Jane Birkbeck, daughter of Joseph and Jane Gurney of The Grove, died in childbirth. Her husband Henry Birkbeck, a partner in Gurneys Bank, was the brother of Joseph John's wife. Meanwhile, the Earlham Gurney siblings were spending as much time as they could with Priscilla, who was being looked after at Cromer Hall.

In a letter to Harness, having written about her father's health and the books she wished to read to him, Amelia gave news of the Gurneys:

> My beloved friend Priscilla Gurney still lives. The funeral of her cousin Jane Birkbeck was overwhelming, but not so much so, as I have known such scenes before. The eldest sister of ye deceased [Hannah Backhouse] spoke at ye grave; the father spoke also and with incredible firmness. The husband said not a word, but looked miserable and corpse like. Mrs Fry prayed at ye grave and her tones quite upset me and once I sobbed audibly. She afterwards preached in the meeting, and in a manner, and in language such as no description can do justice to – the beauty and pathos were unrivalled. All descriptions of religions and persons were there and ye effect

was electric on all.... You, probably, never saw a Quaker funeral. It is ye most touching of ceremonies....

Oh! what a rich and rare assemblage of beauty, talents, virtue and piety in ye course of ye last ten years I have followed to our Quaker burial-ground![19]

In conclusion, Amelia told Harness that, should he wish to see Newgate 'in its reformed state' on a day when Mrs Fry was in attendance, she would get a ticket from her. This was a reference to Elizabeth Fry's pioneering work on reforming the conditions for women prisoners in Newgate Gaol – a project which she had begun in earnest in 1816, despite initial opposition from family and friends. A fortnight later Amelia was writing to her cousin Eliza about the funeral of her beloved friend, who had died on March 31st:

Dearest Priscilla was interred last Monday and a most touching but satisfactory interment it was. Such public testimony borne to her character! She was indeed *perfect*. Joseph John, Mrs Fry and her uncle excelled themselves! There were much above 2000 persons present. I was earnestly invited to dine at Earlham that day but I would not leave my father. Luckily he was going to a consultation and thence to his club so at half past six I set off. It was chiefly a family party.... I have lost in Priscilla a friend who loved me dearly and who loved my *soul* I may say. She left me £5 in her will in proof of remembrance – the first legacy I have ever had! I feel proud to have been so remembered by such a being![20]

Her loss inspired a poem, *Priscilla's Grave*, which was not included in *Lays for the Dead*; Brightwell found a copy in Amelia's papers and reproduced it in her *Memorials*. She also published two prayers written in April, 1821, by the anxious daughter beseeching aid in leading her 'beloved parent' to God.

The London cousins invited her to stay with them in July for the coronation of George IV, but she refused, on the grounds that her absence would cause her father too much anxiety. Passing on family gossip, she said that when news came of the death of Bonaparte (on the island of St Helena) Mrs Alderson (wife of her uncle Robert) said she supposed that Mrs Opie would go into mourning. 'Indeed, I do mourn inwardly,' wrote Amelia.[21] In October she was sending condolences to the sisters on the death of their 'so kind' Durham uncle Dickens Hazlewood. With the letter she sent some Norwich crape as a present for mourning. 'It is very fashionable and I think *pretty* – you may prefer it to bombazine.'[22] A month later she was in mourning again for the loss of Dr Rigby, her father's dear friend and colleague. As she wrote to Dawson Turner, the death affected her father's spirits considerably but not his health: 'You cannot think how *I* miss poor Rigby! He used to come to us every other day, and sit with us while we breakfasted.'[23]

Chapter Twenty-three

With her social life curtailed, Amelia pressed on with her writing. Her next work – published in 1822 – was *Madeline*, a full length novel in two volumes, told primarily in the form of the title character's journal, edited, ostensibly, by her former governess. In a preface, the author assures her readers she is laying before them 'a story which is, in many respects, literally true, and that the characters in it are not entirely the creatures of the imagination.'[1]

The title character Madeleine is the daughter of humble Scots parents who are 'burthened' with a large family; she is brought up as a gentlewoman by a wealthy Sussex couple who take her into their home. The conflict between the two backgrounds is one of the story's themes, Madeline being not quite acceptable to the social class of either. There are many instances of her discomfort when she is obliged to return to her real family, with its lack of taste and ignorance of etiquette; on the other hand she is offended by the patronising attitudes and snobbery of people in the circle of her adoptive parents. Rumours, misunderstandings and deceits pepper the narrative, along with explorations of what it means to be an educated woman in a society which does not always value such accomplishments. Her secret marriage to a wealthy laird takes place in the opening chapter of volume two, but this is no 'happy ever after' love story, for the bride's problems are only just beginning. She still has to contend with financial problems, serious illness, her marital status, anxiety over her brother at Waterloo and a case at the Assizes before the many loose ends are tied up in the final pages.

In the weeks before the novel was published Amelia gave some attention to Lady Caroline Lamb, who had written on New Year's Day seeking advice on two stories she was writing and reminding her recipient she had promised her some unpublished verses. The black edge to the address sheet indicated the writer's mourning for her recently deceased mother:

> I have lost such a friend. Next to William [her husband] I loved her better than any thing in life but if it please God to spare him and I can grow good enough to dare die I shall not consider myself as

unhappy besides which I have passed such a very happy life and enjoyed so many blessings and so much kindness that it is wrong to repine.[2]

Amelia replied promptly, saying she was 'highly flattered' by the writer wishing to submit her work for inspection; she usually refused such requests but was prepared to make an exception because of her regard for Caroline's mother and a conversation they had shared about her daughter's writing:

> There was something so fascinating to me in the mother of whom you have been deprived that I think you must ever miss and regret her as an object of *vision*. It was always delightful to me to see her enter the room where I was and never was there more disinterested admiration than mine, for though her manner was always courteous, it never flattered my self-love.... I could say a great deal more on this subject but I forbear – and now dear Lady Caroline, to answer the rest of your very obliging letter.
>
> I had not forgotten my promise to send you some unpublished lines and last October *twelvemonth* I wrote you a letter and began to prepare the verses – but I thought that you had probably forgotten your request, and the letter was burnt. I have not time just now to revise, and correct the lines in question, but I will do so before long.[3]

To Robert Southey, one of the founders of the influential *Quarterly Review*, Amelia wrote she was going to 'take a great liberty' with him: she had an 'earnest desire' that her new novel should be noticed in the publication:

> where I never *yet* have had the honor [sic] of being *named*... but I am conscious that its writers review for the most part only such works as are of far more strength, importance and excellence than mine can boast and I forbore to ask for admittance where I felt that I had no claim to enter till I saw a novel reviewed in the Quarterly which, though abounding in force and in talents, did not I think deserve the circulation.
>
> ...*if* after reading my story of a *woman's heart*, for such my tale is, you can *conscientiously* raise it into notice by mentioning it in the *Quarterly* you would gratify the first ambition of my heart.[4]

Southey replied promptly, but declined to offer *Madeline* for review in the magazine. Although disappointed, Amelia wrote a courteous response saying she had no right to expect his 'compliance', adding:

My tale is not heart-breaking, as, to oblige my Co. and another person, I altered the catastrophe and have, I think, by that means injured it as a work and weakened my moral. But such as she is, my *Madeline* shall appear before you, and the ladies of your family and happy shall I be if, though I am forced to give up the proud distinction of being reviewed by you, my simple and *true* story calls forth in your domestic circle any heartfelt commendation and kind feelings towards its author...

You tell me that you feel you are growing old. Would that I felt the same but I do not, though older than you and I am almost ashamed of my vivacity and the buoyancy of my spirits. I consider however any continued elasticity of mind and feeling as one of the many blessings vouchsafed me, as I have need of all my cheerfulness to enable me to support the drooping spirits of my father, who till he was turned 78 never knew what pain or lowness was and now, at 79, is confined to the house by a very painful complaint and one which opium alone can render bearable.[5]

Replying a few weeks later Southey told the author:

Your *Madeline* is a great favourite here, and well deserves to be so. The tale is beautifully told, and everywhere true to nature....The tragic catastrophe would, as you say, have made the story more perfect, but it would have made the book painful, instead of pleasing, in recollection.[6]

Southey added that his influence on the *Quarterly Review* was greatly overrated; nevertheless, to convince Amelia that her tale had really interested him, he would write to the editor, and ask him to include an article on it. However, his request was in vain.

Amelia's old friend the Rev Francis Wrangham, now an archdeacon, enjoyed the novel. She wrote telling him his appreciation of the tale was 'a cordial' to her heart, adding she had 'learnt the documents on which y tale is founded' from a dear friend. 'I fear I ought to have killed Madeline and I *had done so* and broke my own heart and so I was easily prevailed upon to alter y Catastrophe. The *real* Madeline died.'[7]

Not only was Amelia a committed writer – both of works for publication and private correspondence – she was also a keen amateur artist. For several years she had been doing 'drawings', as she called them, of people she knew, telling Eliza in one letter of the interest taken in her work by the artist Joseph Clover, who was in Norwich completing the last of three commissions for the civic portrait collection. Clover, a Norfolk man, was inspired to take up painting as a career after getting to know Opie; from 1803 he had made his home in London. When Amelia was out one day, Dr Alderson showed her drawings to Clover, who said she had 'so capital an eye for likeness it ought to be cultivated'. On her return, the artist told her where she had failed in the drawings; he came back in the evening with materials he thought she might use, made a drawing for her to copy and spent some time giving her advice. 'He said he should go crazy if I had any master but himself.'[8] A few weeks later she reported to Eliza that her drawings were going on triumphantly. Dr Wright (Warner Wright, a

Mrs Dawson Turner started work on her etching from Opie's 1798 portrait of Amelia in February 1822. Her husband submitted each attempt to Amelia for comment. The fifth one (shown here) met with her approval, as she confirmed in a letter of May 29th: 'Nothing now can be better than the head, not only according to my own judgement, for of *its* correctness I might doubt, but according to that of everyone who sees it and I am very grateful to the fair artists.' (WL: Dawson Correspondence, O 13 23) (Norwich Castle Museum and Art Gallery)

physician at the Norfolk & Norwich Hospital), had sat for her one evening, with Clover looking on. Although proud of his daughter's skill with the pencil, Dr Alderson was reluctant to sit for her; she told her cousin Margaret she had to catch him unawares, when he was asleep.

She was glad of Clover's support, for this was the time when Mary Turner was working on her etching of Amelia from the 1798 portrait by John Opie. She had some misgivings about the first of Mrs Turner's attempts and hesitated about expressing them. Fortunately, Clover agreed with her and eventually she decided it was 'a duty and justice' to tell the Turners – in some detail – what the two of them thought was wrong with the etching:

> I conclude that this little fault can be remedied but whether it be worthwhile to do it is another thing, as very few will detect it and *altogether* nothing can be better than it is. Still I could not be easy in my mind without putting it in the power of those who are, I know, ambitious of *excellence* in all they undertake.[9]

Joseph John's wife Jane died on June 10th, 1822, leaving him with a young son and daughter, John Henry, aged three and Anna, aged two. Amelia wrote straightaway to Rachel Gurney, who, with her sister Richenda, had been helping at the sickbed:

> Such a happy union to be so *soon* dissolved.... You will easily believe I wish earnestly to see *all* or some one of you – but I will not come over till you tell me I may.... Dear, dear Joseph! I can send no message to him, but he knows my heart....[10]

As always on such occasions the Gurney relations drew together, Betsy hastening to Earlham to be with her family and writing an account of the bereavement in her journal, where she described Jane Gurney as 'an excellent wife, mother, daughter and sister and a great friend to the poor'.[11] Amelia wrote a poem to Jane's memory, calling her 'a bright example of the Christian life'.[12]

Ollyett Woodhouse died in Bombay on June 22nd but it was many weeks before the news reached Norwich. Harriet, his widow, returned to England in 1823, dying herself a year later. Amelia, still grieving the loss of this dear cousin, befriended Ollyett's second son, Henry Alderson Woodhouse, when he left India, possibly with his mother and, apparently, bringing with him one of the Opie portraits of his father, which Amelia offered to care for:

If thou art still willing to let me keep thy beloved father's picture for thee, and to part with it now, my friend Joseph Sparshall will be so good as to get a case for it and convey it to me in safety.[13]

At this time Henry was staying at Great Yarmouth, where he met his future wife, Mary Palgrave, whose aunt was the wife of Dawson Turner. Once married, they went to live in Bombay, where Henry worked as Diocesan Registrar.

Joseph John's interest in Amelia's spiritual welfare persisted; he was also taking an interest in Dr Alderson's views on religion, recording instances in his journal of time spent with father and daughter. He kept his sister informed about Amelia's attendance at Friends meetings, assuring 'dearest Betsy' that her influence was most beneficial. Among the many pamphlets he wrote, *A Letter to a Friend on the Authority, Purpose and Effects of Christianity and especially on the Doctrine of Redemption*, which ran to 15 editions, was thought to have been addressed to the doctor. Amelia herself was sharing her thoughts on such matters with her cousin, writing in one letter that she wished her father, who was 'low in mind', would find comfort and consolation in religious belief.

Early in the new year she wrote to Joseph John saying he would be pleased to hear that her father's heart was more resigned than it had ever been to the divine will and she herself had attained peace of mind:

I have felt more especially today a sort of *repose* such as I have longed for for years – something which when in the world and its most dissipated scenes I wished to feel, but in vain – yet also something which I thought I was formed for and should enjoy *one day* tho' how I was to get it I knew *not* – but it has come to me at last through trials and conflicts – a peace which the world cannot give and which the world cannot take away.... My only fear is that I am thus because I have not had since Monday any intercourse with worldlings.[14]

In February she wrote again:

I wish to tell thee that we are going on more comfortably and that my dear father attributes his present tranquillity to thy printed letter which he reads I find every Thursday morning while I am at Meeting and one passage of which he has nearly gotten by *heart*.[15]

Amelia also told her Quaker friend that she had been visiting 'the *sick*', one of whom was her dear Susannah Taylor, suffering a painful terminal illness which gave her a 'terrible suffocating cough'. The dying woman was insisting on sleeping in her parlour alone at night. Amelia felt it her duty to tell her she risked suffocation from her cough, but, as she reported to Joseph John, her old friend had 'an unconquerable obstinacy and an over directed love of independence'. She was also shocked to note that Susannah* appeared to be preparing for 'a sort of *Heathen philosopher's* death', talking not a word about her Saviour.

Although proud of his daughter's skill with the pencil, Dr Alderson refused to sit for her, so she had to 'catch' him when he was asleep, she told her cousin Eliza. (New York Public Library: Pforzheimer Collection)

With religious matters on her mind she penned a poem, dated April 7th, 1823, to her father:

> And thou art eighty! Tis thy natal day!
> Then, oh! forgive me, if I dare to pray
> (Since, from so dear a tie tis hard to part, A tie, sole treasure of this lonely heart)
> That many a year thou yet may'st with me stay,
> Resigned in pain, and cheerful in decay,
> While the bright hopes redeeming love has taught,

---

* She died on June 5th, 1823, and was buried at the Octagon Chapel.

Prompting each pious purifying thought,
Live in thy love, to tell of sins forgiven,
And plume its pinions for its flight to Heaven.[16]

Although she was moving towards becoming a Quaker, the journey
was never an easy one. In August she sent a painfully honest letter to
Joseph John, writing 'Private' on its address page. She told him she often found it easier to write her thoughts and feelings than to *say* them.
She was full of fear at the prospect of the many trials, temptations and
obstacles she saw before her – impressions which accompanied her to
and at Meeting:

> ...when, as if thine eyes had read my heart, and thine ear been ren-
> dered sensible to the voice of my supplication, thy ministry came
> over my soul like balm poured into a painful wound and I felt
> comforted and encouraged....
>
> To watch and pray lest we enter into temptation is, I am con-
> vinced, necessary at every moment of one's life and in *every situa-
> tion whatever* be it *in* or *out* of the world. Do pity thy poor friend,
> dear Joseph, and let her benefit by thy prayers.[17]

The young Quaker himself was reporting on her progress to his uncle
Joseph and his sister Betsy, telling the former 'My clever Dr A and
Amelia seem to go on nicely,' and the latter 'Amelia goes on steadily.'

The brother and sister united in prevailing upon Amelia to become
involved in prison visiting in Norwich – a new interest which she outlined to her cousin Margaret:

> *Entre nous,* for it is not known here yet, Betsy Fry made me, aided
> by Joseph, join an association of ladies, all friends except their sis-
> ters, to visit the prisons and I am *Secretary*!! I am also y only lady
> stationary here and able to visit always, par conséquence I have
> been on constant duty at y jail (y other prisons we have not yet
> *leave* to visit) and the only fear for me is that the duty should be *too
> interesting*. I feel a strong wish thus to devote myself to this service
> of my fellow creatures, and Betsy thinks I am y sort of person to be
> *effective*.... We read to them, set them things to get by heart, hear
> them spell, give them work and so on – and my jail adventures are
> already very interesting. The jailer and his wife are *charming*, and
> she tells me very curious anecdotes of *sentiment* in the midst of
> depravity – love tokens exchanged at parting between the *profli-
> gate* of both sexes, which affectingly exhibits remnants of *original*

brightness fallen tho' they be.

I had a tête-à-tête y other day with a lad sentenced to Botany Bay for fowl stealing who is brother to my housemaid. I was the bearer of a message from his poor father on whom his bad courses have brought *palsy*. I had also found out that he was attached to, and adored by a girl of the town, seized with him as a receiver of y stolen goods and when I told him she should not be forsaken, that I had visited her in jail and would do so in Bridewell* and we would reclaim her if possible, he burst into tears, and thanked me so fervently! The wretched girl seems very penitent... She and her companion, a noble looking girl, are sentenced to 6 months confinement and hard labour in Bridewell. At ye end of that time we hope to get a room and a man and his wife to keep them, to which we can take these girls (and others) when discharged till we can get them employment, or perhaps we can continue to employ them there to prevent want leading them back to their old courses. This scheme was mine and J.J.G. approves it and Cath Fry [Elizabeth's eldest daughter] says a Miss Neave has done it in London and it *succeeds* wonderfully.[18]

Amelia explained that the association's patroness was Lady Suffield, wife of Lord Suffield, who, with Hudson Gurney would be providing the money for the project. A radical MP, anti-slavery campaigner, prison reformer and friend of the Gurneys and Buxtons, Suffield had a country seat in Norfolk – Gunton Hall, near Cromer – and was a member of the Norfolk Gaol Committee.

The ongoing contact with the redoubtable Elizabeth Fry was of immense value to Amelia as she struggled with her conscience and sensibilities before making the decision to apply for membership of the Society of Friends. By January 1824 she was almost ready to do so, sending a heartfelt account of her position to the Quaker whose example was such an inspiration and whose opinion she so valued. Addressing 'dearest Betsy', she explained that she did not require an answer in the recipient's own hand: '*sufficient* for me is the privilege of writing to thee when I feel disposed to do so'. She told her friend something of her Briggs family's religious background, especially the Wesleyan Methodists whose ideas had impressed her. Thinking things over, she felt she was being called to the Society, yet she feared she could never be allowed to join 'as a convinced person and one will-

---

* The Bridewell is now a museum of local crafts and industries.

ing to resign all for Christ's sake' because she was 'too sinful and too disobedient in many ways'. However, she never felt so *comforted* as she did at Meeting:

> To say the truth, much as I see, or think I see, the hand of my gracious Lord in leading *me,* to whom have been given so many *ties* to a worldly life in the various gifts which have been bestowed on me (I mean accomplishments as they are called), to communion with a sect which requires the sacrifice of them almost in toto is thereby trying my faith to the *uttermost.*[19]

Four weeks later the decision was made. The Rev William Harness was one of the first to be told:

> Since we parted I have undergone a change, for which a length of years had gradually prepared me. I was brought up a Socinian dissenter. But, in 1814 I embraced orthodox opinions, and left that Sect. Since then, I have always, at Norwich, attended ye Friends Meeting House, and worshipped with some of my dearest and best friends.
>
> Three years ago, when my darling friend Priscilla Gurney died, I asked for one of her caps, with a full conviction I should, one day, wear it, but, till last July no one but Betsy Fry, I believe, ever thought I should do so. However, the die is now cast – and all ye preliminary steps, save one, that I have to take, are taken. I am not yet a member of ye Society of Friends, nor do I know when I shall be, but that is of no importance.[20]

Despite all the soul-searching about her religious path, Amelia was also enjoying more worldly pleasures, including visits from literary and artistic friends. Southey paid a visit to Norwich with his daughter Edith for a week in January, inspiring Amelia to write a poem for Miss Southey's album, extolling the pleasures of their stay and regretting it could not have been longer. Later she told Eliza that Southey and his daughter were so delighted with her drawing of Clarkson, the slave trade campaigner, that she was asked to copy that into the album. Henry Crabb Robinson also spent time with Amelia and her father while working in the city. The artist Benjamin Haydon, commissioned to do a portrait of the city's 1822 Mayor, Robert Hawkes, was in Norwich during the summer. Plymouth-born Haydon had become a student at the Royal Academy in 1804 and John Opie was one of the first people he got to know in London. A talented artist, but tactless and opinionated, Haydon enjoyed seeing Amelia again. He recorded in his diary a conversation he had with Mrs Opie, when he was having breakfast with her, in which she reminisced about parties in London and told him that 'Byron's voice was the most exquisite of any mortal's she had ever heard'.[21]

Amelia did this drawing of the artist Benjamin Haydon after he had breakfast with her in August 1824, when he was in Norwich working on a commission to paint a civic portrait. (New York Public Library: Pforzheimer Collection)

Amelia was also preparing her next work for publication – a set of didactic tales about lying – having abandoned a novel which her publishers had already begun to advertise. Anxious to reassure her Quaker friends that her novel-writing days were over, she wrote to Mrs Fry:

> As it is possible that thou may'st have been told that a new novel from my pen called *The Painter & his wife* is in the press, I wish to tell thee that this is a *falsehood* – that my Co. advertised this only begun work unknown to me and that I have written to say the said work is not written or ever will be. I must own to thee however that as several hundred of it are already ordered by the *trade* I have felt the sacrifice, but I do not repent of it.[22]

The sacrifice she felt was the loss of income; however, she was pleased to tell Betsy that Joseph John was 'highly pleased' with her new work and thought it must do *good*.

The two volumes of *Illustrations of Lying in all its Branches* were published early in 1825. Although written before she was accepted into the Society of Friends, Amelia chose to use Quaker-style personal pronouns in her dedication:

> To thee, my beloved Father, I dedicated my first, and to thee I also dedicate my present, work – with the pleasing conviction that thou art disposed to form a favourable judgment of any production, however humble, which has a tendency to promote the moral and religious welfare of mankind.[23]

Possibly her most ambitious and complex piece of writing, *Illustrations*, is made up of moral tales, each demonstrating a particular aspect of telling lies and its damaging, even fatal, effect on the lives of its perpetrators or victims. Each chapter opens with her own views and definitions of the type of lie she is about to exemplify and ends with a moral judgment. Having devoted ten chapters to the tales, she then presents a further seven chapters, which offer essays on the subject, with lengthy assessments of and excerpts from the writings of moralists and philosophers, including her old friend Godwin. Deciding that 'the strongest motive to abhor lying and cleave unto truth [is] obedience to the DIVINE WILL', she explains that she has offered her observations 'with much fearfulness and humility', concluding her work with a summary of the principles she has laid down.

Illustrations ran into three editions in England and achieved great acclaim in America, where it was brought out by a succession of publishers over the next three decades, one of whom produced special Sunday School editions. In Norwich an enthusiastic reader published a 24-page pamphlet in the form of a letter signed 'A Lover of Truth' in which he applauded the work, expressed his own observations about falsehoods and added suggestions for the 'further work' he believed she might be writing.[24]

Mentioning the work in a letter to her friend, the MP Sir William Elford, Mary Russell Mitford focused on the author's move towards the Quakers:

> Pray, talking of tales, have you seen Mrs Opie's *Lying*? She is all over Quakerized, as you of course know – to the great improvement, as I hear (for I have not seen her) of appearance. It is certainly a pretty dress. She *thee's* & *thou's* people; calls Mr Haydon 'friend Benjamin'.... With all this, she is just as kind and good-

humoured as ever; and Mr Haydon told me that, in about a quarter of an hour's chat, she forgot her *thee's* & *thou's*, and became altogether as merry as she used to be. She has really sacrificed upwards of a thousand pounds copy-money for a novel, which she had contracted for; and yet I believe there are difficulties still as to her admission to the sisterhood. You also may have heard say that a certain Mr Gurney is in some sort the cause of this conversion, and that there are difficulties there also; but of this *I* say nothing.[25]

Miss Mitford's comments would indicate that Amelia's potential conversion to Quakerism and the influence of Gurney were common knowledge among the literary, artistic and political circles in which she had been such a popular figure. There was gossip, too, in her home city. Fox, the Unitarian minister, helping out at the Octagon Chapel while the pastor was absent, told his fiancée:

Mrs Opie is exciting much tea-table talk. She has become a regular attendant at Quakers' meetings, and we have to discuss whether she is really to be metamorphosed into a Friend, or only goes there to study manners and characters for a new novel.[26]

As indicated in Amelia's letter to Betsy, there were to be no more novels. But she did write *Tales of the Pemberton Family: For the Use of Children*, a set of 'improving tales' as such works were called in those days, which was published in 1825. The printer for both *Illustrations* and this new work was Simon Wilkin, brother-in-law of Amelia's solicitor Thomas Brightwell. Wilkin had set up his business on Norwich Haymarket, devoting himself to publishing, bookselling, printing, bookbinding and supplying stationery. In 1822 he had helped to found the Norfolk and Norwich Literary Institution, to which Amelia subscribed. His first professional work for her was printing her narrative poem *The Negro Boy's Tale Addressed to Children* (originally published in her first anthology) for the publishers Harvey & Darton as a new slim volume for which she wrote a special introduction explaining the evils of the slave trade.

However, her main preoccupation during the first few months of 1825 was going through the necessary procedures for acceptance into the Society of Friends. She was in correspondence with Alfred Corder, a young Quaker from Ipswich, who was a protégé of Joseph John and accompanied him on some of his ministerial duties in Lincolnshire.* She sent him some verses she had written about his mentor and they began to exchange thoughts on aspects of religion. In April she wrote of being summoned to meet 'the monthly meeting committee', made up of senior Quakers:

> It was a very solemn thing and begun by a sweet encouraging prayer from Joseph Gurney [of The Grove].... On *the whole* I am come away satisfied and *comforted* but as I have to answer *close questions* and will answer *closely* to *the truth* I fear that *in little things* and *by* them it will be long before Friends have unity sufficient with me to admit me a member....
>
> Well I think I have spoken *conscientiously* and I feel my beloved and revered friend Joseph Gurney was satisfied with me and that is a comfort. 'Farewell my dear' he said as he shook my hand when we parted and he never says that but when he is particularly pleased.
>
> Yet, dear Alfred, I could sit down and weep heartily lest this were vain and foolish.[27]

Five weeks later her application for membership was read for the first time at the Gildencroft† an occasion of 'much solemnity' for Joseph John, who listed Amelia and the other applicants and recorded the event in his journal: 'I knelt down to supplicate...that those who were gathering towards us might be kept from the power of their enemy and preserved in the simplicity of truth.' His journal entry for August 18th noted: 'The Monthly Meeting on fifth day was a large, and a good, solid time. Dear A. Opie was received into membership.'[28]

---

* Corder died in the autumn of 1825. Joseph John Gurney said he had loved the young man as a brother and his death brought 'inexpressible grief' to his friends. (Braithwaite, *Memoirs*, Vol.1, p.283)

† The purposed-built Gildencroft opened in 1699 on land adjacent to the Society's burial ground, the first Friends meeting house in Goat Lane having been acquired 20 years earlier. The Gildencroft was destroyed in the Norwich Blitz of 1942; it was rebuilt in 1958 and is now used as a children's centre.

Chapter Twenty-four

Reactions to Amelia becoming a member of the Society of Friends were mixed: Anna Eliza Bray was mystified:

At the time we were visiting her Mrs Opie was not a Quaker. It was many years afterwards that she joined that sect of Dissenters, to be a member of which, her peculiar and uncommon talents seemed to render her unfit.[1]

Harriet Martineau took a derisive view:

...she suddenly discovered that all is vanity: she took to grey silks and muslin, and the 'thee' and 'thou', quoted Habakkuk and Micah with gusto and set her heart upon preaching. That, however, was not allowed. Her Quaker friends could never be sufficiently sure how much was 'imagination'... her utterance was confined to loud sighs in the body of the Meeting.[2]

Crabb Robinson, in Norwich for the Assizes, was not too perturbed:

Called on Mrs Opie who had then become a Quakeress. She received me very kindly but as a Quaker in dress and diction. I found her agreeable and not materially changed. Her dress had something coquettish in it, and her becoming a Quakeress gave her a sort of éclat; yet she was not conscious, I dare say, of any unworthy motive. She talked in her usual graceful and affectionate manner.[3]

Constable's son Thomas, who first met her in 1816, was impressed:

In 1834 I saw her again, when under the attractive influence of the admirable Frys and Gurneys she had joined the Society of Friends. The lapse of 18 years had carried her far beyond middle age, but her manner was cheerful as ever, and in her quaint and becoming attire of lavender and white she appeared to have gained instead of lost in personal comeliness.[4]

Southey wrote: 'I like her in spite of her Quakerism – nay, perhaps the better for it.'[5] And the Quaker garb made an impression on her younger relatives, as her cousin Margaret's daughter recalled:

I can see her now – the soft, plump, rounded figure, perfectly upright, the head exquisitely poised on the shoulders, not even over-weighted by the tall Quaker helmet fastened under her chin by crisp muslin frills which closed round the delicate curves of her cheek. Over her shoulders and across the full lines of her figure was folded the soft white muslin handkerchief, always perfectly dainty and fresh....Then came the flowing skirt of some soft rich silk.[6]

This description of the older Mrs Opie in her Quaker dress was to come much later, but, undoubtedly, her taste for style and quality clothing would have made her wish to do the best she could within the limitations of the Society's ruling on attire. In the weeks follow-ing her admittance, however, her prime concerns were the decline of her beloved father and bereavements within the Quaker community. Only days before her acceptance, a young Friend, Thomas Sparshall, died. Amelia wrote a poem, mourning the loss of one whose presence in her 'darken'd home' had shone 'like a bright lamp at evening' and 'cheer'd away each gathering gloom'.*

In a letter to her cousins Sarah and Eliza, who were staying with friends in Paris, she informed them of the sad event:

> ...a great and most unexpected sorrow came upon us in the death of our beloved young friend Thomas Sparshall, who has been now for many years our constant evening visitor and the kind supplier of my place whenever I dined or drank tea out. Dear fellow! he was here, bright, blooming and happy in y 2nd day (Mon) evening (yesterday 3 weeks). The next morning early he was seized with his mortal malady, bleeding from the intestines and on y 6th day, y Friday following, he bled to death. I saw him die and saw him *dying* and still I feel it difficult to believe that he is *gone for ever!* He was only 20.[7]

Thomas Sparshall was the son of Edmund Sparshall, a Quaker, who traded as a wine and spirits merchant in Fye Bridge Street, just round the corner from Dr Alderson's house in Colegate. Edmund and his wife Judith had an older son, Joseph, whose help was also valued by Amelia, as she explained to her cousins:

---

* A copy of the poem on a black-edged parchment, addressed *In Memory of our beloved young friend Thomas Sparshall*, signed by Amelia and dated August 15th, 1825, is held at Norfolk Record Office (MC/1389/1)

Last Sabbath day evening my father was seized with encreased [sic] pain and a chilly fit accompanied by so alarming a change in his pulse that he *gave himself up* and during the whole night Joseph Sparshall and myself who watched near him believed him in great danger, but he rallied again and now, tho' weaker, he is much as usual....

I sometimes, I own, shrink back appalled from the solitary path that lies before me if I survive my father, but I recollect myself again and feel thankful that I am where and what I am and I rejoice that my religious course is now *sealed.*

She also wrote news of Thomas Sparshall to her friend Hannah Martin, whose husband Simon* became a partner in Gurneys Bank that year. Hannah was the daughter of another of the bank's staff, Thomas Ransome, and had been brought up as a Quaker, but ceased her membership when she married Martin because he was not of the faith. The Martins lived at Bank House in Norwich, but spent their summers at Hill House on Richard Gurney's Northrepps Hall estate. A few weeks after writing to her about young Sparshall's death, Amelia was penning Hannah a letter of condolence on the death of her daughter Emma.† She advised Hannah to take up work and occupation: 'I, who can only do plain work, have in moments of sorrow found great alleviation of them by working whole days at common seaming and hemming when I could do nothing else.'[8]

There was some respite when Elizabeth (now Lady Milman), described by Amelia as 'a darling', came to Norwich with her husband Sir William, a governor of the Old Bailey, and their four older children to stay with her father Robert Alderson. Writing to tell Eliza about their visit she also gave her response to the news that their cousin Margaret Alderson was about to marry John Vincent Thompson, apparently accepting his proposal under some pressure from her father and brothers:

He is an agreeable man, I believe, and has loved her many years

---

* Simon's uncle, Simon Martin senior, son of a Norwich weaver, was working for bankers in London when he was invited to help run the Gurneys Bank when it was set up in 1775. His portrait was painted by John Opie.
† Three years later the Martins had another daughter whom they named Emma. She became a writer under her married name of Marshall. Her older sister Hannah also became a writer under her married name of Geldart: her works included profiles of T.F.Buxton, Elizabeth Fry and J.J.Gurney.

and has learning and talents. *I*, old as I am, could not be talked into marrying any man and I must *love* decidedly ere I so consented and how hurt *I* should be to have *my* father and brothers so eager to get rid of me apparently, as to be so soon satisfied in a husband for me.[9]

After their wedding in Hull, the newly-weds went to Paris. Amelia wrote a letter in which she brought the bride and her husband up to date with all the family news. Margaret's father, Dr John Alderson, had come to stay with his brother Robert, bringing with him gifts of wedding cake for all the family. He had cheered Amelia greatly by saying her father was no more near *dying* than *he* was. She added that the maids were worn out and she herself was suffering fatigue and anxiety, but Joseph Sparshall was 'such a help', sleeping at the house every night. She did not know what they would do without him.

Amelia's drawing of Joseph Sparshall, the young Quaker, who gave her valuable support during the last weeks of her father's life. (Norwich Castle Museum and Art Gallery)

Nothing can exceed my beloved parent's tranquil and resigned state of mind and J.J. Gurney has had most satisfactory conversations with him relative to his entire and *sole* confidence in the merits of his Saviour. He sent for him last first day Eve when he thought himself dying to ask him to promise to *take care of me* and when he did so, he said he should then *die easy* and had not a care in the world.

Her father's condition made it difficult for her to get to the Friends Quarterly Meeting:

> However, if my father is better, I hope to be able to leave him for a few hours and go. I feel deeply thankful that I was admitted before this illness took place as it has been a pleasure to my father. He told me the other night that he had only known three happy periods in his life. The first was when I was born, the next when I wrote y *Father and Daughter* and it *succeeded* and ye third when I became a *Quaker*. What a comfort to me!...
>
> There will be much to see in Paris. Pray write to me from that gay city if thou hast time – but do learn to date thy letters. Tues: morning is *no date at all*! In fear I should lose the orderly and ex-cellent habit of dating I even date *my notes*. Godwin, the author, scolded me into this rational regularity.[10]

Amelia would also miss an important county meeting on the slavery question, which involved three days of activity at Earlham, where many national figures involved in the ongoing campaign to grant free-dom to all slaves in British colonies, were house guests. A week before the event Joseph John told his sister Betsy 'The Doctor declining very gradually, Amelia is capital. Never was anything better timed (in my opinion) than her admission.'[11]

Dr Alderson died on Thursday, October 20th. Although not a member of the Society of Friends, permission was given for him to be interred in their burial ground at the Gildencroft.

Brightwell was only 14 at the time of the doctor's death, but over the years she developed a high regard for Mrs Opie and 'the true ex-cellence of her moral and religious character', which inspired her re-cord of Amelia's 'religious history' in which she told how 'the inmost depths of her nature were stirred' by the illness and death of her fa-ther: 'Filial love was, through life, her strongest passion; and all the affection of which she was capable was centred on her father.'[12]

Despite his preoccupation with guests and meetings on the slavery business, Joseph John found time to visit the dying man. He recalled this last visit in his journal:

> Fifth day (Thursday), amidst its full and eager pursuits, was sad-dened and solemnized by the death of dear old Dr Alderson; after

a night of severe suffering, and after a final struggle of distressing character. I saw him the last time on third day afternoon (Tuesday), when I took the opportunity of his awakening from his usual state of slumber, to pour forth a prayer by his bedside. For this he was very thankful; and the impression left on my own spirit, by the circumstance, was comforting, as it related to this beloved, aged friend....

Dear A.O. is wonderfully helped and supported. I am very thankful that she now belongs to the family of Friends.[13]

The grieving daughter appreciated letters of condolence. Responding to a note from Eliza, she wrote:

Thy few lines were very sweet and welcome tho' short. My heart is very *sore* and at times seems almost broken. I feel my loss more now than I did at first and can scarcely make myself stay where I am till the time for moving comes but you will see me soon, that is in the first week of the first month. I have business in London but must return here before I finally leave my house which is to be *sold* and then the world is all before me.[14]

Although Amelia intended to dispose of the last house she had shared with her father, it would be several years before she did so. As she began to come to terms with her loss, she became more involved with Quaker activities, meetings of the Bible Society and 'good works'. She had been a member of the Norwich Society for relieving the Sick Poor at their own Houses since 1819, serving as a member of the ladies' committee; she continued her commitment to the charity for the rest of her life. It meant attending monthly meetings, visiting the needy in their homes, helping to organise fund-raising bazaars and assessing what provision was needed for families who fell on hard times because of illness and the subsequent loss of income. She also took an interest in the Norfolk and Norwich Magdalen, a home for 'fallen women' which was opened in July 1827, at Life's Green within the precincts of Norwich Cathedral.

In the context of her commitment to the campaign to end slavery she produced a narrative poem for children *The Black Man's Lament* or *How to Make Sugar*. Illustrated with coloured pictures of negroes being sold into slavery and working in the sugar cane plantations, the poem opens with an appeal to its young readers:

Come, listen to my plaintive ditty,

Ye tender hearts and children dear!
And, should it move your souls to pity,
Oh! try to *end* the griefs you hear.[15]

Then follows an account of life from the slave's point of view; his tale concludes with his hopes of an end to his miseries, having learned from 'Christian men' that after death God will wipe every tear away. For Amelia, visiting cousins and their children brought enjoyment and interest. One of her first family visits in the months following her father's death was to Welnetham in Suffolk, where she stayed with her cousin Samuel Hurry Alderson, his wife and 'three magnificent boys'. Thoughts of her father took priority on her return:

> ...today I visited my dear father's grave. He hoped I would some-times do so! I felt peace both for him and myself while I looked on it, and looked forward with cheerfulness to sleeping beside him.[16]

Meanwhile, a great-nephew of her late husband, 16-year-old Edward Opie, wishing to get started on his own career as an artist, arrived in London from Cornwall. After finding somewhere to live, he went straight to the Royal Academy and set about calling on artists such as Northcote who had known John Opie well. He also got in touch with Amelia who invited him to Norwich, where he stayed for three weeks before returning to London to pursue his career. Edward, the grandson of John Opie's older brother William, was only the second member of her husband's family whom she had met. She believed he had talent and did her best to encourage him, reporting to her cousin Sarah that, while staying with her, he had painted 'an admirable copy' of the portrait of John Gurney and portraits of two of Simon Martin's children. She thought he was really good and 'has it in him'.[17]

Amelia was planning to stay with friends in the Lake District. She left Norwich early in September 1826, stopping off in London for Sarah's wedding to Lenon Jean Baptiste De Barbot at St Andrew's Church, Holborn. Amelia was a witness to the marriage, along with Sarah's siblings Eliza and Tom. The service was conducted by Robert Jervis Coke Alderson, who, having graduated at Oxford, had been ordained into the Church of England the previous year.

The joy of that occasion and the subsequent pleasures of her month's stay at Grasmere brought some respite from the grieving process. Amelia enjoyed the three-day journey from London, when she made friends on the first day with a fellow traveller, a witty and interesting clergyman, who left the coach at Coventry that evening. She described him in a letter to Tom as ' a *clerical* Lord Herbert Stuart – the same penetrating look, joyous laugh and keen sense of the ridiculous....'[18] She expanded on her encounter with the clergyman in a much longer letter to friends in London, remarking on 'how satisfactory and how curiously coincidental' was their meeting, for he was a Catholic priest and the very man to whom De Barbot, also a Catholic, had been obliged to apply before he could marry a Protestant:

> He said he disliked such marriages and never chose to have anything to do with them, if he could help it, but he was so pleased with De Barbot, so satisfied of his innocency of mind, purity of intentions and openness, that he said to him, 'My dear, I am pleased to do this for thee.'[19]

A highlight of her stay in the Lake District was a visit to Lowther Castle, the home of William and Augusta Lowther, the 1st Earl and Countess of Lonsdale, who were patrons of the arts. Wordsworth, whom they had helped financially, was a frequent visitor. Lady Lonsdale kept an album in which some of the visiting poets wrote verse. Amelia, writing to Joseph John from the castle, told him that fellow guests Wordsworth and Sir George Beaumont* were 'charming'. Now she must:

> write some lines for the most *splendid* of Albums. I must do it. Lady Lonsdale bids and I *obey*. The cautious *Rogers* [the poet] has given a translation only...Sir Walter Scott has begun the book. If I give ought of my own it shall be of humble pretension – but it were a *meanness* to shrink from competition, and *vanity* not *humility*.[20]

Joseph John was making plans to marry again. During a visit on Friends' business to the west country he had stayed at Elm Grove, near Melksham in Wiltshire with Rachel Fowler, a cousin of his late wife. There he sought her permission to ask Mary, her younger daughter – 14 years his junior – to be his wife. As he understood it, Mary accepted his proposal believing she had 'the sanction of that gracious Lord whom she desired to serve'[21] and he returned to Earlham a happy man, but anxious about his beloved's 'delicacy of health'. Any perusal of the Gurney letters held in the Library of the Religious So-

---

* Beaumont, an accomplished amateur artist, was a wealthy arts connoisseur and collector, patron of the artist John Constable and friend of Wordsworth. He was a founding director of the British Institution and a major sponsor behind the creation of the National Gallery.

ciety of Friends would indicate how widely they shared and discussed matters concerning the activities of family and friends. The Fowlers had been informed of the death of Dr Alderson. Rachel wrote to Joseph John asking him to present her 'kind love to A. Opie' and Mary, recently bereaved of her own father, added a few lines:

> I wish that we were likely to have an opportunity of becoming acquainted with Amelia Opie. She is a person of whom I have heard characters given so widely differing from each other that I long to see and judge a little for myself and from all I have recently learnt I do not doubt being much pleased with her.[22]

Having achieved some peace of mind during the first year following her father's death – much of it due to the resolution of her religious struggle and the comfort of being embraced warmly into the family of Friends – Amelia developed a new life style. On New Year's Day, 1827, she started to keep a diary in which she reported the day's events and, frequently, her responses to what she was reading – mostly hymns, religious works, the poetry of Felicia Hemans and the writings of her old friend Anna Letitia Barbauld,* who had died seven months before Dr Alderson's death.

Free to leave home once more, Amelia spent time with friends and relations and, whenever possible, attended Friends' Meetings and associated with Quakers in other locations. Much of her correspondence about her travels over the next two decades concerned meeting new Friends. There were also renewals of contact with Gurney relations, notably Hannah Chapman Backhouse, the eldest daughter of Joseph and Jane Gurney, of The Grove. Hannah had gone to live near Darlington in 1811, when she married Jonathan Backhouse, a member of the Quaker banking family. As a minister, she made tours across the country and also to Ireland, sometimes accompanied by her husband. She returned to Norwich at intervals, often leaving her children to be cared for by her parents while she was away preaching. In 1826 her youngest sister Emma moved to Darlington, having married Joseph Pease, who later became the first Quaker to be elected

---

* Mrs Barbauld's latter years were far from easy. She and her husband moved to Stoke Newington in 1802, when Rochemont undertook pastoral duties, but he developed a serious mental disorder, becoming violent towards his wife and committing suicide in 1808. Her last published work, a radical poem, *Eighteen Hundred and Eleven*, depicting England as a ruin, was so viciously reviewed that she ceased writing for publication.

as an MP.* Amelia was always pleased when Hannah turned up at Meetings in London or further afield.

In February 1827, Amelia went to stay at Northrepps Cottage as the guest of Anna Gurney and her companion Sarah Buxton – the first of many visits. Anna, the third daughter of Richard Gurney, of Keswick, had suffered what was called 'a paralytic affection' at the age of 10 months, which meant she never stood or walked unaided. But this did not prevent her from leading an active and happy life as a distinguished scholar, traveller and benefactress. Her father died in 1811, leaving his Keswick and Northrepps estates to Rachel, his widow; after her death in 1825 the family estates passed to Anna's brother Richard Hanbury Gurney, who continued to live at Keswick. Anna joined forces with her cousin Sarah Buxton (their mothers were sisters), and they moved to Northrepps where they became affectionately known as 'the Cottage ladies'.† An ardent supporter of the freedom for slaves cause, Anna became an invaluable amanuensis for Sarah's brother Thomas Fowell Buxton, when, in 1828, he moved

Northrepps Cottage, where Amelia was a regular house guest. Built in 1793 by the Norwich banker Bartlett Gurney on his newly-acquired estate in north Norfolk, it was lived in by a succession of Gurneys. It is now an hotel and restaurant.

---

* The Backhouses and Peases were the main underwriters of the Stockton & Darlington Railway, the first public railway to be empowered to use steam locomotives.

† Anna's mother Rachel and Sarah's mother Anna were daughters of Osgood Hanbury, an Essex landowner.

into Northrepps Hall with his wife and family.

Amelia made a trip to Dorset in June where she spent time with Sarah Buxton's sister Anna and her husband William Forster, the Quaker preacher. While in the west country she and Forster spent a day with Hannah More, the celebrated 'blue stocking', dramatist, poet and anti-slavery campaigner, at Barley Wood, her home near Wrington in Somerset. Later in the year she sent Hannah some beef-ins, following up the gift with a letter in which she declared:

> The recollection of my day at Barley Wood is very precious to me. My dear companion and I wished to have seen and heard more of thee and to have arrived at a more quiet time – but we felt, and enjoyed the privilege of being with one of whom we had heard so much, and whose writings and character were so warmly admired and so deeply venerated.[23]

She also attended Joseph John's wedding at Elm Grove in July. In London later that month she dined with J.V. Thompson, giving him a glowing account of her travels, as he related in a letter to his wife:

> Cousin Amelia had been to the friend of all friends whose name is Forster, in order to have his permission *as a minister* (she used this very expression) to publish a work she had been composing. That was the object of her journey to the West of England, and friend Forster being bound probably in his ministerial capacity to attend at Joseph John's wedding, she thought she could not do otherwise than go, and upon her expressing to Joseph John her intention to be at the meeting she received an invitation to be of the bridal party, which she considered a great thing, as she said she found that the lady gave the invitations. I could have told her that. Well she said the meeting at the wedding was highly owned and favoured. Then she had been with friend Forster to Barley Wood, and it was one of Mrs More's public days. But she had a long communication with the mistress of the house....
>
> Talking of Hannah More it is not irrelevant to turn to Mr Wilberforce. I wished to ask him to be godfather to our daughter [Philothea], but I have never known where to direct to him. As his hostess,* you may ask him with propriety....[24]

---

* Margaret was staying in Cottingham Castle, home of her father-in-law Thomas Thompson, where Wilberforce was also a guest. Wiberforce House museum in Hull holds a book inscribed to Margaret as 'a pledge of the friendly regard of W. Wilberforce, Cottingham Castle, 2 August, 1827'.

Soon after Joseph John returned to Earlham with his new wife, the unmarried Rachel Gurney died, after being lovingly tended through a painful terminal illness by her sisters Catherine and Richenda. As was her wont, Amelia wrote verses to mark the occasion.*

The work on which she had consulted Forster was *Detraction Displayed* – a didactic piece which would be her penultimate published work. Still mourning the loss of her father, she introduced herself to the reader thus:

> With more than usual self-distrust, I give this book to the world, and under circumstances of a new and trying nature. The voice of affectionate encouragement, which used to animate me to my task, I can hear no more; and when, from the force of habit, I have sometimes turned round, while writing, to ask as in former times for counsel and advice, I have been painfully reminded, that the judicious critic, as well as tender parent, was removed from me forever.[25]

The book is a series of essays on what she perceives to be the 'sin' of detraction, that is, the undermining of a person's reputation or character by derogatory, damaging, envious or malicious comments. Undoubtedly aware of this kind of behaviour in the fashionable social world in which she had once been an eager participant, she is at pains to explore every possible example of the 'vice'. In so doing she quotes from many published sources and contributes her own recollections of incidents in which detraction was displayed. One of the 18 chapters looks at the most likely people to be subjected to such behaviour – among them 'authoresses and blue-stockings'. She has a great deal to say about her fellow female writers – what impels them to write, how they keep going often in difficult circumstances and how they are exposed to scorn and ridicule; she gives 'a history of bluestockingism' and the stigma attached to women who wish to cultivate their minds. She also looks at the detractors who try to undermine 'converts to serious religion' such as herself. Reviews of the book were kind and she was gratified to have a letter from Wrangham, the archdeacon, acknowledging 'the pleasure and profit' he had gained from reading her book.

During its publication year she continued with her travels and had Quaker friends from Tottenham to stay with her. She rented lodgings

---

* Lines on a late Funeral & on the Funeral day, The Friends Burying Ground at Norwich, by Amelia Opie, 1827, 9th Month. (SoF, MS 100/22

at Cromer, where she invited them to stay, and from where they could visit the Cottage ladies and the Buxtons. Thus Amelia filled her time until she set off once more for another big adventure – a visit to Paris, the city she had fallen in love with in 1802. There she would meet a Frenchman who would become a close friend and correspondent – the sculptor David d'Angers.

Chapter Twenty-five

Amelia's new year began with a stay at Northrepps Cottage. At home – and worrying about money – she decided to dispose of some of her husband's paintings, writing to William Christie in London for his advice. There were two she wished to sell privately – 'excellent specimens of the artist's best manner – a Rembrandtish-looking picture of his mother and the *Detected Correspondence*', a favourite when it was exhibited at the Royal Academy.* The others could take their chance at auction and with Mr Christie as auctioneer, she was satisfied that all would be done for them that could be done.[1]

In London in May for the Quakers Yearly Meeting, she was planning to travel to France, where she would stay with her cousin Sarah, now living in Paris with her husband. According to substantial family correspondence over three months in 1828, De Barbot had found himself in severe financial difficulties, owing huge sums of money and pursued by creditors threatening prosecution. As the tale of woe emerged it became clear that the villain of the piece was his brother-in-law Tom Alderson. Amelia, although owning that the whole business made her ill, offered a generous contribution towards the debt and took upon herself the task of explaining the situation to other Alderson cousins, namely Edward, Sam and Lady Milman, seeking financial help from them. While so doing, they must face facts:

My beloved cousins, attempting to shield poor Tom is *nonsense*. *We know* and *others* know *too much* already – and he is past help – our *united fortunes* could not save *him*....How Tom gets on and continues to live I cannot think! but suppose he goes on *borrowing* money....He is *a mystery*! and to think how fond and proud of him I once was! Oh! it is terrible![2]

---

* Earland listed 'a small portrait' of the artist's mother as having been seen by Edward Opie when he was in Norwich in 1826, but could not say who bought it from Amelia. The other painting, originally known as *The Angry Father*, depicts a father reproaching his daughter after intercepting a clandestine love letter to her. Earland understood that this was sold at Christie's in May 1807, to Dr Alderson. Amelia sold it through Christie's in 1829, to a private collector; it was later donated to the City of Birmingham Art Gallery.

Once the cousins had come to his aid De Barbot made a fresh start. Amelia believed him to be a kind husband to Sarah, now expecting their first child, and looked forward to staying with them. Before leaving for Paris on June 10th, 1829, she received a letter from Southey suggesting that she and Elizabeth Fry might be prevailed upon to take the lead in establishing societies for improving the management of hospitals and infirmaries on similar lines to the latter's prison reform work. She told him she had no time to give an opinion then. In France she made inquiries about the sisters of charity who attended the sick in hospitals; there was further correspondence on the matter over the next few months, followed by consultation between Amelia, Betsy and the medical profession, but nothing came of the project.

Amelia intended to stay in France for four weeks, but found so much to occupy her that she remained there until the third week of October. She had set off with mixed feelings:

> When I last saw it, I was accompanied by my husband, as well as endeared friends, and my pleasant experiences were then communicated to my beloved father. *Now* I am alone in the world, affording, not receiving protection; and in every way my position in life is changed…yet I cannot but recollect that France has undergone changes of far greater importance to itself, and the world. The France which I left a Republic in 1802 has become a Monarchy again, under the dominion of a Bourbon![3]

She was delighted to reach Paris and a welcome from relatives – not just the De Barbots but Lucy and Perronet Thompson, the two oldest children of Thomas Perronet Thompson,* who were joined a few weeks later by their uncle John Vincent Thompson. She wrote letters about her travels and also kept a journal; her writings were a rich mixture of anecdotes about friends, relations, food and fashion, descriptions of places visited (some for the first time, some she had seen on her first visit) and accounts of meeting numerous people in French society, whose names would be known to her correspondents.

The person whom Amelia most wished to meet was the military officer and aristocrat, commonly known in England as Lafayette†, who had taken part in both the American and French Revolutions,

---

* A year earlier the two youngsters, then aged 16 and 15, had accompanied their grandfather Thomas Thompson on his first visit to France, where he had been taken ill and died, aged 74. He was buried at the Père La Chaise cemetery in Paris.
† His full title was Marie-Joseph Paul Yves Roch Gilbert du Motier, de La Fayette, Marquis de La Fayette.

entirely without pay, since he came from an immensely wealthy family of feudal landowners. In a letter to Sarah Rose (a friend who later lived in Norwich) she described him as:

> … the hero of my childhood, the idol of my youth and I have found him far beyond my idea of him – high raised as it was! He's a handsome man of 72, humble, simple and blushing like a girl…with manners the most perfect possible and his bonhomie is so striking that one almost forgets his greatness and his fame.… I brought letters to him I delivered in *person*.… His daughter called on me the next day and I had a note from him inviting me to his *soirée*. I took Sarah with me and was charmed and gratified. Americans and strangers made most of the company.…
>
> The great delight was my friend Margaret Southwell's [of Wroxham Hall] having sent over Davis* to finish Lafayette for her and Davis wishing me to be present to animate the General – accordingly I was at LF's *five* mornings having his precious conversation to myself. I was also at his house in the evening five times.[4]

The letter continued with further name-dropping before she reached the subject of her important new friend, the talented sculptor and medallist David d'Angers. His real name was Pierre-Jean David, but he adopted the name David d'Angers (he was born in Angers) to avoid confusion with the master painter Jacques-Louis David.† By the time he met Amelia he was well established as a leading figure in the French art world. Early in his career he did monumental work on the Arc de Triomphe; later some of his most celebrated sculptures were for tombs at the Père La Chaise cemetery. He was in great demand for his busts and medallions, of which he made more than 500, and his sitters included many illustrious people, among them Victor Hugo and Honoré de Balzac.

My next hero is no *general* but a sceptical *sculpteur libéral* – the

---

* John Philip Davis, the portrait painter, who exhibited at the Royal Academy, and was often in Norfolk. He was a friend of Dawson Turner, whose wife Mary did many etchings from his work, including his portrait of John Sell Cotman. He would certainly have been known to Amelia.

† Macgregor (p.104) believed that Amelia had met David before, having misinterpreted a passage in Brightwell (p.115) about the 1802 Paris visit when Amelia accompanied Opie to the '*Atelier* of David', where she was struck by the artist's painting of 'Brutus returning from the tribunal…' This was one of Jacques-Louis David's most controversial works. At that time David d'Angers was a boy of 14, still living at home.

A signed portrait 'à son illustre amie Madame Opie' from Pierre-Jean David d'Angers, the sculptor and medallist, who became a close friend when Amelia visited Paris in 1829. (New York Public Library: Pforzheimer Collection)

first man of his class here; who before I saw him was desirous of making a medal of me to reward me for having made him cry his eyes out by my writing. *Malgré moi*, he has made me *un medaille*, me and my *petit bonnet* which the artists here say looks like a Phrygian helmet and has *un air classique* but tho' young and flattered, the thing is *like* and David *satisfied*. To this very interesting man I owe some of the most interesting hours I have passed here... he has given me much indeed of his precious time. We were one day five hours at Père La Chaise, where I vainly tried to find my friend Backhouse's tomb – again we went and again in vain...this afternoon we are going again for now it is found. Père La Chaise is a lovely place![5]

On the days when she was not sitting to David for her medallion, he sent her little notes – usually in English but sometimes in French, signed 'your devoted and faithful friend David' or 'celui qui vous aime de tout son coeur D'.[6] Writing to his wife Margaret, John Vincent told her about cousin Amelia's exploits:

David, of the Institut National, has made a medallion of her, which is really very excellent; he has contrived to give her Quaker cap the air of the Phrygian cap in which the ancient Sculptors represent Paris.[7]

Eliza, who would join the family in Paris in September, was told the 'petit cousins' were untidy and wore shabby clothes, but they were 'nice young persons'. She had bought the girl a new gown and hats for both of them and taken them to meet Lafayette. Henry Perronet Briggs, also arrived in Paris in September. Among the compatriots with whom she spent time in France were the writer Mary Berry, Susannah's younger daughter Sarah Austin, who was starting her career as a writer and translator, and Lady Morgan*, who, under her maiden name Sydney Owenson, was a successful novelist who championed women's rights. Of the latter, Amelia told Eliza: 'She says she will turn Friend. My dress is so admired here!'

Soon after arriving in Paris she made herself known to Albertine, the daughter of Mme de Staël, who, as a 16-year-old, had accompanied her mother when Amelia met her in London in 1813 and who, on marriage, had become the Duchesse de Broglie. There was a visit to the French Institute where she 'had to undergo many *presentations* and flatteries' as she reported to Joseph John 'for, as an author, I am as much known, and more admired, perhaps, than in *England*.'[8] The distinguished Paris residents whom she met included Benjamin Constant, the liberal writer on politics and religion, the Marquis de Lally-Tollendal, author of *Defence of the French Emigrants* (1797)

---

* Lady Morgan's bust in white marble by David d'Angers is owned by the Victoria & Albert Museum.

and a member of the Académie française,* and Baron Cuvier, a leading figure in the natural sciences research field, whose stepdaughter
Sophie du Vaucel became a particular friend.

However, the main attraction was Lafayette, who at their first
meeting invited her to visit him at his country home.† Before the visit
could be arranged he was called away to the Auvergne so Amelia
decided to stay on in France until he returned. She wrote a slightly
apologetic letter to Joseph John, fearing he and her beloved friends
at Earlham and Norwich would disapprove of her continued absence
from home, but explained she could not resist 'the *temptation* to stay'
and make the promised visit to La Grange. It was worth waiting for:
she enjoyed walking in the beautiful grounds and visiting her host's
farm. Every day Lafayette led Amelia down to dinner and to breakfast, which meant she sat next to him at the table and could converse
with him. The house guests included Louis Philippe, Comte de Ségur,
a diplomat and historian who had served in the American War of
Independence.

> We dined every day 33 in company.... The first evening I had to give
> an exposition of Friends' principles.... Ségur, who was in America
> with Lafayette, says he is *three-quarters* a Friend *himself*....
>
> Lafayette's library is a very beautiful room... amongst other *in-
> teresting* things for one to see *there*, were some of my own tales
> *splendidly* bound, gratifying to *any* author's vanity – to be in the
> library of Lafayette.[9]

On her return to England she was at pains to write to Coke, telling
him of her visit to Paris, mentioning in particular the time spent with
Lafayette:

> ...with whom I frequently conversed of *thee*, and I even *presumed
> so far* as to assure him that thou wouldst be delighted to see him
> at Holkham!... He is indeed very desirous to see *thee* in the first
> place and thy *farms* in the next and to compare his farming experi-
> ence with thine. But it is comparatively on a small scale, certainly,
> though he has very fine merinos and a thousand sheep in all....
> The ancient round tower on which is the General's beautiful li-

---

* In 1804 Amelia had written verses in French as a tribute to Lally-Tollendal, having read of his attempts to clear the name of his father, Thomas Arthur, Comte
de Lally, who had been executed for treason in 1766. (NYPL, Pforzheimer Collection, O.ANA 0033)
† The Château de la Grange-Bléneau, dating back to the 14th century, was inherited from his wife. Lafayette lived there from 1802 until his death in 1834.

brary, is now covered by an ivy planted in 1802 by our beloved Charles James Fox, and is green and flourishing like his memory....

I conclude thou hast heard that a certain widowed friend of ours sent a painter over to Paris to paint his portrait for her. It was a fortunate circumstance for me, as I was permitted to attend all the sittings. I wonder she has not yet sent for it to Wroxham, but I hear it is still in Norwich.[10]

As the year drew to a close Amelia decided to dispatch 'a little Christmas offering' of Norfolk beefins to Sophie du Vaucel, suggesting they might be presented at one of the Saturday evening soirées of her mother La Baronne Cuvier. Acknowledging how much she had enjoyed the family's hospitality and friendship during her time in Paris, she wrote:

> I often figure you all to myself on a seventh day evening looking over prints and drawings and *caricatures* and then assembling at half past 10 round the tea table! ...
>
> I have been very unwell since my return to Norwich. I over exerted myself and was much worried in mind during my fortnight's residence in and near London and I had not been home many days before I was *forced* to own myself ill and have medical advice....
>
> I am thankful to be able to say that I am now quite well. In a few days I hope to go near the *sea* to my friend Anna Gurney's cottage.[11]

She was concerned about the serious decline in the city's textile industry and its impact on weavers' families. Some manufacturers resorted to putting out work into rural areas at reduced rates of pay which led to riots. Amelia reported the facts to her correspondents, noting that people were starving and she was being 'besieged' by the poor. Joseph John attended a demonstration in the city's Victoria Gardens, where he tried to persuade the rioters to 'desist from disorderly proceedings'; alarmed by their violence of manner he invited them all to breakfast at Earlham the next morning. About 70 turned up; they conducted themselves in an orderly manner and he spoke to them of their Christian duty.[12]

After her visit to Northrepps, Amelia was pleased to hear that Sarah De Barbot, staying with her siblings in London, had given birth to a daughter. Lenon was still in Paris and efforts were being made to find him employment. She was thrilled to receive from Paris her own David medallion, for which she paid 13 guineas, describing it to Eliza as:

my own self in gold, gilt bronze.* It is *really beautiful*, the frame, being black. It is really precious as an ornament and looks well with my pictures.... David has made for me, *smaller* than the original, a *bust* of Lafayette!† He is to bring it to London when he visits in June.[13]

Meanwhile, plans were being made for the wedding of Eliza and Henry Perronet Briggs, who had settled in London, where he was doing well with historical and Shakespearian scenes and as a portrait painter. Amelia invited Henry to stay with her in Norwich in April to meet the Alderson relations, and to introduce him to people who might give him portrait commissions. She was in no doubt about his ability to do justice to his sitters and rejoiced when he was commissioned by the actor Charles Kemble to do a double portrait of his sister Sarah Siddons and actress daughter Fanny Kemble. Amelia told Eliza she had presented her fiancé to 'uncles, aunts and cousins' and all seemed pleased. She was delighted when Henry was asked to paint Joseph John Gurney (for his brother Samuel), Hudson Gurney and Thomas Fowell Buxton, but distressed to hear that Henry might do a portrait of Richard Hanbury Gurney, brother to Anna Gurney and half-brother to Hudson. He was, Amelia told Henry, 'a convicted adulterer, who had just run away with another man's wife' and his name was never mentioned in the Gurney family.

Henry confided in Amelia about his elderly father, John Hobart Briggs, being none too happy about the match with Eliza, but the wedding went ahead in August 1830, at St George's, Hanover Square, and Briggs senior was a witness, along with the bride's brother and sister, and their cousin, Isabella Milman. The service was conducted by Robert Alderson. Amelia had sent waistcoats for Henry and Tom to wear, 'bridal attire' for Eliza and a gown for Sarah; she also sent a silver milk jug and sugar bowl which had been a wedding present for her mother from her uncle John Briggs (Henry's great-uncle). For herself she had a dress made and ordered a bonnet, but in the event she stayed away, telling her cousins not only was she was tired and unwell, but she feared a visit to London would make her idle for weeks.

She was anxious about Sarah, who was ill and fearful for her husband in Paris, where an uprising against King Charles X and the gov-

---

* It is not known how many of the Opie medallions were cast. The National Portrait Gallery, the Louvre and the Metropolitan Museum of Art in New York each own one.

† Amelia bequeathed the Lafayette bust to Thomas Brightwell.

ernment of the Bourbon Restoration – known as the July Revolution – had been taking place. Amelia was working on an account of her 1802 visit, which was eventually published in *Tait's Magazine*. She told Eliza how curious it was

> that I had been *some day* writing of *my* Paris in1802 and describing my *intense interest* in visiting the scenes of the Revolution... *little thinking* some of the same scenes were then acting again in the same places.[14]

Amelia felt very privileged to be the only non-family member at a memorable gathering at Joseph Gurney's house to bid farewell to his eldest daughter Hannah Backhouse, who, with her husband Jonathan, was about to set sail for America on a religious mission which lasted for five years. Later in the summer she stayed at Worlingham Hall in Suffolk, the home of Lord and Lady Gosford, where Fanny Twiss, the eldest daughter of her dear departed friend Fanny, was employed as a governess. From there she went on to Pakefield, where the Rev Francis Cunningham, Richenda's husband, was curate, and then to Lowestoft, where she stayed at the Sparrow's Nest, cousin Edward's summer residence, with his wife Georgina and children.

David did not make his proposed visit to London that summer, but dispatched the promised Lafayette bust to Amelia, who was still working on her Paris memoir and in regular correspondence with her French friends. Fascinated by news from the capital – the overthrow of the repressive régime of Charles X and the proclamation of the popular Louis-Philippe, Duc d'Orléans, as 'King of the French' – she determined to return to Paris in the autumn, telling very few people of her plans. Knowing of her cousin's declining health she hoped to see her en route for France, but Sarah died before she reached London, a loss which she found hard to bear. In her first letter to Eliza from Paris, she said that 'poor Sarah' had been constantly in her thoughts as she crossed the Channel. She added that De Barbot had left his lodgings and nobody knew where he was.

Amelia remained in France from November until the following May, visiting old friends, meeting new ones, enjoying walks down familiar streets, going to exhibitions and lectures, attending Friends' meetings, seeking information about the political situation and ascertaining how the new monarch – known as the 'citizen king' because of his republican policies – was regarded by her liberal colleagues. She kept a journal with detailed accounts of each day's events and lists of people she encountered, among them her favourites Lafayette and David and the hospitable Baron Cuvier's family. She sat in on a debate in the Chamber of Deputies at which Benjamin Constant read a paper; two weeks later he was dead and she found herself at a friend's house watching his exceptionally long funeral procession go past.

Amelia was introduced to the author and educator Madame de Genlis, who had been governess to the new king and his brothers. In her journal she described the 86-year-old woman as 'really pretty and unaffected'. To Joseph John she wrote of a happy tête-à-tête with 'this highly gifted women', recalling 'the delight her works afforded me and my poor mother'. She sat next to her at a dinner party, attended by many distinguished guests, at which the host toasted the King 'hoping he would always act on those admirable principles which he owed to the early instruction of La Comtesse de Genlis!'[15] Three weeks later she called on the elderly writer and hoped for more encounters, but it was not to be, for Madame de Genlis died on New Year's Eve.

Although shocked by this sudden death, Amelia was much more distressed by news from England that Thomas Fowell and Hannah Buxton had lost their 17-year-old son Harry after a long and painful illness. More grief followed with news of the sudden death of Joseph Gurney of The Grove on Christmas Day. She heard later that crowds of people gathered along the streets of Norwich to watch the cortège, with many more crowding the burial ground. His loss inspired a heartfelt tribute to 'a most dear and venerated friend' which was published in *Lays for the Dead*. While in France she arranged for the publication of Joseph John's pamphlet *A Letter to a Friend*, for which he paid 10 guineas for its translation into French. On New Year's Day she distributed copies of the work as gifts to many of her Paris friends. She had already given Lafayette a netted purse she had made for him.

The American writer James Fenimore Cooper had arrived in Paris in August, with his wife and eldest daughter; inevitably they came into contact with Amelia:

> At Lafayette's…they met Mrs Opie, then a converted Quaker, of whom Mrs Cooper wrote that her 'plain gauze Cap and simple Dress, make her appearance very striking among the gay colours and feathers and flowers at Paris'. The meeting with Mrs Opie led to several pleasant exchanges of visits.[16]

Also staying in Paris were Samuel Carter Hall and his wife Anna Maria, who were known professionally as S.C. Hall & Mrs S.C. Hall. He was the editor of *The Art Journal*. Amelia contributed occasional pieces for *The Amulet*, an annual religious publication which the couple had founded, and for Mrs Hall's *Juvenile Forget-me-Not*. Years later they recalled seeing Mrs Opie at 'a memorable evening' in the salons of Lafayette:

> She was habited as usual; in her plain grey silk, and Quaker cap.... No wonder such a vision of simplicity and purity should have startled gay Parisian dames, few or some of whom had the least idea of the nature of the costume; but the good old General selected her from a host of worshippers, and seemed jealous lest a rival should steal the fascinating Quaker from his side.[17]

Possibly Joseph John was aware of the impact Amelia would make in Paris society. He expressed his 'great disappointment' at finding her away from Norwich when he returned to Earlham from ministry work in Scotland and the north of England, having anticipated a quiet winter in which they might enjoy one another's society:

> With the single exception of thyself, I know of no-one who would not find it very difficult to maintain the character of a simple and consistent Friend amidst the politicians and philosophers of Paris, amidst scenes which destitute as they may be of some other ingredients valuable to us, are certainly not devoid either of charm or fascination. But I know the *facilities* which appertain to thy character in this respect; and even thy perfect command of the language may be of great help to thee in making thyself *intelligible* as a Quaker in the midst of this motley society. I also know thy steadfastness and Christian courage. At the same time I do wish, as an unworthy brother, to encourage thee to *constant watchfulness and prayer*.[18]

She assured Joseph John that she believed she had been a good influence on some of the people she spent time with in Paris. She said his translated *Letter to a Friend* had been well received, mentioning a French general, a Catholic, who said 'thy little work is suited to *all* Christians and he is thankful for it'. She said she was cynical about the political scene, but not the royal family:

> The more I hear of the King and his family the more I admire them. But with one great drawback as far as he is concerned. The Queen attends her chapel regularly – He *dares* not go because Charles X by his over devotion, they say, disgusted everyone. Fear of man

conquers fear of God.[19]

Amelia's interest in the royal family received an unexpected boost when she was summoned to the Tuileries Palace and spent the evening 'seated *en famille* by the side of Marie-Amèlie Reine des Francois'. Giving a graphic account of the evening to Sarah Rose, she explained that the Marquise de Dolomieu, a 'dame d'honneur' to the Queen, had attended one of her Saturday morning receptions and told her the Queen desired to see her the next evening. On her arrival, she was led through a long suite of rooms and then ushered into a room in which some ladies were sitting round a table. The Marquise greeted her and as they approached the table:

> the Queen and la Princesse d'Orléans rose and said 'bonjour Madame Opie', the Queen adding, 'Sit down by me, I am glad to see you. I have read your works,' and so forth. My friend, the Marquise, sat on the other side; round the table sat two of the princesses, and some dames d'honneur, and the Dukes of Orléans and Nemours were standing near it. I cannot tell thee all the conversation that ensued, nor all the interesting questions which I had to answer; but I found the Queen a very pious-minded woman.... At length the Queen resumed her work*...'As it is Sunday,' said she, 'I cannot do any other work; but do not like to sit idle, and when one works is its pleasant to know one is working for the poor.'[20]

Returning to England, Amelia spent several weeks in or around London, staying first with Eliza and Henry, who were living in Charles Street. She told Joseph John:

> Little did I ever think that any (probable) circumstances would ever renew for me in the last stages of life the interest and anxieties which so much occupied the former ones. Yet they have done so – and it is to them that my dear Norwich friends owe my lengthened stay in London. I feel a desire which I do not seem at liberty to disregard to *do all I can* to serve my cousin Henry Perronet Briggs in the line of his profession, especially at this period, which will be probably the *turning-point* in his career as a portrait-painter (the only really *lucrative* line) for [Thomas] Lawrence and [John] Jackson's deaths have left a way opened by which he must try to profit *now* or *never* and I am trying all I can to get distinguished persons to *sit to him*.[21]

---

* Using French terms, Amelia explained that the Queen was shredding a sort of silk lint with which to stuff foot warmers for a lottery for the poor.

Henry believed a portrait of Amelia might 'serve him'; Thomas Fowell Buxton, who was also sitting for Henry, thought the result 'exceptionally like' and she herself thought it was beautifully painted. Her cousin Margaret gave a dinner to which she invited some of Amelia's old friends, including Lady Cork; she dined 'tête-à-tête with Lady Charleville'. She visited the Milmans, the Hoares, the Quaker Forsters at Tottenham, stayed for a few days with her friends Sir John and Lady Gurney at Lincoln's Inn Fields and spent a weekend at Upton Park, the home of Samuel Gurney and his family.

By the end of July she was in Norwich, where she settled back into her routine of Quaker activities, charitable work, tending to her elderly aunt Elizabeth, worrying about her uncle Robert who was suffering from dementia, writing copious letters to friends at home and abroad. She declined to go back to London for the coronation of William IV, saying she could not afford it. She was also working towards selling her house and thinking about where she might make a new home.

Chapter Twenty-six

Early in 1832 Amelia rejoiced in the news that her cousin Henry was now a Royal Academician. She dispatched a letter of congratulations, telling him she had approached the Whig politician Lord Mulgrave, who agreed he would sit for Henry 'once the fatigues of the Reform Bill' were over. Amelia and her radical colleagues had followed the parliamentary reform movement over more than three decades and at last it was coming to fruition. Lord Grey (brother of Lady Whitbread), an ardent reformer, had the chance to make his mark, when he became Prime Minister in 1830, the Whigs having defeated the Tories, whose leader the Duke of Wellington was resolutely opposed to reform. It was a long struggle, watched keenly by the general public. Introducing a wide range of changes to the electoral system, the Representation of the People Act, which became known as the Great Reform Act, was passed in June 1832.

Amelia went to London in May for a meeting of the Bible Society, the Friends' Yearly Meeting and the Royal Academy exhibition, where Henry's portraits of her and Thomas Fowell Buxton were to be on show. She confided in Eliza that she had some anxieties about her dress, fearing that the colour might not be 'a Quaker one' and she would be in 'sad disgrace' with Friends who would also 'have something to get over' in the exhibition of her picture: 'I hope the gown is not a blue grey – what looks neat to others may appear gay to Friends.'[1] She also told her cousins that she had decided to sell her house and not to find another home for at least a year; instead she would travel.

When Amelia returned home, she found a parcel of gifts from David and a letter which prompted her to seek advice from Henry:

For y presents I am grateful – but for y letter! He reproaches me painfully to myself for my unkindness in refusing a request in which his heart was so much interested and will not take a denial. He *will* put me in white marble, malgré moi. Seeing my features and face as I see them and knowing therefore how they must look in a bust I *shrink aghast* from his wishes – but be it so! as I have no better motive than vanity to oppose it then.... Now Henry what dost thou say to sending the picture itself to Paris?... The picture *might* help

– a drawing could not. If I could *be sure* the Italian modeller* here would *break* y mask when *taken* (and I might *insist* on it) I would get my face taken off and that he might *beautify* à son bon plaisir.[2]

By the time Henry responded, she had decided to accede to David's wishes and have a plaster model made and sent to him. Meanwhile, she was pressing on with the sale of her house, but the process was delayed by the corporation seeking to alter the terms of the leasehold for her garden which would also substantially increase the ground rent. Amelia was outraged, telling Henry it was 'rank extortion' and she wished to see 'all corporations annihilated'. Her solicitor advised accepting the new lease, but only after trying to obtain better terms:

> This contretemps delays the sale of my house, that is it will do so if I accede to the committee's demand because the decision of the body corporal can't be known till 21st Sept and I want to be off long before then! Thus my plans are *entirely* at a standstill.... I advise thee never to have anything to do with *corporations*.[3]

Keswick Hall, built by Hudson Gurney at the request of his wife Margaret. Work started on the building in 1817 and was completed in 1819. Amelia was a frequent visitor. (Norwich Castle Museum and Art Gallery)

While awaiting the completion of the sale she spent time with the Gurneys at Earlham and with Hudson and Margaret Gurney at Keswick Hall.† The couple lived mostly in London, but in 1817 Marga-

---

* Kristel De Wulf, who is researching Italian immigrants in Norfolk, believes he was Pellegrino Mazzotti, a plaster figure maker from Coreglia in Lucca, Tuscany, who settled in Norwich in the late 1810s or early1820s. He had a studio in Goat Lane from 1830. (Mazzotti website: see bibliography)
† The hall remained in the Gurney family until the 1940s, when Quintin Gurney offered it to the Norwich Training College which had been destroyed by enemy action. When the college became part of the University of East Anglia in 1981, the hall was converted into apartments.

ret persuaded Hudson to have the new hall built on land the family owned near the original Keswick Hall (afterwards known as Keswick Old Hall). Amelia was a frequent visitor when Hudson and Margaret were in residence.

Despite her misgivings, the sale of the house went ahead and by the first week in August – on a visit to Earlham – she was able to write a happy footnote to a letter which Catherine Gurney was penning to Joseph John and his wife who were away from home:

> I will 'add' for I *wanted* to tell you dear friends that, not only have I sold my house *well*, considering all things, but that I have sold it to the very persons whom I should have chosen for my successors. The widow Clover*, and her daughter, and Tom Preston her son-in-law! who *love* my dear father's memory, and prize the house the more for having been *his*. Tom Preston told a friend of mine since the sale, that he would have given £100 *more* because it was Dr Alderson's house, and I *had told* my auctioneer that *I* would *take* less from Tom Preston than from *any one else*. There was *no bid* so there was no *auction*, therefore we are saved auction expenses. I have told my maids that we *must part*, a *grief* to me, but the pang is over, and my mind relieved. I am going forth now, homeless as well as fatherless....[4]

In her letter, Catherine wrote that Amelia had sold the house for £1,000. She also sold Preston many of the fixtures for £30.† Amelia confirmed the sale price of the house in a letter to Eliza before she set off in September 1832 for Cornwall where she would remain for seven months. Her first port of call was Falmouth, where she stayed with the family of Robert Were Fox, whose wife Maria (née Barclay) was a cousin of the Earlham Gurneys.‡ Robert Were Fox was a distinguished scientist and Fellow of the Royal Society, with business interests in mining and shipping. There was a big family group of Foxes who were prominent in local affairs and businesses. Robert and two of his brothers Alfred and Charles acquired estates outside

---

* Sarah Clover, widow of Joseph Clover, a yarn-maker, who was an uncle of the artist Joseph Clover.

† The receipt for the fixtures bears a note from Joseph Preston, the son of Sophia (née Clover) and Thomas Preston, that the building became known as Opie House. (NRO MC 2/11).

‡ Her parents were Rachel (née Gurney) and Robert Barclay. Her brother Charles married into the Kett family who were related to the Gurneys and her sister Lucy married George Croker Fox, a cousin of Robert Were Fox.

Falmouth where they built or extended existing houses for country retreats. Robert owned Penjerrik, Charles took on Trebah and Alfred had Glendurgan (now owned by the National Trust). For Amelia there was much to enjoy in a succession of attractive locations, interesting people with whom to converse and attendance at Meetings.

She travelled by coach, first to Plymouth and then to Falmouth, where she was met by her host's family. Robert Were's son Robert Barclay (always known as Barclay), then 15, wrote in his journal on September 24th: 'Drove down to the Plymouth coach and brought home Amelia Opie to dinner at five. She means to stay here for some time.' He mentioned the house guest again several times – taking 'a very good likeness' of Uncle George Croker when he and Aunt Lucy drank tea with them, dining with Uncle Alfred, walking with Papa and attending Meeting.[5] Amelia enjoyed spending time with Barclay and his sisters, Anna Maria, 17, and Caroline, 13; she told Sarah Rose she had been joining in their writing sessions – prose one week and verse the next – and was having an 'uninterrupted round of enjoyment'.[6]

She was taken on a visit to the Perran Foundry which had been set up by the Fox family to supply machinery to the mining industry. She spent four weeks with the matriarch of the family, Elizabeth Fox (née Tregelles), said by her descendants to be a woman of strong will and rigid principles. While staying with Elizabeth she heard from the Gurneys that 13-year-old Isabella Milman had died. She minded that nobody in her own family had informed her, telling Eliza: 'I should have liked to have appeared to my friends here a little more respected by my kin and kind.'[7]

By November Amelia had reached St Agnes, where she stayed with John Opie's nephew Edward (son of his brother William) and his wife Joanna. It was a successful visit, as she reported to Sarah Rose:

> I am here with my poor husband's nephew and his wife and family which consists of Edward Opie the painter, a boy of 10 [John] and of a gentle pleasing young woman named Amelia after me at the desire of my poor sister [her late sister-in-law Betty Opie]. They have just lost a lively gifted girl of 13 [Johanna], which loss has sunk deep into the hearts of her parents who seem excellent persons and the whole family have soft, pleasing manners. Edward Opie, the father, is a thriving man of business, has a large general shop and is buying land and building homes....
>
> Yesterday I dined at Harmony Cottage, where my husband and

all the family were born and bred. It is a most sequestered cottage, whitewashed and thatched, a hill rising high above it...flower beds in front of it...I am glad I have seen it...it is inhabited by James Opie [another son of William], his wife and four daughters – a fifth is well married at Redruth. My hostess is a sweet woman – the daughter of a surgeon and apothecary and she is gentle, sensible and pious. In short, I like all the family and I have here the most delicious bread, butter and clotted cream possible.[8]

Amelia's cousin Henry was treated to a more detailed letter about the Opies, beginning with her appreciation of his having agreed to take on Edward the budding young artist as a student at a reduced fee. She told him the Opies all had excellent manners and 'not one of the family is at all vulgar (more than I expected)'.[9] She had also met Nancy Opie, the widow of John Opie (another nephew by William),who had kept the White Hart Inn in St Agnes. Nancy, 'a fat, lovely landlady' had continued running it after he died. Before returning to Falmouth, Amelia stayed in Truro and visited business partners of the Foxes. By Christmas she was ensconced in Wodehouse Place, the home of Alfred and Sarah Fox, from where she wrote to Joseph John on Christmas Day.

In the new year she went to Penzance, where she found her lodgings on Regent Terrace 'pleasant' and settled in for a busy few weeks of sightseeing and working on her poems for *Lays for the Dead*. The first news she received from Falmouth was of the death from scarlatina maligna (a severe form of scarlet fever) of Jane Fox, the five-year-old younger daughter of Charles and Sarah. She wrote immediately to the grandmother:

> I venture to express to thee and to those most near and dear to thee how deeply I sympathize [sic] with you all on this truly distressing occasion – distressing to the survivors, for as to the darling child herself I cannot mourn that she is taken away in her sweet and safe innocence! I *always* think early death a mercy and a blessing.[10]

With death much on her mind, she wrote the next day to Eliza, asking her to tell 'Meggie' (Margaret Thompson) she had been searching for the graves of 'the Philotheas'. Her landlady 'a pretty young Methodist' remembered them dying and advised Amelia on where they were buried.[11] To Sarah Rose she wrote a detailed description of Jane Fox's last hours, when, in her delirium, she asked what angels drank. The anecdote inspired a poem which she sent to the parents:

And didst thou wish for angels' drink?
Didst thou for heavenly nectar pine?
Blest supplicant! Oh! Tis sweet to think
What angels feed on now is thine.

The bereaved mother told Amelia she found comfort in these words:

This day the interment takes place in a lovely sequestered dell, a graveyard belonging to a tiny meeting house called the Kea and I do so grieve I could not be there![12]

Amelia also told Sarah of her forthcoming visit to St Michael's Mount (much of it now owned by the National Trust), where (thanks to her friendship with Lord de Dunstanville, whose mother was a St Aubyn), she had an open invitation to stay at the castle, the seat of Sir John St Aubyn, who was away from home at the time. She planned to go 'at the next full moon'. In February, she spent two nights 'alone' at the castle, where the obliging housekeeper showed her 'the *prime* of the house' and she walked round the ramparts. The experience was all she had hoped for, as she wrote in a lengthy epistle to Thomas Brightwell. The housekeeper wished her to stay for a week:

but I thought she would, in her heart, be very glad to get rid of a crazy old gentlewoman, who came to look at the moon from the ramparts of the castle, as if she had no moon in her own country!

Then followed an account of her nocturnal wanderings, with dramatic descriptions of the wind, rain and rough seas, and occasional flashes of moonlight illuminating the dark turrets and walls of the castle:

I walked, and gazed, and leaned on the ramparts, till the consciousness of my solitude became oppressive to me, and I hastened along that corridor, so often trodden, in times long past, by the monk or the warrior, to my repose.[13]

Fascinated by the history of the mount and its spectacular location, she also wrote six poetic 'sketches', which were appended to her book of lays.

Returning to Penzance, she was shocked to receive a letter from Norwich telling her of the death of Sarah Rose, noting in her journal: '...a mercy to her! Still, I *grieve* to see her no more, a friend so long attached,' and two days later, 'Wrote *all* my Lays on my six pictures – very poor, but hope to improve them.' The final versions would be introduced in the anthology as lays *On the Portraits of Deceased Relatives and Friends, which hang around me.* The six were her illustrious ancestor Augustine Briggs, her father Dr Alderson, her teacher John Bruckner, her cousin Ollyett Woodhouse, her friend Fanny Twiss and her husband John Opie. She continued to work on her lays and found time to visit the local jail and workhouse where she gave some money to its fund, which she was told would give the poor people a treat of cake and tea. Thomas Opie, a younger brother of Edward the artist, accompanied her on visits to Land's End and St.Ives, before she left Penzance and returned to Falmouth, where she stayed again with Robert Were and Maria Fox.

She was also a house guest at Wodehouse Place, at Grove Hill, the home of George Croker and Lucy Fox, and at Perran House, home of Charles and Sarah Fox. From Falmouth she wrote to Henry about a picture which Edward Opie had painted of Charles and Sarah's two daughters, Juliet and Jane. Following the death of the younger girl, the mother wished for a small copy of her portrait. Amelia asked Henry to recommend a competent artist and to seek Edward's opinion, adding that the fee would be no object. Within a matter of weeks, all was arranged: Edward would do a copy of his portrait of little Jane Fox for the parents who would themselves take the original canvas to London and deliver it to Henry. Amelia left Cornwall at the end of April, staying with Agatha Hillhouse, another of Rachel Barclay's daughters, near Bristol, on her way to London for the Yearly Meeting.

When she returned to Norwich, she stayed with Joseph Gurney's widow, Jane, at The Grove; Jane was looking after her Backhouse grandchildren, while their parents were in America. Henry Birkbeck had moved into Keswick Old Hall, with his second wife Lucy (from a branch of the Barclay family) and they invited Amelia to stay with them for a few days. Having also accepted an invitation to stay with her cousin Sam Alderson, she was vexed to find Dr Thomas Chalmers, professor of theology at Edinburgh University and a prolific writer on religion and political economy, would be staying at Earlham while she was away. Joseph John persuaded her to delay the family visit and meet the distinguished Scot, who was staying with the Gurneys during a two-months' tour of England. Amelia told Henry she had 'the privilege of a long tête-à-tête walk and sitting with him'; he gave her 'a most pressing invitation' to stay with him and his wife in Edinburgh and sent her 'his last book'.[14]

During his tour, Chalmers wrote letters home to his two daughters. From Earlham, which he described as 'an abode of friendship and piety', he wrote admiringly of:

'another lady, who dined and spent the night – now aged and in Quaker attire, which she had but recently put on, and who in early life was one of the most distinguished of our literary women, whose works, 30 years ago, I read with great delight – no less a person than the celebrated Mrs Opie, authoress of the most exquisite feminine tales.

... the idea of the accomplished novelist and poet was never once suggested by the image of this plain looking Quakeress till it rushed upon me after dinner, when it suddenly and inconceivably augmented the interest I felt in her. We had much conversation, and drew greatly together, walking and talking with each other on the beautiful lawn after dinner. She has had access into all kinds of society, and her conversation is all the more rich and interesting.[15]

From Earlham Amelia went to stay with Sam Alderson and his 'sweet wife', now the parents of six children, at Bredfield, near Woodbridge in Suffolk, where he had a new living. She was pleased to find his sister Elizabeth Milman was staying there with four of her children. Another source of pleasure was meeting the Quaker poet Bernard Barton, a bank clerk, whose father had been active in the anti-slavery movement. Barton had been helped financially by Joseph John Gurney, who set up a fund with donations from friends, the interest of which provided him with an annuity. He and Amelia had been in correspondence for several years but had not met before he and his daughter Lucy dined at Sam Alderson's during her visit. 'What an inconvenient place Bredfield is to go and stay at!' she told Henry, explaining that Lady Milman had come to her aid, giving Amelia a place in her barouche to Lowestoft, where she spent the night and from where she took the 7am coach to Norwich.

The next highlight was an invitation to meet the Bishop of Winchester [Charles Sumner], his wife and family, at Earlham. They had been staying with Richenda and her husband at Lowestoft where Francis had been appointed Vicar of St Margaret's. 'This exquisite Bishop', as Amelia described him to Eliza, and another guest, Charles Wodehouse, a prebendary of Norwich Cathedral, had both attended the funeral of William Wilberforce at Westminster Abbey in July. On

August 1st the Slavery Abolition Bill (to abolish slavery throughout the British Empire) had been passed by the Commons and the Lords; it received Royal Assent on August 29th and would become law a year later. The name of the great anti-slave campaigner was in everyone's thoughts:

> The first night of the Bishop's arrival JJG read us a sketch and memoir of Wilberforce which he had drawn up and its justice and spirit delighted us all...what was read and what described and the conversations which therein resulted, interesting to the mind and beneficial to the soul.

Both the Bishop and his wife expressed their pleasure at meeting Amelia. Mrs Sumner told her 'they put my books in the hands of their children' and that 'she reads, lends and patronizes my book on Detraction *excessively*'.[16]

After visits to Wroxham Hall and to Dan Gurney's at Runcton Amelia returned to Norwich, where she took lodgings in St Giles's Street. As the year drew to a close she sent family news to the cousins: the unveiling of the statue of their uncle John Alderson at Hull, the newspaper report of which she had received from his son James; her poor health which consisted of an erratic pulse and pain in her hip which prevented her from walking; and in December, the death of uncle Robert Alderson. From his home, St Helen's House, she joined his son Robert in writing letters to inform people of the death:

> ...all is happily over – and my poor dear uncle *released* and apparently without suffering in his last moments. Sam is arrived and the Judge [Edward] and Lady Milman are coming tomorrow evening. My aunt Alderson is a good deal affected at times – but she has the comfort of knowing that she has done her duty to him in his sad, sad state, both with judgment and feeling. He is to be buried in the Cathedral.[17]

The death prompted serious reflection about her elderly aunt Elizabeth's lack of religious faith. Edward's wife Georgina had challenged her, saying if Amelia was so 'zealous and eager' to convert people why did she not look at her own flesh and blood, adding 'Look at your poor benighted aunt!' Amelia penned a lengthy letter to Eliza, outlining the aunt's lack of understanding, and her own belief in the necessity of a Saviour. She said the idea of death was frequently on her mind, on account of her 'heart's stopping so oft' and she was praying for her aunt's atonement.

But the letter ended with a burst of the worldly Amelia in gossipy mode, prompted by news of the death of Lady Beechey, wife of William Beechey, the artist, who had been knighted in 1798. The former Ann Jessop was a Norwich girl with whom the married Beechey had formed a relationship when he lived and worked in the city in the 1780s. When he moved to London she went with him and they lived together, getting married in 1793 after his first wife died. There had been a great deal of gossip about the couple when Amelia was in London. A talented artist in her own right, Ann exhibited five drawings at the Royal Academy in 1787 under her maiden name; after that she exhibited under her married name. Farington believed she had given drawing lessons to Mrs Opie, but Amelia made no mention of this:

> Poor Ann Jessop! She was my dancing mistress and so she was of the Earlham Gurneys! Beechey seduced her, but behaved well in marrying her the day after his prostitute wife died and she made an excellent wife and mother...I believe she was kind-hearted and genuine.[18]

In the first weeks of the new year Amelia was caught up in the final stages of selecting pieces for *Lays for the Dead*. Henry agreed to produce an illustration for the frontispiece. In January she sent excerpts from some of the verses with her ideas on how the lines might be depicted. How would Henry feel about drawing the group round Charles Thompson's grave, when his brother Col Thompson had it opened? Or perhaps he might like to draw Amelia visiting Holt church at twilight and kneeling on the stones of the vault holding her mother's remains. From the many suggestions Henry elected to draw Bishop Heber* 'blessing the kneeling Hindoo round the altar at Trichinopoly'. She said that her publishers were 'charmed to publish my lays' but had not responded to her proposal about the art work, so would he go 'on winged steps' to Paternoster Row and lay the case before them.[19]

In February, having updated Henry with further thoughts on his art work, she reported on a forthcoming visit:

---

* Reginald Heber was an English clergyman, traveller, hymn writer and man of letters. He went to India as Bishop of Calcutta in 1823, dying suddenly three years later at the age of 42, only hours after taking a confirmation service at Trichinopoly, while travelling through Madras.

My old devoted friend Sneyd Edgeworth*, Maria E's brother, whom I knew and danced with in 1810, and have not seen since, is so romantic as to be coming down to see me! I think we shall scarcely be able to recognise each other but he is still *youngish*. He was 22 only in 1810 – I was so surprised to receive a letter from him to know whether I cared to see him again.[20]

To Sneyd Amelia responded that she would be pleased to see him:

But will thou really take the trouble to come hither to see an elderly gentlewoman in a Quaker cap, and speaking, as dear Southey says, the 'shibboleth of her sect'? If so, come away and the sooner the better... I cannot give thee a bed under my roof – there is an excellent hotel opposite to my dwelling – there thou couldst sleep – taking all thy *meals* with me.[21]

She sent further information about coach travel and the 'excellent warm bath' of the Norfolk Hotel. Sneyd stayed for a week and his hostess exerted herself to show him around her home city. From several letters which she wrote to him after he had returned home, it would seem that they had greatly enjoyed each other's company, reminiscing about old friends, talking about books and sharing anecdotes about relations. But she also found his visit exhausting:

Before we parted I was sure I had caught the influenza prevalent in our city – and the day after thy departure I took to my bed and I have not been out of my house since.

Today I am going to venture to Meeting and from there to Wroxham Hall. If I *did* make *too many* exertions in order to do the honour of our ancient city to an intellectual and enquiring stranger I cannot be sorry for it because I felt that those exertions were not thrown away on an ungrateful person and that he fully appreciated whatever was worth seeing.[22]

In March she enjoyed a fortnight with the Cottage ladies at Northrepps, but her ill health continued to worry her. In May, when she was in London for the Yearly Meeting and Royal Academy exhibition, she decided to consult the distinguished surgeon and physiolo-

---

* Charles Sneyd Edgeworth, always known as Sneyd, trained as a lawyer. His father, Richard Lovell Edgeworth had 21 children by four wives: Maria, the best-selling author, was his eldest daughter by his first wife; Sneyd's mother was his third wife.

gist Sir Benjamin Brodie* and continued to do so during subsequent visits to the capital. Early in the summer her final poetry book *Lays for the Dead* was published. Admitting in the preface that the subject of death must be 'painfully monotonous', she said she would not have dared to publish the lays had she not been encouraged by friends to do so. Reviewers were kind, rather than enthusiastic. There was approval for Mrs Opie's ability to describe the thoughts and emotions of the bereaved, but coolness towards her style of poetic writing, which some critics thought was outdated. One chose to remind readers of the author's past successes:

> The name of Amelia Opie acts as a talisman upon our memory; it calls back the time when we read her *Simple Tales*, and wept over her *Father and Daughter*, when we repeated her verses, and treasured her books under our pillows. Yet here she is tuning her harp to the sweetest melody, though to a mournful story – one to which there is a chord to respond in every heart; for who is there that cannot number amid the dead those whom long they loved?[23]

She was in Norwich making plans for a trip to Scotland when the Slavery Abolition Act became law on August 1st, 1834 – a day of double celebrations for Thomas Fowell Buxton. Since taking the place of the ailing Wilberforce in the anti-slavery movement, he had pushed the cause in Parliament at every opportunity and at public meetings across the country. On the auspicious day of the Bill taking effect Buxton's eldest daughter Priscilla was married to Andrew Johnston, of Fifeshire, who was MP for St Andrew's. Following a honeymoon in the West Highlands, the newly-weds settled at Rennyhill, overlooking the Firth of Forth from the north, where they welcomed Amelia as a guest a few weeks later. She had planned to 'steam off' from Great Yarmouth to Edinburgh, but was advised to sail from Blackwall (then a thriving port) on the Thames instead.

Despite her painful hip and bouts of severe toothache, Amelia travelled north from Edinburgh to Perth and Aberdeen, back via Stirling to Edinburgh for a scientific meeting, then west to Glasgow and northwest to Oban, from where she wrote an account of her adventures to Lady Charleville. Along the way she attended Quaker Meetings and was accommodated in the homes of friends and acquaintances (some

---

* Brodie's eldest son, Benjamin, married Philothea Thompson, daughter of Amelia's cousin Margaret. His only daughter Maria married Edward Hoare, son of Louisa (née Gurney) and Samuel Hoare.

titled) or in inns. She visited all the places she wished to see and enjoyed the solitude and the scenery:

> ...in such scenes as this, the full heart finds relief and enjoyment in communion with Him whose wondrous hand created them and thoughts become prayer and praise!...
>
> I have gone fearlessly along in boats, chaises, or carts or gigs and I have *trusted* and I have been preserved hitherto from harm.[4]

From Oban she went south to Largs and Fairlie on the east shoreline of the Firth of Clyde, where Dr Chalmers and his wife were taking a holiday, then headed east for Fifeshire, where she stayed with Priscilla and Andrew Johnston. In a letter to her mother Priscilla wrote of outings and visits they arranged for their guest, ending with:

> On Tuesday we took Mrs Opie to St Andrew's, and then to dine and sleep at Largs. She made verses and sang them as we went along. The next morning we went to see her off by the steam-boat to Edinbro'....[25]

Back in Edinburgh Amelia renewed acquaintance with the theatre world, dining with Sarah Siddons's youngest daughter Cecilia, now the wife of George Combe, a phrenologist, and relatives of Sarah's actor son Henry, who had managed Edinburgh Theatre before his death in 1815. She stayed with Quaker friends Robert and Mary Nasmyth,* then took a coach to Melrose on the Scottish Borders. Hiring a post chaise she was driven to Abbotsford, the home of Sir Walter Scott, which in the two years since his death in 1832 had become a literary shrine. Her first account of the pilgrimage was dispatched to Nasmyth. Her respect for 'the great departed' was lowered by seeing the 'treasuring up' of arms which made her wonder how a man so gifted could delight in accumulating 'such bloody memorials' around him. She was even more offended at his having pictures of 'two notorious courtesans, Nell Gwynne and Lucy Walter in all their naked and meretricious beauty'. She believed that such images would have blunted the moral sense of his children.[26]

Her next account of the visit to Scott's house and to Dryburgh Abbey, where he was buried, was to Joseph John. She re-iterated her distaste for the abundance of armoury:

> I could not have lived in rooms so filled....It was with feelings of sadness and I hope with a consciousness of some moral teaching

---

* The Nasmyths named the sixth of their seven daughters Amelia Opie Nasmyth.

that I left this home of past for his last home – and reached with some difficulty, walking over decayed leaves and slippery muddy paths along the path that leads to the precincts of the dead.... The effect is cold and desolate beyond expression and I was glad to hasten away. [27]

From Melrose Amelia headed south, stopping off at Darlington, York and Hull en route for Norwich, where her landlady, who had been obliged to leave St Giles's Street, offered her lodgings at her new home in Lady Lane.[*]

---

* The street and surrounding buildings were demolished to make way for a new Central Library in 1960. The library burned down in 1994 and the site is now occupied by The Forum, which houses the Millennium Library, BBC East, Tourist Centre and restaurants.

Chapter Twenty-seven

Although genuinely sympathetic to the poor and needy, Amelia loved to associate with titled people. She was very fond of three of the daughters of William Hay, 17th Earl of Erroll, whom she got to know through the Gurneys and all three of whom she considered exceptionally beautiful. Lady Harriet was married to Daniel Gurney, the youngest of the Earlham brothers; Lady Jane, wife of the Cathedral prebendary Charles Wodehouse, was a particular friend of Hudson Gurney's wife Margaret; Lady Isabella, married to Lt.Gen William Wemyss, was a lady-in-waiting.

Through Jane and Charles Wodehouse she was introduced to '*the* Prof Sedgwick their new prebendary', as she described him. Adam Sedgwick, who had taken holy orders, was Woodwardian Professor of Geology at Cambridge, where, breaking with tradition, his lectures were open to women. He was said to be a spellbinding lecturer and numbered the young Charles Darwin among his students. Following the Cathedral appointment he gave occasional lecture series in the city and Amelia became an enthusiastic attendee. She continued to pay annual visits to Northrepps Cottage and stayed often at Brooke House, as a guest of George Kett, whose parents, Thomas and Hannah, had entertained the Opies at nearby Seething Hall soon after their marriage. She also stayed with her cousin Robert, now married and rector at Baconsthorpe in Norfolk.

For some time Amelia had hoped to make a journey 'up the Rhine' with her cousins, but the hopes were not realised. Henry was busy with portrait commissions and in 1835, Eliza, having suffered a miscarriage, was anxiously expecting their first child. Amelia stayed with them in May and decided to set off on her own. Her friend Elizabeth Marlay, who lived in Paris, would join her when she reached Brussels at the beginning of August. It was an ambitious journey from city to city – Bruges, Ghent, Brussels, Liège, Aix-la-Chapelle, Cologne, Heidelburg, Zurich and Lucerne. She steeped herself in the history of the places she visited, drank in all the sights, relished taking drives through spectacular scenery and, aware of her charitable duties at home, visited prisons, religious houses and lunatic asylums. Brightwell reproduced a letter sent to her father in which Amelia was in raptures about seeing the Rhine Falls.[1]

A letter to her cousin Margaret gave a graphic account of the recent assassination attempt on Louis Philippe, as reported to her by Madame Marlay, whose cousin was in the royal party. While awaiting her friend's arrival Amelia had been reading the newly-published memoirs of Sir James Mackintosh, who had died in 1832. She was gratified by what he said in praise of her husband, but challenged a passage from a letter Mackintosh wrote to a friend in which he expounded on verses she wrote to him and his belief that she had written verses to William Ashburner (brother-in-law of Samuel Boddington):

> His account of *me*, and my loves and verses, is not at all accurate. The *Forget me not** was *written to no-one* and when I was a happy wife. The first verse was written at Boddington's one evening for Viganoni to set to music but he tried in vain. The second verse was written some time afterwards. William Ashburner was not only *dead* before the song was written but if I would have married him he would *not* have gone to India.... The lines to M were written in consequence of his sending a *message* to me desiring I would write an elegy on his absence. How rare is accuracy in anything![2]

To Margaret's children, Philothea, Vincent and Sarah Isabella (then aged eight, six and two), she wrote on notepaper with a fancy border and a picture of flowers:

> I flatter myself my darling children, that this is *the first letter* which any one of you has ever received from *abroad* – nor, as I believe, did any one of you ever receive before a letter written on such gay and ornamental paper. I bought it at Ghent to oblige a young woman, and I thought to myself as I did so, that I would write on it to P, V, and S.I. Thompson – but alas! not till this moment have I seemed to myself to have time to write.

Having thus begun, she told them about being seasick on her 18-hours sea crossing to Ostend, 'gliding' in a barge on a canal to Bruges and then going by boat to Ghent. Descriptions of a colourful 'fête' at Bruges gave way to something more serious:

> At Ghent I visited the prison and saw 1,300 prisoners, 300 of

---

* Two verses *To the Forget Me Not* by Mrs Opie were published in *The Poetical Forget Me Not* (London: Darton & Clarke, 1839), p.129. The lines are a plea to the flower to bloom round the grave of the writer.

whom were women, who wear a queer ugly bonnet. As there is no punishment of death at Ghent, even murderers are not hanged as in England but they are condemned to confinement for life, to perpetual silence and perpetual labour and to *solitude* at night, each sleeping in a cell alone. I saw *ten* of these murderers and their countenance was very bad indeed. I was glad to get away. A soldier is always with them to enforce silence and work. I also visited the deaf and dumb institution under the care of the Sisters and then the madhouses for men and women....[3]

By the second week in October Amelia had reached Lucerne, where, as she confided to her journal, she was distressed to read a death notice in *Galignani's Messenger* (a daily newspaper published in Paris and printed in English):

A most afflicting and unexpected event! The death of my beloved young friend, Mary, the wife of my dearest and best friend, J.J. Gurney. I had learned to love her dearly.... To her husband she was the heightener of his joys, the soother of his trials, the sharer, and I may say assistant, of his literary labours; to his children she was a most affectionate, kind and judicious mother.[4]

The travelling companions continued on their way for another two weeks, parting at Lille in Belgium, from where Amelia drove on to Calais for the Channel crossing. Wishing to see the new arrival in the Briggs household – whom she thought 'a noble and beautiful boy' – she stopped off in London before returning home.

Although the trip to the Continent was her last visit abroad, Amelia continued to spend time away from home almost until the end of her life – sometimes just an overnight stay at Earlham or Keswick or several weeks away further afield. She enjoyed inviting guests, such as Sedgwick, to dine with her – her new lodgings consisted of a suite of rooms – and having people to stay. Soon after her return to Norwich in November 1835, she was urging Henry to bring Eliza and their baby son, Henry Alderson, to stay with her.

Amelia was still seeking commissions for Henry. In January, after staying at Northrepps Cottage, she went to Wroxham Hall and was pleased when her hostess Margaret Southwell decided she would like Henry to paint a picture of the house. The two women had been friends since childhood. Margaret's maternal grandfather, Dr John Beevor, a colleague of Dr Alderson's, was one of the first physicians at the Norfolk and Norwich Hospital when it opened in 1772. Beevor's daughter Margaret married another medical man, James Crowe, twice mayor of Norwich, a member of the hospital's management team from 1802 and a wealthy landowner. He built The Grove, which became the home of Joseph and Jane Gurney. Margaret, one of the three Crowe daughters, married Sigismund Trafford South-well in 1791.* High Sheriff of Norfolk in 1816, Sigismund owned many properties in Norfolk and Cambridgeshire; in 1820 he acquired Wroxham Hall,† a Georgian house about eight miles from Norwich city centre, where he died seven years later.

John Opie had painted portraits of Sigismund and Margaret. Hav-ing offered work to Henry, she suggested he should stay at the hall for a few days, along with his cousin. Louisa Barwell, one of Amelia's Norwich associates, was an admirer of the artist. The daughter of Richard McKenzie Bacon, editor of the *Norwich Mercury*, and wife of John Barwell, a wine and spirit merchant, Louisa had begun her own writing career as the author of educational works for children. Amelia wrote to her from Wroxham Hall:

> H.P. Briggs assures me today that he shall be able to quit this place on fifth day (Thurs next). I am therefore at liberty to invite friends for the *next* evening and on Saturday he is obliged to return to London. I earnestly hope that thou and thy good man will be able to come to us that evening and I am now going to invite some other friends. He has made a charming picture of Louisa Trafford [wife of Margaret's youngest son Edward Trafford].[5]

Henry was working on a portrait of Hudson Gurney's wife, Marga-ret; later in the year he was commissioned to paint the Duke of Wel-lington. After his return to London, Amelia wrote to tell him that his portrait of Charles Turner, who was Mayor of Norwich in 1834, had been hung in St Andrew's Hall and was highly commended. She went to view it and was approached by 'an underling' who compared it unfavourably with another civic portrait:

---

* At the time of their marriage her husband, was known as Sigismund Trafford. His parents, Sir Clement Trafford, high sheriff of Lincolnshire, and Lady Jane Trafford (née Southwell) separated when he was young. On his mother's death in 1809 Sigismund added her maiden name and his wife became Margaret South-well, as did his daughter Margaret. His second daughter and three sons retained Trafford as their surname.

† The building was taken over by the War Department and used as a hospital for wounded members of the armed forces in the First World War. It was demolished a few years later.

He said the background was not *light* enough to throw the head out as Beechey had done in [John] Patteson's picture. I had a mind to knock him down but I contented myself with saying B's picture was *vile*.[6]

To Eliza she wrote a long account of being taken to Salle Church 'to weep over the bones' of her Briggs ancestors. This had inspired her to consult Francis Blomefield's seminal work on the county's history.

I really think I could make a pretty saleable story out of the real history of one of our ancestors – a Hobart in the time of Cromwell. The account of Briggses and Hobarts in the *History of Norfolk* is very amusing. Henry ought to buy the book. It contains many interesting anecdotes of other families like ours gone to *decay*.[7]

As a dedicated correspondent – she told one of her cousins that she wrote several letters each day – Amelia kept in touch with Hannah Backhouse during the latter's extensive preaching tour in America, sending, with one letter, some 'likenesses' she had done of Hannah's children. Soon after her return to England Hannah's son Henry was taken ill at his Quaker school in Tottenham and died. She hurried to The Grove to be with her widowed mother and three remaining children, Jane, Ann and Edmund. She had already lost Jonathan and Gurney, her first and second sons, and while she was sailing home her sister Elizabeth, who married into the Barclay family, had died. Amelia decided to delay a planned visit to London, telling the Briggs she could not turn her back on her 'poor friends at The Grove in their affliction'.

In America Hannah had made an important friendship with Eliza Paul Kirkbride from a Quaker family in Philadelphia. Miss Kirkbride decided to visit her friend in England, intending to stay with the Backhouses at Darlington, but by the time she arrived Hannah was in Norwich, where she remained for several months. Thus, the American visitor was invited to stay at The Grove from where she was introduced to the Gurneys, their relations and friends. Amelia, 66, was

Amelia signed her letters 'A Opie' or 'Amelia Opie'. She never omitted her surname, even when writing to cousins or close friends.

immediately drawn to the young woman, 30 years her junior.

After her annual visit to London in May, she received a parcel from France, but, as she confessed to Eliza, it was only after three weeks of having 'the box from David' that she had the courage to look at the bust he had created. It had relieved her mind:

> I suspected that it was either so flattered as to lose *all likeness* even more than Henry's picture, or else, so frightful and so *like* that it would offend my taste and feelings to look at it. But I was mistaken. It is *eminently flattered* but in some views like still – the back of the head and throat like and the dress well managed – as a work of art it is valuable. It is much younger than I am and yet *not young*. It has marks of age – the hair is too full for what my hair is *now*, but I wore it so at Paris.[8]

In August, after another bout of poor health, she was off again – this time to stay with a distant Briggs cousin, Charles Smith, a general practitioner, and his family at Bury St Edmunds. Charles was a grandson of Elizabeth (née Briggs), the only sister of Amelia's maternal grandfather. Elizabeth and her husband Joshua Smith had eight children. Amelia tried to keep track of their descendants, and shared news about them with the Briggs cousins. She looked forward to having Henry, Eliza and their son to stay with her in September, but had to write and tell them not to come because 'measles and hooping [sic] cough' were raging in the city; she had consulted four medical men, all of whom advised against bringing the child to Norwich. In the same letters she wrote of her distress at the death of Louisa Hoare (née Gurney) at her home in Hampstead, where she had always been a welcome guest.

At the end of the year she was able to tell her cousins that 'everybody at Keswick' was delighted with the portrait of Margaret Gurney and Hudson was now willing to sit for Henry. Writing to Eliza about fabrics and fashions, she added news of an interesting encounter:

> Richmond (a charming young man) the artist,[*] has been at Earlham to paint Joseph and certainly he has succeeded to admiration! I could not see a fault in it! The best of his I ever saw.... He has also done Anna Gurney and F. Buxton...he is a charming artist. I walked all over Norwich with him.[9]

The meeting made an impression on the 27-year-old Richmond, who

---

[*] George Richmond painted 50 portraits of Gurneys and Buxtons.

recorded the event in his journal:

> Dec 1836 – Met Mrs Opie, the widow of the painter, a very in-
> telligent and pleasing-looking woman, full of life, and *malgré* the
> Quaker's cap, laughed as heartily and talked as much as other peo-
> ple. I led her down to dinner, and talked a good deal about pictures
> and matters of Art, but do not think her judgment very high on
> these subjects.... In the drawing room she talked to me a good deal
> of her husband... she had known him take seven sitters a day, but
> spoke of it as of rare occurrence.... Mrs Opie has an upright fore-
> head and high head, and the face very like Blake the painter,* the
> eyes especially....[10]

Having been a regular house guest at Runcton Hall, Amelia was devastated when Daniel Gurney's wife Lady Harriet died. She was recovering from influenza when she heard the news: 'The blow coming on
an exhausted frame fell heavily on me. For hours I could neither cry
nor breathe – it would have been a comfort to laugh or scream.'[11]
She was able to weep when Joseph John came to see her, along with
his daughter Anna, son John Henry and Rachel Fowler, sister of his
late wife, now a permanent member of the Earlham household. The
comforting presence of Joseph John would soon be absent for three
years, as he had decided, after what he called 'a remarkable measure
of mental conflict' to submit to a project he had been considering
for years 'of crossing the Atlantic, and visiting Friends and others
in America'.[12] Before leaving he was obliged to obtain 'certificates'
from Friends giving him leave of absence. Amelia was at the Norwich
Meeting which granted his request; although he would be a great loss,
she believed it would help to heal his wounded mind:

> He is already quite another creature since he laid his concern before
> the Meeting and received their sanction, and heard the expressions
> of our *unity* with his prospects. Many wept as they expressed it,
> from affectionate reluctance to part with him, but *selfishness* was
> quite subdued....He can't however go without the consent of the
> Yearly Meeting, but we do not think it will be withheld.[13]

Before he left home, Amelia prevailed upon Eliza to go to a shop in
Bond Street and buy:

---

* At 16, Richmond had met, walked and talked with William Blake who had
made a profound impression on him. Two years later he was present at Blake's
death, closed his eyes and took his death mask.

two pieces of the best and sweetest smelling soap going and a round flat perforated thing sold for gentlemen to wear in their waistcoat pockets to regale their noses with when wanted. This and the soap I want for my beloved friend J.J. Gurney as a *resource* on ship-board.[14]

Joseph John sailed from Liverpool in July. A fellow passenger was Miss Kirkbride, returning home, and his first resting place in America was at the home of her uncle John Paul in Philadelphia. Throughout his three years away he kept a journal. On his return he put together an account of his travels entitled *A Journey in North America described in Familiar Letters to Amelia Opie* and printed 'for private circulation' by the Norwich publisher and bookseller Josiah Fletcher. It was a substantial work made up of 28 letters, each addressed to 'My Dear Friend', in which the author described visits to Friends' Meetings, private homes and prisons, the scenery and wildlife, reflecting throughout on customs and morals. In the first letter he explained that he was availing himself of his and Amelia's 'old and intimate friendship' in freely addressing the letters to her.

While he was away Amelia continued to make visits to Earlham and spend time with his siblings and cousins, writing regularly to her absent friend with news of their activities and what was going on in Norwich and Norfolk. Her first letter reported on the arrival of a new Bishop of Norwich,* Coke of Holkham being made Earl of Leicester, the 'new rooms' at Keswick Hall, Judge [John] Bosanquet calling on her and telling her about the new queen.[15] In letters to his children Joseph John invariably made a reference to Amelia, begging them to give her his 'very dear love'. Her drawings were especially pleasing:

I must begin by expressing my unfeigned delight in the portraits of my darling Anna. Amelia's framed profile is capital – *very* like – *very* sweet. I should think her chef-d'oeuvre. Give her my renewed warmest thanks – and beg her to send me her very best of dearest JH.[16]

In November Eliza gave birth to the Briggs's second child, a daughter whom they named Elizabeth Amelia. Their move to a house in Bruton Street off Berkeley Square met with Amelia's approval and she was keen to see it for herself. She hurried to London for two weeks

---

* Edward Stanley and Catherine, his wife, soon became friendly with Amelia and she was a frequent guest at the Bishop's Palace.

in December, when she was concerned to find Eliza and her little boy both unwell.

Over the next few months Eliza's illness caused more concern; Amelia herself suffered sporadic bouts of ill health which she wrote about in considerable detail in her letters. By the new year she was well enough to stay at Northrepps Cottage, where the heavy snow confined her and her hostesses indoors. A few weeks later she received news of the death of Margaret Southwell:

> I am very sorry she is gone. We were playfellows in earliest days, and friends in youth, maturity and age! As a *companion* I have known few women her equal. She had a reasoning mind – on politics we agreed – not so on religion. I had ceased to be an Unitarian; she had become one.[17]

Joseph John Gurney's daughter Anna, drawn by Amelia Opie, who continued to sketch Anna and her brother John Henry, as they were growing up. (© Religious Society of Friends in Britain, 2014) See page 299.

Not long afterwards she heard of the death of another old and dear friend – Anne Pocklington, a daughter of Thomas Harvey, of Catton

Hall, the patron of John Crome and a keen amateur artist.*

In May, 1838, the young Queen Victoria was crowned. Amelia – in London for four months – managed only to see the procession in Parliament Street, her Quaker conscience having prevented her from accepting a ticket for a seat in Westminster Abbey – offered by Lady Milman's brother-in-law, the Rev Henry Hart Milman, rector of St Margaret's, Westminster, who told her she would *see* very little but would hear the music to perfection. She explained her refusal to Joseph John:

> …this assurance made it *incumbent* on me to *refuse* the ticket – I wanted to go to *see* and not to *hear* – and I *refused*, to my cousin Eliza's great sorrow, as she had a ticket for the same Nave – and she saw *all* I wanted to see![18]

From the capital she paid visits to literary friends – Mary Berry and her sister at Richmond and Mary Russell Mitford at Three Mile Cross, the subject of her best-selling volumes entitled *Our Village*. Mitford had taken over from Mrs A.M. Hall as editor of *Finden's Tableaux*, an album which was popular in fashionable quarters; she asked Amelia to write something for her next edition. In its preface the editor gave 'most earnest thanks to the Friends whose Contributions have given to this Volume its literary value', followed by their names, including Elizabeth B. Barrett and 'Amelia Opie, that truest Friend'. Her contribution, *The Novice: A True Story,* was a melodramatic tale set in Paris in the reign of Louis XV. She told Miss Mitford that, as a Friend, she was bound not to *invent* a story.

Amelia's return to Norwich was marred by news of her cousin Robert's wife Sophia dying from puerperal fever and the loss of their premature child. She was also worrying about Louisa Trafford who was staying in Norwich for her 'lying-in' and was 'in great danger'. Her husband was often with Amelia, who told Eliza she felt 'a sort of maternal instinct' for the young couple. Edward Trafford was just one of many callers, as she was confined to her house once more, with painful knees which made walking difficult.

She rallied and, although suffering from recurring bouts of lameness and other disorders, she carried on with her habitual activities. Her next London season was something like a revival of her 'worldly' days, with a succession of parties, visits, dinners and soirées where

---

* Amelia owned two of Harvey's landscapes which she bequeathed to his grand-daughters Mary Anne and Emily Pocklington.

she met many old friends, including Lady Charleville and Lady Cork and met 'new' people, among them the American novelist Catherine Sedgwick, who was staying in London and reported their meeting to her friends:

> I owed Mrs Opie a grudge for having made me in my youth cry my eyes out over her stories; but her fair cheerful face forced me to forget it. She long ago forswore the world and its vanities, and adopted the Quaker faith and costume; but I fancied that her elaborate simplicity, and the fashionable little train to her pretty satin gown, indicated how much easier it is to adopt a theory than to change one's habits.[19]

Edward Maltby, now the Bishop of Durham, obtained tickets for Amelia and Henry to attend the Prorogation of Parliament, an occasion which she thoroughly enjoyed, writing a full account of the proceedings to her sponsor. She was intrigued to see people whom she had known years ago; in particular she mentioned the Prime Minister, Lord Melbourne, once the husband of Caroline Lamb (who had died in 1828):

> I knew William Lamb once for I used to visit at Melbourne House but I had difficulty in recognising him in Lord Melbourne *not* because he is grown grey and old, for old he is not; nor does he look so...but his countenance and manner is altered. He was grave, he is gay. He was dignified, now he seems a merry fellow on ye verge of a laugh or a joke. I could scarcely look at him without laughing myself. Such was my impression and my cousin's also....[20]

Amelia stayed with friends during her first few weeks in the capital before moving into Bruton Street, with the intention of doing what she could for Eliza, now terminally ill. She would read to the patient, at her request, until even that was too much for her. 'Dearest Eliza looks more like death every day,' she wrote to young Anna Gurney 'and poor Henry's health suffers from his sorrow.'[21] Despite his distress, Henry was trying to keep working. One morning Lord Glenelg's valet turned up unexpectedly, saying his master was coming to sit for Briggs. This was due to Amelia having contrived to get the portrait commission through her friendship with Margaret Grant, widow of Glenelg's younger brother Sir Robert Grant, a former MP for Norwich. Amelia, writing to tell Margaret of her pleasure at meeting Glenelg and being invited to remain in the painting room while Henry worked, continued her letter with news of her 'beloved cousin' whom she had not even seen for three weeks:

> She refuses now to see her husband except for a *minute* once a day and she has not for weeks seen her children. I used to have the privilege of reading the Scriptures and prayers and hymns to her but now she cannot bear it, the excitement is too much. But I believe I am here at my proper post because she likes to know I am in the house and because she thinks I am a comfort to her poor husband.[22]

Scarcely had the ink dried on the paper, when Amelia received letters telling her of the sudden death of Sarah Buxton in Bristol. She and Anna Gurney were about to set off on a long-planned trek to Greece and had been visiting Sarah's stepfather in Weymouth before leaving England. Amelia wrote immediately to pass on the news to Joseph John, telling him that the Cottage ladies had called on her in London en route to the west country:

> I had folded dear S in a *last* embrace as it now turns out! Well I am thankful indeed that I did see her then! Her removal is indeed a blight to my future life! I did so rely on the sincerity of her friendship and enjoy her society! but such regrets are *selfish*. Let me *rejoice* that she is taken from a life of suffering to one of cloudless joy!

Amelia quoted substantially from the letters describing Sarah's last hours and how the Buxtons were rallying round to support the bereaved Anna, who wanted to bring her partner back to Norfolk and have her buried in Overstrand churchyard. Sarah's niece Priscilla Johnston and nephew William Edward Forster (whose parents William and Anna had moved to Norwich in 1837) were 'even now, on the melancholy journey' which would take five days, as they would not travel on the first day [Sunday].[23]

Eliza died on September 4th, 1839. Amelia remained at Bruton Street, where the household was joined by Henry's unmarried sister Catherine; she left London 'with painful feelings' which she expressed in her first letter to the widower after her return to Norwich:

> But God's will be done! and I most fully believe that grief on this occasion, though natural and unavoidable, abounds with consolations of the highest order – the conviction that *all is well with her*....Thou hast *another* source of comfort which perhaps *few* can

ask – the consciousness of having been so evidently eminent as a kind and devoted husband.[24]

To Joseph John she wrote explaining why she had not written for several weeks; she was still catching up with correspondence, sitting up till one in the morning to read the letters which had come during her five months' absence. He was given an account of Eliza's deathbed, the impending death of Lady Milman's daughter Elizabeth, news of attending a Friends meeting in London when Betsy Fry spoke of her 'labours of love abroad', her latest visit to Earlham and her decision to go and stay at Northrepps Cottage, Anna Gurney having written her 'the most heartrending letter'.

> Poor Henry Briggs is *deeply* afflicted. He finds his only consolation in reading over and over again all the letters poor E ever wrote to him in the belief that she still looks down on him and his children and that thought cheers his solitude. He sees no-one but on business, and of painting and business he is full and so much the better.[25]

Two weeks later she wrote to Henry: the stay at Northrepps had been 'trying', but friends thought Amelia's visit had done Anna good. To Joseph John she reported that Anna had been persuaded to go ahead with her trip to Greece, accompanied by Thomas Fowell and his eldest son Fowell as far as Rome. It was at this time that Amelia and Henry had the unwelcome task of sorting out the legal problems brought to light after Eliza's death, due to the negligence of her brother Tom over their father's will 40 years earlier. Seeking Joseph John's patronage for a new lunatic asylum which Friends were setting up near London, Amelia owned she thought it a good idea to relieve the expense on families of maintaining any insane relation, as one day she might need to be so helped herself, 'not in my own person but I do positively expect that my poor dear cousin Tom's strange career will end in decided madness.'[26]

Although the problems with Tom offended Amelia's sense of family propriety, she was even more appalled by a scandal in the family of the late Margaret Southwell. Her love of a good narrative made reporting the matter to her correspondents a melodramatic business. The person who brought dishonour to the family was Louisa Trafford, who had, said Amelia 'endeared herself' by her many kindnesses and whom she saw frequently. Joseph John was informed that the young lady was the stepdaughter of his friend Tryphena This-tlethwayte*; Henry was told that his portrait of Mrs Trafford had probably been 'conveyed to a lumber room'. To her Edinburgh friend Mary Nasmyth she composed a full-length report, saying the subject was 'uppermost' in her mind. Having stated that the tale concerned the mother of three young children who 'seemed to have all this world could give', but who was caught 'under *her husband's* roof with a young officer, she continued:

> The husband was *informed* of her suspected bad conduct and pretended to go to London – but he returned at midnight, the chamber door was broken open and the gallant escaped like y man in Hogarth's *Marriage à la Mode* out of y window and had to run barefooted two *miles* in a *fog* to the village inn!...
>
> I hear that when her brother in law and her own brother came to take her away the scene of her parting from her children was fearful to behold![27]

In addition to her prolific correspondence Amelia was writing for *Tait's Magazine* and Chambers' *Edinburgh Journal*-. For the latter she wrote pieces on Harriet Countess of Rosslyn, Sir Walter Scott, Lord Loughborough and George Canning, which were published in January and February as *Recollections of an Authoress*. As she told Henry, she was satisfied to have her name attached to the pieces, which meant she would get 'more pay'.

---

* After her mother died, Louisa's father Thomas Thistlethwayte married Tryphena Bathurst, daughter of the then Bishop of Norwich Henry Bathurst.

Chapter Twenty-eight

The liberation of British slaves had not brought an end to anti-slavery campaigning. There were still demands for slaves across the Atlantic and demands in Africa for manufactured goods which the slave trade supplied. Thomas Fowell Buxton, who lost his Parliamentary seat in 1837, wrote *The African Slave Trade and Its Remedy* and was the driving force behind the setting up of the Society for the Extinction of the Slave Trade and for the Civilisation of Africa, which had the Prince Consort as its president. He believed that the way forward was to deal with the problem on a commercial basis by helping the Africans to develop alternative sources of income. Amelia admired the book and sent a copy to Sedgwick, who responded:

> I read some parts of it again and again till I was heartsick. I am filled with disgust and horror and indignation in turning over the leaves of it; when is this monstrous evil to die from the earth? And for men calling themselves Christians (shame upon them) to do such deeds, which might seem almost an over-match for the powers of darkness, is quite appalling. Many of the facts were known before; but they were never before seen in one glance, or grasped in all their frightful combinations. Mr Buxton has done good service in laying bare this frightful passage in the history of man, and is well entitled to the warmest thanks of every Christian Patriot.[1]

Amelia was also very taken with Harriet Martineau's *Society in America*, about her two years in the country, where she travelled widely and was subject to abuse and even death threats because of her support for abolitionists against a violent pro-slavery movement. Later she read and re-read Martineau's article about the abolitionists, *The Martyr Age of the United States*, in the *Westminster Review*, which she thought was 'masterly'. She was in London in May 1840 for the Yearly Meeting, which was followed in June by two significant events in the anti-slavery calendar – an abolition meeting at Exeter Hall*

---

* Opened in 1831 in The Strand, the building had two halls which were used for philanthropic and religious meetings and became synonymous with the anti-slavery movement. It was demolished in 1907 and the site is now occupied by the Strand Palace Hotel.

and an international convention at the Freemasons' Hall, called by the British and Foreign Anti-Slavery Society to promote the universal abolition of slavery and the slave trade and the protection of emancipated slaves in the British Colonies. She was pleased that Buxton was back in London after his sojourn in Rome, writing to him from Bruton Street:

> Welcome to England! I *must* tell thee how delighted I was to see thee passing in a yellow chariot last second day as I was driving down Fleet Street, and looking so young and *butiful* [sic] and well![2]

After the first event, she started a letter to Joseph John, telling him about the 'never to be forgotten day' of Buxton's meeting, when she was surrounded by 'dear, dear friends', including Betsy Fry. 'The Lion of the meeting was Prince Albert in the chair and thus was the Sovereign of ye realm identified with the philanthropic work'.[3] She resumed the letter after attending the British and Foreign Anti-Slavery Society Convention, which was 'the most interesting period perhaps of my life... *such* a 12 days'. She wrote of the eloquence of the convention speakers – 'I fell under *his spell*', she said of Daniel O'Connell, the Irish politician – and of hearing Joseph John 'named and praised' when extracts from one of his letters were read to the convention by William Knibb, a Baptist minister and missionary to Jamaica. She loved 'the dear devoted American delegates' and, with Henry's 'cordial approbation', invited them to a soirée at Bruton Street. They told her that her book on lying had achieved great sales in America.

Returning home in August, Amelia wrote accounts of the proceedings of the convention, intending them for publication, giving this project as her reason for refusing a request by Mary Russell Mitford to write something for her:

> I have *faithfully promised* to give my whole mind to drawing up, if *I am able*, a sort of *popular précis* of the glorious anti-slavery proceedings and sittings in the Anti-Slavery Convention, where I was daily a delighted auditor; and some of my own Society, distinguished members of that convention, entreated me to *try at least* to draw up something for the committee to publish.[4]

In the Opie papers Brightwell found hand-written reports of the first two days, running into thousands of words. She opted to reproduce an excerpt from the second day's account giving Amelia's impressions of some of the delegates. From the report of the first day she merely offered the concluding paragraph:

> ...if the benefits resulting from it be in any proportion to the in-
> tense interest which (as I believe) it excited in all who were present,
> then Millions yet unborn may bless The meeting of that day.[5]

Amelia's feelings on seeing Thomas Clarkson in the chair were expressed in a letter to Lucy.* Accompanied by his young grandson
and widowed daughter-in-law, the veteran campaigner was led in by
the Quaker Joseph Sturge, a founder of the society which set up the
convention:

> The assembly had been desired to abstain from all applause lest it
> be too much for his feelings but to shew [sic] their respect by stand-
> ing up. It was an affecting sight...the poor boy wept with his aged
> sire and his weak mother, and indeed, I saw many new friends weep
> also. No wonder, for the feelings which Clarkson was actuated by
> and which Joseph Sturge communicated in broken accents himself
> were *real* feelings and not *acted* ones and feelings in which all pres-
> ent sympathised with and respected.[6]

Neither in this letter, nor in the letter to Joseph John did Amelia write
of a long-drawn-out debate on the first day about American women
attending the event, other than mentioning to the latter that 'their
female delegates were not permitted to speak'. She and the other British women attending the event knew their place, which was to sit and
listen. The American delegation included woman who were leading
activists in the abolitionist movement and who expected to participate fully in the convention. The arguments began once the opening
speeches had been made and 'the venerable chairman' had retired.
Wendell Phillips, from Massachusetts, proposed that 'a correct list' of
members of the convention should be prepared, adding that several
of his co-delegates, although admitted to the hall, had been refused
tickets as members. As Amelia wrote in her unpublished account:

> Hitherto a feeling of complete unanimity seemed to prevail over
> the meeting, but on hearing this motion some persons present, who
> knew its tendency, saw that it was 'the flash precursor of the com-
> ing storm' and they anxiously awaited the result.[7]

The debate lasted for the rest of the day. Many were the arguments,
expressed with eloquence and sincerity, both for and against accept-

---

* Probably Lucy Birkbeck.

ing women as accredited members of the convention until, at last, an overwhelming majority voted against. They were permitted to remain in the hall, but not to take part. Amelia's document gave verbatim accounts of the speeches and the conclusion which was reached but she forbore to comment on the feminist issue – a surprising omission for one who had sung the praises of Mary Wollstonecraft (in her bereavement letter to Godwin) as 'a woman who nobly, and *incomparably* fought for the violated rights of her sex'. Brightwell ignored 'the woman question' altogether. But for two of the American delegates, Lucretia Mott and Elizabeth Cady Stanton, it was a turning point; on their return home they began to campaign in earnest for women's rights.

Benjamin Haydon was commissioned by the Society to commemorate the event. He went to the Freemasons' Hall every day 'to sketch heads'. Once the convention was over, he continued to work on sketches of those he wished to include in his painting of the scene, making notes in his diary of who they were and what he thought of them. Amelia, who sat for him three times, was described as 'a delightful creature', but he was less pleased with Lucretia Mott: 'I found her out to have infidel notions, and resolved at once (narrow-minded or not) not to give her the prominent place I intended first.' Buxton was also criticised because he insisted on dictating letters to a clerk and talking to two American delegates, while he was sitting:

> That man so bedimmed my brain, a bad head was the consequence, and what with his dictating letters, signing, correcting and telling, I passed literally a most distracting morning, and told him so.[8]

He finally completed the huge oil painting *The Anti-Slavery Society Convention, 1840*, at the end of April the following year. It now hangs in the National Portrait Gallery.

Soon after Amelia's return home Joseph John Gurney arrived back at Earlham. In October a major exhibition opened in the city under the auspices of the Norwich Mechanics Institute of which Louisa Barwell's husband John was president. A talented artist – he had exhibited at the Royal Academy – Barwell was interested in all aspects of art, design and technology. The Norwich Polytechnic Exhibition was an ambitious venture, designed to show works of art, natural history specimens, antiquities, machinery, models, paintings, sculpture and engravings. Louisa wrote a comprehensive guide to the exhibition which was held in the Royal Norfolk and Norwich Bazaar, an elegant three-storied building which housed a picture gallery.* The catalogue listed 'Mrs Opie' as the exhibitor of two pieces – a 'profile cast' of herself (probably the David d'Angers medallion) and 'a daguerreotype view in Rome', one of only six photographs on show. Examples of the new medium of photography had first been exhibited in public in 1839 and those displayed in Norwich were probably the first ever to be exhibited in the county.

The Rome daguerreotype was probably a gift from Anna Gurney, who had returned home from her travels in Europe, still grieving over Sarah's death. Amelia had written to her while she was in Rome, expressing interest in the eternal city; in October she stayed at Northrepps Cottage, acutely aware of her own loss, but hoping to offer some comfort to her bereaved friend. The experience prompted a poignant poem to Anna about this visit, setting the scene in the opening lines as she lamented the absence from the cottage of the woman they both loved:

> We *met* but oh! how changed our meeting
> From *that* of former happy years!
> Now not in words we gave our greeting
> But, all our language was in *tears*.[9]

A few months later she was grieving for the loss of Jane Gurney of The Grove. Members of the family, including her two surviving daughters, Hannah Backhouse and Emma Pease, were summoned to the deathbed. Amelia was at Earlham when Joseph John and his daughter returned with news of Jane's last hours. Anna told her it was 'the most interesting and comforting scene of death that she had ever witnessed',[10] wrote Amelia.

During his time in America Joseph John had kept in touch with Eliza Kirkbride, who paid a return visit to England in the autumn of 1840, staying with the Backhouses in Darlington. As on her first visit, she endeared herself to all the Gurney relations, who were delighted when, in London for the Yearly Meeting, she accepted Joseph John's proposal of marriage. Amelia sent her a letter:

> I hasten to tell thee how *heartily* I rejoice in the happy prospects of my dearest friend in and by which I trust thy happiness is included and will be through life secured....
> What a pleasure it is to think that if I live till next winter Earl-

---

* Built in 1831 in St Andrew's Broad Street, it later housed the city's first cinema before being demolished in 1964 for road widening.

ham will have even a new attraction for me.[11]

Frequently in her correspondence Amelia would write of the flowers growing in her garden and, according to Brightwell, she loved having cut flowers in her house. She became a member of the Royal Botanic Society which, not long after its foundation in 1839, leased the grounds within the Inner Circle in Regent's Park for use as an experimental garden. It was open to members and their guests and to the general public for a fee on some days. On June 2nd, 1841, Amelia asked Joseph John to be her guest at a 'Promenade' in the gardens when members were invited 'to view the progress of the works previously to the general opening.'* His daughter told his fiancée about the outing:

> Papa was in London all fourth day after, calling on A. Opie and expecting to see some Hoares, was enticed by her to a Botanic garden which turned out to be a most fashionable promenade where they paraded together to their mutual satisfaction. On their way they met Lady Colebrook who asked Papa if that was the lady (meaning A. Opie) whom he was *going to marry*![12]

Joseph John spent the next four months, with Elizabeth Fry and other family members, in missionary work on the Continent before returning to Eliza whom he married at Darlington in October. In November Amelia was pleased to see another old friend, the distinguished sculptor Sir Francis Chantrey, in Norwich with his wife for the placing of his statue of the late Bishop Bathurst in the Cathedral. She dined with them at the Bishop's Palace, although not feeling at all well. Chantrey called two days later to inquire after her. 'In three days he was a corpse and I was *recovering*' she wrote to friends who knew the sculptor.

A few weeks later, while staying at Northrepps, she heard of the death of another old friend, Coke of Holkham. But the main topic of conversation was the ill-fated voyage known as the Niger expedition which had been put in motion at the Exeter Hall meeting in 1840. Buxton still had influence in the Commons and the Whig government was persuaded to support an expedition along the River Niger, where attempts would be made to conclude treaties with tribal lead-

---

* Her invitation survives in a printed card, with names written in her hand – Joseph John on the 'Admit' line and Amelia Opie on 'Introduced by...' (SCFHL, Amelia Alderson Opie papers, SC 088)

ers, offering regular trade in return for an embargo on slave selling. Possibilities for agricultural, commercial and technological development would also be investigated. The project started in high hopes, but ended in failure and disaster, all three vessels limping home after barely seven weeks on the Niger, with more than 40 people dead and others sick and prostrated by fever.

Later Buxton wound up the society upon which he had pinned so many hopes. He suffered greatly in its aftermath, but friends such as Amelia were anxious to express their support. She wrote to his daughter Priscilla, saying she believed (as was the case) that some treaties had been negotiated with tribal leaders and was hopeful of their being maintained She was cheered, too, by the thought that the worst was over:

> And spite of everything (said Dr Hull yesterday evening to a little party of friends here) – the scheme will still remain on record, one of the grandest, noblest, and most benevolent ever conceived by the mind of man.
>
> But alas! I know but too well how these events will affect thy dear father.[13]

To Buxton himself she wrote a poem for his birthday on April 1st, hailing his 'natal morn' and the arrival of spring and hoping 'soon may thy mind from gloom be free'.

During her visit to London in the summer she was flattered by an invitation from the Duke of Sussex. The sixth son of George III and favourite uncle of Queen Victoria, he was a president of the Royal Society and took a keen interest in Bible studies. In the autumn he stayed at Auckland Castle, home of the Bishop of Durham, which prompted Amelia to tell Maltby of her time with the Duke:

> *He* is a good friend of mine and last summer desired a friend of mine to tell 'Sister Amelia', as he calls me, that he wished to see me at Kensington Palace, and I went and had half an hour's tête-à-tête with him. The Dutchess [sic] shewed me what, probably, thou hast seen – the long-room full of closets filled with Bibles in all languages. I was staying in ye house, at Holkham in 1820, four days, with ye duke, who ascended, at some loss of breath, to ye north tower, one day, to see ye Holkham collection of Bibles.[14]

Henry had completed a portrait of the Bishop earlier in the year, which Amelia told him, their cousin Margaret thought was 'splendid'.

She was still taking an interest in his career, but was concerned when he told her he was suffering from 'diseased lungs' and suggested he might go abroad 'for his health'. In October she was cast down by the news that Jonathan Backhouse had died, telling Henry what a kind friend he had always been, sending her 'fine coals' to keep her warm in winter. Hannah, his widow, took her family back to Norwich and remained at The Grove for more than a year.

Now in her 70s, Amelia was often unwell, sleeping badly and taking laudanum to relieve intense pain. She told Henry she had learnt not to wonder that 'persons unrestrained by religion' killed themselves to get away from it.[15] But she tried to keep going. She rallied to the cause of her friend Mary Russell Mitford, who found herself in financial difficulties after the death of her father – an inveterate gambler who had squandered much of his wife's fortune. When her mother died, Mitford's literary work became the family's only source of income; but she was unable to keep it up during her father's declining years as she was taking care of him. After his death in December, 1842, she was penniless and owed £1,000 to creditors. Her friends organised a subscription list and by the end of March had raised more than £1,300. Thanking one contributor for her efforts, Mitford wrote 'my good old friend Mrs Opie has been taking the same kind of trouble at Norwich and with great success.'[16]

Amelia enjoyed her annual London visit – the last summer she would spend with Henry at Bruton Street – and was pleased with an introduction to Elizabeth Stanhope, wife of Leicester Stanhope, who later became the 5th Earl of Harrington. Elizabeth was a minor poet and society hostess, entertaining literary friends at Ashburnham House in Chelsea. In Norwich Amelia was also enjoying frequent invitations to gatherings at the Bishop's Palace, where, as she told Lady Charleville, she always met 'charming people'. The Stanleys introduced her to Sir John and Lady Boileau, of Ketteringham Hall, where she became a welcome guest. Sir John was involved in a wide range of activities across the county and was its high sheriff in 1844. In the autumn she renewed her contact with Caroline Fox from Falmouth, who was staying with the Gurneys.

While visiting Anna Gurney in October she met a former slave who was staying at Northrepps Hall as a guest of Buxton. Born in Yorubaland (now western Nigeria), Ajayi was captured by Portuguese slave traders on the trans-Atlantic route, then rescued by the British and put ashore at Sierra Leone, where the Church Missionary Society was working with liberated slaves. He became a committed Christian and was baptised in the name of Samuel Crowther. Fluent in English and native languages, he was employed as an interpreter on the Niger expedition; when the expedition failed he was brought to England to further his studies at the Church Missionary College in Islington; his visit to Northrepps followed his ordination earlier in the year.

The Rev Samuel Crowther, a former slave liberated by the British, who stayed in Norfolk as a guest of Thomas Fowell Buxton in 1843. Amelia met him when he was a dinner guest at Northrepps Cottage.

As Anna told Priscilla Johnston, she was reading quietly with her guests when the servant announced 'Mr Charles Buxton and a gentleman' and in walked Buxton's son and the Rev Samuel Crowther. Buxton himself joined them later for dinner and the evening was an unqualified success. The ex-slave told them the story of his captivity. 'Mrs Opie was delighted at hearing him,' reported Anna. The rest of his visit to Norfolk included his being taken by Anna to her parish church, where he gave a sermon: 'I may say that a woolly head does not look unnatural now in our Northrepps pulpit,' she concluded.[17]

There were more changes to the family at Earlham in November, when Joseph John's daughter Anna married into the Backhouse family of Darlington. The service took place at the Goat Lane meeting house, followed by a marriage feast at Earlham. Amelia's gift to the couple was a copy of *The Pilgrim's Progress* in what she called 'a bridal binding' of white and gold. As the year drew to a close, although feeling 'dangerously ill', she made an effort to keep in contact with Henry's son and daughter, as he had gone abroad and she thought it appropriate to let them know they were in her thoughts. Henry's sister Catherine was partly in charge of the children, as were his Bell cousins.* Of these, Jacob Bell, founder of the Pharmaceutical Society (later the Royal Pharmaceutical Society) and editor of the *Pharmaceutical Journal* and his sisters Eliza and Anna were stalwart supporters of the youngsters and much admired by Amelia.

---

* Henry's mother Mary (née Oldham) had a sister Sarah who married Frederick Smith, a pharmacist; their eldest daughter Eliza was the wife of John Bell (father of Jacob), who ran a chemist and druggist business in Oxford Street.

Chapter Twenty-nine

When her cousin Henry returned to England from what Amelia called his 'fruitless visit to Malta, Naples and Rome' he was terminally ill and wanted to see her. He died on January 18th, 1844, three days after she arrived in London; she and Jacob Bell were at his deathbed. She remained at Bruton Street until the end of the month, then went to Hampstead Heath to stay with the Hoares, where she was taken ill with severe chest pains which kept her in bed for three days. She returned to the Briggs household at Jacob Bell's request.

From Bruton Street she wrote to Anna Backhouse:

> What a strange position I am in here! I *surviving* my two young and kind relations, the master and mistress of this house and living with their servants and everything as usual here but their dear selves! And *I* too living to see in my old age a scene *nearly resembling* that which I went through in my much younger days, though that scene was more painful.... *The house* to be let or sold! The gallery *dismantled*, the pictures, many of them going to be sold by auction! and this my second London home through so many years about to be closed on me for ever!
>
> Would I were gone! but as he does not approve of breaking up an establishment *so soon* after the death of the master, Jacob Bell, the executor and trustee (the cousin and affectionate nurse of HPB) wishes HPB's sister and myself to remain here as the servants must. The darling children are with his father and sisters at West Hill, Wandsworth, which is to be their home till the little girl goes to school and the boy from school to college.[1]

In the previous year Amelia had been approached by the publisher Grove & Sons, of Southwark, who wanted to bring out new editions of her works. She consulted Josiah Fletcher, who, having ascertained that Groves were 'respectable', said it was a duty she owed herself as it would give her the chance to make corrections. He suggested approaching Simon Wilkin about the project, so she wrote to him, saying she was taking the liberty of asking him a great favour respecting her published works:

All my *egregiously sublime and delightful* books, for such they *undoubtedly* are, are quite out of print in England and, alas! I cannot obtain a set from America where there is a whole new set published in 1838.[2]

She told Wilkin of her consultations with Fletcher, adding that Groves had written to her that very day, asking for an answer to their proposition. As a favour, she wondered if he would negotiate with them on her behalf. Wilkin agreed to act as her agent, whereupon he and Amelia exchanged several letters about her contract with the publishers. Once the project was under way she told Wilkin that Groves wanted 'an advertisement to appear in the Public Papers' and asked him to write it for her. When the advert appeared in the press some months later she was at Bruton Street, dealing with the aftermath of Henry's death, and was distressed to receive a rebuke from Joseph John who said she had infringed undertakings she had made when she became a Friend. She replied immediately, defending her actions:

I never thought, nor do I *now* think that in doing this I have *at all* violated my engagement as a Friend. I promised never to write things of the same sort again, nor have I done so...I never thought that works of fiction were never to be read – on the contrary I believe simple moral tales the very best mode of instructing the young and the *poor*, else why did the blessed Saviour teach in parables?

My own books, which Friends never read and know nothing about, are, in my belief, moral tales and many many proofs have the kind and candid given me of the good they have occasionally done....

I had *prayed much* on the subject when, near a year ago, after some weeks consideration I agreed to the proposal. I got no *money* whatever by this – only the pleasure of knowing that all mention of the great names and other blemishes are to be expunged in the new edition....

Till thy note came my mind was quite easy and satisfied and is now disturbed *only* by the consciousness that I have given pain to thee. I hope I have written clearly but I have coughed all night nearly, and have not long been rouzed [sic] by thy note from my late morning slumbers.[3]

Having remained for several weeks in London in response to Bell's request. Amelia was back in Norwich in time to attend the Lent Assizes*, still one of her favourite occupations, and this time she was invited to dine at the Bishop's Palace at the end of the week to meet the judges. Her old friend Lord Abinger was to be the presiding judge and would be a guest at the Stanleys. She first met the judge during her early days in London, when he was James Scarlett, newly called to the bar and a friend of James Mackintosh. He entered Parliament in 1819 and was MP for Norwich for three years from 1832; his illustrious legal career brought him a peerage in 1835 when he was created the 1st Baron Abinger.

Their encounter was not what she expected and caused her to write detailed accounts to Joseph John and his daughter. Anna was given a summary of their exchanges at Bishop Stanley's dinner party:

> ...he was very irritating to me in his expressions of dislike of my dress and my diction and spoke of Friends so ignorantly as well as so queerly, owning however they were excellent people, though not strong-headed. I was very gentle with him, though I hope and trust I was firm and honest in my replies. He said he must come and live a week with me to know all about us and perhaps I should convert him....When we parted he said 'Farewell! Pray remember our conversation,' and I assured him I could never forget it.[4]

A few days later Amelia wrote again to Anna, telling her that Abinger was dead.

Joseph John, in France fulfilling Friends' duties, was treated to a much longer report of the Abinger situation, beginning with Amelia's recollection of an earlier meeting with him at the House of Lords, when he mocked her Quaker use of 'thou' and 'thee' and she had turned her back on him. At the recent Assizes she had conversations with Judge John Patteson and other court officials, but not Abinger who she believed was ignoring her because of her rudeness. 'This was *very silly of me* and conceited too.' When she left the court on the second day, she was called back by the Baron and found him 'with hands stretched out to greet me and saying, 'Why did you not speak to me? How could you be so unkind?' He then told her he was blind since having an operation to remove 'incipient cancer' and stood in the lamplight turning on her 'his dreadful eyes'. They talked for a while and then again at the Bishop's Palace. After she had challenged his judgement on a particular case, 'he began to abuse *my cap*, my

---

* When Amelia was a girl the Assizes were only held once a year, but from 1832 they were twice yearly and known as the Lent and Summer Assizes.

language, my nonsense in having given up music and singing and so he went on.' However, before she left the party she made a point of bidding him farewell. News of his fatal stroke was a shock. 'Now I can't get him out of my mind.'[5]

The elderly Elizabeth Alderson was thought to be on her deathbed, so Amelia decided she must not travel too far afield for the time being in order to be with her aunt if needed. She declined invitations from her Thompson cousins to spend summers at their London address and took only brief breaks closer to home for the next four years, while her aunt lingered on. In the autumn she travelled on Norfolk's first railway line from Norwich to Yarmouth,* from where she took a coach to Lowestoft to see her cousin Edward and his family. Her self-imposed detention in Norwich gave her more time for reading and writing.

Elizabeth Stanhope's social circle and literary interests made her an ideal correspondent for Amelia, who enjoyed passing on gossip, anecdotes and opinions about acquaintances old and new. She expressed distress when Lady Charleville's young grandson James Marlay was drowned in the Thames at Hampton Court in the summer of 1843; she was gratified when the boy's mother, the widowed Catherine Marlay (Lady Charleville's only daughter) called on her at 'the house of death', a few days after Henry's passing; she grieved over the deaths of Sir John Gurney and Sydney Smith; she alerted Elizabeth to the sale of her cousin Henry's pictures at Christie's, telling her later that Hudson Gurney had bought the portraits of Henry Hart Milman, Sydney Smith and herself and 'the one of the Duke of Wellington that was unsold'.

A book which Amelia admired was George Borrow's *The Bible in Spain* (1843), writing in her journal: 'Long live Don Jorge! He is my delight both night and morning, and my happiest hours are spent in his society.'[6] Born at East Dereham in Norfolk in 1803, the son of an army recruiting officer, Borrow spent much of his early life on the move. By 1817 he was settled in Norwich, where he became a protégé of William Taylor, the German scholar. An inveterate traveller, with exceptional linguistic skills, he made many trips abroad, walking from place to place and getting to know the inhabitants. As an agent for the British and Foreign Bible Society, he spent two years

---

* When the service opened on May 1st, 1844, thousands of people thronged to places along the route to get a view of the trains. The Norwich to London service started in June 1846.

in Russia, followed by nearly five years in Spain. The book which Amelia so admired was a huge success. As she informed Elizabeth Stanhope, Borrow was the main topic of conversation one morning at the Bishop's Palace:

> I think thou hast not yet met him. He is, I think, more clever and learned in language than agreeable. Still, he is worth meeting. I think some of thy habitués know him. He is writing his own life which will be, I am told, his chef-d'oeuvre. He once lived among the gipsies and if he tells *all the truth*, probably his account of that period of his life will be the most amusing. He was a Norwich man and his sensible mother lives here. He was the lion of last year in certain circles.[7]

Since the winding up of his anti-slavery activities Thomas Fowell Buxton had retreated from public life and spent most of his time at Northrepps Hall. He died in February 1845, with his family gathered round him. Amelia told Lady Catherine Boileau that she had:

> the melancholy satisfaction of following in the funeral procession of my loved and honored [sic] friend, while crowds of all ranks surrounded the burial place among the wild ruins of Overstrand Church and I saw him laid in the family vault by the side of his beloved sister and son.[8]

There was some joy at Earlham when Anna Backhouse and her husband returned to her old home in March, bringing her six-month-old baby son John Henry, who was shown off to all his Norfolk relations and family friends. Amelia had taken to signing her letters to Anna 'thy loving friend and granny' and calling her 'my grand-daughter' when she mentioned her in letters; now she adopted 'my great grandson' when referring to the baby. Joseph John also used this term, suggesting to Amelia, when he was on a visit to the Backhouses a year later, that a trip to Darlington would do her good: 'How thou wouldst enjoy the rapidly developing faculties and affections of thy great grandson.'[9]

Betsy Fry, although still actively involved in her prison reform work and Quaker ministry, had returned to her home county to support her bereaved sister Hannah Buxton. Exhausted and unwell, she was persuaded to spend a few restorative weeks at Earlham. Amelia, although unwell herself, was pleased to spend time with her dear friend, who commented on a 'very handsome Barcelona handkerchief'* she was wearing, saying, 'Why Amelia looks like a *bride*!'[10] It was the last time they saw each other; Betsy was terminally ill. Her devoted husband Joseph took her to Ramsgate, where she died in October 1845. She was buried in the Friends Burial Ground at Barking in Essex, next to the grave of her little daughter Elizabeth, who had died 30 years earlier. Joseph John said a prayer at the graveside, while more than 1,000 people stood in tribute.

As the year drew to a close Amelia was surprised to receive a gift from Mrs Bray – a new edition of her short stories, with a dedication to Mrs Opie, in which she recalled the pleasure of being 'hospitably received' by Amelia and her father and expressed her 'unfeigned thanks' for the delight she had received from so many Opie writings:

> Feeling that, in treating of the heart, I could never dedicate a work of such a description to one who has more deeply searched its most hidden recesses, nor more powerfully depicted its feelings than yourself, I venture to inscribe to you the following pages. Should you trace in them anything akin in spirit, however much inferior to your own admirable story of *The Confessions of an Odd-Tempered Man* or the *Simple Tales*, I shall consider it the highest praise that could be bestowed upon *Trials of the Heart*.[11]

Amelia responded, 'Well indeed do I remember the visit to my beloved father and myself; and I can see the party at this moment clearly before me!' She had maintained an interest in Mrs Bray and enjoyed reading her books, especially *The White Hoods*, which she had bought when it first came out and had read *four times*.

> Hadst thou asked my leave to do me the favor [sic] to dedicate thy *very* interesting and excellent book to me I should have requested thee not to insist on my compliance – because I have always declined the distinction when offered me with one single exception. Therefore, I am glad that thou didst 'buckle fortune on my back' as Richard says, without my knowing what awaited me and a *prettier*, better turned, though undeserved dedication I never read – and I *thank* thee.[12]

More often than not she was having to decline invitations to dine or stay overnight with friends, due to ill health. But, as she wrote

---

* A handkerchief of soft, twilled silk from Barcelona, used as a neckerchief in the 18th and 19th centuries.

to Sir John Boileau, when telling him she was ill and could not fulfil an engagement she had with him and his wife at Ketteringham: 'The kind attention and kind visits of my friends have been bright stepping stones lately on the otherwise perhaps clouded path which leads me to the grave.'[13] Her Alderson cousins were solicitous and welcoming when they were at Lowestoft, and she was pleased to receive a visit from her cousin Richard Woodhouse. She kept in touch with the orphaned Briggs children, writing letters full of family news and sending them books.

Amelia's loyalty to the Earlham Gurneys was tested when Joseph John's son John Henry fell in love with the daughter of Richard Hanbury Gurney. He was the black sheep of the Gurney family, the man whom Amelia had not wanted Henry to paint. Richard, who became master of Keswick Old Hall when his father died, had begun an affair with Mary, the young wife of his neighbour Joseph Muskett, of Intwood Hall. Muskett banished his errant wife to the home of her father William Jary at Burlingham in Norfolk; she was never allowed back to the marital home, nor permitted to see her daughter by Muskett. The affair with Richard was resumed and when she became pregnant he took her to London, where their daughter Mary Jary was born. Once the Musketts were divorced, the runaway lovers were free to marry; they returned to Norfolk and went to live at Thickthorn Hall a few miles out of Norwich. Mary was not brought up as a Quaker, her father having left the Friends many years previously. John Henry, who had been absenting himself from Quaker Meetings, was willing to be disowned by the Friends for marrying 'out'.

The young couple – John Henry was 26, his bride only 16 – were married at All Saints' Church, Langham Place, on June 15th, 1846. Mary's parents were witnesses, as was Margaret Gurney, wife of Richard Hanbury's older half-brother Hudson. Although Joseph John was not present, he conveyed good wishes to the pair, which John Henry acknowledged from the London hotel where he was staying before the wedding:

I am happy to say we are going on comfortably and I trust we shall get well through on Monday [June 15] in all respects – as there seems to be everything that we could wish to enable us to do so and I think you may think of us on the day with very easy minds on *all points* as everything seems to be arranged as satisfactorily as I can possibly wish....Mary was much pleased with thy charming note to her and sends her dear love.[14]

322

Two days after the wedding Amelia wrote to Joseph John, saying she had thought much about him on the 15th but had not written to tell him so because she felt it 'a *difficult* task, all things considered'. But now she felt differently on the subject:

> I *may* congratulate thee on the event in question and I trust that a blessing will attend the union.... I am writing this at 7 in the morning that is, before post *time* when I expect a letter from Margaret Gurney and I will not close this sheet as I hope to be able to tell thee what she says of the wedding party.... Post man come and gone, no letter from MG, so farewell. PS. I have received wedding cake and cards.[15]

The new father-in-law wrote in his journal about the couple, who set up home at Easton Lodge, only a few miles from both sets of parents: 'Dined and lodged at Easton... we alone with dear JH and Mary. The impression on the whole, comforting and satisfactory, and nothing can exceed their love and tender attention.'[16]

At the end of August Amelia was glad to see Anna Backhouse and her little boy, who spent five weeks at Earlham – a very happy period for all concerned, as Anna recorded in her journal five months later, when Joseph John was no longer with them:

> I never saw him [her father] more delighting in Earlham, then in its flowery beauty. One day, I remember particularly, J.H. and Mary were there – the latter, in youthful glee, her dog Keeper and my Johnny gambolling by her on the lawn – he walking about in his cloak and cap, his beautiful hair blowing about it, really taking hearty pleasure in this dear girl, and delighted to be able to do so, while everything glowed with sun and beauty, and his own countenance shone with *heavenly peace*![17]

Amelia's close association with the Earlham Gurneys, whom she regarded as her family, was indicated simply in one of the last entries Joseph John made in his journal in December, 1846, noting 'an agreeable dinner party, the Ketts, and A. Opie, and the Birkbecks, *en famille*'. Soon after this gathering Amelia was saddened by news of the death of her friend Lady Elizabeth Whitbread, followed three weeks later by the loss of the widowed Samuel Hoare, who had been a staunch supporter of his brother-in-law's philanthropic works. On December 22nd Joseph John attended a meeting in Norwich; on leaving it, he was thrown from his horse. Knowing that Amelia would be anxious if she heard of the fall from somebody else, he called at her lodgings to reassure her that he was all right before returning home. He carried on with his many duties but a week later felt too unwell to continue and took to his bed. At this stage nobody believed that the master of Earlham was seriously ill.

Amelia, unwell and in bed herself, wrote to thank Eliza for the jelly she had sent her, mentioning, in passing, she was glad 'dearest Joseph' was being attended by Dr Dalrymple. But his condition deteriorated and he died on January 4th. The only member of the family attending his deathbed was Eliza, his wife of five years. Once the news got out there was an unprecedented flurry of letter writing from siblings, nieces, nephews, friends and colleagues, all paying tribute to a man they loved, honoured and respected.* The grief-stricken Amelia wrote first to the widow:

> I cannot help writing to thee dearest E, yet I know not what to say. However, I feel assured that thy mind even now is alive to the Mercies vouchsafed and I, to comfort *myself*, will only dwell on the bright side for it appears to me a mark of Divine favour that his was a *short* illness, that he knew not his danger and that he escaped the agony of a parting scene to friends and those whom he most tenderly loved.[18]

The weekly *Norfolk Chronicle* (January 9th) reported:

> We have the very painful task of recording an event, which may strictly be said to fill the hearts of all around us here with grief and regret, whilst it has invested our whole city with the outward signs of universal mourning – a mark of public sympathy and sorrow, unprecedented with regard to this, or perhaps to any other large and populous place, as shewn [sic] in the instance of a private individual – Joseph John Gurney *is no more*!

On the following day Bishop Stanley devoted his sermon at the Cathedral to the subject of Gurney's character as 'a Christian *Quaker*' and there were sermons on similar lines at other places of worship in Norwich.

The funeral two days later was reported in full by the *Norfolk Chronicle*. It outlined the route taken from Earlham Hall to the Gildencroft, through the city where all the shops and businesses were

---

* Augustus J.C. Hare devoted 12 pages to excerpts from family letters. (*The Gurneys of Earlham*, Vol.2, pp.221-32)

closed 'in a spontaneous universal tribute of respect', all the city church bells 'pealed forth their solemn knell' and the Earlham road was thronged with multitudes from the city and thousands from country districts. The report listed the names of relatives and friends who rode in the carriages following the hearse, which was drawn by two horses. Mrs Opie was in a carriage with Lucy Aggs (whose mother was a Gurney). After a full report of the funeral procession's route, the graveside speeches and the burial, the account concluded:

> During part of the afternoon the grave was left open, and the Friends kindly allowed the thousands of people who crowded into the burial ground, to view the coffin, and to mutually express their sorrow over the remains of the philanthropist.
>
> The police arrangements throughout the day were excellent. The whole city day-force was in attendance, at or around the burial ground, to prevent too great a rush of people or any interruption of the solemn proceedings. The conduct of the people, though congregated to the number of at least 20,000, was orderly and decorous.

Such was the demand for copies of these two newspapers they sold out. The proprietors rose to the occasion by bringing out a 24-page pamphlet containing not only the obituary and funeral report, but a list of Gurney's published works, the full text of the Bishop's sermon and of another given by the vicar of St Michael's Coslany Church in Norwich.[19] Amelia, suffering from a heavy cold and infected finger, wrote her own report of the events in letters to friends, including Lady Boileau who was away from Norfolk at the time.

> I *attended* the funeral of my best and dearest friend and did not leave Earlham till late in the evening. The next day I was in bed all day and there I have remained ever since.... But what is bodily compared to mental suffering! I have lost the most attached friend that I ever had and though I feel *sure* that he is gone to Glory I am as yet selfish enough not to feel my sense of his life swallowed up.... The *last time* I saw him, he and his dear wife (it was last Sunday three weeks) came to visit me in my chambers and he and I met no more.
>
> If honor [sic] done to the memory of a beloved object could reconcile me to losing him *I* ought to be already cheered for I believe no man in his station of life was ever so honored [sic] before and by *all sorts* of persons.[20]

Two weeks later she wrote to Elizabeth Stanhope saying, 'Pain, illness and sorrow have been for many many weeks mine and still are.' She believed she was still staggering under 'the stunning blow' of the death of her best, dearest and most attached friend:

> I left my bed to go to the house of mourning and drive in the long, long procession from his seat near Norwich to the place of interment and the duties of that day over, I took to my bed again, and never left it for a week. Then I had a relapse and only since last Sunday have I been allowed to go out again....
>
> I have seen here the mourning widow, his son and daughter and brothers and sisters and many kind friends came to see me. But alas! for the best of all I mourn, tho' I rejoice that he is gone undoubtedly to Glory and is taken from evil to come![21]

Amelia also took the trouble to write a letter, sharing her thoughts on the death of their friend, to William Forster, who was away from Norwich on Quaker work in Ireland:

> Thou will readily believe dear friend how *promptly* and *deeply* I thought of and *felt* for thee when the *stunning* and *unexpected* blow was announced to me! [Eliza] bears up, that is, supported wonderfully but I believe she is only as yet in the *vestibule* of her grief. She has not yet ventured into the *interior*. I went over to Earlham twice before y funeral and she had me alone and told me *every* minute of y *last hours* to y *end* and then persuaded me to *go with her* to *see him* in his coffin where he lay like one asleep and so beautiful![22]

She continued to mourn Joseph John's death, but, despite increasing lameness, tried to get out and about, visiting her Aunt Elizabeth (now 93) every day when possible, helping at the Sick Poor Society's annual fund-raising event and attending the Lent Assizes. Her Thompson cousins Margaret and John brought two of their daughters to stay in the spring in order to see their old aunt. Her doctors advised her that sea air and a 'hot sea bath' would be good for her 'rheumatic affliction', she told Elizabeth Stanhope, so she took lodgings at Cromer for a few days in June. But, although feeling better physically, she still felt the loss of her dearest friend: 'It is an enduring affliction. I miss him every day.'[23]

Chapter Thirty

In January, 1848, Elizabeth Alderson died; as her conscientious niece, Amelia had persisted in trying to bear the old lady's awkwardness and negativity with patience and respect. Only a few weeks before the death she had written to her cousin Edward about their aunt's decline, adding: ' How grateful I sometimes feel when I remember my dear father's last illness. A pattern he of humble resignation, full of gratitude to me and those who waited on him.' Once the aunt had died, Edward wrote to Amelia:

> I enter completely into your feeling of a want of interest arising from the failure of your dutiful occupation of so many years. I am sure that you may feel satisfied that you have done all that an affectionate child could do, and this surely is a great consolation....[1]

Anna Backhouse had given birth to a daughter, Eliza Jane, in the spring of 1847. Her visit to Earlham that summer, with her husband and two children, brought some comfort to Joseph John's family. Amelia joined them several times, telling friends how pleasing it was to see her 'darling grand-daughter'. Anna was unwell ill during much of her time at Earlham and her husband decided to take her to a warmer climate for the winter months. They travelled south through France and on to Italy. Not only was Anna seriously ill, her baby daughter was poorly throughout their travels and died on November 26th. The grieving parents buried Eliza at Leghorn and continued on their way; in January they were in Palermo, Sicily, but soon after their arrival a revolution broke out and all English visitors were advised to leave. The Backhouses were taken aboard a British warship, where Anna died two days later. The English captain arranged for her body to be taken ashore for burial at Palermo cemetery.*

Amelia and the grieving relatives comforted themselves in the belief that Anna was now re-united with her father. Once again there was a plethora of letters to and from the family members, many of whom were worried about the impact of Anna's death on Catherine Gurney. She was devoted to Joseph John's children, having seen them through

---

* Her remains were later disinterred and re-buried next to her baby daughter's grave at Leghorn.

the loss of their mother and first stepmother and being there for them during their father's frequent absences from home. Like Richenda she had become a member of the Church of England and she spent her last few years at Lowestoft, in a house adjacent to the Cunninghams.

With no aged aunt to care for, Amelia was free to return to London, travelling for the first time on the railway from Norwich and thrilled by the speed of the service, compared with the many long journeys by coach which she had made over the decades. She attended the Yearly Meeting, the annual Royal Academy exhibition and the wedding of Samuel Gurney's youngest daughter Richenda to Henry Ford Barclay, whose mother was Elizabeth (née Gurney) of The Grove. She stayed first with the Bell family in Langham Place, from where she wrote urgent notes to Josiah Fletcher who was binding 'in white and gold' an illustrated book of poems as a gift for the newly-weds. In September she ordered books bound in linen as a bridal gift for Juliet, the daughter of Charles and Sarah Fox of Falmouth, who was to marry Edmund Backhouse, son of Hannah Backhouse. At Langham Place she enjoyed spending time with the Briggs orphans – 'they are very pleasing and good children', she told Fletcher. Later she sought his advice on a book for Elizabeth Briggs – did he think Captain Marryat's *Masterman Ready* was a proper present for a girl of 11 years?[2]

A highlight during her first month in London was an invitation to call on Marie-Amèlie, the former Queen of France, who was living in exile in Surrey. During the February Revolution, when rioters calling for social reform surrounded the Tuileries Palace, King Louis Philippe had abdicated and fled to England with his family. Amelia told Thomas Brightwell about the Royal summons:

I hired a clarence and two horses, and borrowed J. Bell's servant; and, in a broiling hot day, set off on my 15 miles journey!... I cannot express my feelings, when I thought of the change in her position since we met! I could scarcely speak, while she pressed my hands most affectionately, and called me 'ma chère, bonne Opie, que vous êtes bonne de venir me voir!'...The first question was 'I hope you are writing? you know I read, and like all you write.' I replied that I did *not* write and so on....[3]

Amelia spent half an hour with Marie-Amèlie and could hardly voice a farewell, as she was on the verge of tears.

From the Bells she went to stay with Judge Gurney's widow and her son Russell, a QC, who became a judge a few years later. Throughout

Amelia's pride in her home on Castle Meadow is reflected in this letter to her friend Lady Charleville, dated September 24, 1849, in which she explains her choice of notepaper: 'I send thee a print of my Castle – but I live on the other side to the view represented there.' (Manuscripts & Special Collections, The University of Nottingham: Marlay Collection, My 148). *See also next page.*

her 14 weeks in the capital she was warmly welcomed by old friends and the younger generation of Gurneys, Buxtons and Barclays. At the private view of the Academy exhibition she met the soprano Jenny Lind, who made her London debut in Meyerbeer's opera *Robert le Diable*, attended by Queen Victoria, in May 1847. In September she gave two concerts in Norwich, when she was a guest of the Stanleys. Amelia was at Northrepps at the time and sorry not to have met the woman who was known as 'the Swedish Nightingale'. Mrs Stanley told her that Miss Lind sang to the Cathedral choristers, who cried when she went away, and had them sing to her. She also gave the Bishop £200 for local charities. Amelia had the chance to hear her sing when she returned to Norwich for two concerts in January 1849.*

At the end of July Amelia returned to Norwich and her new home on Castle Meadow, which she described, with great delight, in her correspondence. One letter to Lady Charleville was written on notepaper headed with an illustration:

> I send thee a print of *my* Castle – but I live on the other side to the view represented there. That paling and those trees form a circle round the bottom of the Hill on which the Castle stands and there is a shrubbery round its bank *into* the *lofty* trees of *great varied* beauty surrounding the shrubbery.... My drawing room windows are exactly opposite to them and as a wood *not* a street is before my house I am as if I were in the county and the grey Castle and its turrets rise grandly above the trees – the two together form a lovely picture which I am never tired of looking at.[4]

One of her passions was for reflected light. Years earlier she had assembled a collection of prisms – the first having been a gift from her cousin Henry – which were mounted on frames and placed where they might best catch the light. She took them with her from house to house. Writing to Eliza when her boy was a toddler she wished he was there at that moment:

> The room is full of the glories of the prisms and, what I have never seen before in such profusion, the drops of the candlesticks being set in motion, they cast on the walls the prismatic colours in the shape of little birds, like the birds of the tropical climes.[5]

Whether or not the young Henry Briggs ever saw the prisms is not recorded, but to some children taken to visit the elderly Mrs Opie in her Castle Meadow house they made a lasting impression. Josiah Fletcher's youngest child Lucy, born in 1842, writing the family memoirs when she was in her 70s, recalled:

---

* The soprano was devoted to charitable causes throughout her career. Money raised at her Norwich concerts was put towards the Jenny Lind Infirmary for Sick Children which opened in the city in 1853 – only the second children's hospital in the UK. It no longer exists as a separate entity but the Norfolk & Norwich University Hospital retains the name Jenny Lind for its children's departments.

I well remember being taken by my mother to the tiny, tall house in what is now Opie Street* and the trying climb to little legs up those many steep stairs. The shining of the many prisms on the stairs and in the drawing room was rather alarming too and the elderly lady who did not rise from her chair to greet us, seemed to me very awful in her tall white cap.[6]

Amelia's last home on Castle Meadow in Norwich. It was demolished in the 1860s. The wall and railings at the foot of the Castle mound opposite the house were removed at the end of the 19th century, when the road was widened for the installation of a tramways system. (New York Public Library: Pforzheimer Collection)

Janet Ross, also born in 1842, a great grand-daughter of Susannah Taylor, recalled visits to Norwich with her grandmother Sarah Austin:

I called Mrs Opie 'Rainbow Grandmother', and invented fairy tales about her in which sunlight and rainbows played a great part. Years afterwards, whenever I remembered the charming soft-man-

---

* Amelia's house was demolished a few years after death so that the original narrow alley adjacent to the building could be widened. It was named Opie Street. The house which was next to Amelia's bears a commemorative plaque suggesting she 'lived in this or an adjacent house'. A correspondent to the *Eastern Daily Press* (January 1924) wrote: 'While I honour the spirit which brought about the construction of the memorial I regret seeing an unnecessary doubt perpetuated in stone.'

nered old lady in her pretty quaint dress, I had a dim memory of curious rays of light flashing about her room. It was not until I read Miss Brightwell's memoir of Mrs Opie that I found out that she had a love for prisms, and understood why I had associated her with rainbows.[7]

Amelia suffered from poor health during the summer and autumn, which meant she refused invitations from Charles Muskett – another of her Norwich bookseller and publisher friends – to a water party on the River Yare at Thorpe village and from the Boileaus to the 21st birthday celebrations for their eldest son John Elliott. At the end of the year she was horrified to learn of a double murder at Stanfield Hall. The victims were the owner, Isaac Jermy, the Recorder of Norwich, and his son Isaac; Jermy's daughter-in-law and a maid called Eliza Chestney were both shot at but not killed. Within a day Jermy's tenant farmer James Rush was arrested on suspicion of murder; Sir John Boileau was one of the magistrates who examined Rush before remanding him at Norwich Castle* to await his trial the next year. Local and national newspapers were full of the story. Amelia passed on to Lady Charleville what she knew of:

> the dreadful murders six miles off at Stanfield Lodge where, in the days of the poor murdered man's parents†, I used to be a staying guest. We are now recovering the shock and ceasing to talk of it. The poor young man and his wife were the *happiest of the happy*. It is a tale as curious as it is horrible....
>
> Jermy succeeded my uncle as Recorder some years ago. He was just and honorable [sic] in his dealings, a good brother and affectionate father....[8]

Although an ardent follower of the Assizes, she chose not to be present during what was called in her day 'a capital case'‡ but she was well aware of what was going on in the court room at the Shirehall (next to the Castle), when Rush's trial began on March 29th, 1849. Reporters from national newspapers flocked to the city, crowds gathered round the entrance from early in the morning and extra police

---

* Part of the castle was at that time used as the county jail with a governor's house and room for 224 prisoners.

† The Rev George Preston and his wife Henrietta. His son Isaac took the name Jermy as required in the will of a previous owner of the Stanfield estate.

‡ A case in which a successful prosecution for murder brought the death penalty for the accused.

were in attendance. Throughout the six days' trial Amelia made notes for about what she saw from her window:

> What hundreds are passing to and fro; and what various sounds I hear! Now children and boys laughing and shouting; then men, congregated under my windows, and talking; but always, within those walls, *I* see that wretched man, writhing in mental agony, and against what, I fancy, he now *believes* inevitable doom![9]

The *Norwich Mercury*, published on a Saturday, brought out extra weekday editions during the trial and, when the 'Guilty' verdict was delivered, it announced that orders were being taken for *The Stanfield Hall Assassination* 'handsomely printed and bound in cloth boards'. Books, pamphlets and leaflets from hacks and publishers across the country followed. In July the *Norfolk Chronicle* announced that a model of 'Rush the murderer, taken from life' had been added to the Chamber of Horrors at Madame Tussaud & Sons' Exhibition in Baker Street.*

Outraged to learn that her cook wished to go and watch the execution of Rush, Amelia wrote to Eliza:

> I exclaimed and remonstrated – and then she owned that she had seen ever so many men and women hanged for murder! and seemed to think there was nothing disgusting or improper in a woman's *indulging* such a taste or in her *having* it....
>
> I think of telling her I cannot keep her if she persists in going to such a show....
>
> I mean to convince the girl if I can how disgustingly *unfeeling* and *vulgar* such a taste is and how disgraceful to reputable parents which hers are – but Nixon [Amelia's maid] tells me the girl's father used to take her on his shoulders when he went to see an execution – else I had thought of writing to *him* on the subject.[10]

Local people set up subscription funds for Emily Sandford, Rush's housekeeper (but believed to be his mistress), who had been the chief witness for the prosecution and Eliza Chestney, the injured maid. Amelia told Lady Charleville that one of her concerns was what would happen to Rush's children, so, two days after the hanging, she sought an interview with the governor and his wife:

> I went up to the Castle at 11 in a chair and was there two hours I believe. The good people were very kind and communicative and

---

* Norwich Castle Museum has a plaster death mask of Rush.

the chaplain to the jail, hearing I was there, came in and helped the others to answer all my questions....

It is hoped the family will be helped to go to Australia and Emily Sandford also....

The subscription for Eliza Chestney is already £600 – that for Sandford £400.[11]

In June she was able to tell her friend of happier things, while promoting her loyalty to Norwich craftsmen. Writing to remind Lady Charleville of 'a lovely satin gown and a handsome shawl', which she had bought from the Norwich shawl maker Edward Blakely, she said he had asked her to recommend a new venture in London. His son was about to open an exhibition of new and beautiful shawls in a room in Conduit Street. Amelia told her friend she had been present when Mr Blakely handed to the Bishop the shawl he ordered as a gift for Jenny Lind when she was last in the city 'and it was the most beautiful I ever saw'.[12]

In September there was another bereavement to come to terms with – the death of Bishop Stanley while on a short tour in Scotland with his wife and daughter. His body was taken by sea to Great Yarmouth, where the colours on the ships were at half-mast, and then to Norwich where he was buried in the Cathedral. When his memorial stone was placed in the nave, Amelia copied out its inscription and sent it to Jenny Lind, who replied thanking her for the great kindness she had shown:

> It was thus a delicacy I never will forget and although I am unable to write down my real thoughts and feelings upon the subject yet I hope that you, most respected Lady, may kindly receive the plain but true words from my thankful heart.
>
> So highly I ever feel the loss of that venerable Bishop at the same time do I thank God for his being safed [sic] from this troublesome life because I am convinced that the Bishop was worthy to die *in* our Saviour Jesus Christ.[13]

Eliza Gurney had moved from Earlham Hall to The Grove; before she left she invited the 80-year-old Amelia to pay a final nostalgic visit to the home which had played such an important role in her life. The two women continued to correspond. Amelia wrote to Eliza about a visit to see the Bells, who were staying at Lowestoft in April 1850. She went on the train with her maid and was pleased to spend time with the Briggs orphans. She also called on 'dearest Catherine *once*... she said I brought with me such a train of early and dear associations.'[14] In May there was news of the death of Hannah Backhouse in Darlington; Catherine died a few weeks later. Amelia decided she was 'too lame to be other than a burden to someone' if she went to the funeral at Lowestoft:

> Yet it would have been a *melancholy* gratification, but one to reflect on with satisfaction. *I*, the oldest of the precious one's friends should have paid her the last tribute of affection & respect! Dear Dan was with me yesterday. I was *glad* he had sense enough to perform his *duty* to his mother-sister.[15]

Amelia's interest in literature never waned; many of her notes to Fletcher were queries about titles she had been recommended to read or orders of books she wished for gifts to friends. She had read Charlotte Brontë's *Jane Eyre* when it was published in 1847 under the nom-de-plume Currer Bell. Harriet Martineau was one of the first people to whom Brontë made herself known and she passed on the information to Amelia. Brightwell wrote in her diary (March 1850) that Mrs Opie had told her about the revelation, but chose not to publish the account in her *Memorials*. Having recorded that Mrs Opie had read to her two letters from Miss Martineau, she reported on the meeting in London with Charlotte Brontë and a brief history of her tragic background. She continued with Amelia's opinions:

> On the subject of the alleged immoral tendency of *Jane Eyre*, Mrs Opie said that she was conversing with Lord Denman and Justice Earle when she remarked that it did not appear to her immoral, but certainly coarse and indelicate in some parts. In which opinion Lord Denman expressed his concurrence.[16]

Early in 1851 Amelia entered into correspondence with Charles Muskett about John Britton, an antiquary and prolific author, who had approached her for a subscription to his autobiography which was to take the form of a review of his publications with anecdotes about authors, artists, publishers and patrons connected with the works. She told Lady Boileau she would subscribe to the book, Britton having told her he had called at Berners Street, when she lived there, even though she had no recollection of this. She read and admired the first part of the work, but the second part filled her with 'justifiable indignation' as she expressed it to Muskett:

If thou has not read the second part of his publication thou mayst not be aware that in his account of English painters, he has made no mention of Mr Opie neither as a painter, nor a writer on art and he not only had the impudence (as I *think*) to ask my name as a subscriber but in his *letter* to me (*unanswered* yet) he asks me if I knew Peter Pindar and Jack Taylor, two of my poor husband's intimate associates *before he knew me* and who did all they could to prevent his forming a connexion [sic] which they feared would free him from their influence![17]

After much soul-searching about how to deal with the matter – should she 'answer his letter coldly' or would it be more *dignified* not to mention her indignation – she told Musket she had decided to send Britton 'a very civil note, with no allusion to his fancied offence'.

In July Eliza did a round of farewell visits to her husband's relations and friends, having decided she must return to America. The loyal William Forster accompanied her to Liverpool where she embarked for her journey home. In April 1851, Amelia wrote to Eliza, telling her she intended to go to London for, probably, the last time. She had accepted an invitation from her 'kind and faithful friend Russell Gurney' to stay with him in Russell Square where she was last a guest of his late mother. He had put a bed in one of his drawing rooms to save her from the pain of 'going aloft'. It would give her the chance to be measured for some 'spring crutches' only made in London and to buy 'a chair on wheels'. Her 'dear and lamented friend Lady Charleville' wrote to her not long before she died (in February) and told her where she bought *her* chair in Bond Street for £2. 'I shall like to see the Chrystal [sic] Palace, the *outside* of it I mean. I cannot see the inside but I should have gone up had there been *no* Exhibition.[18]

She was invited to attend the private view of the Royal Academy exhibition but was not well enough to leave home at that time. Sir Charles Eastlake, the RA president and husband to Elizabeth (née Rigby), was one of the Commissioners appointed under the presidency of the Prince Consort to plan the Great Exhibition. On the eve of its opening Amelia wrote to Lady Eastlake, thanking her and her husband for their messages and 'kind considerations' for helping her at the Academy:

I deeply regret that I now may never be able to attend the private view again, but had I been able to reach London, I should probably have *tried* to get as far as the *Statuary* room, but certainly *no far-*

ther. Here am I writing to thee while all is still around me. What a different scene I dare say surrounds thee! and what will tomorrow be! Perhaps not a few in London while remembering what the next day is, viz. the first of May, will, on rising, quote Shakespeare and say 'Would it were bed time and all well!' Certainly there is much to hope and perhaps there is something to fear, but I look to the hopeful side of the question and trust that Sir Charles and thyself do the same.[19]

Amelia travelled to London on May 7th, remaining at Russell Square for six weeks. She attended Friends Meetings, paid calls on old friends and went to her favourite fashionable shops. The splendid new 'chair on wheels' gave her entry to the Great Exhibition, where she found several friends also in wheelchairs, among them Sydney Smith's widow and Mary Berry. When Miss Berry said how she envied the chair and asked where it came from, Amelia playfully proposed a chair race. She remained sitting in her chair in the Transept – one of the glories of the building, letting in light through its high arched and glazed roof – for an hour, enjoying the scene, before moving on. On her way home to Norwich she spent two days with Samuel and Elizabeth Gurney at Upton Park in Essex.

In November she paid her last visit to Northrepps Cottage; by the following January she had developed such severe pain in her feet she was obliged to stay in bed for two months. In September 1852, she decided on a trip to Cromer, where she took lodgings for a fortnight – two rooms on the ground floor of a house where she could lie in bed and watch the sea. Members of the Hoare family, staying at their seaside home, called on her every day. She returned home with a streaming cold, saying she did not regret one hour spent at the coast and 'more enamoured of Cromer than ever'. From that day she never left her house again.

Her last bed-ridden months were cheered by visits from many who knew and loved her. The surviving Earlham Gurney siblings, their cousins, descendants and relations rallied round: John Henry and Mary Gurney, now parents of 'a most lovely boy' sent gifts of wine and flowers. Amelia was grateful for the attentions of her rector cousin Robert, who called often (and was with her on the night she died), and for the warmth and kindness of friends from all walks of life. She found comfort in hearing prayers read aloud and, to those who attended her, seemed calm and composed about her approaching death.

Hudson Gurney noted in his diary he visited Mrs Opie on November 9th, when 'She was partially clear and talked a great deal, at other times confused and her recollection partial.' On November 25th when his wife called 'She was greatly altered, but Margaret thought she knew them...[her] speech was so low that she could not gather what she said.'[20] Hudson mentioned 'a Miss Brown' who was with Mrs Opie. This was Mary Browne, a Quaker friend, whom Dr Hull had summoned, at the dying woman's request. She was on duty at the Castle Meadow house until the end. Amelia died at midnight on December 2nd, 1853, and was buried a week later in her father's grave at the Friends Burial Ground at the Gildencroft.

Browne made it her business to write to fellow Quakers and other friends, telling them of Amelia's death, with accounts of her final weeks of 'severe suffering'. Over the next few weeks, in consultation with Nixon, she dispatched various items from Amelia's effects to her friends as 'remembrances', seeking advice and information from Robert Alderson where appropriate. She was at pains to explain the provenance of the gifts: Elizabeth Stanhope was offered 'a miniature locket of Hayley the poet', which he himself had given to Amelia, and a Dresden bowl, the only item remaining from her home in Berners Street.[21]

Announcing her death, the *Norwich Mercury* (Dec 10th) stated:

We gather from those called away before her, Mrs Opie was accomplished and possessing great mental attraction. She sang with elegance and feeling, and shone in conversation alike through her acquirements, her intellectual power, keen perceptions her grace of manner. Mingling in high society, and in that we include those who adorn it by their high intelligence, skill in art, science, and literary attainment, as well as by elevated position, the deceased lady possessed a fund of anecdote, which nobody knew better how to use, delightfully and appropriately.

The *Norfolk Chronicle* (Dec 10th) chose to focus on the fact that Amelia was the daughter of Dr Alderson, the cousin of Baron Alderson, the wife of John Opie (with a resumé of his character and work) and 'intimate with' the late J.J. Gurney's family. Of Mrs Opie, the writer, it concluded:

Several of her novels have been very popular and gone through many editions but are now thrown into the shade with many others widely circulated half a century ago, by more powerful fictions and the more masculine character of the imaginative literature of late years. During the last quarter of a century Mrs Opie was a consistent member of the Society of Friends and she lived in comparative seclusion, highly esteemed and beloved by all who were acquainted with her.

Both papers reported a week later on her funeral, stressing its lack of ceremony. 'There were neither mourning coaches, suits of black, nor hat bands; but a plain hearse, followed by 10 private carriages,' said the *Mercury*. Stating that the funeral was 'as plain as possible', the *Chronicle* added: 'as quietly as she had lived, the deceased was buried; very few persons excepting her friends knew of her funeral.' Both listed 'some' of the mourners, who included the Rev R.J. Alderson, Thomas Brightwell, John Gurney, Josiah Fletcher and several clergymen. The *Chronicle* noted that her grave was 'in the corner opposite to that where the late Mr J.J. Gurney was buried'. The mourners stood in silence before adjourning to the Gildencroft; 'when all were seated an impressive silence reigned for some time'.

To the *Chronicle's* funeral report were appended obituary notices from national publications. *The Daily News* paid tribute to Mrs Opie's devotion to her father and her bounty to the poor: 'Her majestic form moved through the narrowest streets of the ancient city and her bright face was seen lighting up the most wretched abodes.' *The Athenaeum* reminded readers that 'In their day [her novels] were cherished and wept over, as moving and truthful.' It was left to *The Spectator* to point out, in a thoughtful consideration of her early life, work, character and later years, that 'this venerable Quaker lady was the once dashing Amelia Opie'.

In fact, the dashing Amelia had never gone away; nor had the sterling qualities of the venerable Quaker emerged only in the aging widow. The girlish Amelia, eager for life and love, was the elderly woman excited about travelling on the new railroad and seeing the Crystal Palace; the young Miss Alderson giving money to the asylum inmates was the worthy old lady visiting the poor and needy. The flirtatious girl who gazes knowingly from John Opie's most famous portrait of her was also a loyal wife, dependable friend, earnest devotee of good causes and steadfast daughter. The serious matron in a Quaker bonnet, depicted in the David d'Angers medallion, was also an adventuress who loved dancing, parties and fashionable society. Well into her seventies, after spending a happy evening at Earlham Hall, where she had been invited to a family celebration, she reported to Sir John Boileau: 'I suffered a little for my *dancing* – however I do not regret it, for the proverb says "Nothing venture, nothing have"....'[22] An apt maxim for a woman who, throughout her long life, seized the opportunities which came her way and made the most of them.

Appendix

Most of the known portraits of Amelia Opie were by her husband, the Royal Academician John Opie. The originals and engravings or etchings created in her lifetime are reproduced (where possible) in the pages of this biography. So, too, are images of the bust and medallion by David d'Angers and Amelia's portrait by her cousin Henry Perronet Briggs.

However, there are gaps, which the author has been unable to fill:

Photograph of Amelia

It is known that at least one photograph was taken of Amelia. In a diary entry, dated July, 1849, Brightwell notes: 'A person from Cambridge here taking daguerrotypes. We had Papa and I and Elizabeth done, also Mrs Opie.' (NRO, MS 69, *Diary of Cecilia Brightwell 1842-1866*). In *A Book of Sybils* (1883), Miss Thackeray writes: 'Some of Mrs Opie's family have shown me a photograph of her in her Quaker dress, in old age, dim, and changed, and sunken, from which it is very difficult to realise all the brightness, and life, and animation which must have belonged to the earlier part of her life....'

Miniature of Amelia

In a letter to her cousin Henry Perronet Briggs, writing of family pictures which she might use to fill 'a wide naked frieze' Amelia says: '...myself by Beechey is *too small* tho' new gilded on purpose.' (HL, Opie MSS, Op 127). 'Miss Alderson' is on a list of miniatures found in a William Beechey account book. His biographer, W. Roberts, believed the miniatures were painted by his second wife Ann Beechey. However, Mrs. Opie, with her regard for correct forms of address is unlikely to have named Ann as 'Beechey'. When Macgregor was working on her Opie biography, she applied to *Notes and Queries* for information; one response came from Ethel Carr, daughter of Elizabeth Amelia Carr (née Briggs), listing Opie memorabilia in her possession, including 'one miniature'. (*Notes & Queries*, February, 1931)

Drawing by Julie von Egloffstein

Julie von Egloffstein, a German countess and artist, who was in London in 1838 to study English painting, did a drawing of Amelia in her Quaker dress, as she told Joseph John Gurney (SoF, Gurney MSS,

1/360). Amelia sought a copy of her husband's *Lectures on Painting* as a gift for the countess, telling her publishers the recipient was 'an admirable painter by profession'. (NRO, MS 20814).

Painting by Lady Charleville

Amelia's friend Lady Charleville painted her portrait. When their mutual friend, Elizabeth Stanhope, wished for a copy, Amelia wrote she was flattered to think Lady Charleville thought it worth her while to paint her: 'but I know so well how unavoidably my face and person run into caricature that I have always disliked to see myself on canvas. However I duly appreciate the kindness which led her to paint me and *thee* to request a copy of her performance.' (BL, Stanhope (Harrington) Papers, 82737, Vol vii)

Sitting for Galignani

Brightwell indicated that Amelia sat 'to an artist for Galignani' while she was in Paris in 1829 (*Memorials*). The Italian publisher Giovanni Galignani had lived in London before moving to Paris where he started an English library and, in 1808, a monthly publication, *The Repertory of English Literature*. In 1814 he launched *Galginani's Messenger*, a daily newspaper printed in English, which Amelia read while travelling abroad. Galignani's two sons took over the paper when he died in 1821.

Henry Perronet Briggs drawing

It appears that Amelia's cousin Henry Perronet Briggs did a drawing of her which he gave to Madame Marlay, who lived in Paris. Amelia told Henry her friend wished for the drawing to be framed in oak, adding '...she is very much obliged as it is not only a drawing of *me*, but *by thee*.' (HL, Opie MSS, OP148)

Opie portrait

The BBC Your Paintings website shows an Opie portrait of Amelia Alderson Opie acquired by Chawton House Library in 1996. This may be the portrait listed by Earland, as belonging to James Parsons, who received it from his uncle Edward Opie (the artist). She described it 'nearly full face, looking over left shoulder, very penetrating eyes, hair piled high on top of head with band of blue ribbon parted in the middle....' It is likely that this portrait was the one owned by Elizabeth Opie who bequeathed 'the picture of Mrs.Amelia Opie, widow of my brother John' to her nephew James Opie. (CRO, AD102/58) James Opie was uncle to the artist Edward Opie and his sister Amelia Parsons.

Endnotes

References

The authorities and collections which hold manuscripts transcribed and quoted in the text are identified in the Chapter notes by the abbreviations listed below.

BL   British Library, London
BodL   Bodleian Library, Oxford
CL   Chapin Library. Williams College, Williamstown, Massachusetts
CRO   Cornwall Record Office, Truro
GL   Guildhall Library Manuscripts Section, London Metropolitan Archives, Clerkenwell
HL   Huntington Library, San Marino, California
HCL   Haverford College Library: Quaker & Special Collections, Haverford, Pennsylvania
ML   Morgan Library: Literary & Historical Manuscripts, New York
NHC   Norwich Heritage Centre, Millennium Library, Norwich
NRO   Norfolk Record Office, Norwich
NYPL   The Carl H. Pforzheimer Collection of Shelley & his Circle, The New York Public Library, Astor, Lenox & Tilden Foundations, New York
RHL   Rhodes House Library, Oxford
SoF   Library of the Religious Society of Friends, London
SC   Swarthmore College: Friends Historical Library, Swarthmore, Pennsylvania
UN   University of Nottingham: Manuscripts & Special Collections, Nottingham
WFM   Wisbech & Fenland Museum, Wisbech
WL   Wren Library, Trinity College, Cambridge

Introduction

1   NRO, MS6181, 17 March, 1848.
2   Cecilia Lucy Brightwell, *Memorials of the Life of Amelia Opie* (Norwich: Fletcher & Alexander, 1854), p.48

Chapter One

1   Brightwell, *Memorials*, p.9.
2   Amelia Opie, *Poems* (London: T.N. Longman & O. Rees, 1803), pp.167-179.
3   Brightwell, *Memorials*, p.13.
4   BL India Office records, N/1/1 ff.329, Bengal burials register.
5   Brightwell *Memorials*, p.8.
6   ibid.
7   ibid, p.4.
8   HL, Opie MSS, OP 176, 16 February, 1842.
9   NRO, MS6181, 28 February, 1842.
10   Zachary Clark, *An Account of the Different Charities belonging to the Poor of the County of Norfolk* (London: Longman, Hurst, Rees, Orme & Brown, 1811), pp.154-55.
11   NRO, PD/674, Deposition regarding Alderson property.
12   ibid, FC13/23, Octagon baptism register.
13   Edmund Gillingwater, *An Historical Account of the Ancient Town of Lowestoft* (London: C.G.J. & J. Robinson, 1790), pp.366-67.

14 NYPL, O'ANA 0031, 10 & 11 October, 1759.

15 ibid,, O'ANA 0032, Letter, 20 October, 1759.

16 Edward Copeman, *Brief History of the Norfolk & Norwich Hospital* (Norwich: Charles Muskett, 1856), p.5.

17 NRO, NNH1/1, Norfolk & Norwich Hospital Committee Book (1770-1773).

18 *Rules & Orders for the Norfolk & Norwich Hospital* (Norwich: Chase & Co., 1786).

19 ibid, pp.3-4.

20 SoF, Gurney MSS, 1/105, 2 June, 1773.

21 Brightwell, *Memorials*, p.3.

22 ibid, p.64.

Chapter two

1 Brightwell, *Memorials*, pp.13-14.

2 ibid, p.14.

3 ibid, pp.15-16.

4 J.W. Robberds, *Memoirs of the Life and Writings of the late William Taylor of Norwich* (London: John Murray, 1843), Vol.1, p.6

5 NRO, NNH1/57, N&N Hospital Committee Book (1790-1805).

6 Ada Earland, *John Opie and His Circle* (London: Hutchinson, 1911), p.266.

7 Horace N. Pym, *Memories of Old Friends – being extracts from the Journals and Letters of Caroline Fox, of Penjerrick, Cornwall, for 1835-1871* (London: Smith Elder & Co., 1882), p.185.

8 Brightwell, *Memorials*, p.75.

9 Amelia Opie, *Lays for the Dead* (London: Rees, Orme, Brown, Greene & Longman, 1834), pp.99-100.

10 Edward Taylor, *Some Account of the Life of Mr John Taylor of Norwich* in *The Monthly Repository*, August, 1826.

11 Lucy Aikin, *The Works of Anna Laetitia Barbauld, with a Memoir* (London: Longman, Hurst, Rees, Orme, Brown & Green, 1825), Vol.2, pp.103-104.

12 SoF, Gurney MSS 434/150.

13 Opie, *Poems*, pp.51-69.

14 Edith J. Morley, editor, *Henry Crabb Robinson on Books and their Writers* (London: J.M. Dent & Sons, 1938), Vol.1, p.2.

15 ibid.

Chapter three

1 Thomas Sadler, ed., *Diary of Henry Crabb Robinson* (London: Macmillan & Co., 1869), Vol 1, p.25.

2 Penelope J. Corfield & Chris Evans, eds., *Youth & Revolution in the 1790s: Letters of William Pattison, Thomas Amyot & Henry Crabb Robinson* (Stroud: Alan Sutton, 1996), p.117.

3 Trevor Fawcett, *Some Aspects of the Norfolk Book-Trade 1800-24* in *Transactions of the Cambridge Bibliographical Society*, Vol.4, edited by Bruce Dickins, Richard Vaughan & John Harrison (Cambridge University Press, 1968), p.391.

4 Frank Arthur Munby, *Publishing and Bookselling, Part One*, (London: Jonathan Cape, revised edition 1974), pp.183-4.

5 Amelia [Alderson] Opie, *Dangers of Coquetry* (London: W.Lane, 1790).

6 Margaret Eliot Macgregor, *Amelia Alderson Opie: Worldling and Friend* (Menasha, Wisconsin: The Collegiate Press, 1933), p.13.

7 HL, Opie MSS, OP 61, 23 March, 1801.

8 *Norfolk Chronicle*, Saturday, January 8, 1791.

9 ibid, Saturday March 5, 1791.

10 *Norwich Mercury*, Saturday, September 6, 1788.

Endnotes

Chapter four

1. BodL, Abinger MSS, Dep.e.201, 1793-94.
2. ibid.
3. Brightwell, *Memorials*, p.43.
4. BL, 1856.d.1. (72) Boddington Pedigree, complied by Reginald Stewart Boddington, 1890 .
5. Brightwell, *Memorials*, pp.43-44.
6. Dr George A. Goulty, *The Registers, Monuments & other Miscellaneous Records of St Margaret's Church, Old Catton, Norwich* (Peterborough: G.A.Goulty, 1997).
7. Herschel Baker, *John Philip Kemble: The Actor in his Theatre* (New York: Greenwood Press, 1969), p.178.
8. Brightwell, *Memorials*, p.44.
9. HL, Opie MSS, OP 3, September, 1794.
10. *The Cabinet*, by a Society of Gentleman, 3 vols (Norwich: Printed & sold by J. March), Vol.1, p.i
11. ibid, pp.iv-v.
12. Brightwell, *Memorials*, p.41.
13. ibid, p.48.
14. Caroline E. Williams, *A Welsh Family from the Beginning of the 18th Century* (London, Women's Printing Society Ltd., 1893), p.140.
15. *The Cabinet*, Vol 2, pp.137-143.
16. Macgregor, *Amelia Alderson Opie*, p.11.
17. *The Cabinet*, Vol.1, pp.309-10.

Chapter five

1. Brightwell, *Memorials*, pp.40-41.
2. Thomas Jones Howell, compiler, *A Complete Collection of State Trials and Proceedings for High Treason* (London: Longman, Hurst, Reese, Orme & Brown, 1818), Vol.24, p.1392.
3. Brightwell, *Memorials*, p.44.
4. ibid, pp.45-46.
5. HL. Opie MSS, OP 59, 1794.
6. ibid
7. Brightwell, *Memorials*, p.23.
8. ibid, p.24.
9. ibid, pp.25-26.
10. ibid, pp.26-27.
11. ibid, p.52.

Chapter six

1. Brightwell, *Memorials*, p.53.
2. GL, Ms 10823:4. Journal kept by Benjamin Boddington, 1747-1791.
3. Williams, *A Welsh Family*, p.98.
4. Eastlake, Lady Elizabeth, editor, *Dr Rigby's Letters from France in 1789* (London: Longmans, Green & Co., 1880), p.28.
5. GL, Ms 10823:5B. Samuel Boddington letters, 1789.
6. *The Times*, July 9 & July 12, 1790.
7. Edmund Burke, *Reflections on the Revolution in France* (London: Penguin, 1986), p.92.
8. Anon, *A Look to the Last Century: or The Dissenters weighed in their own Scales* (London: B. White & Son & R. Faulder, 1790), pp.120-21.
9. *The Life of John Thelwall* by his widow (London: John Macrone, 1837), p.202.

Chapter seven

1   HL. Opie MSS, OP 59, Letter 1794.
2   Howell, *State Trials*, Vol.24, p.572.
3   ibid, p.934.
4   *The New Annual Register or General Repository of History, Politics & Literature for the Year 1794* (London: G.G. & J.Robinson, 1795), p.275.
5   ibid, p.275.
6   Morchard Bishop, editor, *Recollections of the Table Talk of Samuel Rogers* (London: Richards Press, 1952), p.88.
7   Howell, *State Trials*, Vol.25, p.8.
8   *The New Annual Register*, pp.283-4.
9   *Norfolk Chronicle*, Saturday, November 8, 1794.
10 NRO, Family papers, RQG 380 491x4.
11 Mrs William Sidgwick, *Recollections of Mrs Opie* (Pamphlet printed for private circulation, from three articles in *The Manchester Guardian*, 1884), p.15.
12 William Beloe, *The Sexagenarian, or The Recollections of a Literary Life* (London: F.C. & J.Rivington, 1817), Vol.1, p.414.
13 Thomas Constable, *Archibald Constable and his Literary Correspondents: A Memorial by his Son* (Edinburgh: Edmonston & Douglas, 1873), Vol.2, p.277.
14 ibid, pp.278-9.
15 Howell, *State Trials*, Vol.25, p.747.
16 ibid, p.746, footnote.

Chapter eight

1   Brightwell, *Memorials*, pp.33-4.
2   ibid, p.36.
3   Jacobine Menzies-Wilson & Helen Lloyd, *Amelia: The Tale of a Plain Friend* (London: Oxford University Press, 1937), p.57.
4   V.S. Pritchett, *The Quaker Coquette* in *A Man of Letters* (London: Chatto & Windus, 1985), p.43.
5   Paula R. Feldman, editor, *British Women Poets of the Romantic Era* (Baltimore: John Hopkins University Press, 1997), p.523.
6   NRO, Family papers, RQG 380 491x4. .
7   Robert James Mackintosh, editor, *Memoirs of the Life of the Rt.Hon. Sir James Mackintosh* (London: Edward Moxon, 1836), Vol.1, p.165.
8   Janet Ross, *Three Generations of English Women: Memoirs & Correspondence of Mrs John Taylor, Mrs Sarah Austin & Lady Duff Gordon* (London: John Murray, 1888), p.8.
9   Harriet Martineau, *Autobiography* (London: Smith, Elder & Co., 1877), Vol.1, pp.297-99.
10 Brightwell, *Memorials*, pp.59-60.
11 NYPL, AO2, 17 March, 1795.
12 BodL, Abinger MSS, Dep.e.202, 1795-96.
13 Brightwell, *Memorials*, p.60.
14 ibid, pp.64-5.
15 A.M.W. Stirling, *Coke of Norfolk & His Friends* (London: John Lane The Bodley Head, 1908), p.294.
16 Earland, *John Opie*. p.128.

Chapter nine

1   BodL, Abinger MSS Dep.b. 210/6, 28 August, 1795
2   ibid, 12 February, 1796.
3   ibid, 5 February, 1796.
4   ibid, 12 February, 1796.

Endnotes

5   ibid, 1 April, 1796
6   Claire Tomalin, *The Life and Death of Mary Wollstonecraft* (London: Penguin Books, 1992), p.243.

Chapter ten
1   BodL, Abinger MSS Dep.b.210/6, 28 August, 1796.
2   ibid
3   Janet Todd, ed., *The Collected Letters of Mary Wollstonecraft* (New York: Columbia University Press, 2003), p.345.
4   BodL, Abinger MSS Dep.b.210/6, 1796 [probably September]
5   ibid.
6   John Thelwall, *An Appeal to Popular Opinion against Kidnapping & Murder, including a narrative of the atrocious proceedings at Yarmouth* (London: J.S. Jordan, 1796)
7   ibid, p.36.
8   BodL, Abinger MSS Dep.b.210/6, 1 November, 1796.
9   ibid, 13 November, 1796.

Chapter eleven
1   BodL, Abinger MSS Dep.b.210/6, 18 December, 1796.
2   James Greig, ed., *The Farington Diary by Joseph Farington RA* (London: Hutchinson & Co, 1922-28, eight volumes), Vol.1, p.170.
3   Todd, *Collected Letters*, p.198.
4   Earland, *John Opie*, p.14.
5   Algernon Groves, *The Society of Artists of Great Britain 1760-1791* (London: George Bell & Sons, 1907), p.185.
6   Earland, *John Opie*, p.29.
7   ibid, p.31.
8   ibid, p.34.
9   *Memoir of James Northcote* in *The Gentleman's Magazine*, August 1831.
10   Ernest Fletcher, ed., *Conversations of James Northcote RA with James Ward on Art & Artists* (London, Methuen & Co., 1901), p.199.
11   *A Memoir by Mrs Opie*, prefixed to John Opie's *Lectures on Painting* (London: Longman, Hurst, Rees & Orme, 1809), p.41.
12   John Taylor, *Records of my Life* (London: Edward Bull, 1832), p.303.
13   Greig, *Farington Diary*, Vol.1, p.170.
14   BodL, Abinger MSS Dep.b.210/6, 18 November, 1796
15   ibid, 18 December, 1796.
16   ibid, Abinger MSS Dep.c.507/15, undated.
17   C. Kegan Paul, *William Godwin: His Friends and Contemporaries* (London: Henry S.King, 1876), Vol.1, p.240.
18   Brightwell, *Memorials*, pp.61-2.
19   ibid, p.63.
20   ibid, pp.63-4.
21   Menzies-Wilson & Lloyd, *Amelia*, p.67.

Chapter twelve
1   Paul, *William Godwin*, Vol.1, p.276.
2   BodL, Abinger MSS Dep.c.507/14, undated.
3   ibid, Dep.b.215/2, 11 October, 1797.
4   ibid, Dep.b.227/7, 23 October, 1797.
5   Brightwell, *Memorials*, p.33.
6   Harriet Martineau, *Biographical Sketches 1852-1875* (London: Macmillan, 1883), p.333.
7   Beloe, *The Sexagenarian*, Vol.1, p.414
8   Martineau, *Autobiography*, Vol.1, p.301.

9 NRO, Louisa Gurney Journals, MC 1593/1
10 ibid, MC 1593/2
11 Augustus J.C.Hare, *The Gurneys of Earlham* (London: George Allen, 1895), Vol.1, p.73.
12 Earland, *John Opie*, p.138.
13 Brightwell, *Memorials*, p.68.
14 Thelma Morris, *Made in Norwich: 700 Years of Textile Heritage* (Norwich: Nick Williams, 2008), p.24.

Chapter thirteen
1 Beloe, *The Sexagenarian*, Vol.1, p.414.
2 Earland, *John Opie*, p.127.
3 Opie, *Memoir*, p.38.
4 ibid, pp.41-2.
5 NRO, Family papers, RQG 380 491x4.
6 John Thomas Smith & Wilfred Whitten, ed., *Nollekens and His Times*, (London: John Lane The Bodley Head, 1920), Vol.2, p.221.
7 Fletcher, *Conversations*, p.215.
8 Opie, *Memoir*, pp.25-6.
9 Elbridge Colby, ed., *The Life of Thomas Holcroft, Written by Himself* (New York: Benjamin Blom, 1968), Vol.2, p.187.
10 NYPL, AO15, 8 August, 1798.
11 Sydney D.Kitson, *The Life of John Sell Cotman* (London: Rodart Reproductions, 1982), p.9.
12 WL, Dawson Turner correspondence, O.13 19, 13 November, 1837.
13 James Reeve, *A Catalogue of the Portraits & Paintings in St Andrew's Hall & other public buildings* (City of Norwich, 1905)
14 ibid.
15 Frank Sayers, *Collective Works of the late Dr Sayers, to which have been prefaced some biographical particulars by W. Taylor of Norwich* (Norwich: Matchett & Stevenson, 1823), p.lxxxi.
16 Katharine Fry & Rachel Cresswell, eds., *Memoirs of the Life of Elizabeth Fry with extracts from her journals & letters* (London: Charles Gilpin, 1847), vol 1, p.39.
17 HL, Opie MSS, OP 60, 12 December, 1800.
18 NYPL, O'ANA 0014, 27 February, 1854.
19 Amelia Opie, *The Father and Daughter, A Tale, in Prose* (London: Longman & Rees, 1801), p.23.
20 HL, Opie MSS, OP 63, 1801.
21 ibid, OP 61, 23 March, 1801.
22 BodL, Harding Mus. G231 (9)
23 HL, Opie MSS, OP 62, 22 June, 1801.
24 Opie, *Memoir*, p.27.
25 ibid, p.31.
26 WL, Dawson Turner correspondence, O.13 23, 2 February, 1822.

Chapter fourteen
1 Opie, *Memoir*, p.32.
2 Mrs Opie, *Elegy to the Memory of the late Duke of Bedford, written on the eve of his interment* (London: T.N.Longman & O.Rees, 1802).
3 NYPL, O'ANA 0006, 1802.
4 Brightwell, *Memorials*, pp.101-2.
5 ibid, pp.102-3.
6 ibid, pp.111-12.
7 HL, Opie MSS, OP 61, 23 March, 1801.
8 Earland, *John Opie*, p.185.

9   Stirling, *Coke of Norfolk*, p.297.
10   Brightwell, *Memorials*, pp.107-8.
11   ibid, pp.108-9.
12   Greig, *Farington Diary*, Vol.2, pp.7-10.
13   Brightwell, *Memorials*, p.114.
14   Sidgwick, *Recollections*, p.13.

Chapter fifteen
1   Colby, *Life of Holcroft*, p.289-90.
2   Greig, *Farington Diary*, Vol.2, p.10.
3   ibid, p.104.
4   Hare, *Gurneys of Earlham*, Vol.1, pp.130-31.
5   Ernest Betham, ed., *A House of Letters* (London: Jarrold & Sons, 1905), pp.82-3.
6   Opie, *Memoir*, pp.43-44.
7   NRO, MC257/159, Poster, 1802.
8   NHC, Colman Collection, *The Iris*, Saturday, April 28, 1804
9   HL, Opie MSS, OP 328, 9 February, 1837.
10   ibid, OP 151, 20 April, 1837.
11   NHC, Colman Collection, *The Iris*, Saturday, May 26, 1804.
12   ML, MA Unassigned PML 7580, undated.
13   Greig, *Farington Diary*, Vol 2, p.247.
14   Opie, *Memoir*, pp.45-6.
15   *Catalogue 1806: Works just published by Longman, Rees, Hurst and Orme, Paternoster Row*, p.5. (St.Bride Printing Library: T1)
16   NHC, Colman Collection, *Mrs Opie* in *Biographical Memoirs 1757-1879* (cuttings of magazine & newspaper articles bound in one volume)
17   BodL, Abinger MSS Dep.b.210/6, 28 August, 1796.
18   Julia Kavanagh, *English Women of Letters: Biographical Sketches* (London: Hurst & Blackett, 1863), Vol 2, pp.276-277.
19   Miss Thackeray (Mrs Richmond Ritchie), *A Book of Sybils* (London: Smith, Elder & Co., 1883), p.177.
20   Mackintosh, *Memoirs*, Vol 1, p.255.
21   HL, Porter MSS, POR 482, 7 March, 1805.
22   Franklin Fox, ed., *Memoir of Eliza Fox* (London: N.Trubner & Co., 1869), p.204.
23   Sidgwick, *Recollections*, p.8.
24   Allene Gregory, *The French Revolution and the British Novel* (New York: G.P.Putnam's Sons, 1915), p.210.

Chapter sixteen
1   Opie, *Memoir*, p.14.
2   BL, Opie, John, RP 3144, 7 October, 1801
3   *Treachery and Adultery. Trial of Benjamin Boddington* (Eighteenth Century Collections Online: Print Edition).
4   BL, Stanhope (Harrington) Papers, 82735, Vol v, April 1847.
5   Brightwell, *Memorials*, pp.124-5.
6   BL, Opie, John, RP 3144, 7 October, 1801
7   Robberds, *Memoirs*, Vol.2, p.122.
8   ibid, p.129.
9   ibid, p.121.
10   HL, Porter MSS, POR 1584, 21 February, 1806.
11   Longman, Rees, Hurst and Orme catalogue. (St Bride Printing Library: T1)
12   Rev A.G. L'Estrange, ed., *The Life of Mary Russell Mitford Related in a Selection from her Letters to her Friends* (London: Richard Bentley, 1870), Vol.1, p.36.
13   NYPL, O'ANA 0014, 27 February, 1854.

14   Allan Cunningham, *The Life of Sir David Wilkie* (London: John Murray, 1843), Vol.1, p.109.
15   ML, MISC Artists MA Unassigned, undated
16   HL, Opie MSS, OP 42, 1806.
17   A. Opie, *Recollections of an Authoress: Harriet Countess of Rosslyn* in *Chambers' Edinburgh Journal*, No.417, 25 January, 1840.
18   Opie, *Memoir*, p.28.

Chapter seventeen
1   HL, Opie MSS. OP 280, 7 March, 1833.
2   BL, Mackintosh Papers, 52451 f.133, 22 January, 1807.
3   ibid, 78765 f.92, 27 January, 1807.
4   Lady Holland, his daughter, *A Memoir of the Reverend Sydney Smith* (London: Longman, Brown, Green & Longmans, 1855), p.129.
5   BL, Mackintosh Papers, 27 January 1807
6   Opie, *Memoir*, p.10.
7   Stirling, *Coke of Norfolk*, p.332.
8   Opie, *Memoir*, p.47.
9   Robberds, *Memoirs*, Vol.2, pp.187-8.
10   Opie, *Memoir*, p.49.
11   ibid, pp.50-51.
12   NYPL, 14 November, 1842, insert in grangerised Brightwell *Memorials*, p.346
13   Opie, *Memoir*, p.52.
14   Ben P. Robertson, ed., *The Diaries of Elizabeth Inchbald* (London: Pickering & Chatto, 2007), Vol.3.
15   CRO, St Agnes Deeds, AD102 Family Papers: Opie
16   NYPL, AO4, undated.

Chapter eighteen
1   Mackintosh, *Memoirs*, Vol.1, p.441.
2   HL, Opie MSS, HM 1840, 5 June, 1807.
3   *The Annual Anthology*, Vol.1 (London: T.N. Longman & O. Rees, 1799). Amelia also had a poem published in Vol.2 (1800).
4   Mrs Opie, *The Warrior's Return, and other Poems* (London: Longman, Hurst, Rees & Orme, 1808), pp.49-50.
5   HCL, Autograph letters, 115 British poets: Amelia Opie. 12 December, 1808.
6   ibid
7   Opie, *Memoir*, p.5
8   ibid, pp.1-2.
9   ibid, p.54.
10   Mackintosh, *Memoirs*, Vol.2, p.27.
11   HCL, Call No.861, Opie Mss, 19 March, 1809.
12   HL, Opie MSS, OP 4, 30 March, 1809.
13   Brightwell, *Memorials*, p.139.

Chapter nineteen
1   William St Clair, *The Godwins and the Shelleys* (London: Faber & Faber, 1989), p.174.
2   Cecilia Lucy Brightwell, *Memoir of Amelia Opie* (London: Religious Tract Society, 1857)
3   Brightwell, *Memorials*, p.144.
4   Sidgwick, *Recollections*, p.5.
5   UN, Marlay Collection, My 129, 3 June, 1810.
6   Martineau, *Biographical Sketches*, p.334.
7   L'Estrange, *Mitford Letters*, Vol.3, p.294..

Endnotes

8   Macgregor, *Amelia Alderson Opie*, pp.56-7.
9   Cecilia Lucy Brightwell, *Memorials of the Life of Mr Brightwell of Norwich* (Norwich: Fletcher & Son, 1869, for private circulation), pp.41-2.
10   Mrs Opie, *Temper, or Domestic Scenes: A Tale* (Longman, Hurst, Rees, Orme & Brown, 1812).
11   HL, Opie MSS, OP 72, 18 September, 1812.
12   BL, William Hayley letters, MS Add.30805: 38, 23 January, 1813.
13   ibid, 40, 29 January, 1813.
14   ibid, 46, 12 February, 1814.
15   Mrs Opie, *Tales of Real Life* (London: Longman, Hurst, Rees, Orme & Brown, 1813),
16   L'Estrange, *Mitford Letters*, Vol.1, p.231.
17   Brightwell, *Memorials*, p.146.
18   Mrs Roberts, *Duty: A novel interspersed with poetry and preceded by a character of the author by Mrs Opie* (London: Longman, Hurst, Reese, Orme & Brown, 1814), Vol.1, pp.20-21.
19   BL, William Hayley letters, MS Add 30805: 46, 12 February, 1814.
20   NYPL, AO26, 15 March, 1814.
21   Sidgwick, *Recollections*, p.4.
22   Brightwell, *Memorials*, p.158.
23   ibid, p.164.
24   ibid, p.168.
25   Sidgwick, *Recollections*, pp.4-5.

Chapter twenty
1   Brightwell, *Memorials*, pp.172-3.
2   SoF, Gurney MSS, 1/325. Letter, 13 June, 1814.
3   Kenneth Povey, *Amelia and the Hermit* in *The Sussex County Magazine*, Vol.3, No.1, January 1929, p.41.
4   SoF, Gurney MSS, 1/326A, 4 August, 1814.
5   ibid
6   ibid, 1/327, 10 August, 1814.
7   Povey, *Amelia and the Hermit*, p.43.
8   Fry & Cresswell, *Memoirs*, Vol.1, p.225.
9   NRO, MC 1627/1, *Memoirs of Rachel Gurney 1809-1814*.
10   Brightwell, *Memoir*, p.21.
11   Macgregor, *Amelia Alderson Opie*, p.72.
12   SC, Amelia Alderson Opie papers, SC 088, 5 June, 1815.
13   SoF, Gurney MSS, 1/328, 9 July, 1815.
14   ibid, 1/329, 9 August, 1815.
15   ibid, 1/330, 15 August, 1815.
16   Povey, *Amelia and the Hermit*, p.43.
17   Macgregor, *Amelia Alderson Opie*, p.76.
18   ibid, p.77.
19   HCL, Autograph Letters, 115 British Poets, Amelia Opie, 27 November, 1815.
20   SoF, Gurney MSS, 1/331, 31, December, 1815.
21   Macgregor, *Amelia Alderson Opie*, p.65.
22   ibid, pp.65-6.
23   SoF, Gurney MSS, 1/332, 15 June, 1816.
24   BL, William Hayley letters, MS Add 30805: 49, 25 July, 1816.
25   Constable, *Archibald Constable*, Vol.2, p.270
26   ibid, pp.273-4.
27   HL, Opie MSS, OP 194, 20 December, 1816

Chapter twenty-one
1   HL, Opie MSS, OP 167, 168 & 169, 1839.

2   NRO, MC 19/44, 443x2, Windham & Batt Papers, Title Deeds: Gresham.
3   NYPL, AO15, 8 August, 1798.
4   Sidgwick, *Recollections*, p.10.

Chapter twenty-two
1   HL, Opie MSS, OP 195, 30 January, 1817.
2   WFM, 252 Opie: WISFM 2003.35.243.1
3   Joseph Bevan Braithwaite, *Memoirs of Joseph John Gurney* (Norwich: Fletcher & Alexander, 1854), Vol.1, pp.120-21.
4   HL, Opie MSS, OP 196, 1 May, 1817.
5   NRO, MC 519/1-2, Elizabeth Fry Journals 1816-22.
6   John Johnson, ed., *Memoirs of the Life & Writings of William Hayley Esq.* (London: Henry Colburn and Simpkin & Marshall, 1823), Vol.2,.p.191.
7   WL, Dawson Turner Correspondence, O. 13 17, 19 January, 1819.
8   HL, Opie MSS, HM 25784, 1 December, 1818.
9   Macgregor, *Amelia Alderson Opie*, p.67.
10 Mrs Opie, *New Tales* (London: Longman, Hurst, Rees, Orme & Brown, 1818), Vol.4, p.162.
11 Edward Fitzball, *Thirty-five years of a Dramatic Author's Life* (London: T.C. Newby, 1859), Vol.1, pp.61-63.
12 Derek Hudson, ed., *The Diary of Henry Crabb Robinson* (London: Oxford University Press, 1967), pp.59.
13 John A. Kempe, ed., *Autobiography of Anna Eliza Bray* (London: Chapman & Hall, 1884), pp.138-40.
14 Published by Longman, Hurst, Rees, Orme & Brown in four volumes.
15 BL, Letters of Lady Caroline Lamb, 50142, f.4, 1820.
16 NRO, NNH1/10, N&N Hospital Committee Book (1817-1822).
17 ibid, Opie MC118/1, 29 January, 1821.
18 ibid, Family papers, RQG 380 491x4.
19 NYPL, 11 March, 1821, insert in grangerised Brightwell *Memorials*, p.183.
20 HL, Opie MSS, OP 209, 6 April, 1821.
21 ibid, OP 212, 13 July, 1821.
22 ibid, OP 215, 1 October, 1821.
23 WL, Dawson Turner correspondence, O 13 22, 7 November, 1821.

Chapter twenty-three
1   Mrs Opie, *Madeline, A Tale* (London: Longman, Hurst, Rees, Orme & Brown, 1822), Vol.1.
2   BL, Letters of Lady Caroline Lamb, 50142, f.8, 1 January, 1822.
3   HCL, Call No.861, Opie mss, 4 January, 1822.
4   HL, Opie MSS, HM 23043, 10 March, 1822.
5   NYPL, AO 13, 16 March, 1822.
6   Brightwell, *Memorials*, pp.190-91.
7   NYPL, AO27, 30 April, 1822.
8   HL, Opie MSS, OP 217, 7 February, 1822.
9   WL, Dawson Turner correspondence, O 13 23, 7 March, 1822.
10 SoF, Gurney MSS, 1/334, 10 June, 1822.
11 NRO, MC 519/1-2, Elizabeth Fry Journals 1816-22.
12 SoF, Gurney MSS, 1/334A
13 ML, Misc Ray MA 4500, 12 December, 1824.
14 SoF, Gurney MSS, 1/335, 9 January, 1823.
15 ibid, 1/336, 11 February, 1823.
16 SC, Amelia Alderson Opie papers, SC 088
17 SoF, Gurney MSS, 1/337, 4 August, 1823.
18 Private family papers, 29 October, 1823.

Endnotes

19 HL, Opie MSS, OP 48, 19 January, 1824.
20 NYPL, 16 February, 1824, insert in grangerised Brightwell *Memorials*, p.183.
21 Willard Bissell Pope, ed., *The Diary of Benjamin Robert Haydon* (Cambs, Massachusetts: Harvard University Press, 1960), Vol.2, p.490.
22 HL, Opie MSS, OP 47, 9 December, 1823.
23 Amelia Opie, *Illustrations of Lying in all its Branches* (London: Longman, Hurst, Rees, Orme, Brown & Green, 1825).
24 Anonymous, *A Letter addressed to Mrs Opie with Observations on her recent publication "Illustrations of Lying in all its Branches"* (Norwich: Printed & sold by Matchett & Stevenson).
25 L'Estrange, *Mitford Letters*, Vol.2, p.199
26 Fox, *Eliza Fox Memoir*, p.75.
27 SoF, Port 30/55, 7 April, 1825.
28 Eliza Paul Gurney, ed., *Extracts from the letters, journals &c of Joseph John Gurney* (printed for the family, 1848), p.209.

Chapter twenty-four

1   Kempe, *Bray Autobiography*, p139.
2   Martineau, *Biographical Sketches*, p.334.
3   Morley, *Crabb Robinson*, Vol.2, p.277.
4   Constable, *Archibald Constable*, Vol.2, p.270.
5   Hare, *Gurneys of Earlham*, Vol.1, p.260.
6   Sidgwick, *Recollections*, p.3.
7   HL. Opie MSS, OP 226, 30 August, 1825.
8   NRO, MS6181, 10 September, 1825.
9   HL, Opie MSS, OP 226.
10 Private family papers, 23 September, 1825.
11 SoF, Gurney MSS, 3/416A, 12 October, 1825.
12 Brightwell, *Memoir*, p.38.
13 Gurney, *Extracts*, p.213.
14 HL, Opie MSS. OP 227, 12 November, 1825.
15 Amelia Opie, *The Black Man's Lament* (London: Harvey & Darton, 1826), p.2.
16 HL, Opie MSS, OP 50, 26 March, 1826.
17 ibid, OP 67, 4 July, 1826.
18 ibid, OP 76, 15 September, 1826.
19 NYPL, 15 September, 1826, insert in grangerised Brightwell *Memorials*, pp.198-99.
20 SoF. Gurney MSS, 1/339, 29 September, 1826.
21 Braithwaite, *Memoirs*, Vol.1, p.304.
22 SoF, Gurney MSS, 1/339, 21 October, 1825.
23 ML, Misc English, MA 3018, 9 February, 1828.
24 Private family papers., 26 July, 1827.
25 Amelia Opie, *Detraction Displayed* (Norwich: S.Wilkin; London: Longman, Reese, Orme, Brown & Greene, 1828)

Chapter twenty-five

1   NYPL, AO17, 19 March, 1829.
2   HL, Opie MSS, OP 69, 25 March, 1828.
3   Brightwell, *Memorials*, pp.229-30.
4   HL, Opie MSS, OP 52, 27 July, 1829.
5   ibid.
6   ibid, OP 11-16
7   Private family papers, 22 August, 1829.
8   SoF, Gurney MSS, 1/344, 16 June, 1829.
9   ibid, 1/346, 19 October, 1829.
10 Stirling, *Coke of Norfolk*, pp.524-25.

11   SC, Amelia Alderson Opie papers, SC 088.
12   Gurney, *Extracts*, p.278.
13   HL, Opie MSS, OP 241, 19 February, 1830.
14   ibid, OP 248, 4 August, 1830.
15   SoF, Gurney MSS, 1/347, 29 November, 1830.
16   James Franklin Beard, ed., *The Letters & Journals of James Fenimore Cooper* (Cambs, Masachusetts: Harvard University Press, 1868), Vol 2, pp.4-5.
17   S.C. Hall & Mrs S.C. Hall, *Memories of the Authors of the Age: Amelia Opie* (*The Art Journal*, Vol.27, 1865, pp.287-88)
18   NRO, Family papers, RQG 595/1, 24 November, 1830.
19   SoF, Gurney MSS, 1/347, 29 November, 1830
20   HL, Opie MSS, OP 55, 7 March, 1831.
21   SoF, Gurney MSS, 1/349, 9 July, 1831.

Chapter twenty-six
1   HL, Opie MSS, OP 273, 27 March, 1832.
2   ibid, OP 110, 30 June, 1832.
3   ibid, OP 111, 9 July, 1832.
4   SoF, Gurney MSS, 2/36, 8 August, 1832.
5   R.L. Brett, ed., *Barclay Fox's Journal* (London: Bell & Hyman, 1979), p.33.
6   HL, Opie MSS, OP 56, 14 October, 1832.
7   ibid, OP 278, 24 October, 1832.
8   ibid, OP 57, 24 November, 1832.
9   ibid, OP 113, 24 November, 1832.
10   BL, Fox-Backhouse Papers, 61712/f.156, 11 January, 1833.
11   HL, Opie MSS, OP 279, 12 January, 1833.
12   ibid, OP 58, 14 January, 1833.
13   Brightwell, *Memorials*, pp.297-98.
14   HL, Opie MSS, OP 116, 2 August, 1833.
15   Rev William Hanna, *Memoirs of the Life & Writings of Thomas Chalmers* (Edinburgh: Thomas Constable & Co., 1852), Vol.3, pp.399-400.
16   HL, Opie MSS, OP 288, 27 August, 1833.
17   ibid, OP 290, 6 December, 1833.
18   ibid, OP 291, 23 December, 1833.
19   ibid, OP 293, 25 January, 1834.
20   ibid, OP 117, 4 February, 1834.
21   BodL, MS.Eng.lett.c741, 165, 24 January, 1834.
22   ibid, 169, 20 February, 1834.
23   *New Monthly Magazine & Literary Journal*, July, 1834, p.376.
24   UN, Marlay Collection, My 131, 29 September, 1834.
25   E. MacInnes, ed., *Priscilla Johnston's Journal & Letters* (Carlisle: Charles Thurnam & Sons, 1862), p.85.
26   SC, Jenkins Autograph Collection: MSS 031, 27 November, 1834.
27   SoF, Gurney MSS, 1/352, 16 December, 1834.

Chapter twenty-seven
1   Brightwell, *Memorials*, pp.325-328.
2   Private family papers, 22 August, 1835.
3   ibid, 15 August, 1835.
4   Brightwell, *Memorials*, p.330.
5   NRO, MS20813, 24 February, 1836.
6   HL, Opie MSS, OP 141, 11 March, 1836.
7   ibid, OP 315, 3 April, 1836.
8   ibid OP 319, 6 July, 1836.
9   ibid, OP 326, 19 December, 1836.

Endnotes

10 A.M.W. Stirling, *The Richmond Papers – from the correspondence & manuscripts of George Richmond RA & his son Sir William Richmond RAS, KCB* (London: William Heinemann, 1926), pp,38-39.

11 HL, Opie MSS, OP 328, 9 February, 1837.

12 Braithwaite, *Memoirs*, Vol.2, p.70.

13 HL, Opie MSS, OP 329, 8 March, 1837.

14 ibid, OP 335, 29 June,1837.

15 SoF, Gurney MSS, 1/355, 23 August, 1837.

16 ibid, 3/689, 27 November, 1838.

17 HL, Opie MSS, OP 348, 26 March, 1838.

18 SoF, Gurney MSS, 1/358, 19 July, 1838.

19 Miss Sedgwick, *Letters from Abroad to Kindred at Home* (London: Edward Moxon, 1841), Vol.1, p.92.

20 NYPL, August, 1838, insert in grangerised Brightwell *Memorials*, p.346.

21 NRO, Family papers, RQG 527 492x8, August, 1839.

22 BL, Mss Eur E308/33, Papers of Sir Robert Grant & family, 14 August, 1839.

23 SoF, Gurney MSS, 1/369, 23 August, 1839.

24 HL, Opie MSS, OP 163, 28 September, 1939.

25 SoF, Gurney MSS, 1/370, 6 October, 1839.

26 ibid, 8 August, 1839.

27 SC, Jenkins Autograph Collection: MSS 031, 16 December, 1839.

Chapter twenty-eight

1 RHL, Thomas Fowell Buxton Papers, MSS Brit.Emp.s.444, Vol.18, 14, 1 April, 1839.

2 ibid, Vol.19, 279 a-d, 20 May, 1840.

3 SoF, Gurney MSS, 1/374, 2 & 27 June, 1840.

4 Rev A.G. L'Estrange, ed., *The Friendships of Mary Russell Mitford, as recorded in letters from her Literary Correspondents* (London: Hurst & Blackett, 1882), Vol.2, p.64.

5 Brightwell, *Memorials*, p.341.

6 SoF, MS Box10 (19) 5, 13 June, 1840.

7 CL, Amelia Opie ms: *British & Foreign Anti-Slavery Society Convention 1840*, pp.12-13

8 Pope, *Haydon Diary*, Vol.4, p.661.

9 SoF, Gurney MSS, 4/43. Poem *To Anna Gurney*.

10 NRO, MS6181, 28 February, 1841.

11 SoF, Gurney MSS, 1/353, undated.

12 ibid, 3/122, 3 June, 1841.

13 RHL, Buxton Papers, MSS Brit.Emp.s.444, Vol.20, 437 p-s, 22 January, 1842.

14 NYPL, 14 November, 1842, insert in grangerised Brightwell *Memorials*, p.346.

15 HL, Opie MSS, OP 185, 17 November, 1842.

16 Henry Chorley, *Letters of Mary Russell Mitford* (London: Richard Bentley & Sons, 1872), Vol.2, p.5.

17 RHL, Buxton Papers, MSS Brit.Emp s.444, Vol.20A, 462-9, 10 & 12 October, 1843.

Chapter twenty-nine

1 NRO, Family papers, RQG 527 492x8, 7 February, 1844..

2 ibid, MS 4281, Wilkin papers, 18 January, 1843.

3 SoF, Gurney MSS, 1/380b, 23 February, 1844.

4 NRO, Family papers, RQG 527 492x8, 1 April, 1844..

5 SoF, Gurney MSS, 1/381 a&b, 7 April, 1844.

6 Brightwell, *Memorials*, p.349.

7 BL, Stanhope (Harrington) Papers, 82736, Vol.vi, 22 March.1844.

8 NRO, MS6181, Boi 63/5/11, 7 March, 1845.

9 ibid, Family papers, RQG 595/2, 4 February, 1846.

10 UN, Marlay Collection, My 138, 21 December, 1845.

11   Mrs Bray, *Trials of the Heart* (London: Longman, Brown, Green & Longmans, 1845).

12   HCL, Call No.861, Opie Mss, 19 December, 1845.

13   NRO, MS6181, Boi 63/6/14, 25 November, 1845.

14   SoF, Gurney MSS, 3/242, 12 June, 1846.

15   ibid, 1/384, 17 June, 1846.

16   Gurney, *Extracts,* p.702.

17   Eliza Paul Gurney, *A Brief Sketch of the Life of Anna Backhouse* (Burlington, New Jersey: John Rodgers, 1852), p.119.

18   SoF, Gurney MSS, 1/387, 6 January, 1847.

19   *Record of the death of J.J. Gurney Esq., of Earlham* (Norwich: Stevenson & Matchett)

20   NRO, MS6181, Boi 63/5/32, 19 January, 1847.

21   BL, Stanhope (Harrington) Papers, 82735, vol.v, 3 February, 1847.

22   SoF, Forster correspondence, MS 100/15, 5 February, 1847.

23   BL, Stanhope (Harrington) Papers, 82735, vol.v, 19 July, 1847.

Chapter thirty

1   Charles Alderson, *Selections from the Charges & other Detailed Papers of Baron Alderson, with an Introductory Notice of his Life* (London: John W. Parker & Son, 1858), pp.103-4.

2   NRO MS5252, Opie letters & notes to Josiah Fletcher pasted into his copy of Brightwell *Memorials,*

3   Brightwell, *Memorials,* p.381.

4   UN, Marlay Collection, My 148, 27 September, 1849.

5   HL, Opie MSS, OP 358, 19 December, 1838.

6   NRO, MF/RO 528/1, *Lucy Massey's Memories 1842-1865: Reminiscences of the Fletcher Family of Norwich* (Handwritten, 1918)

7   Janet Ross, *Early Days Recalled* (London: Chapman & Hall, 1891), p.27.

8   UN, Marlay Collection, My 143, 9 December, 1848.

9   Brightwell, *Memorials,* p.385.

10   SoF, Gurney MSS, 1/394a, 16 April, 1849.

11   UN, Marlay Collection, My 144, 22 April, 1849.

12   ibid, My 146, 4 June, 1849.

13   NYPL, O'ANA 0029, 28 December, 1849.

14   SoF, Gurney MSS, 1/399, 12 April, 1850.

15   ibid, 1/401, 2 July, 1850.

16   NRO, MS 69, *Diary of Cecilia Brightwell 1842-1866* (Handwritten)

17   Private collection, 30 April, 1851.

18   SoF, Gurney MSS, 1/404, 18 April, 1851.

19   ibid, 30 April, 1851.

20   Private collection.

21   BL, Stanhope (Harrington) Papers, 82737, Vol.vii, Letter, 1 January, 1854.

22   NRO, MS6181, Boi 63/6/13, 14 November, 1845.

Bibliography

Works by Mrs [Amelia Alderson] Opie

Adeline Mowbray (Longman, Hurst, Rees, Orme & Brown, 1805), 3 vols

Adeline Mowbray, intro. by Jeanette Winterson (London: Pandora Press, 1986)

A Memoir, prefixed to John Opie's *Lectures on Painting* (London: Longman, Hurst, Rees & Orme, 1809)

Dangers of Coquetry (London: W.Lane, 1790), 2 vols

Detraction Displayed (Norwich: S.Wilkin; London: Longman, Rees, Orme, Brown & Green, 1828)

Elegy of the late Duke of Bedford, Written on the Evening of His Interment (London: T.N.Longman & O.Rees, 1802)

Illustrations of Lying in All Its Branches (Norwich: S.Wilkin; London: Longman, Hurst, Rees, Orme, Brown & Green, 1825), 2 vols

Lays for the Dead (London: Longman, Rees, Orme, Brown, Green & Longman, 1834)

Madeline, a Tale (London: Longman, Hurst, Rees, Orme & Brown, 1822), 2 vols

New Tales (London: Longman, Hurst, Rees, Orme & Brown, 1818), 4 vols

Poems (London: T.N.Longman & O.Rees, 1803)

Simple Tales (London: Longman, Hurst, Rees & Orme, 1806), 4 vols

Tales of Real Life (London: Longman, Hurst, Rees, Orme & Brown, 1813), 3 vols

Tales of the Heart (London: Longman, Hurst, Rees, Orme & Brown, 1820), 4 vols

Tales of the Pemberton Family: for the Use of Children (London: Harvey & Darton; Norwich: S.Wilkin, 1825)

Temper: or Domestic Scenes (London: Longman, Hurst, Rees, Orme & Brown, 1812), 3 vols

The Black Man's Lament or *How to Make Sugar* (London: Harvey & Darton, 1826)

The Father and Daughter (London: Longman & Rees, 1801)

The Father and Daughter with *Dangers of Coquetry*, edited by Shelley King & John B. Pierce (Broadview Press Ltd., 2003)

The Warrior's Return: and other poems (Longman, Hurst, Rees & Orme, 1808)

Valentine's Eve (London: Longman, Hurst, Rees, Orme & Brown, 1816), 3 vols

Biographies, autobiographies, memoirs, diaries, letters

A Grandson [of Alfred Fox], *Two Homes* (Plymouth: William Brendon & son, 1925) Printed for private circulation

Aikin, Lucy, ed., *The Works of Anna Laetitia Barbauld with a Memoir* (London: Longman, Hurst, Rees, Orme, Brown & Green, 1825), 2 vols

Alderson, Charles, *Selections from the Charges & Other Detached Papers of Baron Alderson, with an Introductory Notice of His Life* (London: John W.Parker & Son, 1858)

Asleson, Robyn, ed., *A Passion for Performance: Sarah Siddons and Her Portraitists* (Los Angeles: The J.Paul Getty Museum, 1999)

Backhouse, Hannah Chapman, *Extracts from the Journal and Letters* (London: printed by Richard Barrett, 1858) not published.

Baker, Herschel, *John Philip Kemble: The Actor in his Theatre* (New York: Greenwood Press, 1969: reprint from Harvard University Press edition 1942)

Baker, John Milton, *Henry Crabb Robinson of Bury, Jena, The Times and Russell Square* (London: George Allen & Unwin, 1937)

Barcus, James E., ed., *The Literary Correspondence of Bernard Barton* (Philadelphia: University of Pennsylvania Press, 1966)

Barnard, Mrs Alfred, ed., *The Life of a Negro Slave* (Norwich: Charles Muskett, 1846)

Barton, Lucy, ed., *Selections from the Poems and Letters of Bernard Barton* (London: Hall,Virtue & Co., 1849)

Batty Shaw, A., *Norfolk & Norwich Hospital: Lives of the Medical Staff 1771-1971* (Norwich: University of East Anglia, 1971)

Beard, James Franklin, ed., *The Letters and Journals of James Fenimore Cooper* (Cambs, Masachusetts: Harvard University Press, 1968), 6 vols

Beloe, William, *The Sexagenarian, or The Recollections of a Literary Life* (London: F.C. & J.Rivington, 1817), 2 vols.

Betham, Ernest, ed., *A House of Letters* (London: Jarrold & Sons, 1905)

Bishop, Morchard, *Blake's Hayley: The Life, Work and Friendships of William Hayley* (London: Gollancz, 1951)

Braithwaite, Joseph Bevan, *Memoirs of Joseph John Gurney* (Norwich: Fletcher & Alexander, 1854), 2 vols

Brett, R.L., ed., *Barclay Fox's Journal* (London: Bell & Hyman, 1979)

Bridgeman, June, & Hudson, Briony, *Jacob Bell 1810-59: A useful and honourable life* (Friends of Woodbury Park Cemetery)

Brightwell, Cecilia Lucy, *Memoir of Amelia Opie* (London: Religious Tract Society 1857)
Memorials of the Life of Amelia Opie (Norwich: Fletcher & Alexander, 1854)
Memorials of the Life of Mr.Brightwell of Norwich by his daughter (Norwich: Fletcher & Son, 1869) Printed for private circulation

Brown, Ford K., *The Life of William Godwin* (London: J.M.Dent & Sons Ltd., 1926)

Buxton, Charles, ed., *Memoir of Sir T.F.Buxton* (London: John Murray, 1849)

Buxton, Hannah, *Memorials of Hannah Lady Buxton from papers collected by her grand-daughters* (London: Bickers & Son, 1883). Printed for private circulation.

Chorley, Henry, ed., *Letters of Mary Russell Mitford: Second series* (London: Richard Bentley & Sons, 1872), 2 vols

Clemit, Pamela, ed., *Lives of the Great Romantics III: Godwin, Wollstonecraft, Mary Shelley by their contemporaries*, Vol.1: *Godwin* (London: Pickering & Chatto, 1999)

Clifford, Derek, & Clifford, Timothy, *John Crome* (London: Faber & Faber, 1968)

Colby, Elbridge, ed., *The Life of Thomas Holcroft, Written by Himself* (New York: Benjamin Blom, 1968), 2 vols

Cooper, James Fenimore, ed., *The Correspondence of James Fenimore Cooper* (New York: Books for Libraries Press, 1922, reprint 1971), 2 vols

Bibliography

Corder, Susanna, *Memoir of Priscilla Gurney* (Philadelphia: Henry Longstreth,1858)

Corfield, Penelope J. & Evans, Chris, eds., *Youth and Revolution in the 1790s: Letters of William Pattison, Thomas Amyot and Henry Crabb Robinson* (Stroud: Alan Sutton, 1996)

Cozens-Hardy, Basil, and Kent, Ernest A., *The Mayors of Norwich 1403-1835* (Norwich: Jarrold & Sons, 1938)

Cunningham, Allan, *The Life of Sir David Wilkie* (London: John Murray, 1843) 3 vols

Curry, Kenneth, ed., *New Letters of Robert Southey* (New York & London: Columbia University Press, 1965), 2 vols

Earland, Ada, *John Opie and His Circle* (London: Hutchinson & Co., 1911)

Eastlake, Lady, ed., *Dr.Rigby's Letters from France in 1789* (London: Longmans, Green & Co., 1880)

Equiano, Olaudah, *The Interesting Narrative of the Life of Olaudah Equiano or Gustavus Vassa, the African* (8th edition, Norwich. Printed for & sold by the author, 1794)
The Interesting Narrative and Other Writings (London: Penguin, 1995)

Field, the Rev.William, *Memoirs of the Life, Writing and Opinions of the Rev. Samuel Parr* (London: Henry Colburn, 1826), 2 vols

Fitzball, Edward, *Thirty-five years of a Dramatic Author's Life* (London: T.C.Newby, 1859), 2 vols

Fox, Franklin, ed., *Memoir of Eliza Fox* (London: N.Trubner & Co., 1869)

Fry, Katharine, & Cresswell, Rachel, eds., *Memoirs of the Life of Elizabeth Fry with extracts from her journals and letters* (London: Charles Gilpin, 1847), 2 vols.

Fulford, Roger, *Samuel Whitbread* (London: Macmillan, 1967)

Geldart, Mrs. Hannah Ransome, *The Footmarks of Charity: Sketches of Sir Thomas Fowell Buxton, Elizabeth Fry and Joseph John Gurney* (Norwich: Josiah Fletcher, 1853)
Memorials of Samuel Gurney (London: W.& F.G.Cash, 1857)

Goodman, Nigel, ed., *Dawson Turner: A Norfolk Antiquary and his Remarkable Family* (Chichester: Phillimore & Co., 2007)

Greig, James, ed., *The Farington Diary by Joseph Farington, RA* (London: Hutchinson & Co., 1922-28), 8 vols

Gurney, Eliza Paul, ed., *A Brief Sketch of the Life of Anna Backhouse* (Burlington, New Jersey: John Rodgers, 1852)
Extracts from the letters, journals &c of Joseph John Gurney (Printed for the family only, 1848)

Gurney, Joseph John, *A Journey in North America: described in familiar letters to Amelia Opie* (Norwich: Josiah Fletcher, 1841) Printed for private circulation

Hall, S.C., ed., *The Art Journal, Vol. 27* (London: George Virtue, 1865)

Hanna, the Rev.William, *Memoirs of the Life and Writings of Thomas Chalmers* (Edinburgh: Thomas Constable & Co., 1852), 4 vols

Hare, Augustus J.C., *The Gurneys of Earlham* (London: George Allen, 1895), 2 vols

Hatton, Jean, *Betsy: The dramatic biography of prison reformer Elizabeth Fry* (Oxford: Monarch Books, 2005)

Hendra, Viv, *The Cornish Wonder: A Portrait of John Opie* (Truro, Cornwall: Truran, 2007)

Holmes, Richard, ed., *Godwin on Wollstonecraft* (London: Harper Perennial, 2005)

Hudson, Derek, ed., *The Diary of Henry Crabb Robinson*, (London: Oxford University Press, 1967)

Jenkins, Annibel, *I'll Tell You What: The Life of Elizabeth Inchbald* (Lexington: Kentucky: University Press of Kentucky, 2003)

Jewson, Charles B., *Simon Wilkin of Norwich* (Norwich: Centre of East Anglian Studies, University of East Anglia, 1979)

Johnson, John, ed., *Memoirs of the Life & Writings of William Hayley, Esq. The friend and biographer of Cowper, written by himself, with extracts from his private correspondence and unpublished poetry* (London: Printed for Henry Colburn & Co. & Simpkin & Marshall,1823), 2 vols

Jones, Mrs.Herbert, *The Worthies of Norwich* (Norwich: Jarrold & Sons, 1892) Reprinted from *The Edinburgh Review*.

Kavanagh, Julia, *English Women of Letters: Biographical Sketches* (London: Hurst & Blackett, 1863), 2 vols

Kempe, John A., ed., *Autobiography of Anna Eliza Bray* (London: Chapman & Hall, 1884)

Kitson, Sydney D, *The Life of John Sell Cotman* (London: Rodart Reproductions, 1982)

L'Estrange, the Rev.A.G., ed., *The Friendships of Mary Russell Mitford, as recorded in letters from Her Literary Correspondents*, (London: Hurst & Blackett, 1882), 2 vols
The Life of Mary Russell Mitford related in a Selection from her Letters to her Friends, (London: Richard Bentley, 1870), 3 vols

Locke, Don, *A Fantasy of Reason: The Life and Thought of William Godwin* (London: Routledge & Kegan Paul, 1980)

Macgregor, Margaret Eliot, *Amelia Alderson Opie: Worldling and Friend* (Menasha, Wisconsin: The Collegiate Press, 1933) Reprinted from *Smith College Studies in Modern Languages*, Vol XIV, Nos 1-2, October 1932-January 1933

MacInnes, E. ed., *Priscilla Johnston's Journal and Letters* (Carlisle: Charles Thurnam & Sons, 1862)

Mackenzie, Kathleen, *The Great Sarah: The Life of Mrs. Siddons* (London: Evans Brothers, 1968)

Mackintosh, Robert James, *Memoirs of the Life of the Rt. Hon. Sir James Mackintosh* (London: Edward Moxon, 1836), 2 vols.

Marshall, Peter H., *William Godwin* (New Haven & London: Yale University Press, 1984)

Martineau, Harriet, *Autobiography with Memorials by Maria Weston Chapman* (London: Smith, Elder & Co., 1877), 3 vols.
Biographical Sketches 1852-1875 (London: Macmillan, 1888)

Menzies-Wilson, Jacobine, & Lloyd, Helen, *Amelia: The Tale of a Plain Friend* (London: Oxford University Press, 1937)

Morgan, Dr. G.W., *An Alderson family of Ravenstonedale, Lowestoft, Norwich,etc.* (Alderson Family History Society, Newsletter, December, 1987).

Morley, Edith J., ed., *Henry Crabb Robinson on Books and their Writers*, (London: J.M.Dent & Sons, 1938), 3 vols

Mott, Richard F., *Memoir and Correspondence of Eliza P.Gurney* (Philadelphia: J.R.Lippincott, 1884)

Mottram, R.H. *Buxton the Liberator* (London: Hutchinson & Co., 1958)

Bibliography

John Crome of Norwich (London: John Lane The Bodley Head, 1931)

Painting, Vivienne, *John Boydell* (London: Guildhall Art Gallery, 2005)

Palmer, Charles John, *Memorials of the Family of Hurry, of Great Yarmouth, Norfolk* (Norwich: Miller & Leavins, 1873)

Paul, C.Kegan, *William Godwin: His Friends and Contemporaries* (London: Henry S.King, 1876), 2 vols

Pearson, Hesketh, *The Smith of Smiths* (London: Hamish Hamilton, 1934)

Pease, Sir Alfred, *Rachel Gurney of the Grove* (London: Headley Brothers, 1907)

Pollock, John, *Wilberforce* (London: Constable & Co.,1977)

Pope, Willard Bissell, ed., *The Diary of Benjamin Robert Haydon* (Cambs, Massachusetts: Harvard University Press, 1960), 5 vols

Pritchett, V.S., *A Man of Letters* (London: Chatto & Windus, 1985)

Pryor, F.R., ed., *Memoirs of Samuel Hoare by his daughter Sarah and widow Hannah* (London: Headley Bros., 1911)

Pym, Horace N, ed., *Memories of Old Friends – being extracts from the Journals and Letters of Caroline Fox, of Penjerrick, Cornwall, for 1835-1871* (London: Smith Elder & Co., 1882).

Reid, T.Wemyss, *Life of the Right Honourable William Edward Forster* (London: Chapman & Hall, 1888), 2 vols

Robberds, J.W., *Memoirs of the Life and Writings of the late William Taylor of Norwich* (London: John Murray, 1843), 2 vols

Roberts, Mrs., *Duty, A Novel*, preceded by a character of the author by Mrs.Opie (London: Longman, Hurst, Rees, Orme & Brown, 1814), 3 vols

Roberts, W., *Sir William Beechey, RA* (London: Duckworth & Co., 1907)

Robertson, Ben P., *The Diaries of Elizabeth Inchbald* (London: Pickering & Chatto, 2007), 3 vols

Robinson, Arthur R.B., *The Counting House: Thomas Thompson of Hull 1754-1828 and his Family* (York: William Sessions, 1992)

Robinson, Henry Crabb, *The Diary of Henry Crabb Robinson*, abridgement edited by Derek Hudson (London: Oxford University Press, 1967)

Robinson, William, ed., *Friends of Half a Century: Fifty Memorials with Portraits of Members of the Society of Friends 1840-1890* (London: Edward Hicks, 1891)

Rogers, John Jope, *Opie and His Work* (London: Paul & Dominic Colnaghi & Co.; Truro: Netherton & Worth, 1878)

Ross, Janet, *Early Days Recalled* (London: Chapman & Hall, 1891)

Three Generations of Englishwomen: Memoirs and Correspondence of Mrs. John Taylor, Mrs.Sarah Austin and Lady Duff Gordon (London: John Murray, 1888), 2 vols

Sadler, Thomas, ed., *Diary of Henry Crabb Robinson* (London: Macmillan & Co., 1869), 3 vols

St Clair, William, *The Godwins and the Shelleys: The biography of a family* (London: Faber & Faber, 1989)

Sanders, Valerie, ed., *Harriet Martineau: Selected Letters* (Oxford: Clarendon Press, 1990)

Sayers, Frank, *Collective Works of the late Dr.Sayers, to which have been prefaced some biographical particulars by W.Taylor of Norwich* (Norwich: Matchett & Stevenson, 1823)

Sedgwick, Miss, *Letters from Abroad to Kindred at Home* (London: Edward Moxon, 1841), 2 vols.

Seebohm, Benjamin, ed., *Memoirs of William Forster* (London: Alfred W.Bennett, 1865), 2 vols

Sidgwick, Mrs William, *Recollections of Mrs.Opie* (Printed for private circulation from three articles in the *Manchester Guardian*, July, 1884)

Smith, John Thomas, & Whitten, Wilfred, ed., *Nollekens and His Times* (London: John Lane The Bodley Head, 1920) 2 vols

Southey, Rev.Charles Cuthbert, ed., *The Life and Correspondence of Robert Southey* (London: Longman, Brown, Green & Longmans, 1849-50), 6 vols

Stanley, Arthur Penrhyn, *Memoirs of Edward and Catherine Stanley* (London: John Murray, 1880)

Stephen, Leslie, & Lee, Sidney, eds., *Dictionary of National Biography, 1882-1900* (Oxford: Oxford University Press, 1917)

Stirling, A.M.W., *Coke of Norfolk and His Friends* (London: John Lane The Bodley Head, 1912)

The Richmond Papers – from the correspondence and manuscripts of George Richmond, RA and his son Sir William Richmond, RA, KCB (London: William Heinemann, 1926)

Stoddard, Richard Henry, *Personal Reminiscences by Barham, Harness and Hodder* (New York: Scribner, Armstrong & Company, 1875)

Swift, David E., *Joseph John Gurney: Banker, Reformer and Quaker* (Middletown, Connecticut: Wesleyan University Press, 1962)

Taylor, John. *Records of my Life* (London: Edward Bull, 1832)

Thackeray, Anne, Lady Ritchie, *From the Porch* (London: Smith, Elder & Co., 1914)

A Book of Sybils (London: Smith, Elder & Co., 1883)

Thelwall, Mrs., *The Life of John Thelwall* (London: John Macrone, 1837)

Todd, Janet, *Mary Wollstonecraft: A Revolutionary Life* (London: Phoenix Press, 2001)

ed., *The Collected Letters of Mary Wollstonecraft* (New York: Columbia University Press, 2003)

Tomalin, Claire, *The Life and Death of Mary Wollstonecraft* (London: Penguin Books, 1992)

Vansittart, Jane, ed., *Katharine Fry's Book* (London: Hodder & Stoughton, 1966)

Wardle, Ralph M., ed., *Collected Letters of Mary Wollstonecraft* (Ithaca & London: Cornell University Press, 1979)

ed., *Godwin and Mary: Letters of William Godwin and Mary Wollstonecraft* (Lawrence: University of Kansas Press, & London: Constable and Company, 1967)

Mary Wollstonecraft: A Critical Biography (Lincoln, Nebraska: University of Nebraska Press, 1966)

Warter, John Wood, ed., *Selections from the Letters of Robert Southey* (London: Longman, Brown, Green, Longmans & Roberts, 1856) 4 vols.

Williams, Caroline E., *A Welsh Family from the Beginning of the 18th Century* (London: Women's Printing Society Ltd., 1893)

Wilson, Ellen Gibson, *Thomas Clarkson: A Biography* (York: William Sessions Ltd., 1989)

Bibliography

Art, history, literature, publishing, directories

Anon, *Rules & Orders for the Norfolk & Norwich Hospital* (Norwich: Chase & Co., 1786)

The History of the City of Norwich (Norwich: William Allen, 1869)

The New Annual Register, or General Repository of History, Politics and Literature for the Year 1794 (London: G.G. & J.Robinson, 1795)

Allthorpe-Guyton, Marjorie, *A Happy Eye: A School of Art in Norwich 1845-1982* (Norwich: Jarrold & Sons, 1982)

Barham-Johnson, C.M., *Keswick Hall 1817-1957* (Norwich: Modern Press, 1957)

Barringer, Christopher, ed., *Norwich in the 19th Century* (Norwich: Gliddon Books, 1984)

Bateman, Frederick, & Rye, Walter, *The History of the Bethel Hospital at Norwich (Norwich: Gibbs & Waller, 1906)*

Bayne, A.D., *A Comprehensive History of Norwich* (London: Jarrold & Sons, 1869)

Bentley, E., *Genuine Poetical Compositions on Various Subjects* (Norwich: Crouse & Stevenson, 1791)

Poems (London: Darton & Harvey, 1821)

Bidwell, W.H., *Annals of an East Anglian Bank* (Norwich: Agas H.Gooch, 1900)

Blyth, G.K., *The Norwich Guide & Directory* (London: R.Hastings 1842)

Blagden, Cyprian, *Fire More than Water: Notes for the Story of a Ship* (London: Longmans, Green & Co., 1949)

Blakey, Dorothy, *The Minerva Press 1790-1820* (London: Biographical Society, 1939)

Browne, P., *The History of Norwich from the earliest records to the present time* (Norwich: Bacon, Kinnebrook & Co., 1814)

Buhle, Mari Jo & Paul, eds., *The Concise History of Woman Suffrage: Selections from the Classic Work of Stanton, Anthony, Gage and Harper* (Urbana, Chicago & London: University of Illinois Press, 1978).

Burke, Edmund, *Reflections on the Revolution in France* (London: Penguin, 1986)

Butler, David M., *The Quaker Meeting Houses of Britain* (London: Friends Historical Society, 1999), 2 vols.

Chandler, David, *Norwich Literature 1788-97* (unpublished doctoral thesis, University of Oxford, 1997)

Chase, W., ed., *The Norwich Directory of Gentlemen & Tradesmen's Assistant* (Norwich: W.Chase & Co., 1783; Fax edition, Michael Winton, King's Lynn, 1991)

Clark, Zachary, *An Account of the Different Charities belonging to the Poor of the County of Norfolk* (London: Longman, Hurst, Rees, Orme & Brown, 1811).

Cole, Timothy, and Van Dyke, John C., *Old English Masters* (London: Macmillan & Co., 1902)

Copeman, Edward, *Brief History of the Norfolk & Norwich Hospital* (Norwich: Chas Muskett, 1856)

Cox, Harold, and E.Chandler John, *The House of Longman 1724-1924* (London: Longmans, Green & Co., 1924) Printed for private circulation.

De Caso, Jacques, *David d'Angers: Sculptural Communication in the Age of Romanticism* (Princeton, NJ: Princeton University Press, 1992)

de Montluzin, Emily Lorraine, *The Anti-Jacobins 1798-1800* (London: Macmillan Press, 1988)

Douglas, James, *Glimpses of Old Bombay and Western India, with other papers* (London, Sampson Low, Marston & Co., 1900)

Eddington, Arthur J., *The First 50 Years of Quakerism in Norwich* (London: Friends' Historical Society, 1932)

Emden, Paul H., *Quakers in Commerce: A Record of Business Achievement* (London: Sampson Low, Marston & Co., 1939)

Fawcett, Trevor, *Some Aspects of the Norfolk Book-Trade 1800-24* in *Transactions of the Cambridge Bibliographical Society,* vol iv, 1964-68, edited by Bruce Dickins, Richard Vaughan, John Harrison (Cambridge: Cambridge University Press, 1968).

Ferguson, Moira, *Subject to Others: British Women Writers and Colonial Slavery 1670-1834* (New York & London: Routledge, 1992)

Feldman, Paul R., ed., *British Women Poets of the Romantic Era* (Baltimore: John Hopkins University Press, 1997)

Forby, Rev.Robert, *The Vocabulary of East Anglia* (Newton Abbot: David & Charles Reprint, 1870; first published London: J.B.Nichols & Son, 1830)

Gibbs-Smith, C.H., *The Great Exhibition of 1851* (London: Her Majesty's Stationery Office, 1950)

Gillingwater, Edmund, *An Historical Account of the Ancient Town of Lowestoft* (London: C.G.J. & J.Robinson; J.Nichols, 1790)

Gregory, Allene, *The French Revolution and the English Novel* (New York: G.P. Putnam's Sons, 1915)

Goulty, Dr.George A., *The Registers, Monuments and other Miscellaneous Records of St.Margaret's Church, Old Catton, Norwich* (Peterborough: G.A.Goulty, 1997)

Groves, Algernon, *The Society of Artists of Great Britain1760-1791* (London: George Bell & Sons, 1907)

Gurney, Gerard Hudson, *Portraits at Keswick Hall* (Norwich: A.E.Soman & Co., 1922)

Hooper, James, *Norwich Charities* (Norwich: Norfolk News Co., 1898)

Howell, Thomas Jones, compiler, *A Complete Collection of State Trials and Proceedings for High Treason and other Crimes & Misdemeanors from the year 1783*, vols 24 & 25 (London: Longman, Hurst, Rees, Orme & Brown, 1818)

Jewson, Charles B., *The Jacobin City: A Portrait of Norwich 1788-1802* (Glasgow & London: Blackie & Son, 1975)

Johnson, Frederic, ed., *A Catalogue of the Collection of Engraved Norfolk and Norwich Portraits in the Possession of Russell J.Colman* (Norwich: H.W.Hicks, 1911) Printed for private circulation

Jorns, Auguste, *The Quakers as Pioneers in Social Work*, trans. by Thomas Kite Brown (New York: Kennikat Press, 1969)

Kelly, Geoffrey I., *Gurney Court Norwich: A History* (unpublished typescript 2005)

Kent, Ernest A., *The Gildencroft in Norwich* in *Norfolk Archaeology: The Centenary Volume*, ed. by Percy Millican (Norfolk & Norwich Archaeological Society, 1946)

Lidbetter, Hubert, *The Friends Meeting House* (York: The Ebor Press, 1961)

Linnell, Rev.C.L.S. & Douglas, A.B., *Gresham's School History and Register 1555-1994*

McCarthy, William, & Kraft, Elizabeth, eds., The *Poems of Anna Letitia Barbauld* (Athens & London: University of Georgia Press, 1994)

Bibliography

Mitford, Mary Russell, ed., *Finden's Tableaux of The Affections* (London: Charles Tilt, 1839)

Morris, Thelma, *Made in Norwich: 700 Years of Textile Heritage* (Norwich: Nick Williams, 2008)

Munby, Frank Arthur, *Publishing and Bookselling, Part One* (London: Jonathan Cape, revised edition 1974)

Nixseaman, Rev.A.J., *The Intwood Story* (Norwich: R.Robertson, 1972)

Palmer, Charles John, *The Perlustration of Great Yarmouth: with Gorleston and Southtown* (Great Yarmouth: George Nall, 1872-1875) , 3 vols.

Parker, Graham, *A History of Holt Hall* (Norfolk Education Authority, 1990)

Pearson, Jacqueline, *Women's Reading in Britain 1750-1835* (Cambridge: University Press, 1999)

Peck, Thomas, *The Norwich Directory* (Norwich: J.Payne, 1802)

Platt, Joan, *The Quakers in Norwich* (Norwich: Goose & Sons, 1926)

Plumptre, Anne, *A Narrative of A Three Years' Residence in France, principally in the southern departments from the year 1802-1805* (London: J Mawman; J.Ridgway; J.Clarke; B.Crosby & Co.; Constable & Co., 1810)

Radford, Lewis B., *A History of Holt* (Holt: Rounce & Wortley; Norwich: Goose & Son, 1908)

Rawcliffe, Carole, & Wilson, Richard, eds., *Norwich Since 1550* (London: Hambledon & London, 2004)

Reeve, James, *A Catalogue of the Portraits and Paintings in St.Andrew's Hall & other public buildings* (City of Norwich: 1905)

Reiman, Donald H., *Romantic Context: Poetry: Significant Minor Poetry 1789-1830* (New York & London: Garland Publishing, 1978)

Reinis, J.J., *The Portrait Medallions of David D'Angers: An Illustrated Catalogue of David's Contemporary & Retrospective Portraits in Bronze* (New York: Polymath Press, 1991)

Rigby, Edward, *Further Facts Relating to the Care of the Poor and the Management of the Workhouse in the city of Norwich* (Norwich: Bacon, Kinnebrook & Co., 1812)

Society of Gentlemen, *The Cabinet* (Norwich: J.March, 1795), 3 vols.

Society of Universal Goodwill in London & Norwich, *An Inquiry into the origin, progress & present state of Slavery, with a plan for the gradual, reasonable & secure Emancipation of Slaves* (London: John Murray, 1789)

Spender, Dale, *Women of Ideas* (London: Routledge & Kegan Paul, 1982)

Stacy, John, ed., *A topographical and historical account of the city and county of Norwich* (Norwich: John Stacy, Market Place; London: Longman, Hurst, Rees, Orme & Brown, 1819)

Taylor, John, & Taylor, Edward, *The History of the Octagon Chapel, Norwich* (London: Charles Green, 1848)

Todd, Janet, ed., *Mary Wollstonecraft: Political Writings* (Oxford: Oxford University Press, 1999).

Ty, Eleanor, *Empowering the Feminine: narratives of Mary Robinson, Jane West and Amelia Opie, 1796-1812* (Toronto: University of Toronto Press, 1998)
Unsex'd Revolutionaries: Five Women Novelists of the 1790s (Toronto: University of Toronto Press, 1993)

Wornum, Ralph N., *Lectures on Painting by the Royal Academicians: Barry, Opie and Fuseli* (London: George Bell & Sons, 1889)

Amelia Opie

Documents, leaflets, pamphlets and newspaper & magazine articles

A Catalogue of the Norwich Polytechnic Exhibition (Norwich: Josiah Fletcher, December, 1840)

A Letter addressed to Mrs.Opie with Observations on her recent publication 'Illustrations of Lying' (Norwich: Matchett & Stevenson, ca 1825).

A Letter to a Friend on the Authority, Purpose & Effects of Christianity by Joseph John Gurney (Bradford: T.Inkersley, 1824)

A Look to the Last Century: or The Dissenters weighed in their own Scales (London: B.White & Son and R.Faulder, 1790)

An appeal to Popular Opinion against Kidnapping & Murder & a narrative of the atrocious proceedings at Yarmouth by John Thelwall (London: J.S.Jordam, 1796)

Amelia and the Hermit by Kenneth Povey (*Sussex County Magazine*, Jan 1829)

A Notice of Mrs Opie (*Biographical Memoirs, 1757-1879*: NHC: Colman Collection)

Clark's Edition of the trial of James Blomfield Rush (London: W.M.C.Clark. 1849)

Dawson Turner FRS (1775-1858) by Warren R.Dawson (*Society for the Bibliography of Natural History Journal*, December, 1958)

Full particulars of the trial of James Blomfield Rush (Norwich: Walker, 1849)

Harriet Countess of Rosslyn by A.Opie (*Edinburgh Journal*, January, 1840)

Last will & testament of Amelia Opie (Public Record Office, Kew)

Longman, Rees, Hurst and Orme catalogues (St.Bride Printing Library)

Memoir of James Northcote (*The Gentleman's Magazine*, August 1831)

Mrs.Amelia Opie Administratrix of the personal estate of the late John Opie (St. Agnes Deeds, Cornwall Record Office)

Mrs Opie (*The Cabinet or Monthly Report of Polite Literature*, June 1807)

Record of the Death of J.J.Gurney Esq., of Earlham, from the *Norfolk Chronicle* (Norwich: Stevenson & Matchett, 1847)

St.Andrew's Church, Holt, Norfolk, by Charles L.S.Linnell, 1956

Some Account of the Life of Mr.John Taylor of Norwich by Edward Taylor (*Monthly Repository*, August, 1826)

The Forsters of Bradpole & Norwich by Arthur J.Eddington (*Friends Quarterly Examiner*, October 1933)

The House of Longman (1724-1924) by Harold Cox (*The Edinburgh Review, Oct 1924)*

Treachery and Adultery: Trial of Benjamin Boddington (Eighteenth Century Collections Online: Print Edition)

Websites

Oxford Dictionary of National Biography (Oxford University Press): www.oxforddnb.com

Family history records and information: www.ancestry.co.uk

Pellegrino Mazzotti website: https://sites.google.com/site/pellegrinomazzotti/home

Index of Names

(fn = footnote)

Index of Names

Index of Names